INDIA : FROM INDUS VALLEY CIVILISATION TO MAURYAS

The Author

Gyan Swarup Gupta (*1929-*) has a deep interest in History, specially unsolved puzzles of the ancient Indian History. After stint with teaching English Language and Literature for a few years he joined the government administrative service. His job took him to various parts of the country but mainly in Rajasthan to remote areas, to lowly cottages and tribal habitations. The people of Rajasthan have an instinctive habit of painting the outer walls of their dwelling with frescoes and old symbols. He was surprised to find the symbols of Indus Valley Civilisation on the walls, further surprised to find the rituals and religion of the Indus Valley Civilisation in their rituals, religion and even in language. This gave him the idea that the cultural and religious ancestry of these people was not some unknown invading tribe but the Indus Valley Civilisation. Reflections on this aspect and observations of the tribal life gave him a glimpse of the society of Indus Valley Civilisation however fleeting it may be. Eight years were spent in writing, recording his observations, study and reflections on paper. The result is this book. He is a prolific writer and his articles on various unsolved problems of history, the correct history of various historical sites have appeared in a very large number of magazines, journals, etc., both in Hindi and English. He is also associated in writing of books, contributing chapters on the state of society from the ancient times to the present one.

CONCEPTS IN COMMUNICATION
INFORMATICS & LIBRARIANSHIP -81

General Editor : **S.P. Aggrawal**

INDIA
FROM INDUS VALLEY CIVILISATION TO MAURYAS

GYAN SWARUP GUPTA

CONCEPT PUBLISHING COMPANY, NEW DELHI - 110059

ISBN : 81-7022-763-1

First Published 1999

Published and Printed by

Ashok Kumar Mittal
Concept Publishing Company
A/15-16, Commercial Block, Mohan Garden
NEW DELHI-110059 (India)
Phones : 5648039, 5649024
Fax : 091-11-5648053

Dedicated
to
All those Scholars who believe that History is a Science based on logical conclusions derived from records and excavations and not on myths and legends found in a religion born in far away lands.

FOREWORD

It is an admitted fact that our rulers, both Mughals and specially British, made original efforts to distort and colour Indian History with ulterior motives and make "Indian Intellectuals" mentally slave, incapable of collecting facts impartially, arrange them in a natural order and interpret them correctly. They succeeded admirably. Even fifty year after Independence, these scholars repeat, like a parrot, that India was never one country, or one nation with one culture; it was British who tried to unite India and make it a country; Aryans came from Middle East; and so on. But when excavations at Mohenjodaro and Harappa stare them at face, they look bewildered, unable to explain they prefer to keep mum. Their condition becomes miserable when excavations have revealed that a Dwarka exists under the sea. What a pity for a country like India which has given light to the world.

Shri Gyan Swarup Gupta, without pretension of scholarship has done well to make a new scholarly beginning in his book, *India: From Indus Valley Civilisation to Mauryas.* He gives a new methodology also. He starts with the study of Vedas without any prenotions, but with an open mind. He gets the impression that Vedas also give an idea of the development of our history. So, he hurriedly scans through other connected literature—Brahmanas, *Purans, Aryanaks, Valmiki Ramayan, Mahabharat* etc. This new methodology threw a flood light which stands amply collaborated by the finds of Indus Valley Civilisation. For example, Shri Gupta seems to compile various hymns in Vedas on various animals (Horse, Tiger, Bulls, Goats etc.), birds (Shyena, etc.), plants, trees etc. A reading of all the hymns on one animal, or bird, or tree or plant gives him the impression that probably in the Vedic period different wandering tribes lived in different parts and the land of the five rivers and the desert now known as Sindh, Punjab and Rajasthan. Each one of these tribes picked up one animal, or bird, or tree of their area, which was considered most important as their totem. For example, the hymns on horse show that horse was just a horse in a few verses, then it was praised which was an ordinary praise, thereafter it was imbued with divinity and ultimately elevated to godhead. Same is true of all animals, birds, trees, plants etc. Shri Gupta, on the basis of these findings rightly concludes that this shows the different stages of development. He makes a very potent conjecture in this connection. He argues that with time, these wandering tribes started settling down and began to befriend some other tribes. So, at one stage, two tribes might have become so close as to lose their individual identity and so agreed to combine their totems. This may explain, for example, God Ganesh's present form or the Shiv family.

In a similar way, Shri Gupta attempts to explain, who was Mudgal and why was he so much praised in *Vedas*. He explains that Mudgal invented a weapon DRUGHAN (a wooden club) which was lighter and more effective in a war. With this weapon, he could protect his tribe, vast hinterland of Indus Valley and its animals and drive out the enemies. Again, Shri Gupta found out, on the basis of his studies, that not only the names of the rivers changed but their courses also went on changing; that most of the towns were located on these rivers, and with the changing course of rivers, the names of the towns also changed, while some towns were ruined. Today, after the Ecologists and Geographers have with the help of Satellite imaginery and field study scientifically established the course of the river Saraswati and that most of the important sites including the town of Kalibangan were located on its banks, none will dispute Shri Gupta. A day may not be far off when the other conjectures of Shri Gupta, viz that river Jamuna flowed through Rajasthan and joined the Saraswati at Kalibangan, and that it changed its course later may prove correct. Further Shri Gupta infers from available evidence that Pushkar Raj was a centre of stone armoury. It is likely that further excavation work may confirm it.

Mr. G.S. Gupta through his studies tries to connect

convincingly the finds of the Indus Valley Civilisation at Mohenjodaro and Harappa with the developments of Vedic period. It will be difficult to refute his several conclusions such as Aryans did not come from anywhere. Hindi existed much earlier than what is attributed to it as at least 70 Hindi words are found in Sumerian language in Parts I and II of Volume 'A' of Sumerian Dictionary indicating that the number of words in Sumerian language may exceed 1000 words. If so many words which are obviously loan words from Indus Valley Civilisation which had intimate relations with the ancient and contemporary Civilisation of Sumer, it is natural to infer that language of Indus Valley Civilisation was Hindi. So the language which is written on Indus seals must be Hindi. He has also succeeded in finding from the Puranas specially *Mahapuran,* which gives in detail various incidents of the life of Rishabhdev which in turn are depicted on the Indus seals as scenes, that the deity in Pashupatinath seal is likely to be Rishabhdev and not Shiv. Similarly, he has collected the material on Alexander's invasion of India, on the Mauryan period and giving a rational and coherent interpretation indicates the likely answer to the old question —"Who were the Mauryas". Thus Shri Gupta gives lot of material on possible historical development from Indus Valley Civilisation to Mauryas, on various themes like festivals (Holi etc.), deities like Pashupatinath, Rulers, Heredity, Towns etc.

This study of Shri Gupta compels us to conclude that what is needed is that a team of genuine historians, with open mind and eyes, together with scholars of Sanskrit may scan through Vedic literature, in its comprehensiveness, and then try to discover true history of India.

S.S. GUPTA
Ex. Vice-Chancellor
(Agra University)

GENERAL EDITOR'S INTRODUCTION

Indus Valley Civilisation, which was highly developed Civilisation, has opened a new Chapter in the ancient history of India and makes an interesting reading. It is shrouded in a number of mysteries which the scholars of both India and Europe have been making strenuous efforts to unravel for decades. A large number of seals has been discovered by excavators in the Indus towns. The most prominent seal is that of deity Pashupatinath which appears in different settings. Various incidents of his life seem to have been depicted on other seals. There is a group of scholars which believes that the hordes of Aryans who came from Central Asia invaded India and exterminated the earlier race which was Dravidian. It was Marshall who first propagated this view. Marshall identified the deity Pashupatinath as Shiv. Since Shiv is the principal deity of Dravidians, it were the Dravidians who inhabitated in the Indus Valley and who were mercilessly slaughtered and driven out. In the support of this theory Marshall cited the case of Brahui tribe of Quetta in Baluchistan. Brahuis speak a language in which 90 per cent of the words are Baluchi and the remaining 10 per cent can be called the derivatives of Dravidian languages. These Brahuis people, who were subsequently displaced by the invading Aryans, belonged to Indus Valley. Opposed to this is another group of scholars which is critical of this theory of migration of Aryans from Central Asia and extermination of Dravidians. The scholars of this group believe that Aryans did not come from anywhere, but were the original inhabitants of this Valley and Indus Valley Civilisation was nothing but Vedic Civilisation. In view of this they maintain that the principal deity Pashupatinath must be either Indra or Agni, the Fire God. Shri Gyan Swaroop Gupta also subscribes to this view and rules out the migration theory.

He holds that there is no physical evidence to show that the people had migrated in such a large number in those times. The people of Indus Valley were Aryans themselves who were compelled to abandon their land and migrate to other places due to natural calamity of a great magnitude. In the 19th Century B.C. the Saraswati river which was the mainstay of this Civilisation became dry; its major tributaries the Satluj and Yamuna along with other minor ones changed their courses. As a result of this change of courses of the rivers and also due to drying up some minor rivers, the life of the people of the towns that stood on their banks or near them became so difficult that they were forced to leave their hearth and home and migrate to other suitable places. As regards the identification of Pashupatinath seal the author has taken great pains in critically examining the mythologies associated with Jainism, Buddhism and the Hindu religion and has come to the conclusion that the deity in question is none other than Rishab, the first Tirthankar of the Jains, elaborately described by *Mahapuran*, the authentic *Puran* of the Jains. Marshall has erred in identifying it as Shiv as he has studied the seal of Pashupatinath is isolation of other seals. Not all but some of them have depicted the incidents of the life of Rishab as recorded in Jain mythologies. Ofcourse Shiv has close resemblance to this deity. But he has no connection with the scenes shown in other seals. In regard to Brahui people of Baluchistan the author is of the view that they are not displaced persons of Indus Valley. Most probably they are the deportees of Kalinga War as the Kingdom of Kalinga had probably the mixed population of Oriyas and Dravidians. In this connection it may be stated that in Kalinga War, as recorded in one of the Ashokan edicts, hundreds of people were killed and a large number of them were subjected to penal deportation as was the practice of the olden days. Is not that Jews were deported, to Babylon from Palestine by Assyrians in ancient times.

The language written on the seals has also baffled our scholars. Some say that it should be Tamil as Dravidians were the original settlers of Indus Valley Civilisation. Opposed to this view are those who regard it as Sanskrit. There are also a few scholars who have advocated the case of Hittitite.

Despite best efforts of the scholars and linguists the Indus script remains undecipherable. The author has made a startling point that Indus language is neither Tamil nor Sanskrit nor Hittitite. It is akin to Hindi as spoken by the masses of those days. It cannot be Sanskrit as it was the language of the elite. The author explains the reason for advocating the case of Hindi in this regard. He believes that there existed a close relationship between the people of Indus Valley Civilisation and of Sumer in matters of trade and culture. There are many evidences of such relationship between the two old Civilisations. The evidence of language is one of them. The author has scrutinised the Parts I and II of the Volume A (five parts) of Sumerian Dictionary (published by University Museum, University of Pennsylvania) and identified a pretty large number of common words in Sumerian language and Hindi. There is every possibility that as and when all the volumes of this Dictionary are published and common words sorted out they may exceed one thousand.

Shri Gupta has also tried to provide answer to the question of the identity of Mauryas and the founder of this dynasty Chandragupta Maurya, who was a military genius and strode the world like Colossus. It was he who halted the march the Greek army under Salecus, the great general of Alexander and forced the general to cede large tracts of his territory to Chandragupta and give one of the daughters in marriage to him.

Shri Gupta has also thrown a new light of Alexander and his invasion of India. His comments on Court Chroniclers are very much true and interesting. Since these chroniclers have to serve their masters they would try to show their masters' weaknesses as their strengths, their failure as grand success and their utter defeat as glorious victory. It is most surprising that there is no mention of Alexander and his invasion in all the records available in those days. What we get about Alexander we get through the writings of Greek Chroniclers whose statements may be taken with a pinch of salt. There is every likelihood that Alexander might have got stiff resistance or might have been repulsed by Porus. Shri Gupta doubts the story of Alexander's generosity towards Porus. Alexander was ruthless in dealing with his enemies. He had shown utmost cruelty and barbarity towards the defeated Persians. Hence, it is not expected of him to show such magnanimity.

On the whole the present publication has attempted to give a new angle to the ancient history in a simple but forceful and elegant language and tried to solve certain knotty problems which have baffled the historians and the scholars alike.

S.P. AGRAWAL

ACKNOWLEDGEMENTS

I must acknowledge the contributions the numerous authors of various books and articles on the subject of Indus Valley Civilisation and ancient History of the World made towards the preparation of this book for they made me realise that probably I may be able to unravel the mystery that is the Indus Valley Civilisation and the origin of the Mauryas. They are my unnamed teachers.

The help and support I received from my wife, Veena, and my children Amita, Anjali, Anu and Alind have made the writing of this book possible. They have absolved me from all the mundane activities required in running a household and other social requirement and thus I could devote myself exclusively to the book. I was again fortunate in my brother Shanti. He is a tower of strength for me. Because of his full support and interest in the subject I embarked on this perilous venture. Without his encouragement and interest, I doubt, if at all this work could have been so executed. Again this book could not have been before the readers without the help of Dr. S.P. Agrawal, a friend of more than forty-five years, but more a brother than a friend.

Sh. M.W.K. Sherwani has very painstakingly gone through the manuscript, looking into spellings of every word, the grammar, and construction of every sentence and the logic of every argument. Can one sufficiently acknowledge his help? I would also like to thank Sh. Amal Kar of the Central Zone Research Institute, Jodhpur, for help in searching relevant maps and information for this book.

GYAN SWARUP GUPTA

CONTENTS

Foreword 7
General Editor's Introduction 11
Acknowledgements 15
List of Plates, Maps and Tables 19
List of Abbreviations 20
How I View the History 21

1. **The Vedas** 31
Prologue; Vedas
2. **Stirring for Civilisation** 66
Discovery of Fire
3. **Mature Phase of Indus Civilisation** 88
Genesis; Founding of Cities; Religion; Deity of Pashupatinath Seal; Life of Rishab; Indus-Sumer Relations
4. **Post-Indus Interregnum** 141
Who Were the Aryans; Common Features in Indus and Later Civilisation; Probable Reasons of the Migration of Indus People; Settlement of Indus People in new Homes; Life in Iran; Vedas and Avesta; Contribution of Indus People to Civilisation as a Whole
5. **The Age of Enquiry and the Rise of Monarchy** 167
Situation in North-East India; Rise of Monarchy in Eastern India; India in the North-West
6. **The Age of Reason** 204
Religion; Religion in Eastern India; Shiv and His Family; Language and Literature; Sanskrit Literature
7. **The Mauryan Age** 236
Chandragupta; Ashoka; Successors of Ashoka
8. **People and Society in the Mauryan Age** 289
Administration; Religion; Religion Prior to Mauryas; Religions of the Living God; Philosophical Religions or Revealed Religions; Language and Literature

Appendices

A : Mahābhārat—Historical and Political Context 329
B : The Age of Gitā 344
C : Likely Influences of Hinduism and Other Religions on the Religion of the Jews 354
Influence on Jews in Haran and Egypt Till They Came to Sinai; Jews in Palestine; Influence of Zorastrianism on the Jews; Contact with Buddhism
D : Indus Script and Language : Was the Language Hindi? 377
Script of Indus Valley Civilisation; Script and Language; Hindi Words in Sumerian Language
Index 399

LIST OF PLATES

1. Buddha 219
2. Krishna Teaching *Gita* to Arjuna 334

LIST OF MAPS

1. Principal Sites of Indus Valley Civilisation 29
2. Map of Western India showing the River Ghaggar System and the Archaeological Sites 69
3. Oldham C.F. 1893. The Saraswati and the Lost River of the Indian Desert 89
4. India in the time of Sixteen Mahajanapadas 168
5. Ashoka's Empire and the places where his Edicts were found 262

LIST OF TABLE

1. Common Hindi and Sumerian words 394

LIST OF ABBREVIATIONS

M.I.C.	Mohanjodaro and Indus Civilisation
F.E.M.	Further Excavations at Mohenjodaro
E.H.	Excavations at Harappa
R.V.	Rigveda
Rig V.	Rigveda
D.V.	Dipvansha
M.V.	Mahavansh
JRAS	Journal of the Royal Asiatic Society of Great Britain and Ireland, London

HOW I VIEW THE HISTORY

The history of India is a myriad mosaic of incidents which are woven into a large continuous carpet interesting in its contours, its variety, its colours, sometimes depressing, sometimes bright but always interesting and at the same times having a unity seldom perceived in the history of other countries or regions of the world. Unfortunately in the huge archives of written word available in India from the ancient Vedas to modern times we find everything on any topic except history. Whatever history is available today is a history written by foreigners with their own outlook whether it is Ibn Batuta or Maxmulleur or Sir Mortimer Wheeler. They have their own ideas, their outlook as seen from their own countries and their own times. No doubt there can be objectivity but at the same time as they cannot observe the grass and land beneath it will lack the objectivity expected of a historian. Only an Indian will have the emotional attachment to look at things with interest which outsiders regard superfluous. Obviously there will not be any objectivity so desired by scholars but can there be any objectivity in any history. History is a subject in which there cannot be any objectivity. It can only be seen by coloured glasses and I do so through my own colours and they can only be bright and loving.

Every nation has its own personality which is quite different from that of any other nation. This is so because when different people started on the road of development and civilisation each met different challenges, faced different vicissitude and each had a different response to each challenge resulting in a different development of skill, a different mental make-up and a different outlook. Hence a nation's personality is made of different but successive layers of social, religious, political and economic influences in successive generations beginning from paleolithic age to the modern times. In fact it is the influence of these layers that makes a nation and which distinguishes it from the other one. Modern Iraq has as its foundation the cultures of Sumer, Accad, Assyria, Babylon and Greek, while modern Iran has as its base the cultures of Aryan, Indus, Achaemenians, Parthians, Arabic etc. Similarly Egypt will have as its base its own ancient past, followed by Greek and Roman cultures, while Arabia between Egypt and Iraq has none of the influences which constituted its neighbours and if it had, it must be a mild one. All the four are today Muslim nations and except Iran all claim to be Arab nations, yet all the three are different in their outlook, in their culture, in their response to different issues and as seen as a whole, in their personality. This is true of every nation including India. If we have to see a nation we must see these various layers in its life and if we have to see a nation at a particular time, then we should peel off the layers above that time. A nation which forgets its past loses its own soul and its own identity. If some conquerer or somebody else wants to pervert a nation, he has only to stress upon that people a past which is different from what it actually was.

If we peel off successive layers of cultural influences, we will find that the base of Indian culture and religion was certainly Indus but the people who would like to interpret things in their own way or who are ignorant otherwise, try to deny it and substitute it with a brutal beginning and thus perverting the personality of the nation. Such attempts had been made in the past also. It is the job of the historian to unravel the past and to point out the correct trend in the life of the nation.

The historical incidents or the social and cultural life of different nations recorded by contemporary writers are no longer available probably due to the fragile nature of the material on which it was written and also due to neglect. The only available records are usually those recorded as inscriptions on stones, on copper plates or fired clay tablets. Some do come to us as legends mutated and distorted. Inscriptions on stones or copper plates are usually composed by the court poets which, to a large extent, cannot be relied upon. The usual experience is that the records of court poets are highly distorted in favour of their masters and sometimes utter routs are described as glorious defeats, while at another times the defeats are shown as victories and only circumstantial evidence or a reading between the lines bring out the fallacious nature of the record. A classical example of such a description is the invasion of India by Alexander. According to the writers in the train of Alexander he met a stiff resistance on the banks of Jhelum by Porus but Alexander somehow managed to defeat him and in his generosity he handed back the kingdom to Porus. He wanted to make a little advance but his troops refused to advance further and on his retreat he had faced a coalition of five tribes led by Yaudheyas. He managed to fight the four tribes which constituted the coalition of Mālavas, Shudraks, Katha and Shibis separately defeating them to the point of annihilation taking about half a million prisoners along with him, while the fifth and most important tribe, the Yaudheyas evaded fighting him. Also that Chandragupta Maurya met him in his camp urging him to attack the Nandas of Magadh. Who was Chandragupta Maurya and how he managed to meet such an important person as Alexander is not indicated which is noteworthy as just after Alexander's withdrawal Chandragupta Maurya became master of the whole of North-Western India as a prelude to his mastery of the whole of North India including Magadh. Inspite of the wealth of literature of this period including poetry, dramas, commentaries on grammar and religious literature including *Puranas* and Buddhist mythologies, the invasion or even the name of Alexander is not mentioned. As if he had not entered India and even if we accept the Greek version it might be only a border raid or a defeat at the very start. Greeks mentioned that he carried away half a million men as prisoners but fail to mention the place where they were carried or settled nor do we find them anywhere in the world. We should take such stories by the court chroniclers with scepticism at the start unless proved otherwise. Similarly, the mention of Chandragupta Maurya as having met Alexander may indicate that he was a very important person, may be the head of the Yaudheyas and leader of the coalition. The Indian history can thus be interpreted in various ways.

Ancient Indian literature available to us today mentions that an important branch of knowledge was history and points out the existence of volumes of history but unfortunately they have been lost. What is left today are only references sometimes oblique to various incidents in the poetry, drama, commentaries on grammar, inscriptions, in Puranas and in Buddhist and Jain mythologies. These incidents can be interpreted in various ways as we had seen in the incident of Chandgragupta being mentioned by the Greeks. Foreign scholars have seen them in their own way and interpreted them as per their outlook. I do not agree with a large number of them and believe that for a proper appreciation of their significance and the reasons for that happening we will have to analyse the cultural, religious, political, social and economic forces working at those times being based on the foundations of earlier such layers in the life of the nation. I may see it with coloured glasses but they are my own.

Seen in this light if we look at the earliest phase of the civilisation of the present day Aryans of North India or as a matter of fact the people of whole of India, we find them not the hordes of Central Asia who invaded India and destroyed the Indus Civilisation as has been alleged but are, in fact, the actors of that civilisation. We will see it in the next phase of the life of the Indus people when they were forced to disperse from the areas where their civilisation took birth i.e. Indus Valley Civilisation area. Uprooting of a people has always a deep influence on their future behaviour, their beliefs, their thoughts and their life style. They not only lose their hearths and homes but also lose their fixed ideas about their deities, their philosophy, their way of life which, in turn, moulds these thoughts, beliefs and way of life into new patterns. In a way the Indus people, when they underwent this process of displacement from their old homes and moved into a different climate and life, also changed and their culture and life blossomed into a richer life. We find this in the culture and thoughts of the period which culminated in the Age of the Mauryas. Full flowering of the thoughts of the *Vedas* can be seen in the teachings of the Buddha and the Jains. However, the period also saw the emergence of new philosophy and new religion whose foundation is the *Mahābhārat* and which by the end of the Mauryan age swept away the religion of the Buddha and the Jains from India. The religion of the Buddha found a new ground for flowering in Central Asia where it emerged into Mahāyān and in the area surrounding India where it was recognised as Hinyān. Thus I perceive the Indus Valley Civilisation as the nucleus of the culture, thought, religion and life in the succeeding ages upto the Age of the Mauryas i.e. upto 2nd Century B.C. I also believe the same period is the foundation, though in a different way, of the religion, thoughts and culture of the succeeding generations of Indians upto the present period. However, different the two may be the latter could not have been possible without the benign influence of the Indus Civilisation.

The contribution of the Indus Valley Civilisation to the growth and enrichment of Indian culture and society is only one of its myriad achievements. In the ancient world three civilisations, the Egyptian, the Sumerian and the Indus almost simultaneously came into being. They flourished and then disappeared. However, the two, the Egyptian and the Sumerian failed to give a strong and vigorous succession and completely vanished. The Egyptian did not have any influence on the people of Egypt or even on their immediate neighbours, the Greeks and the people of Turkey or Palestine. Similarly, Sumerians did not leave any influence on the land of its birth and development nor on the neighbouring areas of Iran or Palestine or Arabia. The whole world from Iran to Greece and beyond on one side and South East Asia on the other speaks one variety or the other of the Indian language, Sanskrit. This is not all, the gods they worshipped have a very strong resemblance to the gods of the Vedas. The seven Prohibitions prescribed in the *Rigveda* are the Seven out of Ten Commandments of the Judaism and Christianity. If we remember the mythology we find that Moses had seen God on Mt. Sinai only in the shape of Fire. Fire is named in the *Rigveda* as 'Yahweh', the god of the Jews. Indus Valley Civilisation had given birth to Indian culture and religion and nurtured it. It had also influenced the whole of the surrounding world, giving life and sustenance to the people of the old world.

I have undertaken a study of the Indus Valley Civilisation, its birth and growth to the development of the nation upto the time of Mauryas. However, it is with trepidation that I took the task, trepidation as the records available are so few and scanty that proper deductions may not be possible and the phases or events can be explained in more than one way. There is a continuous process of excavations going on and any new discovery can change the whole concept. If we can come across due to some fortunate chance a text which may be in two scripts, Indus and the succeeding Brahmi script it will explain many things and may change much of our speculations. Similar is the case with period upto the end of the age of Mauryas. So it was not an easy task for though attempt may be made to take into account the available information, yet the thoughts, perceptions and speculations may become outdated soon due to new discoveries. However, it had to be written and attempt had to be made to sift the available information, put a gloss over it by one's coloured imagination and speculation and attempt to give a systematic history of the times. It was necessary to do so. The history of the period is so sketchy and incomplete that it is almost lifeless. As an example we may take up the advent of the Mauryas. History describes Chandragupta Maurya to have appeared on the scene as if from nowhere. At the most he is given as of a low origin. Yet within three years of this appearance in the court of Alexander he becomes master of North-Western India and in a further few years master of the whole of Northern India. Surely he cannot come from nowhere and succeed so quickly. He must be having a well established base of operations and systematic army ready to fight for him and serve him loyally. As for *Mahābhārat* with the Jewel at its crest, the *Gitā* we may ask as to when it was written, by whom it was written and what are its essential features? With regard to the *Vedas,* we may question what life and what history are they describing and which period they are referring to? Mohenjodaro and Harappa are the two major towns of the Indus Valley Civilisation. We have no knowledge why it is that there is no civilian rural population in their vicinity but the whole of the rural hinterland including the urban ones is far away in the interior on the banks of the river Saraswati hundreds of kilometers to the interior? Who is the deity depicted on the Indus seals and does he have a counterpart in the mythologies of the present day Indians? He is described as Shiv Pashupatinath but is the identification correct or can he be seen in his original form in any mythology of Hindus or of Jains? These are some of the questions left not only unanswered but not even raised. Hence is the compulsion to not only to raise them but to try to give answer based on available information. The present study is in this direction.

First stirring of Civilisation arose among the tribes living and moving about in arid and semi-arid areas with their herds of animals and those animals which were their totems. Those totems played an important part in the development of their psyche, their religion and their beliefs. With the growth of civilisation those totems assumed more and more powers of nature in the imagination of tribesmen and ultimately became deities. Some of them were identified with the Sun. Even today they play a part in Hinduism. If we find the sacred day of the god or a goddess when it is worshipped we find that it invariably falls during the mating period of their mount. Why it is so? Is it because the mating period of the totem had a special significance for them. After the first stirrings the life developed rapidly and agricultural society was established along the river Saraswati. There were agricultural villages and there was agricultural produce stored. To get that produce the wild tribes from the Hindukush mountains started the era of plunder. Was it to thwart their attacks that the two garrison towns of Mohenjodaro and Harappa were founded far away in front of hinterland. Were those garrison towns founded to protect the hinterland which became the centre of later Empires. What happened when the rivers either ceased to flow or changed their courses thus ruining the established villages and the towns. The dispersal of Indus people made the expansion of Indus Civilisation imperative in all the directions even outside the Indian sub-continent. They gave the people of India the language, their culture, their religion and a way of life. What happened really nobody knows but by the time of the Buddha India was divided into a number of tribal states which were really oligarchies. They were systematically extinguished by first Bimbisar and Ajatshatru rulers of Magadh and later by Nandas on one side and by the Persian Empire under Darius I on the other. In between were the few tribes among whom Yaudheyas had a pre-eminent position. They formed a coalition with Yaudheyas at their head to protect them from Nandas of Magadh and the Persians. Chandragupta Maurya was probably head of the Yaudheyas and the head of the coalition. It may be that in that capacity he met Alexander and in that capacity first captured North West India and then Magadh Empire. His being a Yaudheya decided succession as well. Ashoka even though a younger son succeeded to the throne because probably he was born of a Yaudheya mother. When Yaudheyas became enfeebled or the last Emperor failed to have a son through a Yaudheya mother, the succession passed from Yaudheyas to the other partner of the coalition Mālavas and the head of the Mālava Republic became the king. He was Pushyamitra who prided in calling himself not the king but 'Senāpati', the designation of head of the Mālava republic. He was not the Senapati of the army but was that of Mālavas. These are some of the main points which emerged in my study and which I had dwelt at length with the evidence which first I indicated then. Though my views may be regarded as coloured ones, yet I believe that I am nearer to truth in describing events which actually happened.

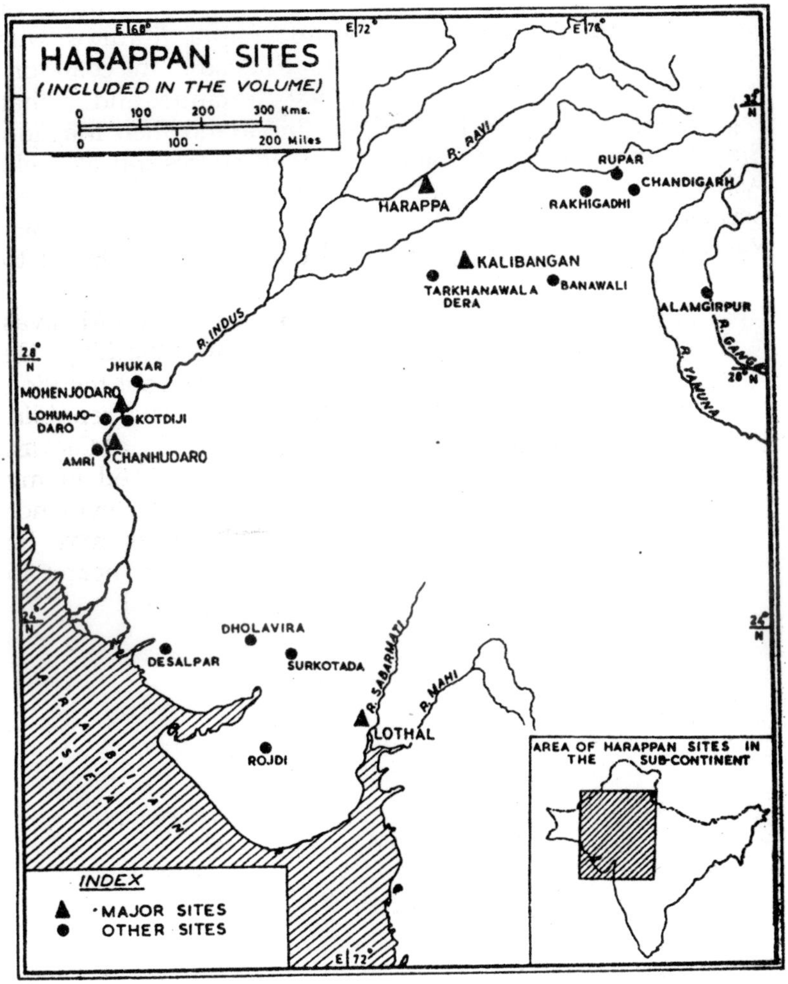

Map 1: Principal Sites of Indus Valley Civilisation

1

THE VEDAS

PROLOGUE

History of India, it is said, began with the *Vedas*. But what are the *Vedas*? Are they just a scripture? Or are they a record however fragmentary of an era spanning a couple of a thousand years? If they are a record of an era, then the understanding of the history of that era becomes important simply because the society, its facets revealed in the *Vedas* or not so far revealed by them, is the progenitor of the later ages. These ages cannot be separated from it and treated as an independent identity with its parents unknown. The later times of Buddha or the Mauryas must have evolved out of it.

A number of monographs with minute details have been written by eminent scholars on various aspects of the *Vedas*. Some have dealt with the religion, some with the various gods, some with rituals and some with various secular aspects mentioned in it. Secular aspects included the society, the politics, various kings and their battles, the inter-relation with mythical enemies and culture, all lumped together. However detailed and scholarly the monographs may be they cannot comprehend the state of society and people, for each aspect interacts with each other and is moulded accordingly. Synthetic treatment of their interaction is needed to understand the *Vedic* age.

What if the society depicted in the *Vedas* is actually that of Indus Valley Civilisation which culminated at about 1600 B.C. In that case the enquiry into the state of society, its evolution as found in the *Vedas* together with the history and religion inter-reacting with each other becomes far more important. We are aware of the physical aspects of the Indus Valley Civilisation so laboriously unearthed by archaeologists. The *Vedas* will, in that case, reflect the spirit of the age, the portrait of the society. The physical aspects found in the Indus Valley would explain some of the unexplained portions of the *Vedas* as well as of the significant aspects not found in the *Vedas.*

We may, therefore, begin with enquiry into the various facets of the *Vedas,* the state of society, its evolution if it is there, the stage of society from which it evolved and upto the stage where it matured, the various states and their rulers, the relations between them, the rituals, the religion and the various gods and what they mean. We have to study the inter-reaction of each of these facets with each other and the synthetic whole which is found in *Vedas.* We will then enquire whether this society is the society of the Indus Valley Civilisation and whether there is proof of the same in the *Vedas* itself. The enquiry will have to be undertaken in that case into the Indus Valley Civilisation itself as the precursor of the history of the Indian people. If as a result of the enquiry we find that the incidents mentioned in the *Vedas* along with their geographical locations overlap the then known geography of the Indus Valley and if it is reasonably established that the *Vedas* are the record, however fragmentary of the era which ended with the end of Indus Valley Civilisation, then the study of the *Vedas* would assume a very important character. A large number of incidents which are taken as mythical and mysterious in the *Vedas* could have been explained as a historical evolution of a developing society and some of the matters unearthed there by archaeologists would unravel the growing complexities of the evolving Indian society which has left its mark on the ancient Indian society, religion and culture as well as on history. The study of that evolution will help us in understanding the consequent history of Indian people in the subsequent ages upto the advent of Mauryas and beyond.

THE VEDAS

What are the *Vedas*? What do they contain? Why they are so important? *Vedas* are the earliest religious books of the Hindus. They are in fact the earliest works known to us. The most ancient of the whole volume are the *Vedic Sanhitas, Rigveda, Yajurveda, Samveda* and *Atharvaveda.* The *Vedas* are essentially a collection of hymns addressed to various gods. Originally it is said that the collection of hymns was a single one but was later divided into four volumes now known as *Rigveda, Yajurveda, Samveda* and *Atharvaveda.* The earliest of the four is said to be *Rigveda* which alone contains 1028 hymns and is almost equal to Homeric poems. The other three have hymns, a large number of which are taken from *Rigveda* itself, taken out of context and added to other original poems. When *Vedas* were divided, we do not know, but probably the division was made in the *Vedic* period, *i.e.,* when the *Vedic* hymns were being collected. We find the mention of the four *Vedas, Rigveda, Yajurveda, Samveda* and *Chhanda* in the Purush Sukta of the *Vedas* and the Purush Sukta is retained in all the four *Vedas.* So the probability is that this division was made in the period when they were formulated and collected. These four *Vedas* are further divided into various books, *Rigveda* containing ten books called Mandals. Some of the Mandals contain hymns attributed to a single family. Thus Mandal 3 pertains to the family of Vishwamitra and Mandal 7 to the family of Vashist. Every Mandal begins with hymns to Fire followed by those to Indra and then to the Ashwini Twins. In fact the bulk of hymns are addressed to these three gods, the Twins being treated as acting together and almost acting as one. In addition to hymns to these gods we also find hymns to various other gods namely Sun, Sky, various Adityas, Dawn, Earth, River Saraswati, etc. We find hymns addressed to all the gods of the world. These hymns contain almost the same matter reciting with monotonous regularity the features of the gods, their benevolence, their kind deeds to certain individual and then favour to certain kings in their battles. However, besides these hymns to gods there are some other hymns addressed to animals, to various trees, plants, and references to various battles which indicate the status of society, even its phases of evolution that must interest us. These hymns and the references to various battles, various kings, various social problems and conditions of society, the secular content of the *Vedas* tell us the most about the state of society and various phases of its evolution which the *Vedas* record.

I

There are a few hymns to animals in *Rigveda* and *Atharvaveda*. In fact there are seven in *Atharvaveda* and eight in *Rigveda*. In *Rigveda* there are five hymns addressed to horse, one to goat, one to a bird and one to bull. In *Atharvaveda* two are addressed to a horse, one to a tiger, one to a bird (Shyena), two to a bull and one to a goat. Mere songs praising animals may not interest us for after all in every age poets have sung songs and written poems in praise of their pets or the useful part an animal plays in society. What, however, arouses our curiosity is the changing tenor of the matter in various hymns. We may examine first *Rigveda*. There are two hymns addressed to a horse in Mandal I (Sukta 162 and 163). The first hymn No. 162 is just a poem describing the horse and praising it. However, the second consequent one No. 163 praises it as something imbued with divine powers. In Mandal IV we have three hymns (Sukta 38, 39, 40) pertaining to horse called 'Dadhrika' meaning horse. The first one, No. 38 just describes the horse and praises it in general terms. The second one No. 39 praises it as imbued with divinity. However, the third one deifies it to the Sun. In Mandal VI we have one hymn to goats, who are yoked to the chariot of Pushan who is identified as Sun god. The goats are not just animals but are divine beings carrying the chariot of the Sun god. In Mandal X we have one hymn addressed to a bird Tārkshya which is difficult to identify. This bird is treated as if it is imbued with divinity. There is another hymn in Mandal X, hymn 102 which is about wooden club but it is also addressed to bull. This is an interesting one and we will examine it a little later.

In *Atharvaveda* there are seven hymns. Kanda IV hymn No. 3 is addressed to a tiger. However, it is not in praise of this animal but threatens it with death, through torture. Kanda VI, hymn 92 is devoted to a horse merely describing it. Similarly, the hymn relating to horse in Kanda XIX, hymn 25 also describes horse as such. The hymn in Kanda VII, number 41 is addressed to a bird (Shyena) which is not possible to identify. But here the bird is treated not as a bird but imbued with the divinity as Sun. Hymn in Kanda VII, number 111 relates to a bull and elevates it to some divinity. However, the hymn number 4 in Kanda IX elevates it to a kind of divinity and treats it as such. Every part of its body belongs to a different god. The subsequent hymn number 5 which is addressed to a goat is also of the similar nature. It deifies the animal to a god and endows it with power of helping its devotees.

What is the meaning of these hymns, some addressing the animals or birds as just animals and birds, some treating them as imbued with divinity and some later identifying them with the Sun? Are we witnessing the evolution of society from a totemic one to a later advanced one when with the growth in their conception of divinity and world, the character and powers of their totems also change? Let us examine the available hymns in this regard. However, our problem is that the hymns of the *Vedas* were collected and divided into various *Vedas, Rig, Sam, Yajur* and *Atharva* and also in the various books of these *Vedas* arbitrarily without regard to their time-sequence. We do not know if the later ones were placed first and the earlier ones later. Similarly it is conjectured that the hymns were lumped together under the authorship of one Rishi or one family whereas it was not necessary that those were written by that Rishi or his family. Subject to these limitations let us analyse them in relation to the evolving society.

As mentioned earlier we may first examine the interesting hymn 102 of Mandal X of *Rigveda*. It is interesting because it throws a flood of light on the puzzle in regard to the hymns to animals and birds. Simply stated it is addressed to 'Drughan', a wooden club. The singer is the wife of Mudgal and in brief the hymn reveals that Mudgal and his wife won a decisive victory over enemies with the help of a single bull. They readied the bull and made it attack the enemies with themselves accompanying with a wooden club. The enemies were defeated and a thousand cows were won. How can a single bull defeat numerous enemies armed with weapons? It appears that the bull mentioned here is not meant to be a single bull but is mentioned as the totem of the tribe and stands for the whole tribe. If it means that bull is meant to be a totem, then it implies that the whole tribe to which Mudgal and his wife belonged got prepared for battle and Mudgal and his wife armed them all with wooden clubs. This tribe attacked and defeated the opposing tribe and captured the cows. We may note that *Puranas* mention that Mudgal was the founder of a dynasty of kings. One of his descendants Divodas is mentioned in *Rigveda* as a king and later another Sudas is mentioned again and again in *Vedas* for his wars and victories. We get from this hymn that bull here stands not for bull as such but as a totem of a tribe. Totemic animal in those early times stood as part of the being of an individual as well as of the whole tribe. Even today in the tribal society which is existing in some parts of India, it is believed that a particular animal, a particular bird and a particular plant or tree is a part of their being. Those animals and birds are not to be killed and that particular plant or tree is neither to be cut nor to be weeded out. It also means that wherever we find a hymn addressed to an animal or a bird we may take it as addressed to the totem and thus to the tribe identified with that totem. Wherever it is mentioned we may also believe it to be a reference to the totem. Another interesting thing is the reference to the wooden club. It probably points to that evolutionary stage of society when it was coming out of Stone age. It appears that in those early times whose remembrance it is, people still fought with stone clubs and stone weapons. They were heavy and short. The wooden clubs with which Mudgal and his wife got their people armed, should be longer and lighter and hence with greater mobility they could defeat the opposing army. For this discovery probably Mudgal got hereditary chieftainship which turned into kingship under his descendant Divodas. This is only a conjecture based on this hymn. Probability is that it may be true, looking to the dynasty which ruled over wide areas as mentioned in the *Vedas* and probably over large tracts of Indus Valley if our conjecture that *Vedas* are a fragmentary account of Indus Valley Civilisation, is correct.

We may next examine the three hymns 38, 39 and 40 of Mandal IV of *Rigveda* about the horse under the name of

'Dadhrikā'. Each is certainly addressed to the horse as a totem but there is something more. Unlike the earlier hymn, as discussed above, which was addressed simply as a a totem standing for the tribe, these hymns contain some additional qualities of the totem which are almost divine not possessed by the horse. Although the hymn 38 mentions the horse as representing the whole tribe and says that the enemies dread it when they see it and that it is capable of killing the enemies, yet it mentions that it also fulfils our desires. The next hymn 39 raises the horse to divinity and prays that it may save devotees from committing sin, may protect our body and increase our age. However, the succeeding hymn 40 raises the horse to divinity and treats it as god. Similar is the case with other hymns exclusively addressed to animals or birds. In some it is treated as a totem representing the tribe, in some it is imbued with some divine powers and in some it is dealt with as a divine being almost as a god and identified with either Sun, or Fire or with Indra, the god who brings rain. However, it is not that the animals are referred to only in hymns exclusively addressed to them. They are more frequently found in other hymns addressed to gods but there they are either associated with them closely or else the animals are treated as if they are the gods. Fire god is compared to a bull with thousand horns in *Rigveda* (5.1.8) as well as in *Atharvaveda* (13.1.12). Similar is the case with the horse and the goat etc. which are treated as if they are gods. Bull is also treated as Sun[1]. Among all this mass of hymns which, it appears, are devoted to totem either treating it as representing a tribe, or imbued with some divine powers or treating it as god identifying it with some deity, there is one interesting hymn which is quite different in nature. The hymn in *Atharvaveda* (4.3) is about a tiger but its contents are different. Instead of praising tiger or identifying it with the tribe, it curses it and declares that his face will be destroyed and all its nails torn. It is not a hymn even cursing the opposing tribe represented by the tiger as totem but appears to be a ritual hymn before going on a tiger hunt. In the tribal societies before going on a hunt it was a usual practice to draw a picture of the animal they were going to hunt or its likeness in mud and to kill it symbolically while reciting a ritual hymn. This appears to be one such hymn.

We have seen the hymns to animals. Let us examine some hymns to birds and to vegetables, and plants. There are two hymns exclusively devoted to birds. One is the hymn to Shyena in *Atharvaveda* (7.41) and the other to Tārkshya in *Rigveda* (10.178). Identity of these birds is unknown. Shyena is treated as Sun in the hymn while Tārkshya on the other hand is called as the bringer of the divine drink, Soma and bestower of wealth. He is imbued with divinity. In other hymns too the birds are referred to sometimes as Suparna and all are treated as divine beings or as Sun. What about hymns to vegetation including plants and trees? We have plenty in both *Rigveda* and *Atharvaveda,* in *Atharvaveda* having much more than in *Rigveda.* What do hymns state? They are full of praise for these trees or plants and imbue them with divinity.[2] It probably helped the tribals to feel strong when the vegetation with which it claimed kinship was tied to their body; even a piece sufficed.

We, while reading the *Vedas,* find ourselves in the midst of an evolving tribal society. A very large number of hymns are either addressed to animals and birds or to trees or plants or references to them. We find the tribal society as it is when we find the animals or birds or plants or trees as depicting them representing the tribes alone. But as the people get moving towards civilisation and their minds and sensibilities get developed, they realise that there are certain supernatural powers too which help or mar their efforts. They need to placate them and worship them. It is but natural for them to colour their own totems with that of supernatural power or divinity. This they do by elevating their totem to divinity. A time comes when they discover fire, the system of seasonal rain and realise the power of the Sun. They feel that the Fire, Sun and the one who gives rain are divine and they must propitiate them. Naturally their own totems must be identified with these divine beings. So these totems must be identified with these gods. Bull, goat, bird, horse, etc. must be identified with Fire, Sun, Rain god Indra, Wind god, etc. or else must be in some close association with them as either their mounts or yoked to their chariots. This can be seen in the fact that the names for Sun Āditya, Pushan, Savitā, Mitra were separately identified with the different animals as their mounts and later lumped together as Ādityas, the names of Sun. We can see the elevation of animals as totems to divinity even in a curious phenomenon in the still existing Hindu society. Even at present there are a large number of gods and goddesses in the Hindu world distinguished by their separate mounts. All these gods and goddesses have their separate sacred days or months. The remarkable things to be noted about these sacred days or months are that they invariably fall only during the mating period of these animals. We should note that the mating period of the totems were a sacred period and a period of rejoicing among the tribes. Thus we have the month Pausha in the Hindu Calendar which is actually the mating period for goat, the mount of Pushan, the Sun god. Similarly, the month Ashwin is the mating period for horses, the Shitla Ashtmi in the month of March-April, or Chaitra according to Hindu Calendar is sacred to Shitlā Mātā whose mount is the donkey, and this day falls during the mating period of the donkeys. So is the case with the sacred days of every god, which invariably fall during the mating period of their mounts.

Do we have any reflection of this state of society as noticed in the study of the *Vedas*, in the archaeological remains found in Indus Valley Civilisation? We may have to confine ourselves to an examination of the seals found there as all other material excavated does not give us much information in this regard. In an examination of the seals we are proceeding with an handicap and that is our inability to understand the meaning of the script and hence the meaning of the inscriptions. The animal and birds are a conspicuous feature of the seals. Most of the seals do contain the picture of one or other animal or bird or tree on one side of it and in few seals where there are other scenes probably showing the then current mythology these animals or birds or even trees are a conspicuous part of the scene. There are 3455 seals found so far. Of them 1159 contain the figure of a Unicorn, a curious animal horse-like but having a single horn on his head, 156 contain the picture of a bull, 14 of a buffalo, 56 of an elephant, 21 of a tiger, 40 of a rhinoceros, 36 of a goat antelope, 10 of a hare, 49 of a gharial, 14 of an animal in the shape of fish, 1 of a tortoise, 1 of an animal in the shape of tortoise, 1 of a frog, 10 of a serpent, 4 of birds in flight, 34 of a tree generally within a railing or on a platform. There are about 100 seals which contain an animal whose body contains limbs from different animals. About 60 seals are the ones containing various mythological scenes but they contain animals playing some meaningful part. It is difficult to say whether these animals are totems or not. However we may examine if they can be treated as such.

There is no doubt that they must mean something to have been depicted on the seals. They occupy a conspicuous central place on the seal. In the absence of our ability to read the inscription which would have told us if they were invocation to some god and hence to be identified with some deity, it is difficult to definitely point out their significance. But before discussing them we may first examine the 60 seals which contain mythological scenes to see if they can throw some light on the problem. These seals contain scenes of some mythology but what that mythology is we are unable to say. But the scenes on some are clear enough to give us some idea. The most famous seal is the seal known as the Pashupatinath seal, seal No. 420 from Mohenjodaro (MIC). In this there is a man sitting nude in a yogic posture on a stool. He is having the face of a bull and horns of bull. Beneath his stool are shown sitting two goats or ibexes, while around him are shown four animals, which are a tiger, an elephant, a rhinoceros and a buffalo together with a man. All these animals and man are shown to be in motion. It implies that they were going round the central figure, a ritual unique among the Hindus showing reverence to the figure round whom one moves. The bull-faced deity must be the one who must be originally a bull totem and elevated to divinity. We again find this same deity with horns of a bull standing between the branches of a tree and worshipped by a similar dressed man and seven figures. Before him stands a ram whose body is made of the limbs of several animals. This seal No. 430 from Mohenjodaro (MIC) has the similar import as the seal known as Pashupatinath seal. We have other seals showing the same person with having the features of a bull having tails, horns etc. (seal Nos. 227, 319, 471, 914 from Mohenjodaro, 305 from Harappa). We have in the seal 815 from Mohenjodaro[3] a man shown worshipping a tree. What does the tree denote? It should denote the same thing which the tree shown surrounded by a railing or on a platform denotes, *i.e.,* the raising of one's special tree to divinity or identifying it with the totem raised to divinity. These are some of the more conspicuous seals in which we get a definite indication that in the developed Indus Valley Civilisation society, the totem of some people were definitely raised to godhead, and were worshipped as such. May be they were identified with the Sun, the Fire, the Rain god, the Wind god, or some supernatural higher being ruling over the world.

In view of above it will be fair to state that the Indus Valley Civilisation began with tribes having as their totems some animals, together with birds and trees. Later as they came into contact with each other and began thinking they felt that there were some powers greater than man, some mysterious powers. They, feeling the mystery, imbued their own totems with these powers. When they realised the power of Sun, they imbued their totem with that power and identified the image of totem with the Sun. Similarly, when Fire was discovered and its mystery and power was realised, the totem got it coloured with that mystery. The rain making god, Indra was transferred to the totem too in course of time. As more and more of mysterious powers of nature came to be known, their totem came to be regarded as god and thus was worshipped. Ultimately one single deity, the figure in Pashupatinath seal came to be regarded as the universal deity in Indus Valley times. What about 100 or so seals with an animal in the central place having limbs from different animals. This can be fusion of the people of different tribes having different totems? When the people became one, naturally their totems should become one too. Either they can adopt one common animal as totem or having an animal having the limbs of the different totems combined into one animal, a composite animal which we find on the seals. Thus Savitā, Pushan, Mitra, Surya became one Āditya called by different names by different tribes during their evolution of speech. *Vedas* appear to be a faithful record of the evolution of the totem-turned-deity in the Indus Valley Civilisation.

II

As stated earlier of the four *Vedas, Rigveda, Sāmveda, Yajurveda* and *Atharvaveda* the oldest one is the *Rigveda* which is divided into ten books or Mandals. Of the ten books or Mandals of *Rigveda,* the hymns in Mandals 2-7, are each assigned by tradition to a single family. These are in order the hymns of Gṛtsamada, Vishvāmitra, Vāmdeva, Atri, Bharadvāja, Vashishta and their descendants. The eighth book contains the hymns of Kanva clan. The book ninth contains hymns to Soma alone. The first book contains hymns of fourteen groups or families. The tenth contains the rest of hymns of different persons and is probably the latest. In these books or Mandals the pride of place is always given to the hymns to Agni, the god of Fire. This is followed by those to Indra and then to Ashwin twins and then to various other gods. The largest number of hymns are addressed to Agni, Indra and Ashwin twins. This plan is scrupulously followed even in the first book, where in the hymns of fourteen families the first hymn goes to Agni. In these hymns the gods are praised, they are invoked to protect the singer and the clan, and some of their achievements are described which incidentally give the names of kings and individuals. If these names are also found in the Indus Valley seals as and when they are deciphered, then we can be certain that the *Vedas* are a record of that period. However, as it is not yet deciphered, we look at other evidence to see if we can still link the *Vedas* with the Indus Valley Civilisation.

Let us examine the hymns to Agni—the god of Fire—which are given the pride of place in the *Vedas.* Why were they composed? What was the occasion when they were recited? What is the other information that we get about Agni in the *Vedas?* What can be the link between the worship of the god of Fire, and the Indus Valley Civilisation? Was Agni, worshipped in Indus Valley Civilisation period? If so what is the evidence? The evidence of special importance given to Fire in the towns of Indus Valley Civilisation are plenty in the remains revealed by excavation of Mohenjodaro, Harappa and Kalibangan. In all these towns we find that there are some fire-pits in public places both in what is guessed to be the rich men's quarters, in ceremonial area and in poor men's area. In Kalibangan we find a special area enclosed, near an area supposed to be the quarters of priests and other special personages. In this special area are found a large number of fire-pits in rows meant for ritual fire-worship by a large number of men. We also find that a very large number of houses contain rooms other than kitchen where there was fire-pit probably meant for keeping it burning all the days and all the year round. Probably fire was kept burning ceremonially in public places and in homes and that it too was ignited whenever required only ceremonially. It is also probable that fire could be ignited by the only known method of rubbing two sticks together for a pretty long time. There was no other known method of igniting fire known to men in those remote times. If fire is kept burning in a pit however big and wooden sticks fed to it for a long time, then surely a time must come when the ash produced and gathered in it will smother the fire and there will be a necessity to extinguish it and after cleaning the pit to rekindle it. We may believe that it was the natural thing to do in the fire pits of the towns of Indus Valley Civilisation. However, if they regarded it as god, then it must be done ceremoniously and on some particular day. It appears if we regard the Indus Civilisation to be an Aryan Civilisation and *Vedas* to be its record and the present day Hindus to be their descendants and successors that they chose a full moon day in the period when the winter passed and summer was yet to begin and counted the beginning of the new year or time cycle from that day. On this day they extinguished the fire everywhere, cleaned the fire-pits everywhere even in domestic hearths, and ceremoniously rekindled the fire by rubbing the two sticks together. As the fire came to life, there must be recitation of hymns composed for the occasion. After the recitation of hymns composed by a number of persons, the fire must have been worshipped and sticks taken out of it were taken to various homes to kindle the ceremonial fire kept there and the domestic fires. Then there must be rejoicings. This is known as renewal or rejuvenation of fire which was prevalent in tribal societies everywhere in the world. There is no reason to believe that it was not so in Indus Valley. The hymns to Agni, must have been composed for this purpose and recited on this occasion. The select few, out of a mass of poems, liked and known for their qualities must have been preserved and selected for inclusion in the *Vedas*. Do we have the same occasion of this renewal of fire in India today? We do have such a festival in Holi where the same ritual is performed. There is the same ceremonial lighting of fire at a conspicuous public place, the taking of fire to every domestic hearth and with it the lighting of fire in domestic hearths.

We may look at the name of the god of Fire. Among its various names two names, *i.e.*, Agni and Vaishavānar are rather interesting. According to Yāska, the first etymologist of the Vedic words, the meaning of Agni is 'Agranirbhavati' meaning the leader and one who is always in the front.[4] The meaning of Vaishavānar, according to Yāska, is 'Vishvān Narān Nayati. Vishvé Énam Narāh Nayanti Iti Vā', he takes all the men forward or he is taken by all the men.[5] Why is such peculiar meaning of the word Agni for Fire? We have to look for it to the era of tribal wanderings in Indus Valley, a semi-arid area. When the fire was discovered, the people not knowing how to kindle it, but knowing its mysterious qualities had to keep it with them during their wandering. They found that with fire in the forefront, they could find way even when darkness fell, in its light it kept beasts away, it kept them warm in cold and close in kinship to each other. With already elevating it to be a deity, they treated it as the leader which led them and also naturally it had to be carried by the tribe while in movement. We have two symbols in the undeciphered Indus Valley script. We have a symbol of a men carrying a huge weighing balance sort of thing on his shoulders meant for carrying something. It is similar to the one used by water-carriers in India of today. The symbol is used 220 times in the seals and is fairly common. The other symbol again shows two men moving with a bamboo over their shoulders and from the middle is hanging something like a palanquin in which they are carrying something. This symbol is shown only once in seal 518 from Mohenjodaro[6].

What is the thing which is supposed to be carried in these two symbols? We may not be far wrong in assuming it to be fire and nothing else which may make these symbols to be used by Indus people as an important symbol in their script. While the former symbol may actually denote either god of Fire himself or the priest who alone may be authorised to carry fire or may be the leader of the tribe, the latter one may mean god of Fire himself. Whatever it may be the names Agni and Vaishavānar appear to link *Vedas* and the language to the Indus Valley Civilisation.

Before discussing the geographical setting and historical evidence which is common to Indus Valley Civilisation and the *Vedas,* which we will discuss later, we would like to examine the mode of observing the last rites of a person, *i.e.,* rites performed after one's death. The *Vedas* tell us that both the rites, burial and cremation were prevalent in the Vedic Age. Sukta 16 of Mandal (book) X of *Rigveda* tells us about the cremation of the dead while Sukta 18 of Mandal X of *Rigveda* speaks about elaborate ritual observed prior to burial. In the Indus Valley Civilisation the excavations at cemetery H and cemetery R-37 at Harappa point out both the types of last rites. While some of the graves were of persons who were first cremated and their bones collected in a pot and buried, others were full burials. Thus both the rites were practised and *Vedas* record the both.

III

Do the physical features and geographical area described in the *Vedas* correspond with the area and physical features of the Indus Valley Civilisation? Are the courses of the rivers as described in the *Vedas* the same as they were in the Indus Valley Civilisation times or do they show those changed courses which came into being long after the end of that civilisation? Do we find some indications of the three cities, Harappa, Mohenjodaro and Kalibangan of the Indus Valley Civilisation or at least of their sites or existence? Do we get some indication of other habitations of the Indus Valley Civilisation? From the various sites discovered so far we found that the Indus Valley Civilisation area comprised the

North-Western part of Indian sub-continent including parts of modern day Afghanistan, Baluchistan and Saurashtra peninsula. This area comprised river system of the Indus with all its tributaries flowing from the Himalayas and Afghanistan, and the river Saraswati. Nothing can more truthfully and amply describe this river system than the Nadi-Stuti as mentioned in hymn 75 of Mandal X of *Rigveda*. It described the major rivers of the Punjab and all the rivers flowing from the Hindukush mountains in Afghanistan and strictly in the order in which they joined the river Indus. The river par excellence in this hymn is the river Indus. In some other hymns too the more important river is Indus. However, in some other hymns the river par excellence is the river Saraswati which is lovingly described as the mother. Why is it that in some Suktas Indus is described as the main river while in the others it is the Saraswati? Can it be that the composers of the various Suktas treated the issue on the basis of the region where they lived? Those living in Mohenjodaro which is on the banks of the river Indus treated Indus as the river with prime importance while those living in Harappa, Kalibangan or near about gave naturally importance to the river Saraswati.

A thing of interest to note is that sometimes names of rivers are changed. Usually it takes a long time that the name of the river is changed to another one. Similarly in course of time that name too is changed to something else. Yāska has pointed out that the name of the river Beas was Vipāshā, Ārjikiā and an earlier one was Uranjirā. (*Nirukta* 9.20). Similarly the name of Parushni was Irāwati as well (*Nirukta* 9.20) and today it is known as the Rāvi. All the names Vipāshā and Ārjikiā for the Beās and Irāwati and Parushni for the Rāvi are found in *Rigveda*. Interestingly the earlier name mentioned by Yāska of the Beās, *i.e.*, Uranjirā is not there in the *Vedas*. Why different names of the same river are mentioned in the *Vedas*? Can it be that those particular Suktas were written in different times? We face another problem with this frequent change of names. We get a number of names of rivers Rasā, Kubhā, Krumu, Sarayu,[7] Pāviravi, Kanyā, Chitrāyu, Virpatni,[8] Āpayā, Dhrisdwati[9], Anjasi, Kulishi, Virpatni[10], and of course Ganga and Yamuna[11]. Can it be possible that in this list the names of the same river are given differently and some one river or the other may be the Gangā and Yamunā, which names were later on transferred to the major rivers of India. Similarly it happened with the name of Sarayu. On the banks of the river of the name of Sarayu in modern Uttar Pradesh is situated the city of Ayodhya, the most sacred town of Hindus.

Do the *Vedas* indicate the courses of the rivers as they were in the times of the Indus Valley Civilisation or as they were after the period? We know that the courses of the rivers as they flowed in the Indus Valley Civilisation times were not the same as they were in later times and as they are today. In those times the river Rāvi flowed to the South of the present course and on its Southern bank was the town of Harappa. While the river Beās which now joins the Satluj at the present site actually flowed independently much further parallel to the Rāvi. At one point it flowed just 8 miles away from the Ravi. Similarly the Satluj which now joins Ravi then joined the Saraswati pouring its water into it. Yamunā also instead of its present course then had a different course joining the Saraswati through the bed of the river Dhrishdhwati. The waters of the two rivers Satluj and the Yamuna which had perennial waters made the Saraswati into a mighty river and a perennial one. The course of the river Indus was changing constantly as can be seen from the numerous river beds in Sind Province. Thus the rivers had changed courses probably due to tectonic changes and this shift in the position of rivers may enable us find out if the *Vedas* described the rivers in their courses which were in the times of the Indus Valley Civilisation or which were of the later period when they had changed their courses. How to find out if they describe the rivers flowing in their previous courses or later? If there is an important landmark such as the city which might be on the bank of the rivers and the *Vedas* indicate that landmark, then alone we can determine whether the river described is flowing in its old course in the times of Indus Valley Civilisation or later. As we know that these three towns of the Indus Valley Civilisation were situated on the banks of rivers, *i.e.*, Mohenjodaro on the banks of Indus, Harappa on the southern bank of Rāvi while just 8 miles south of Harappa flowed the Beās and Kalibangan which was situated where the river Dhrishdwati joined the Saraswati. Let us examine if the *Vedas* indicate any of the towns mentioned above.

Vedas have not mentioned any town in the hymns. As a matter of fact they are just hymns and in them to show the benevolence of the deity they have given the names of kings and tribes who were protected or helped by that deity. We get a very large number of names of kings and of various tribes without getting any idea whatsoever of the place where they lived. However, in a very few cases we are given some idea of the area where they lived or ruled. We may see if that can help us in identifying the place or the course of river. Divodās and his descendant Sudās are the ones often mentioned in various hymns and specially Sudās is praised for his valour, his generosity and as being protected by almost all deities. Though generally no place name is given in most of them, yet a few do give his area of operation and rule. In hymn 18 of Mandal VII of *Rigveda* we are told how Indra helped Sudās in his fight. However, the detailed description of the fight given in the hymn is interesting. It tells us that the enemy consisting of a number of tribes attacked Sudās and even tampered with the bank of the river Parushni (Rāvi). The tribes who attacked were ten in number and among the names given was Pakta, a tribe which can be identified with the modern day Pakhtoon tribe which inhabits the area to the North of the Rāvi and some parts of Afghanistan. It is stated that Sudas crossed the river and with the help of Indra defeated them and even destroyed some tribes.[12] We may note that the only town on the banks of the Ravi in those days was Harappa. No other site had so far been discovered on the then bank of Ravi which belonged to Indus Valley Civilisation. We may take it that the *Vedas* were referring to Harappa and to the old course of the river Rāvi. We get confirmation of this from Sukta 33 of Mandal III of *Rigveda*. In this Sukta which is addressed to the river Beās and Sutluj by Vishwāmitra, it is said that Vishwāmitra laden with gifts from Sudās came to the rivers and prayed to them to allow him and the people of Sudas to cross both the rivers, a prayer which, according to the hymn, was granted by the rivers. This hymn tells us about two things. Firstly, that while coming from the city of Sudās, *i.e.*, Harappa, one had to cross the two rivers the Beas and the Satluj which in view of the courses of rivers in those times was only 8-11 kilometres away. Secondly, at that time when the hymn was composed there were to the South of Harappa two rivers, the Beās and the Satluj while at a later time the Beās joined Satluj much earlier and there was only one river at that place. This clearly points out that the *Vedas* were giving the then courses of the rivers, not the ones which came into being slightly later. We also thus get the position of Harappa and that one of the dynasties which ruled over it was that of Divodās and Sudās. Purānās mention that the founder of the dynasty was Mudgal who is mentioned in *Rigveda*.[13] We do not get the names of towns of Indus Valley Civilisation but in this case there is a solitary reference to a name 'Udvraj'[14] which may be the name of the area or of Harappa even.

In Sukta 31 of Mandal VI of *Rigveda* we are informed that Indra had destroyed Kuyava to help Kutsa while in another Sukta 49 of Mandal X of *Rigveda* we are told that Indra had given the country 'Bétsu' to Kutsa. It gives us the information that a country or city known as 'Bétsu' was given to Kutsa after destroying 'Kuyava'. In Sukta 104 of Mandal I we get the information that Kuyava ruled over the area of eastern rivers. Thus the area of eastern rivers cannot be Indus but can be near Kalibangan which was situated at the junction of the Saraswati and Dhrishdwati. It may be a conjecture only but we note that the area where the mythical Saraswati joins the Gangā and the Yamunā, *i.e.*, near the town of Allāhābād was in the times of Buddha, *i.e.*, in 6th century B.C. known as 'Vatsa', a Sanskritised version of the name 'Bétsu'. May be that Vatsa and Bétsu were connected with the river Saraswati. If this conjecture is correct then 'Bétsu' must be connected with Saraswati and might be the area around Kalibangan or even Kalibangan itself. Dynasty of Kutsa is not given in the *Puranas* though Kutsa finds a mention. We find another mention of King Chitra ruling near at a place on the banks of the Saraswati and the place can only be Kalibangan.[15] We may also point out that throughout the Vedas the Saraswati is treated as a living and mighty river which only indicates that the rivers must be flowing in their old courses when the Satluj and the Yamunā were pouring their perennial waters into Saraswati. It was, as we have seen above, that after the period of Indus Valley Civilisation the rivers changed their courses with Yamunā joining the Gangā and flowing East and the Satluj joining the Rāvi, thus marking the death of the river Saraswati. We get a solitary reference to a king on the banks of the river Indus. We find that King Bhāvya was ruling on the banks of the Indus but we do not find any further reference to him or his dynasty in the *Purānās*. Obviously the reference is to the King of Mohenjodaro. But for further details we are in the dark.[16]

IV

The *Vedas* on the one hand give us a plethora of names of kings and various rulers and warriors but on the other they fail to give us the names of places where they ruled, the tribes to which they belonged and any indication of the political or administrative structure of the territory and the system of political governance. They give us the names of at least twenty or more tribes but again they fail to give us the territory where they inhabited or the kings or chiefs who led them. They do give us the names of fathers of kings who were named but that is the extent to which they go and that does not help us in reconstructing the ruling dynasty. They do give us the names of some tribes who were allies like the Yadu, Turvasu, Druhayu, Anu and Puru who were later described as belonging to Lunar dynasty and children of five brothers in the *Purānās*, or the tribes who were at war like Vrichivants and Pārthavas, etc. But we do not get much out of these random names of kings or tribes. Can it be possible to make out a complete picture of the political structure and find out the ruling dynasties of the Vedic period even if for a part of the thousands of years of its long existence?

Can the later works the *Brahmanas* and the *Purānās* help us in any way? No doubt for any understanding of the Vedic political structure and history we will have to depend on the *Purānās*. However, we will have to keep in view some of the difficulties which we will encounter while seeking the help of the *Purānās*. *Purānās* were composed at least more than a thousand years after the end of the Vedic period, and some of the incidents or the kings mentioned in the *Vedas* might have existed even more than two thousand years before the first Purānic dynasty was thought out. We may take the example of the Mauryas who existed about two thousand years ago, or the Guptas who ruled about one thousand and five hundred years earlier but we do not know much about them. Even there is controversy about the successors within the dynasty, when we have much more materials available about them than was available to the composers of the *Purānās*. Similar must have been the case with the history of the Vedic period. *Purānās* could have faced the same problem of the real events remaining as shadows in memory and might have incorporated some of the things which must have appeared to them to be all right and authentic but in fact might have been otherwise. Dynastic lists given in the *Purānās* could not be relied upon, just as we cannot rely even on the list of the Mauryan dynasty given so differently by different scholars. There are some obviously gross errors in the lists. We may take the case of Sudās, the king so prominently mentioned in the *Vedas*. *Purānās* gave him as belonging to the Lunar dynasty and among the descendants of Puru and belonging to Puru tribe. He is shown as the thirty-third descendant of Puru but in the *Vedas* it is otherwise. He is mentioned as leading the Bharat and Tritsu tribes against a coalition of tribes among whom the prominent tribe was the Puru tribe. Sudās could not have been a Puru. It has also to be kept in view that most of the names of kings mentioned in the *Vedas* are not found in the Purānic lists of various dynasties and hence it is difficult to understand the history of that period fully. We also are faced with the problem of the cities and regions where these people ruled for though the *Purānās* give us the names of cities, yet *Vedas* do not. We may, however, keeping the geography of the Indus Valley Civilisation in mind within which the *Vedas* had confined themselves, try to reconstruct the history as disclosed by *Vedas* howsoever it may be confined to a small area and even a smaller period.

What parts of the Indus Valley were inhabited in those times? How far removed were the cities of Mohenjodaro, Harappa and Kalibangan from the rural areas and what could be the relationship between the cities and the populated areas? A look at the map of the sites of the Indus Valley Civilisation will reveal that most of the sites were situated on the banks of the river Saraswati. In fact out of 800 and odd sites discovered so far 530 are on the river Saraswati and rest are scattered widely in rest of the area, far removed from each other. Mohenjodaro and Harappa, the two major towns are far removed from the Saraswati, Harappa on the river Ravi and Mohenjodaro on the river Indus. In between Harappa and river Saraswati are two major rivers the Beās and the Satluj. In the vicinity of the two cities, however, there were no sites which only indicated that the hinterland of the two cities was far removed from them showing that probably their origin was that of 'guardians of the frontiers' rather than that of the administrative capital. As there are no Indus Valley sites discovered so far on the Rāvi, the Beās or the Satluj it reinforces the belief that Harappa was founded basically to guard the hinterland from the wild tribes which attacked from the North and North-West, *i.e.,* from the Hindukush mountains and which took away the cattle and the agricultural produce of the people living on the banks of the Saraswati. Later on it might have constituted the administrative Capital of the region. Similarly the purpose of the founding of Mohenjodaro must have been to protect the hinterland from being plundered by the tribes from the Baluchistan region and beyond. To the South of the river Saraswati must have roamed the nomadic tribes with their cows, sheep and goats moving from site to site and settling for a short period of intense heat on the banks of the rivers. Surely it is due to them that we find the uniformity in the religion, script, pottery and other artifacts throughout the Indus Valley Civilisation. It is to protect both the settled population as well as the nomadic ones that the two cities were founded and their chiefs acted only as the Guardians of the Frontiers. But what about Kalibangan which was situated on the banks of the river Saraswati itself? Probably it was meant to keep internal order only or as a trading post. Was it because of this that it could not grow to dimensions to which Harappa and Mohenjodaro had grown and developed?

As we had seen above Sudas, according to *Rigveda,* was to be identified as the ruler of Harappa. We find in the *Purānās* a list of eight generations of persons from Vridhayāshva to Somaka. The prominent persons in this list are Mudgal, Divodas and Sudas. Mudgal is second, Divodas the fourth and Sudas the seventh in this list. We know something about Mudgal, Divodas and Sudas as given in the Vedas. All the three had worked in different scenarios. Do their exploits give us any idea of the development of Harappa and the political scene of the Indus Valley Civilisation? Some idea we do have if we look at the incidents associated with them in the changing face of the political and social growth of the Indus Valley. We meet Mudgal[17] in the early stages of the Indus Valley Civilisation when the tribes were fighting each other with stone clubs and stone weapons and used to plunder the other tribes depriving them of cattle and probably of agricultural produce. Mudgal invented the wooden club and if not invented at least used it effectively. We find that a tribe had robbed his tribe of its cows and ran away. Mudgal armed all the people with wooden clubs as seen above and attacked them not only defeating them but recovering the cows from them. This probably made Mudgal the hero and chief of the tribe and others settled on the banks of the river Saraswati might have asked him to defend them against such plunder in return for some contribution in terms of cattle and grain. Guardianship of frontier or 'Wardenship of the Marches' came to his tribe and his descendants probably retained the hereditary chieftainship. We find that the particular site of Harappa was given to Divodas by Indra, after defeating Shambar. It appears that actually Divodas selected the site to be the most suitable for a permanent headquarters and founded the city. We also get the name of the area or city too 'Udvraj'[18]. Later came Sudās whose exploits were so vividly described in the *Vedas*. When again some tribes, among them Pakta that could be identified as the Pakhtoon tribe residing in Pakistan and Afghanistan, attacked again, they were repulsed by Sudas inflicting heavy losses and Sudas became secure[19]. From then on he performed many sacrifices including Horse Sacrifice[20]. He also gave away gifts to Rishis[21]. It was at that time that probably he became the ruler of nearby areas too due to Horse Sacrifice. There are a number of references in the *Vedas* to link some members of this dynasty to each other. We are informed that Divodas was ancestor of Sudas[22]. We are also informed that Vridhayāshva was ancestor of Divodas[23]. We do not know whether they were called kings, but both Divodas and Sudas were known as 'Atithigva'. Was it their designation? Sudas was succeeded by his son Somaka and after him there are no names. Has the dynasty come to an end and some others have succeeded them? We are not aware of. We get another reference to Shrutarvā, son of Riksha who was ruling at the Ravi[24]. *Purānās* are silent about him and the dynasty to which he belonged. The dynasty of Mudgal to Sudas belonged to the Bharat tribe and not to Puru tribe as mentioned in the *Purānās*. Did so much development in the political and social life take place during the period when the seven persons of that dynasty had acted as Warden of the Marches or Guardians of the Frontier? We cannot say whether names of some other members of the dynasty are missing from the list, but it appears that such development could have taken a much longer period.

Some such development must have taken place in the establishment and development of Mohenjodaro but *Vedas* are silent about the events at Mohenjodaro. We get a solitary name of Bhāvya ruling over a place on the Indus which obviously must be Mohenjodaro[25]. But we know nothing more about it. There is reference to a major battle at Hariyupiā in which the tribe Varshikh was defeated by Abhyāvarti of the Pārthav tribe. But we are left in the dark about the location of Hariyupiā or about the Pārthava tribe. *Purānās* do not indicate anything about it.

Of the three cities only Kalibangan is situated on the banks of Saraswati river where all along are settlements. It could not, therefore, be a March or an active frontier. It could have been only an administrative centre. About the kings ruling there we have no indication in the *Vedas*. We get only one name of King Chitra ruling on the banks of the Saraswati which may mean only Kalibangan[26]. To which dynasty he belonged or which tribe was inhabiting the area we have no information. If, as we have stated earlier, Kalibangan could be the ancient Bétsu, then another name of Kutsa is mentioned as the ruler. But who was he? The dynasty or tribe to which he belonged has not been indicated. Both *Vedas* and *Brahamanas* tell us that he was as brilliant as Indra himself, that he acted as the charioteer of Indra and that on his behalf Indra fought the Sun. But that is the only information that we have about his rule.

What about the large number of names of other kings and other tribes? Where did they live and where did they rule? Could they be the rulers of any of the three cities? Names in the *Vedas* are found in plenty. Some of the names are mentioned in hymns to various gods where it is said that they were protected by them. Other names are given in what are called 'Dān-Stutis', the hymns to the kings who gave gifts. These kings must have been quite wealthy for they gave gifts and must have been the patrons of learned ones. Most of them are just names in the *Vedas*. *Purānās* do tell us of the dynasty to which they belonged but where these dynasties were ruling we are left in the dark. We may get a comprehensive picture only when the place and the age when they were ruling is discovered if ever in the Indus Seals. One interesting feature is that the *Vedas* do not give the names of the either the heroes of *Rāmāyana* or their immediate ancestors. However, the name of the great grandfather of the warriors of the *Mahābhārata* war, Shāntanu, is given in the *Vedas* as performing a sacrifice for rain[27].

V

Vedas reveal a society through various phases. They reveal a society which has grown from one honouring its totems into worshipping them and raising them to divinity, from the worshipping a pantheon of gods into believing ultimately to the existence of an unseen, all powerful and indestructible Supreme God who is the *Creator* as well. They show a society which has grown from a nomadic life into a sedentary agricultural life, from a tribal life into a highly organised urban life and from a close fighting tribes into the setting up of kingdoms and probably to an empire with peace for all. However do we find that these various facets growing in isolation are without any impact on the other facet? Probably not. All this growth is there due to the effect of one on the other, in a cumulative growth of all in synthesis. Probably society advanced from one phase to another combining all those facets and ultimately to the final growth, indicating the growth of all the facets of life. Do the *Vedas* indicate the various phases of its development?

We find in the *Vedas* the earliest tribal life where the tribes moved about the land along with animals mainly cattle and their totems. They used to honour their totems and certain plants, specially they used to carry a small portion of these plants as amulet which were dear to them and which they honoured. During that period while moving about they became friendly with certain tribes like Yadu, Turvasu, Drahayu, Anu and Puru, while they fought with others. The fight was mainly for the possession of cattle and probably of women. They fought with stone implements. It was during their wanderings that they discovered Fire and worshipped it, carrying it with them as they were unable to relight it. Fire became their leader, one which showed the way, hence they named it Agni and Vaishwānar. They were used to worshipping their totem. When they realised the power of the Sun, the totem gained the divinity of Sun as well. Their totem became the Sun god as well. When they compared their Sun god with Sun god of other friendly tribes they realised that their god and the god of other tribes have the same attributes except their names and their forms. Thus arose the concept of Ādityas, most of whom are various names of Sun and Fire which they probably thought to be linked, together. The allied tribes thus worshipped Ādityas together. Probably this concept gave rise to the worship of 'Vishwedevās,' all the gods of the world. A number of hymns are addressed to the 'Vishwedevās'.

During their wanderings they must have come to know of the existence of the river Saraswati. Inevitably they must have made their way to the banks of the river Saraswati during the scorching heat of the summer. They got plenty of water and shade of the trees along its banks as well as fodder.

Saraswati became the mother and hence the various hymns extolling it. It might be that on the banks of the Saraswati and nearabout they had noticed that during the rains some grains sprouted and after the rains when again collected were good for food. Also after some time noticing that if during the rainy season these grains were sown again, they sprouted and gave abundant grains. Thus they might have learnt the method of farming and taken the practice of sowing grains and reaping the harvest. Rains became food-giving and nourishing benediction. Surely for them it must have been the work of a god who gives rain and as such the rain-god Indra became their new deity, and was added to the pantheon of Agni, Ādityās and Saraswati. Very large number of hymns are addressed to Indra. After some time a number of tribes sick of their wanderings must have decided to live on the banks of the river Saraswati and take to agriculture. They must have discovered the use of plough[28]. At first their sojourn on the banks of the Saraswati must have been limited to summer and rainy season only. After reaping the harvest the tribe must have moved for their annual wanderings to return in the beginning of summer season. During the course of time some among the tribe must have decided that it was preferable to stay permanently at one place on the bank of the Saraswati and depend on agriculture and protection of cattle. May be at first such persons were confined to older persons. But later on a group of families must have turned sedentary and settled at one place or a village. Such villages belonging to a tribe must have sprung up near each other. Thus a part of the tribe must have lived in a cluster of villages all the year round while a part must have lived there during summer and rainy seasons only and the rest of the time they must have spent in wanderings. This practice also must have given way later to the whole of the tribe living in villages and taking to agriculture and keeping cattle, specially cows. As for the other tribes who must have continued wandering their function must have also changed to carrying goods produced in one area to another as well as carrying tales.

In this second phase of development when the tribes settled in villages and took to agriculture, the new challenges must have arisen. They must have required permanent structures as their homes, enclosures for their cattle including cows. They must have also required pottery to keep their household goods and specially grain. Houses must have been built at first of only mud walls and thatched roofs to be followed by sun-dried mud bricks. They must have been long aware that mud baked in fire becomes hard as stone. Somehow they might have also discovered that they could make pottery by making a pot of mud and baking it in fire. New pottery must have been made. A new god of pottery making Ribhu emerged and we have quite a few hymns to Ribhu in *Rigveda*. Fire must have been used for cooking and it found a permanent home in each household. However, instead of keeping it in a pot as done earlier during their wanderings it was now kept permanently in dug fire-pits where it was kept fed by wood continuously. Public fire-pits for public worship in each village must also have been dug and kept burning throughout the year. These public fire-pits must have been used for propitiation of Fire. How to propitiate other gods? At this time the thought must have emerged that Agni or Fire is the mouth of gods and that they could also be propitiated through feeding it to Fire in their names. The rituals must have become more elaborate and time consuming. However, a problem must have arisen that of accumulated ash which tends to smother fire. So it must be cleaned. They must have decided to clean the fire-pits after the winter season. A particular day must have been selected for the purpose. After cleaning the fire-pits a new fire must have been kindled amidst chanting of hymns and great rejoicing. Probably the hymns sung at that time were preserved and are the hymns to Agni, the Fire god in the *Vedas*. This ritual of cleaning of fire-pits and relighting of Fire or renewal of Fire developed into an annual feature in India through the festival of Holi, one of the main festivals of India celebrated even today. Another celebration must have been the day of departure of tribe on their annual wanderings after the rainy season and harvesting of crops. In the night before the day of their departure the tribe must have made preparations for departure and packed their goods. Among them they must have kept fire to be taken along by each family in small earthen pots and kept them outside their houses. The sight must have gladdened them and inspired them to celebrate it with joy. They must have celebrated it and it continued down to this day in India when people light fire in small earthen pots and keep them outside their houses during the night. This festival is Diwali, another most popular festival of India.

When the tribes were in a wild state and perpetually moving, they must have been faced with the problem of the sick, the wounded, the disabled and old persons who could not move along with the tribe. They must have left them behind to die or if recovered to rejoin them. However, in the settlements of the villages they could not so neglect them. New remedies and various herbs must have been tried and found effective. The sick and disabled were cared for. They must have been amazed at the powers of the herbs and we find so many hymns devoted to various particular drugs in the *Vedas*, mostly in the *Atharvaveda*. They must have felt that only a god could have inspired them to use the drugs for healing the sick and wounded. Hence, a new god or in fact two gods were added to their pantheon, the Ashwin Twins. Hymns were regularly addressed to them. In fact the hymns to the Ashwins are the third largest in the *Vedas* after those to Agni and Indra.

During this second phase of their development the people settled on the banks of the river Saraswati. They had to face a formidable challenge in the shape of raids by wild tribes who took away grain, cows and probably women. When the attack came, the whole tribe stood like one and undivided to fight them and beat them back. But what happened when they stealthily attacked them in the night and took away grain which was stored, cows and women. The tribe required some time to gather its people from neighbouring villages and organise rescue operation. Where had the attackers gone? They must take a long time in locating the attackers and rescue. Some day the problem must have been solved in a miraculous way by a faithful dog who must have gone out to trace the cows by his power of the smell and led the warriors to the exact spot where the cows were kept hidden. The dog became their eternal friend and was used both as a watchdog and one who could help them in recovery of their cattle. A hymn was addressed to dog in the hymn known as that to 'Sarma Paṇat'[29]. In this the divine bitch finds out the cows and leads Indra to rescue them.

This state of permanent alertness and continuous raids by wild tribes could not have continued. The tribesmen had to find a way to meet that challenge. How could they meet that challenge? They must find out someone who could protect them from the surrounding tribes. They must have found such a man in the person of Mudgal who, if we believe that he was the ancestor of Sudās, must have been the leader of Bharat tribe. He had used a long wooden club in place of heavy, shorter stone club and with it had easily defeated the attacking tribe and rescued the cows[30]. On their request he must have agreed to guard the frontier to the north from where almost all the attackers came and thus he became the Warden of the March probably on the condition that grain and cows which his tribe needed must be supplied proportionately by various tribes. They must have agreed to this proposal and the job must have been entrusted to his tribe and his descendants. Now we come at the third stage of development which has been described by the *Vedas* in greater details.

What are the developments and details we find in the *Vedas*? What steps the Bharat tribe had taken in guarding the frontier? How they had prepared themselves for this task? We find, as seen above, that one of his descendants Divodās selected the site of Harappa for his permanent camp. The site must have been ideal in that it was situated in the neck between the Rāvi and the Beās rivers where the distance between the two rivers is only eight miles or eleven kilometers. That had protected him from a surprise attack from either side. Moreover, on receipt of information that the enemy had crossed over they also could cross the rivers in a short time and pursue the raiders. Later the grand design for the city must have been prepared and built. As they were not to take to agriculture or rearing of cows or bother about other necessities, the tribe was a standing army preparing for war and developing armaments. They must have discovered that instead of stone pellets they could make effective pellets of baked mud. They must have discovered the use of copper and bronze and must have developed the battle-axe and equipped their army with it. The pride of place in armament must go to bow and arrow. With it they became invincible. With it they had to develop armour to protect their body, gloves to prevent injury to their hands while discharging arrows, and beating battle drums and such other musical instruments to inspire their army, to gather them and to celebrate victory. We have hymns to bow[31], cord tying the bow Jyā[31], arrow[31], case in which arrows were kept, glove[31], and the musical instrument Dumdubhi, something like a bugle[32]. They also discovered the chariot and the hymn to chariot[32] and those to the cane used to drive the horses were added. In fact chariot became the principal mode of carrying men and goods as seen in the hymn to the two rivers Beās and the Satluj[33].

What was the effect of that permanent encampment of the well-prepared army? Even when peace was restored and dangers of raiders removed did the army remain in their camps? That state could not have remained static for long. We have no knowledge if the city founded to provide for a habitation of the army contained only the warriors of the Bharat tribe or there were other representatives of various other tribes but we find that in the *Vedas* the names of Bharats and Tritsus are only given[34]. With such a large standing army the idea of conquests must have entered the minds of rulers. We find that Sudās conquered a large number of tribes and places. He defeated four different tribes Brahmu, Kavash, Shruta, Vridha and conquered two places among them Vaikarna and another place near the river Yamunā[35]. Other tribes Shigra, Yaksha and Aja also gave tributes[34]. We also find that Sudās undertook a Horse Sacrifice which is a prelude to a campaign for conquest and universal sovereignty[35]. The third phase of development as seen in *Vedas* was the establishment of cities and later Empires. This was the most mature and developed phase as is found in the *Vedas*. We also find that the consciousness of belonging not to different tribes but to a single country had also taken hold of people's mind. This could be seen in two hymns in praise of king where he has been exhorted to keep the country stable and prosperous[36].

Did the growing urbanisation consequent to the setting up of small kingdoms and later empires affect the social, cultural and religious ethos and thinking of the people? It must affect them either to a smaller or to a larger extent. Does it find reflection on the *Vedas*? The effect of urbanisation in the first place is in that it produces leisure and consequently love of pleasure. In the second place it induces a desire for sophistication which implies adornment and beautification of females. Both of them have been indicated in the *Vedas*. Love of pleasure giving games sometimes induces men to take to such games like gambling which ultimately turns out to be a vice. Apparently one such game was the game of dice for we have a hymn to dice which praises as well condemns it[37]. Similarly we have a hymn to gold indicating that Vedic society was familiar with it and was using gold ornaments[38]. Both gold ornaments and dice were recovered in the excavations in Indus Valley Civilisation towns. There was definitely an advancement of culture with a large number of ritual sacrifices probably extending to many days and consequent large scale gift of cows, chariots, horses and even girls by the performers who appear to be mainly chieftains and kings. A very large number of 'Dānstutis' or hymns in praise of gifts are found widely scattered in the *Rigveda*. It is these Dānstutis which give us the names of a large number of important men, both givers and receivers.

Do we have any idea of these elaborate rituals? What was the practice and what was the method? Probably these sacrifices which had those rituals consisted of giving of oblation to various gods through the medium of fire by pouring it into the fire in the names of various gods. Hymns were composed for the purpose of naming the god or gods and the incantation used for pouring it into the fire. A collection of such hymns is in *Yajurveda*. A large number of hymns sung at these sacrifices and at other times are collected in what is known as *Sāmveda*. A very large number of hymns of *Rigveda* are found in both *Yajurveda* and in *Sāmveda*. Both these *Vedas* reveal the large extent to which the ritual-based religion advanced. Was there a conceptual change in the religious thought as well? Should there be a change in the status of various gods in the imagination of people? There should be a change for earlier various chieftains of tribes were treated as equal but were no longer treated as equal with the establishment of an empire or a pre-eminent king. Just as there was a prê-eminent king or an emperor so there must be god among various gods. Indra was chosen as such a leader of gods and moreover being treated as the god of war as well became the chief. Did he become in the eyes of people the Creator of this earth and its inhabitants? No, he did not. He was merely one who brought rain, made the rivers flow, helped people in distress and helped in dispelling the enemies but no more. However, the idea of the Creator of the Universe was agitating the minds of the people and questions were raised about his identity[39]. Attempts were made to answer that question in the Hiranyagarbh Sukta[40]. However, ultimately it appears that the people admitted that there is a Creator but His identity is unknown. In the Nāsādiya Sukta or the Hymn of Creation[41] it comes out that there is a Creator but His identity is not known nor the hymn asserts that it can be known for both the gods and the seers were created afterwards and they simply did not know Him. That hymn also indicates that the people were also interested in knowing how the universe was created. It gives an interesting answer that either He alone knows or may be that even He does not know implying that the universe might have been created in a fit of absent mindedness. Or may be a thought came into His mind and with that thought the universe came into existence. The concept of an unknown Creator is a unique achievement of the society as recorded by the *Vedas* fragmentarily. This concept alone shows the heights to which the imagination and thought of the society had soared.

VI

The *Vedas*, our enquiries reveal, are the record of a developing civilisation which is none other than the Indus Valley Civilisation. Every hymn revealed much more than a plain reading of it tells us. We saw in the Sukta 102 of tenth Mandal of *Rigveda* that Mudgal with a bull and wooden club recovered the cows. But it tells us more. It shows that he had either invented the wooden club or if already invented used it to equip his tribe with it, which is an advancement in development of armament and thus successfully routed the enemies. It also shows that he had proved himself to be capable of being the guardian of the frontier and laid the future greatness and prosperity of his tribe and his successors. Sukta 18 of Mandal seventh of *Rigveda* which describes a later period of the same tribe tells that Sudas leading the Bharat tribe completely routed the coalition of ten tribes who tried to raid his capital but also defeated a number of other tribes in various other parts. The Sukta reveals that the Bharatas had not only vindicated their responsibility as guardians of the frontier but by annihilating the major part of the enemies made it secure for a long time to come. Not only that the Sukta informs us that they had established suzerainty over a large tract, it also shows the Bharatas' bid for power, for pre-eminence among their peers, for world dominion. The world in their case consisted of the known world which was the area of the Indus Valley Civilisation. Every hymn is pregnant with the meaning if seen in the context of the particular growth phase of the Civilisation it records. Every Sukta is of pure ore of gold. It has only to be assessed, weighed and valued. If, only if we may know when the hymn was composed, why it was composed and where in the wide expanse of Indus Valley it was composed. Also if we can find out whether at the time of collection of various hymns in the four *Vedas*, certain hymns were deliberately left out. If so WHY?

REFERENCES

1. *Atharvaveda*, 4.5.1.
2. *Atharvaveda* 3.6, hymn to Ashwattha or *'Pipal'*; *Atharvaveda* 3.5 hymn to Parnamani.
3. F.E.M. Pl. XC, 24(a).
4. Nirukta; Yaska 7.14
5. Nirukta; Yaska 7.21
6. F.E.M. Pl. XCVI.
7. *Rigveda* 5.52.
8. *Rigveda* 6.49.
9. *Rigveda* 3.23.
10. *Rigveda* 1.104.
11. *Rigveda* 10.75.
12. *Rigveda* 7.18.
13. *Rigveda* X.102.
14. *Rigveda* 6.47.21.
15. *Rigveda* 8.21.18.
16. *Rigveda* 1.126.
17. *Rigveda* X. 102.
18. *Rigveda* VI. 47.
19. *Rigveda* VII. 18.
20. *Rigveda* III. 53. 11-12.
21. *Rigveda* III. 33.
22. *Rigveda* VII. 18.25.
23. *Rigveda* VI. 61.
24. *Rigveda* VII. 74.
25. *Rigveda* I.126.
26. *Rigveda* VIII.21.

27. *Rigveda* X.98.
28. *Rigveda* 4.57.
29. *Rigveda* X.108.
30. *Rigveda* X.102.
31. *Rigveda* VI.75.
32. *Rigveda* VI.47.
33. *Rigveda* 3.33.
34. *Rigveda* VII.18.
35. *Rigveda* III.53.
36. *Rigveda* X.173, X.174.
37. *Rigveda* X.34.
38. *Atharvaveda* XIX.26.
39. *Rigveda* I.164.
40. *Rigveda* X.121.
41. *Rigveda* X.129.

2

STIRRING FOR CIVILISATION

When did Civilisation begin in India? When did history begin in India? These are the eternal questions raised in India. Till 1935 books of history taught that the Indian civilisation began when the Aryan tribes migrated into India in the 13th Century B.C. and colonised it. However, by 1940 the textbooks changed and began teaching that India had a flourishing Civilisation, the Indus Valley Civilisation, since 3000 B.C. and that the invading Aryan tribes in the 13th Century B.C. destroyed it and after driving out its inhabitants to South India made it an Aryan land and Aryan civilisation. Mercifully nobody suggested that the Aryans came in India prior to 3000 B.C. and established the Indus Valley Civilisation itself. All are agreed that the Indus Valley Civilisation developed in the land itself and by the inhabitants of the area. Also the modern excavations and the modern satellite imagery indicates that the Indus Valley Civilisation died in 19th Century B.C. and of its own due to natural causes and that it was not destroyed by any invading tribe. The persistence of the view of Aryan invasion may be traced to the rise of Christian fundamentalism which believed in the Biblical story of the Great Flood described in the *Bible* and the story of Noah's Ark descending on Mt. Ararat in Central Asian region of Caucasian mountains, where Noah settled and his descendants grew and multiplied to such an extent that they began migrating to other lands. Out of that grew the legends that one branch moved to Europe and the other to India and Iran. However, mythology is just mythology and nobody should accept it without some proof which is lacking in this theory of Aryan invasion. We will have occasion to see later that the Indus Valley Civilisation was nothing but a predecessor of the later day Hindu Civilisation and nothing else.

We may, therefore, accept that the history of India began with the establishment of a government in some area of Indus Valley Civilisation. However, we cannot give a definite or even a tentative date except that it may be somewhere near 3000 B.C. because the towns of Harappa and Mohenjodaro were founded sometime in the 25th Century B.C. about five hundred years might be the time taken to reach that stage. It might have taken a longer time. Nothing can be said definitely about it. For the question that when civilisation began we are unable to give even a tentative time period. It might have begun much earlier. If we look at the map of the ancient world, we find that the three earliest Civilisations, Egyptian, Sumerian and Indus lie in the same region, have the same climatic conditions and are in the vicinity of each other. The first stirrings in the three Civilisations must have begun at the same time. They must have begun thousands of years prior to the beginning of their history. We may have a look at the first stirrings of civilisation in the then purely tribal society.

History of India is like a river going on its never-ending course moving in a zigzag way but its beginning is also like the river in a streamlet in a far-away mountain. The history of India began millions of years ago when human life found itself in the shape of tribes all over the world. How these tribes lived, surmounted difficulties, moved forward with and thus made the history of that land depended on the geography of the land where that particular tribe or tribes resided. Hence to understand the history of India it is necessary that we understand the geography of the then India, specially that period when its history is supposed to begin. From the archaeological excavations it appears that the Indian history began in the age called neolithic age which began about 10,000 years before Christ. At that time whole of India from the Himalayas to the Cape Comorin in the South, from Assam in the East to a little to the West of Delhi in the North India was one huge forest. South India was covered with forests and so was India North of the river Ravi. India which was not under forest was the area which today comprises the state of Rajasthan except its Eastern and Southern fringe, the state of Haryana, the part of the Indian state of Punjab to the South of the river Ravi, Pakistan to the South of the river Ravi and parts of Baluchistan. This whole area, the Thar desert and the surrounding area probably had some more rainfall than at present which made it into a grassland bereft of forests and trees. Because of forest all around it and in India as a whole and also probably because of world climate there was an abundance of rainfall in India on the Himalayas resulting in more water in rivers and rivulets.

North-Western India had the same number of rivers but their course and alignment was different. River Beas was flowing slightly to the North and was a major river flowing for some time parallel to the river Ravi very near to it almost touching it, its distance from Ravi at Harappa being only about 8 miles (11 kms). To its South in the Southern part of modern state of Haryana and Northern Rajasthan flowed the mighty Saraswati charting an independent course throughout in Rajasthan in an East-Western course, turning South on entering the state of Sind and flowing parallel to Indus into the Gulf of Cutch. It was not as dry as of now but full of water for at that time the river Satluj, which now joins Beas and flows independently for some time before joining Ravi, was a tributary of the Saraswati. Similarly the river Yamunā which is now a tributary of the river Gangā, was at that time a tributary of the Saraswati. In addition, a large number of small rivers and rivulets which flowed from the Himalayas because of plenty of rainfall also contributed their water to the Saraswati. It was, therefore, a mighty river flowing into an arid land and had a significant influence on the growth of civilisation in India.

We may look a little closely into this geographical scene and the evidence on which it is based, specially the existence of the Saraswati. In the maps photographs of which are taken from the modern techniques of remote sensing and also of physical verification we find the old bed of the Saraswati in the state of Haryana and Northern Rajasthan from the East

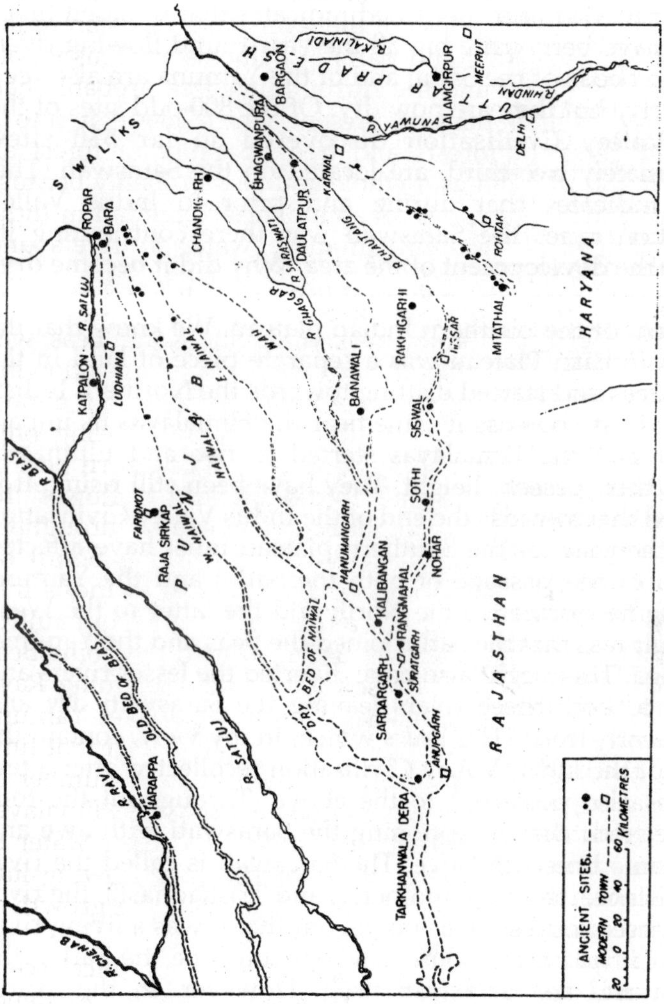

Map 2: Map of Western India showing the River Ghaggar System and the Archaeological Sites

Source: Ecology and Archaeology of Western India

to West and in Pakistan Sind from North to South, known by its modern name of Hakra. This old bed is uniformly wide and at places its width is a few kilometers. It is now a dry river but its wide and deep bed indicates that in olden times it must have been quite big all-the-year-round flowing river.

The old beds of the Satluj and of the Yamuna are also seen very clearly but they are now dry. Of the 800 odd sites of the Indus Valley Civilisation discovered so far 530 sites, approximately two-third, are located on the Saraswati. This clearly indicates that during and prior to Indus Valley Civilisation times the Saraswati was there contributing its share to the development of the area. Why did it become dry? The reason again is geographical, *i.e.*, due to tectonic movement of the Southern Indian plateau. We know that the Southern Indian Plateau was a separate piece of land in the remote ages and started drifting towards the Northern Indian mountains. As soon as it came near the Himalayas its impact was felt and the Himalayas started to rise and ultimately reached their present height. They have been still rising. It is surmised that towards the end of the Indus Valley Civilisation period the push of the Southern plateau must have affected the area of the passage of both the Satluj and the Yamuna diverting the former to the North and the latter to the West. The result was that the Satluj joined the Beās and the Yamunā, the Gangā. This might also have diverted the lesser rivers and rivulets to both these rivers leaving the Saraswati dry and subsequently dead. The *Vedas* which, in my view, contain the history of the Indus Valley Civilisation recollected after a few centuries also point out to the above. Throughout the four *Vedas* we find them mentioning the Saraswati with awe and at the same time with love. The Saraswati is called the river par excellence, the most motherly, and Trishadhastā, the river having three sources. This points out that it was a living river and that it had three sources which could be the Satluj, the Yamuna and the Saraswati itself. However, in the 'Nadi-statuti' hymn of the tenth Mandal of the *Rigveda* we do find the mention of the name of the Saraswati but the praise is confined to Indus, its swift flowing current. Again in the third Mandal of the *Rigveda,* we find the Rishi Vishwāmitra invoking the Beās and the Satluj together points out that at that time both the rivers flowed. Probably the drying of the river Saraswati or its disappearance marked or caused the end of the Indus Valley Civilisation.

After thus looking at the then geography of India we may have a glance at the prehistoric India, the India prior to the establishment of the Indus Valley Civilisation. About 10,000 years ago man was found all the world over, only in the state of primitive tribes. That included the areas of Sumer and Egypt, the lands of the earliest civilisations of the world. Those tribes were so primitive that their only means of sustenance were either gathering fruits, digging roots or hunting animals or fish. They had no fire and no tools and did not know the art of cooking. Thus we had two types of tribes, the food gatherers or hunters or both. In the area covered by dense forests where fruits could be found in abundance on trees or shrubs the gathering of food was an easy job. The tribes inhabiting this region were just food gatherers. In the North West India in the area where there were no forests but a vast arid plain covered by grass whose monotony was only broken by the Saraswati and its tributaries and the river system of Luni, another small river, the tribes could only be hunters. Unlike the food gatherers of the forests who remained sedentary in their forest, the hunters had to be always on the move going after their prey and when the animals, because of the change in climate, moved to other areas, the hunters also had to move along with them. That movement along with the animals as well as hunting was to affect them in more ways than one. Firstly, they had to innovate the means of hunting. They might have used the stones in the shape of club, then small stones to hit animals and thus to bring them down. Then a stage might have come when they might have learned the use of sling and lastly bow and arrows which they might have improved with the use of copper head. The same gradual improvement in the technique of skinning, they must have evolved.

The movement of the tribes must have brought them into contact with other tribes on the move. With some they must have fought and with others they must have formed friendship and sometimes alliance. This friendship or alliance with other tribes must have made them exchange experience and learn things and the fight must have taught them the use of better weapons. The skinning of the animals after a hunt must have produced difficulties but they must have seen the use of a sharp stone and must have made them develop the art of sharpening the stone at first, but they or somebody else must have seen the usefulness of breaking the stone in such a way that it became a handy tool. That art of making a stone into a tool must have spread rapidly among the tribes of that region. They must have learned rapidly that the stone meant for that purpose was found at certain particular places and they could prepare tools only where they could stay for a certain period and which required, in addition to the availability of a special type of stone, shelter and water. This could be had only either on the banks of the rivers or near lakes. We thus find that there were only a few sites where they had prepared their tools. One of the sites was Burha Pushkar lake near Ajmer in the centre of Rajasthan where a large factory was found for preparation of these primitive tools. We find from the pottery found there that the tribes from as far away as Ahar near modern Udaipur and Bagore in District Bhilwara in Rajasthan visited Burha Pushkar for the production of tools. From this we find that the tribes in this region used to traverse the whole of the region and in the course met other tribes. In that process they learnt from others, taught them what they knew and thus a uniformity was achieved and a uniform development took place.

We may now look at the other tribes in the region who were not nomads of the desert. We may remember that the Saraswati was flowing through that desert along with its tributaries. It was a mighty river which during the monsoon season must have been flooding the areas along its bed. Thus along the banks of the Saraswati and its tributaries and of other rivers there must have been forests and also areas, where after the summer floods, some vegetation must come up seasonally. Naturally in these forests and in that seasonal vegetation wild-life must have sprung up. On the basis of the Indus Valley seals we can safely say that that wild-life must have consisted of lion, tiger, elephant, rhinoceros, bull, water buffalo, goat, stag, monkey, camel, etc. The tribes living in that areas must have sustained themselves on that wild-life but must have also learnt to catch fish and also to go into the river in crude boats made of the hollowed trunks of the trees, or planks etc. During the course of time they must have learnt to cultivate crops. They must have seen the growth of numerous plants growing wildly, some of which gave them food, the roots of other must have been delicious. While some grains like wheat, barley and rice must have appeared appetising if grinded into a paste and allowed to be baked in the sun or on fire. It was that second and third type of food which required replanting and cultivation. Somehow these tribes learnt to cultivate those crops and the first step was taken in the direction of civilisation. Cultivation means the storing of seed, the understanding of the season when the crop is grown and the identification of the proper time when it should be sown.

We may visualise the scenario of these times. We may visualise that the whole of the plain which is today a desert might have been covered with small grass and wild beasts must have wandered over them and among them the wild tribes hunting them. As with the seasons the wild animals must be moving and with them the tribes. During their wandering they must have come across other tribes, with some they must have fought and with others they must have become friendly and exchanged pleasantries, some gifts of their prey and their experiences. During their wanderings they might have come across the mighty Saraswati and must have wondered at its majesty and its vast expanse of water. They might have met more tribes whose staple food must have been fish and fruits from the trees growing on its banks and from the roots of some plants. They must have exchanged their food with them and might have wondered at its deliciousness while the tribes on the river banks must have tasted their food consisting of raw meat and must have wondered at their covering of skin so useful at least in winter. Such a life must have gone on for thousands and thousands of years. However, a time arrived when that placid but pleasant life came to an end and the tribes all around had to think seriously of an alternative to the food they were accustomed to eat and to move ahead on road to civilisation. Sometimes in four thousand years before Christ or about six thousand years ago those tribes might have faced the scarcity of food. That situation might have developed suddenly or might have taken a few centuries, we do not know for certain. What we know for certain is that the whole region from the Nile Valley in modern Egypt through the Euphrates and Tigres Valley to the Indus Valley had taken to agriculture. Why this was so? The reason must have been the shortage of food all over the world and that could have happened obviously due to certain climatic conditions which go on changing. We are apt to assume that the climatic conditions were the same as they are today but in fact they were not so. Arnold Toynbee in his *A Study of History* feels that the climate in the period prior to the fourth millennium B.C. was different. There was an ice cap over whole of Europe and Alps and Pyrenees were covered with ice and consequently because of the high pressure due to the Arctic conditions the Atlantic rain storms which pass over Central Europe today were deflected towards the Mediterranean Basin, and Northern Sahara and continued over Arabia, Persia and the Indus Valley. Thus over that whole region there was not only more bountiful rain but it was also distributed over the whole year instead of either in winter or in monsoon season. The result was that the whole area was covered by grass and it was thickly populated by men and the animals. In the fourth millennium B.C. that ice melted and the rain clouds instead of coming to Sahara, Arabia, and the Indus Valley passed over the Central Europe as today and thus the area gradually became as desiccated as today. Arnold Toynbee has quoted V. Gordon Childe and we may reproduce here the same.

> While Northern Europe was covered in ice as far as the Harz, and the Alps and the Pyrenees were capped with glaciers, the Arctic high pressure deflected southwards the Atlantic rain storms. The cyclones that today traverse Central Europe then passed over the Mediterranean Basin and the Northern Sahara and continued, undrained by Lebanon, across Mesopotamia and Arabia to Persia and India. The parched Sahara enjoyed a regular rainfall and further east the showers were not only more bountiful than today but were distributed over the whole year, instead of being restricted to the winter.....
>
> We should expect in North Africa, Arabia, Persia and the Indus

> Valley parklands and savannahs, such as flourish today north of Mediterranean....While the mammoth, the woolly rhinoceros and reindeer were browsing in France and Southern England, North Africa was supporting a fauna that is found today on the Zambesi in Rodhesia.....
>
> The pleasant grasslands of North Africa and Southern Asia were naturally as thickly populated by man as the frozen steppes of Europe, and it is reasonable to suspect that in this favourable and indeed stimulating environment man would make greater progress than in the icebound north.[1]
>
> Faced with the gradual desiccation consequently upon the reshift northward of the Atlantic cyclone belt as the European glaciers contracted, three alternatives were open to the hunting populations affected. They might move northward or southward with their prey, following the climatic belt to which they were accustomed; they might remain at home eking out a miserable existence on such game as could withstand the drought; or they might—still without leaving their homeland—emancipate themselves from dependence on the whims of their environment by domesticating animals and taking to agriculture.[2]

It appears that with the onset of desiccation, the people adopted all the three alternatives. Some moved to the South of the great plain which was becoming a desert and went into the forest with its huge downpour. Some went to the North and reached the great river basin with its linear belt of forest. Here they and the animals who also moved there must have met some other tribes and other riverine animals and other animals living along the linear forest. Their reception must have been both hot and warm. Some of the tribes must have opposed the new comers and there must have been battles between them, while some of the tribes, probably their old acquaintance, might have welcomed them. This is simply a speculation. It is difficult to say definitely as to what had actually happened. However, we can say that the new tribes as well as old ones must have settled into marked areas separate from each other. In their separate areas they must have continued their former lives of hunting and picking up the new habit of fruit-gathering. But for how long? They must have noticed after some time that the prey was getting scarcer and scarcer and fruits were also available for a season of a few months. They might have also noticed that newer variety of fruits too lasted a season. These too could not be preserved. The third alternative too was adopted by some who could not give up the old practice of nomadic life, *i.e.*, moving from place to place. But they too must have found that they had to change their earlier habit and had to stay at one place during the hot summer when they could not get water for hundreds of miles.

We may now visualise what those people did who settled on the bank of rivers and who were in a majority and a few people who continued with their wandering for it were those who created the great Indus Civilisation. Those who settled on the banks of the rivers found after some time that they were facing a scarcity of food and would have to find some way out to get over that problem. It was at such a moment that they must have noticed that after the rainy season during which there might have been a flood a large number of plants sprouted which during the course of a few months had developed into grain and that grain if crushed into powder and made into a paste and baked in the sun could be eaten and that cycle was repeated every year. Some plants different in taste also grew with a surprising regularity during the rainy season. Some men of genius might have thought of collecting some of these grains and replanting at the favourable time. Thus the Indus people started on the new technique of agriculture and so did the people of ancient Sumer and of Egypt almost at the same time. The difference of a few centuries is immaterial in this span of time. So also did a few people in the hills of Baluchistan and of the North-West Frontier Province in Pakistan. How this idea of agriculture spread through the length and breadth of the land? We may visualise the nomads playing their part in the spread of the ideas of agriculture. We may visualise the nomads visiting the new agriculturists and getting wonder-struck at their feat. They might have asked their hosts of that wonder and might have been given the details of the operations. When they might have visited another tribe during their next visit, they might have asked their new hosts about the agriculture and on their admitting ignorance might have explained the process and thus they might have put that tribe also on the road of agriculture. We may visualise that in no time agriculture became the general practice. The first great step towards civilisation was taken and that must have taken place in the fourth millennium before Christ.

The extent of the development can be guaged from the fact that all along the Saraswati basin from the Himalayas to the Indian Ocean there were 296 sites where agriculture was taken up prior to the coming into being of Indus Civilisation or in other words the pre-Harappan sites. While in the Punjab there were only 24, in Jammu and Kashmir there was only 1 and in Baluchistan hills there were just a few. When the first tribes met the challenge of desiccation and shortage of food by discovering agriculture a number of consequent problems confronted them challenging their ingenuity and those people rose to the occasion and met them. We may visualise those problems.

When these agriculturists harvested their crop, they found that they had to store them for they could only sow them at the proper cyclic time. They also found that they could not keep them in the open because if the grain became wet, it could not be used as seed. Hence the need to have a covering with storage facility. They also found that the climate changes from extreme of heat to extreme of cold. They could withstand heat by remaining under the shade of trees, but for cold they required some place which was to be closed on all the four sides with a roof over its head. This must have inspired some hut made of wood and leaves. Thus the first houses must have been built. At the same time they must have noticed that mud if left to dry in the sun becomes sufficiently hard. This must have given someone among them the idea of a sun-baked brick. Soon the idea caught on and the people in the 300 and odd Indus sites were having the houses made of sun-baked bricks. All the houses in the Indus Valley found in the pre-Harappan sites were found to be made of sun-baked bricks. Later they were in turn replaced by fired bricks.

The second problem which arose was the necessity of firstly of the storage and secondly of the cooking requiring the use of pottery. Pottery and the fired bricks imply the use of fire.

When they discovered fire, how they kept it and what uses they got out of fire should be our next subject of enquiry.

Discovery of Fire and its Consequences

No body can say with any certainty when the fire was discovered by the people who created the Indus Valley Civilisation. Fire must have been there all right for any body to see. The tribals must have seen it when dry woods of the trees in a forest rubbed against each other during high velocity winds caught fire which must have kept burning for a long time or when stones were thrown against hard surface and produced sparks. But its preservation and subsequent uses were a discovery which changed the society. Who was responsible for that discovery and whether it was found out during the nomadic stage or when the tribes settled down to a sedentary life after the discovery of agriculture, are questions difficult to answer. We can only take recourse to mythology and try to find out an answer. The earliest known records are the *Vedas* whose hymns too are believed to be composed during several centuries. Almost the whole of them syncronised with the period of the Indus Valley Civilisation.

We may see what the *Vedas* speak about the discovery of fire. The *Vedas* in a number of references have declared that the fire was brought by Mātarishwā. We have no knowledge about Mātarishwā. He may be another ambiguous person like Prometheus of the Greek mythology but with a difference. The Greek Prometheus gave the fire to men in defiance of the gods for which he was punished as the secret of the fire was jealously kept by the gods. However, in case of Mātarishwā it was not so. He was not only not punished but was honoured. Moreover according to the *Vedas* fire was not a possession of the gods but was a deity itself, in fact the first of the gods. *Rigveda* has this to say about the discovery of fire by Mātarishwā

> O Fire! You were brought by Mātarishwā through the sky, while Soma was brought by bird over the mountain.[3]

We also learn from the *Vedas* that the fire is produced by

the rubbing of two sticks, a practice still followed by Hindus when producing a fire for religious and ritualistic purposes, *i.e.*, yagna. According to *Rigveda* when generated from the rubbing of sticks, the radiant Agni bursts forth from the woods like a fleet courser.[4]

We may, therefore, visualise the first intelligent encounter of tribal man with fire. No doubt he has seen fire produced by the friction of dry wood of a tree or trees during a strong gale and noted its generation. His compatriots must have fled away in terror to some distance but he might have returned back after some time and seen that the fire was still burning and not only that instead of harming him gave away pleasant heat. He might have noted that if fed with more wood or leaves or such combustible waste it continued burning. These observations must have given ideas and he must have explained to his tribes that fire is a benign god who must be continuously fed and who would give them warmth during the winter season. During the course this fact must have been realised by the tribe and they must have kept the fire burning continuously during the winter when they had to face a grim winter. The fire must have appeared to the primitive man as a benevolent deity and it appears that the fire was regarded by them as the impersonation of the Sun on earth. But the problem must have appeared when the tribe had to move from their winter sojourn. This they must have solved by the technique of producing it by rubbing two sticks in imitation of the fire produced in the forest. But that was a tedious process. It appears that when the tribes settled down they kept the fire burning continuously at one place by feeding it with wood and consequently some class of persons were entrusted with the job of attending to the fire. It was at that time probably that they must have noticed that if mud was kept near the fire or else if fire was kept on mud it became as hard as stone and that must have given them the idea of making bricks and also pottery. The bricks they could use for the building of huts and houses and pottery in a number of domestic uses, *i.e.*, for storage of water, for storage of grain, for cooking and other domestic purposes in the preparation of food and drinking water, etc. Pottery also gave them the idea of the means of carrying of fire from one place to another.

In order to understand the contribution which fire made to the development of the society we may look into the extant festivals of India. As stated earlier there are two festivals among the Hindus which are apparently connected with fire. These are Holi and Diwali. The rituals of Holi are very elaborate. On the occasion of Holi all the people of the area gather at one place where a fire is ceremoniously lighted and then it is worshipped with all solemnity. Thereafter the people who gather there take away the burning logs from that fire and take it to their homes and light their domestic hearths from that burning log. The implication is that this is the festival where fire is renewed or regenerated. It appears that during the year, specially in the winter months, the fire which is fed with large logs of wood is so covered with ash that it dims and does not give much heat.

The ash so collected requires to be removed. To the primitive mind it must have appeared that the fire was dying and should be reborn. Hence, it was extinguished or allowed to be extinguished. The place was cleaned and so were the domestic hearths. The fire was again lighted in the original way, *i.e.*, by rubbing two sticks and when the fire was lighted it was worshipped and hymns composed for the purpose were recited. Probably there was competition for the purpose. These hymns to fire were preserved and were used whenever fire was worshipped. In the *Vedas* there are a considerable number of hymns to fire and they are given in the beginning of every Mandal. Probably these hymns are actually those hymns which were composed at the time of that renewal of fire. This festival comes immediately after the winter season on a full moon day. Subsequently priests must have decided on the particular day to coincide it with celebrations throughout the land. The second festival is Diwali. In this festival just after the rains on the day fire is lit in the evening in a large number of small earthen pots and kept outside the house. This is done by everybody, in every house. Thereafter Lakshmi, the goddess of wealth and Ganesh, the god of wisdom are worshipped. We may not forget that in ancient times Ganesh was a god who warded evil and was worshipped before every enterprise and Lakshmi was regarded as the goddess of luck. The festival of Diwali may mean two things. When fire in small earthen pots was lit and these earthen pots were kept all around every house and were numerous, they might have created an illusion of sky on earth. They might have also meant that after the rainy season for the tribes who had to remain perforce in a single place near a river during the hot summer months due to the desiccation of the desert and during the rains when the grass had reappeared on the sand dunes, the time to depart had arrived and at the time of their departure the fire was put into the earthen pots so that they might take the fire with them. In course of time the day was fixed on a single day when Ganesh, the god who warded evil and Lakshmi, the goddess of luck were propitiated before their departure. Both the alternatives are a possibility, the first in terms of their religious beliefs as we will see later and the second because of the necessity of carrying fire with them. Which one was the real cause of the festival it is not possible to say.

Inspite of the increasing agricultural activities, nomadism was widely prevalent. This can be said with certainty in view of the uniformity of the language over the whole expanse of area of the Indus Valley Civilisation. We cannot be certain about the language but looking at the uniformity of the script it can be said that whatever language was spoken it was a uniform one throughout the area. As for nomads they moved over the whole area, sometimes at one place and at another time another place and whenever they visited a settled place they had to exchange their goods with those of the settled people, and they had to communicate with the people of the settlement. The barter of goods was also a necessity for they had to give things which the settled people wanted and took those things which the settled people could give and which they required. The goods which they could give to people of the villages could be stone-implements meant for cutting, crushing or grinding things or else for fight. In addition, they could give skins either for wearing in winter or for making sacks. The things which they required could be wheat, rice or such produce of agriculture, fruits dried or fresh but mostly dried, and cotton when it was begun to be grown and subsequently cloth when it was made. Cotton was certainly used, grown and cloth used, in the Indus Valley as revealed by the excavations. They must be also carrying tales and folklore developed in the villages and in later times mythological stories too. When they were carrying tales and mythological stories we can assume that their arrival must have been looked forward eagerly by the village societies and their arrival must have caused excitement and must have been an occasion for celebrations. Such visits by nomads over the whole area brought, if anything, at least a uniformity of language and a uniformity of the script. When first script came into use, then it is reasonable to assume that either the pot maker or the user made designs or pattern on them to make them look beautiful. In course of time they must have given some idea of making of such pattern or picture which might have some meaning or might give some meaning, *i.e.*, fish indicating water, round circle indicating the sun etc. Those signs indicating meaning, during the course of time must have evolved into a script when the necessity of script arose. The uniformity of script must have been the contribution of those nomads for they must have taken the symbols as and when they evolved to the distant and even obscure places in the area.

One other contribution of the nomads must have been the introduction and supply of copper implements and copper goods to the people of the area. In the vicinity of the Ganeshwar hills in Sikar District of Rajasthan is the site from which it is supposed that all the copper used in the Indus Valley was supplied. This is based on the excavations supported by Carbon dating and finds of copper tools with the marking of Indus symbols on them. Near that area were the small rivers and rivulets flowing into the Saraswati. It appears that in some remote times when fire was introduced in the area it was kept burning on stones which were in reality ores of copper. Probably the fire was supposed to be kept burning for the full year. It must have happened that after some period of time had passed somebody might have noticed that out of the ore-stone some liquid had come out and had become as hard as stone. He might have pointed out to others that discovery. They might have experimented with other stones out of curiosity by throwing them into fire and getting more metal. On collecting it they might have found that is was malleable and with it tools and utensils just like those made of stone could be made more easily. When they started making them they might have noticed that the tools had better cutting edge and that the pottery—like utensils were lighter and more useful. Thus probably came into existence the copper industry. Of course the job of carrying and propagating it to the remote corners was done by the nomads who took those things from those people in exchange with things they supplied and again gave them to other people whom they visited in exchange for the things they needed. Those nomads learnt the art of business and acted as merchants in that early era. They might have been called Van-char as per our early Sanskrit literature for the modern term Banjarā also denotes those who moved from place to place and sold goods.

Before proceeding further, we may again see the contribution made by the nomads in the discovery of the art of making tools, their propagation, subsequent manufacture and thus giving a fillip to the development of civilisation. Throughout the length and breadth of the area of the Indus Valley Civilisation we find a few places where the stone tools and implements were made. Among them was Burhā Pushkar as mentioned above. It is a fresh water lake situated among hills covered with forests. On this site as ascertained by excavations and carbon dating was an important tool making factory being operated since at least 10,000 years earlier. There is no evidence of a permanent residence at any period. It appears that when the first nomads who made the discovery that stone implements could be made came to that place, they found a large number of stones lying scattered as usual. Somebody playfully started throwing them about and somebody started chipping a stone with another stone. After chipping that stone he might have found it useful, may be in cutting or cleaning skin. He might have shown it to others who might have realised its usefulness and that must have given them the idea of making implements. They might have made several such implements and on their move might have shown to other nomads who might have also found them useful and might have asked them the place where they could be made. In that way the idea of tool making must have spread to all other tribes. For making of tools it was necessary that the site must be such where there must be plenty of stones, fresh water to drink, trees under which they could live for some time and animals whom they might hunt and whose meat they might eat. All those conditions were met in Burhā Pushkar and similar other sites. It appears that the sites were used by the tribes and they used to come here, stay for some days, make tools in large quantities, first for their own use and later for trading. Those tools they traded first with other nomads and later when agriculture was discovered and people settled in villages, with them. Thus the nomads brought a uniformity in the whole area in the use of tools and such other goods and that all because of the semi-desert conditions in the south and west of the Saraswati river which permitted or rather forced nomadism. In the rest of India there were no arid areas and hence as nomadism was not possible, the development of civilisation at that stage was not possible and the subsequent development must have been due to diffusion of the ideas later from that area.

A similar contribution must have been made by the tribes living on the banks of the Saraswati river. A desert or an ocean or a giant river plays almost a similar role in the spread of ideas and civilisation. Just as desert brought forth nomadism because the tribes had to move perforce in search of food, similarly an ocean or a navigable river also encouraged people to move. In the beginning people must have noted that when trees fell into the river they floated. After some time children or even grown-ups must have found that even if they sat on the floating log of wood it did not sink but floated along with them. They must have enjoyed floating on it. Some times later some body must have thought of hollowing it and a number of persons moving in it. When once the idea of boat emerged, it spread and soon people must be moving all along the river. It must have been preferred to journey on land simply because it was quicker and easier and in those time safer too for on land they had to encounter a number of tribes not all friendly with them. Soon boats must have emerged as the principal means of transport and communications and must have in its way contributed to bringing uniformity in the lives and culture of the people on the banks of the Saraswati.

Lastly we may have a look at their religious beliefs, their view of the mysterious atmosphere all around them and the awe-inspiring forces of nature and their reaction towards them. We do not know anything about them nor have we unearthed anything regarding it. Our only clue can be the slender evidence of the small things recovered from the Indus Valley sites. We may assume that the tribes must be having all the beliefs which a primitive possessed. They must be having beliefs in the benevolent and malevolent spirits all around. They must always propitiate the evil spirits. They must have beliefs in the spirits of their ancestors. They must be worshipping the forces of nature, the Sun, the moon, the rain, the clouds, the wind, the river. They thought that they must be gods and should be worshipped as such. The most important god must have been the Sun and when fire was discovered, then the fire as the personification of the Sun on earth or may be as a separate god in its own right. They must be having totems just as every tribe in times remote had. What were those totems? We do not know unless they may be the animals depicted on the seals. They must be having a belief in what is called black magic. We have no knowledge about them excepting imagining or visualising, and much of it might not be true. We can be certainly correct when we visualise them to be led by men who were adept in the magic, in the interpretation of things supernatural, in understanding the position of stars and through their help in finding their path and knowing the times of the beginning of seasons.

We can be certain that they were led by such men and when fire was discovered it was kept in the charge of those men who became its priests. When the agriculture was discovered, then in turn it were these people who indicated the time for their sowing and harvesting and in the sacrifices to spirits, the ancestors and the gods. But who were the gods they worshipped? We do not know and may not know. The presiding deity of the Indus Valley was the horned deity depicted on the seal No. 420 from Mohenjodaro and whose representation was also found from other sites among them Kalibangan. Was this god the god of the earlier tribes also?

Rationally thinking we can say that every tribe must be having a different totem and different god and goddess but after centuries, may be thousands of years, when a homogeneity and harmony was brought about among the whole area through the medium of the nomadic tribes, which reflected on every aspect of life, then only a single god or goddess who might be the harmonius blend of the variety might have emerged. That could have happened only by the time of the full maturity of the civilisation. It could not happen at the stage we are visualising. If we require proof of the blending of different animals into a single animal, we can find it on the various seals of the Indus Valley Civilisation. We find many experiments of this attempt to blend various animals into a single one. We find animals with three heads; we find six heads of different animals united in a circle; we find animals whose every limb is made of the limb of a different animal and whom we call a composite animal. The culmination of all that might have been that composite animal standing before the horned deity mentioned above. Just as the composite animal was actually a blend of the totems of various tribes, the horned deity might be the blend of the various gods of the tribes or might be the supreme deity among them arrived at by the common consensus.

We thus find that when the desiccation struck, some people in the land met the challenge successfully while some not so innovative migrated into the forests. Some went to the South and never emerged because of the great barrier of the desert between them and the new civilised area while some crossed the river Saraswati and the subsequent rivers, Ravi and the Beas and went into the forests of the Punjab and might have returned back subsequently when they found that the people who remained had met the challenge of desiccation successfully. The people who did not migrate had brought about the civilisation by first meeting the challenge of lack of food by introducing agriculture and settling into sedentary life. That gave rise to problem in habitation, in tilling, in storage, etc. which they met by building huts, by inventing pottery, by discovering fire, by domesticating animals, specially cow, and in introducing barter system to procure tools. The problems arose one by one and were solved by them which subsequently gave rise to other related ones which again were solved by them giving rise to further subsequent ones and so on till they brought the pre-Harappan civilisation into being and led to the mature Harappan civilisation. In that great adventure both the people leading a sedentary life and nomads played their parts. We may now look at the mature and the most developed phase of the Indus Valley Civilisation.

REFERENCES

1. V. Gordan Childe; *The Most Ancient East*, Chapter II.
2. V. Gordon Childe : *The Most Ancient East*, Chapter III.
3. *Rigveda* I.93.6.
4. *Rigveda* V.29.6.

3

MATURE PHASE OF INDUS CIVILISATION

If a metropolis of today like New York, Tokyo, Delhi, Calcutta or even Jaipur is buried in earth and after lying buried for four to five thousands of years is then excavated what we can expect to find? The cement concrete will turn to dust, the iron will oxidise and will also be reduced to dust and so will things made of other metals. The clothes, the articles made of wood, other perishable ones will also vanish. What will be excavated will be again bricks, pottery which will include decorative pieces of china, toys made of clay and a few pieces of jewellery which may survive. If there is no surviving information about those metropolises, then the excavators may be left making intelligent readings of the type of pottery and its maker and the type of bricks used and may be wondering at the dolls of both men and women and making learned guesses about the male and female deities represented by those surviving dolls and the kinds of men who worshipped them. Such is the position of the mature towns of the Indus Valley Civilisation so far excavated. The towns discovered and excavated so far are Mohenjodaro, Harappa, Kalibangan and Lothal. Another major town suspected to be is Dwarka submerged under the sea and where excavations have just been started. We find there bricks and the structure made of them, pottery, toys made of clay, seals made of clay and fired and certain remnants of jewellery made of beads and gold, some articles of copper and sea-shells or things made of shells. It is precisely the things one can get after excavating any of the towns for all the other things will perish.

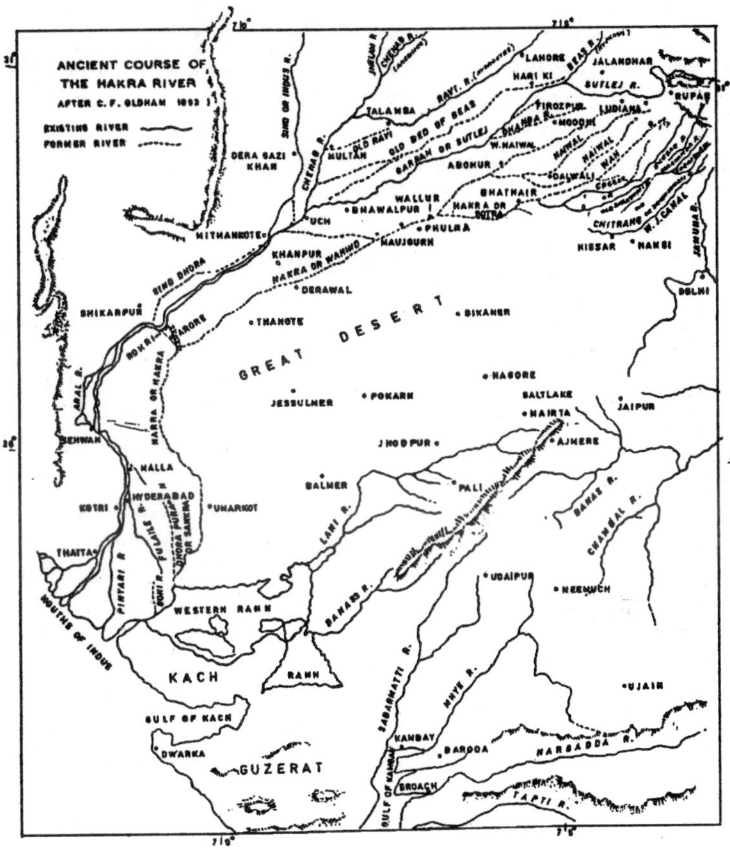

Map 3: Oldham C.F. 1893. The Saraswati and the Lost River of the Indian Desert

Source : *Journal of the Royal Asiatic Society* (*JRAS*) 1893. 49-76.

We do not know what they ate, what they wore, whether they wore clothes made of cotton or of skins, what profession they pursued, what gods they worshipped, what mythology they had and whether they had a well-developed language and if so whether it was Sanskrit or Tamil, and what they wrote and if they wrote whether it was only on clav tablets and seals which were discovered or whether they wrote on cloth and wood which had perished. It is only out of the things which were discovered and recovered in excavation that we can base our theories about their lives. The things recovered are so scanty that different scholars have seen and interpreted them differently and therefore the conception of the people and the state if there was a state is so different in case of everybody and hence we have to take recourse to the subjective conception in our interpretation.

If we look at the location of those major towns of the Indus Valley we would be wonder-struck and would be kept guessing at the reasons which led them to be founded at the places which were really far beyond the periphery of the area of the civilisation. We have seen that of about 800 Indus sites discovered so far about 530 sites are on the Saraswati, about 200 in Kutch and Saurashtra and less than 100 in Sind and Baluchistan. Overwhelming majority of the sites were on the Saraswati but Harappa was situated on the Southern bank of the river Ravi. In between flowed the Beās and the Satluj.

Mohenjodaro, another major town, was situated on the western bank of the Indus river which flowed parallel to the river Saraswati in the Sind. The location of the third town Lothal in Saurashtra is also interesting as it was situated at the Southern end of the neck which joins Saurashtra with the mainland and was the Southern end of the Indus Valley Civilisation area. Only Kalibangan was situated in the area at a place where one of the tributaries of the Saraswati, the Drishdwati joins the river itself. If we look at the then map, we will find that the Harappa was situated at the place where the Ravi and the Beās were flowing nearest to each other, in fact the distance between the two was at that place only 8 miles (11 km.). Thus Harappa and Mohenjodaro were situated at places which were even beyond a natural barrier of the major rivers without many sites of the Indus Valley in sight.

They give the impression of garrison towns founded at the sites most suitable for the defence of the country. Similar is the situation in regard to the site of Lothal. It was situated on the narrow neck which joins Saurashtra with Mainland and could thus be a bastion for defence. Another interesting feature of the site of these towns was that they all stood on major waterways or ocean. Were they so founded so that they could patrol through the length of the rivers and keep an eye on the raiders or intruders?

The Indus Valley Civilisation found at its zenith its fullest expression in these towns of Mohenjodaro and Harappa. In order to understand the highly developed Indus Civilisation it is necessary to learn everything about those towns. We may, therefore, first consider their genesis.

Genesis

When a civilised society has barbarians at its border and the border becomes active, then either of the two can happen. The society by an effort organises itself for an armed conflict and pushes the frontier far into the barbarian territory civilising some of the barbarians in the process and annihilating others. If the society does not so organise itself and the border is left unprotected, it goes to the disadvantage of the society as the raids will increase and the barbarians will become strong and ultimately they will destroy the stability of that society. In the process the barbarians will get civilised and together with the remnants of the old society they are likely to create a new one. When the third millennium B.C. began the Indus society had already reached a high degree of agriculture along the banks of the Saraswati and its tributaries and was in perfect harmony with the nomads of the Thar desert in Rajasthan. But what about the nomadic tribes who fled to the North into Punjab and also those who were there and those who fled to the West into Baluchistan including some who were there? They must have been watching the developments in the Saraswati Valley and must have felt that the villages possessed plenty of animals whose flesh they would like to eat and also plenty of fruits and roots and grain. They did not have anything to offer them for a barter deal and must have felt that they could take those things by force. Hence, the raids began. With the increased frequency of the raids alarm must have sounded in the whole of the Valley. The society must first have panicked and later the elders of the whole area must have convened a meeting and must have decided to entrust the job to some people to drive away the raiders and to see that no raider ever penetrated to raid again. Further they must have also agreed to pay certain portion of their produce to the band of people or its leader who was to guard the frontiers in exchange for their protection. That was necessary because those who would guard could not produce for themselves and would have to depend on others for their sustenance. That must have been the first tribute paid to a king, for the leaders in time actually became kings. It must be said to the credit of the people who were entrusted with the job of guarding the frontiers that they did a thorough job. They cleared the border to the North by either driving the raiders between the rivers Saraswati and Beās and between the Beās and the Ravi and towards the West between the rivers, the Saraswati and the Indus, beyond those rivers or else annihilating them. They must have also noticed the routes taken most frequently by the raiders and must have established garrisons permanently at those places. They must have chosen the sites carefully so that they themselves might not be taken by surprise. Thus the garrisons were stationed at the sites known today as Harappa and Mohenjodaro. Similar garrisons must also have been established at Lothal at the neck of land joining Saurashtra with the mainland. Another garrison must have been put at Kalibangan on the Saraswati itself. In course of times those garrison sites became towns but all their necessaries of life were supplied from the main areas around the Saraswati in case of Harappa and Mohenjodaro. They did not develop any agriculture in the area around them to support themselves. They must have been given protection money in the shape of a share of crops and must have built granaries for the purpose.

Is there any proof for the above conjectures? The proofs of the above are lying widely scattered in the *Vedas*. The *Vedas* are the spiritual history of the times of the Indus Valley

Civilisation. They also contain a large number of allusions to the events and references to other historical events. It is presumed that the hymns of the *Vedas* were composed during a couple of centuries and probably some were composed during the period when the Indus society was very much alive and some were composed afterwards containing recollections of the historical events. In a very large number of hymns addressed to various gods, Fire, Indra, Ashwini Twins, Varuna, Mitra, etc. their protection was sought against their enemies, Dasyus and Asurs mainly who were taking away their cows and in very large number of hymns about their victory over those enemies was sung. The general impression they convey is that the enemies were mainly cow stealers and must necessarily be the raiders against whom those garrisons were established. What is more of interest is that in the *Vedas* there are certain pointed indications of those two cities, Mohenjodaro and Harappa and also that the major battles mentioned in the *Vedas* were fought at those places. The indication to Harappa is very clear while to Mohenjodaro is rather vague. But because of the major battles which were sung repeatedly and remembered it is even possible to recognise them. We may begin with Harappa. The most important battle sung repeatedly was the Dāshrāj battle or the battle of the ten kings. It is mentioned in the Suktas 18, 33 and 83 of the 7th Mandal of the *Rigveda* and the singer is Vashist. It is most vividly described in the Sukta 18. According to the description Kings of ten tribes attacked from beyond the Ravi after putting obstruction on the river Paroshni (Ravi). Obstructions implying that either they tried to divert the waters of the river or they tried to put stones to make a bridge. The tribes mentioned are Turvasu, Druhyu, Anu, Puru, Yakshu, Pakta, Bhālān, Alin, Shiv and Vishāni. The first four are often mentioned together with Yadu in the *Vedas* and according to the later *Purānās* were the sons of King Yayāti of the Lunar race. We do not get any indication of the reasons of Yadu not joining the others in the fight. About the others nothing is known except that from the name Pakta it is surmised that they had gone to the Northern hills after the battle and their descendants are now known as Pakhtoons who live in the modern day Afghanistan and North-West

Frontier Province of Pakistan and known as Afghans and Pathans respectively. According to the Sukta King Sudās leading Bharat and Tritsu tribes faced them on the banks of the river Paroshni along with their priest Vashist. Sudas in that battle routed the ten kings completely. In fact it was a slaughter with Anu and Druhyu tribes annihilated leaving only their names in the later *Purānās*. Probably the raiders who were barbarians and only cattle raiders or cattle lifters were no match for these well-prepared garrisons kept for the sole purpose of keeping these raiders away. The obstructions were removed and water flowed as usual, so says the Sukta. For that deed Sudās was repeatedly praised and mentioned in a large number of Suktas. His was an honoured name in the *Vedas*.

We may now look at the other references which pinpoint the city of Harappa as the seat of Sudas and the *Vedas* as the history of the Indus Civilisation. These are the Sukta 33 and 53 of the 3rd Mandal of the *Rigveda*. This time the singer is Vishwāmitra. In Sukta 33 Vishwāmitra prays to the two rivers Vipāshā and the Shatudri (The Beās and the Satluj) to lower their water to such an extent that the Bharatas may cross the rivers and that the waters may be so lowered that even the axles of their chariots may not be touched by water and as per the Sukta the prayer was granted and the Bharata tribe crossed safely. We are told that protected by Vishwāmitra the armies marched to the south.[1] The release of the horse alluded to the Ashwamédha or Horse sacrifice in which according to the tradition a horse was released and protected by armies was allowed to wander at will. Wherever it wandered the people of the area were to submit themselves to the king who released it. If the people were not willing and seized it as a token of their refusal, they were made to submit by the army accompanying it. After a year it was brought back and sacrificed. This exploit of Sudās is further alluded to in Sukta 18 of Mandal 7 already referred to above where it is mentioned that Sudās also, in addition to winning the battle of ten kings, subjugated the tribes of Matsya, Sindhu, Vaikarna, Bheda, Aj, Sigmu and Yakshu and had conquered territories upto the river Yamunā. We may remember that Yamunā was a tributary of the Saraswati in those times and with this reference we may assume it to be the Southernmost one. We thus find that the armies of Sudās crossed the Beās on the one hand and had fought the ten tribes on the banks of the Ravi on the other. His seat must have been between the rivers Ravi and Beās. The only town between the two rivers was Harappa which was fit enough to be a seat of an empire. We will not be wrong to conclude that the place mentioned as the seat of Sudās was Harappā and he was its king. It also proves that the *Vedas* are really talking about the Indus Valley Civilisation. The name Harappa given in *Rigveda* is Udvraj.[2]

The next question which will arise will naturally be as to which dynasty Sudās belonged, how many kings of that dynasty ruled over Harappa and the time when they ruled and lastly what was the name of Harappa in the Vedic times? The reference to the ancestors of Sudas are found scattered in *Rigveda*. From these references it is possible to make out some history of the dynasty. Divodās is mentioned as the ancestor of Sudas. In Sukta 18 of Mandal 7 of *Rigveda*, Vashist prays to Indra that he may protect Sudas as he had protected his ancestor Divodas. In Sukta 61 of Mandal 6 of *Rigveda* it is mentioned that the Saraswati blessed Vadhrāshva with a son, Divodās. In Sukta 47 of Mandal 6 Indra is said to have defeated Shambar at Udvraj and gave the land to Divodās. In Sukta 48 of Mandal 10 we are informed that Sudās was given the land of 'Gungu' where he ruled, whereas in Sukta 32 of Mandal 2, we are told that Gungu was a goddess. Implication of the 'land of Gungu' is uncertain. Whether goddess Gungu was the presiding deity of the land and whether Udvraj where Shambar was defeated is the same land or different land is not certain. Also whether Harappa is the land of Gungu or Udvraj cannot be said with certainty. *RV* 8.68.16-17 mentions that Indraut, the son of Sudas, bestowed a large number of cows upon Priyamedha. We thus find the names of Vadhrashva, Divodās, the son of Vadhrashva, Sudas and Indraut, son of Sudas, as definite names of this dynasty. Sudas is called a Bharat, *i.e.*, a descendant of Bharat, or a Tritsu. The name of Bharat is sometimes referred to in the *Rigveda* but the problem arises regarding his identity. There are two Bharats mentioned in the *Purānās*; one is the son of Rishabh, a descendant of Manu and the other is the son of Shakuntalā and Dushyant of the Puru dynasty. Puru is frequently mentioned in the *Rigveda* and the list of dynasties given by the *Purānās* show Divodās and Sudās as descendants of Bharat of the Puru Dynasty and Puru himself is shown to be belonging to the Lunar dynasty. We find in *Rigveda* 7.18.13 and 7.8.4 that Sudās fought and defeated Puru. This version of the *Purānās* does not appear to be correct. His belonging to the dynasty of Bharat, son of Rishabh, appears to be more plausible. Rishabh is regarded by the Jains as their first Tirthankar and by the Hindus as an incarnation of Vishnu. However, the more important point is that he was the presiding deity of the Indus Valley Civilisation as we will see later. He was a mythical figure in the Indus Valley times and probably so was Bharat and if Bharat was a real figure it is difficult to make out his history at this stage and in the present stage of our knowledge, specially the lack of decipherment of the Indus script. What we can make out regarding the founding of Harappa from these scanty references can be summed up as follows. Sometimes in the very early phase of the maturity of the Civilisation the barbarians started their raids and started lifting domesticated cows and other cattle. At one time they raided and seized a large number of cows. When they had collected about a thousand cows and were returning with them, Mudgal and his wife could not bear that sight and taking a chariot chased them along with the whole tribe. The cattle lifters were defeated and fled leaving the cows behind. Probably that gave the ideas to the whole society to set up outposts to guard the frontier. The place where Harappa later stood was one such place and the wardenship of the march was given to Mudgal and his tribe, the Bharats. Divodās is said to have received the land from Indra. He strengthened it and guarded it. The tribes beyond the river Rāvi (Paroshni) found the presence of that garrison most inconvenient as well as irksome. They could not penetrate the barrier and singly could not get the better of the guardians of the frontier. After trying singly for some time and having failed, they combined into a massive force collecting ten tribes and attacked the garrison. The fight called the battle of ten kings or the Dashraj took place on the banks of the Rāvi (Paroshni). The barbarians had number on their side but the defenders were battle-hardened and probably better armed. They had chariots as we find from *Rigveda* 3.33 and horses[3]. They knew the use of bow and arrow and might be having battle-axes made of copper as against the weapons of stones with the barbarians. It was a most unequal battle if it can be called a battle for it was probably a slaughter. Probably they then accepted Sudas as their king or sovereign. Probably they agreed to give him larger tribute of their produce and their labour as well. It was probably at that time that plans were made to build the city of Harappa. Also Sudas felt now bold and strong enough to subjugate those people who had not yet accepted him as the king. Hence, the Ashwamédha or Horse Sacrifice mentioned so frequently in the *Vedas.* He probably established his per-eminence in the whole of Indus Valley including Mohenjodaro. Bharatas became the most important and ruling tribe in Indus Valley.

What was the name of the town now known as Harappa? The name could not be ascertained from the *Vedas*. They do not contain many names, the only ones being Hariyupiā, Udvraj, Betsu, the land of Gungu in the *Rigveda* and Ayodhyā in the *Atharvaveda.* We even do not know if the above names are the names of towns or of areas. As we had seen above Udvraj and the land of Gungu are the places given to Divodās to rule. Whether any one had the name of Harappa cannot be said with certainty in the present state of our knowledge. It could not be Hariyupia simply because though it is mentioned only once in *Rigveda* in Sukta 27 of Mandal 6, it was mentioned in a totally different context. At Hariyupia a battle between Abhyāvarti, son of Chāyman and Varchies, sons of Varshikh was fought in which the Varchies were annihilated and this victory of Abhayāvarti is mentioned repeatedly in the *Vedas.* Abhayāvarti who had also defeated Turvasa is called in the Sukta *RV* 6.27.8. a Pārthava meaning a descendant of Prithu, the dynasty founded by Dhruva as has been mentioned in the *Purānās*. Sudas is variously described in the *Rigveda* as Atithigva, Painjvana, Bharat and Tritsu. The dynasties of Bharat and of Dhruva or Prithu were different; hence as we find Sudas to be ruling over Harappa the place where Abhayāvarti defeated Varchies must also be different. It may be near Mohenjodaro.

Kalibangan is a smaller town than Harappa or Mohenjodaro and is situated on the Dhrishdwati near the place where it joins the Saraswati. It is the only town situated in the Indus heartland. The reference to its situation is not as clear as that of Harappa, yet looking to the various references in the *Vedas* it is reasonable to assume that they refer to Kalibangan. Let us see the various references. We may look at the following reference:

> Ava tmna bharate ketaveda ava tmna bharate phenmudam
> Kshiram snatah Kuyadasya yashe hate te syatan pravene shifaya
> Yuyop nabhiruparasvavoh pra purvabhistarte rashta shoorah
> Anjasi, Kulishi, Virpatni payo hamvana udbhirbharnte.[4]

Just as foam rises from water itself so Indra is our support. Women of Kuyava bathe with milk; they may drown. Mighty Kuyava rules beyond the eastern rivers. His rivers, namely the Anjasi, the Kulisi and the Virpatni bring milk along with water. The singer of the hymn is Kutsa Angiras. The question arises as to which place he is alluding to. There are 19 Suktas of Kutsa Angiras 94-115 in the first Mandal of *Rigveda* in each of which while concluding he had honoured the river Indus along with other gods and goddesses.

> Tanno Mitro Varuno manhantamditih Sinduh prithvi ut dyoh[5]

Mitra, Varuna, Aditi, the Indus, earth and sky may protect us, thus sang Kutsa Angiras. Kutsa Angiras was familiar with the Indus and appears to belong to a region where the Indus was treated as a deity. Again in Sukta 108.

> Tadindragni yadushu Turvasisu yad Dhruhushanvanushu Purushustha
> Ath pari vridanava hi yatmatha somasya pivante sutasya[6].
>
> O Indra and Fire/You live among Yadu, Turvasu, Druhu, Anu and Puru come from there and drink soma.

We may recollect that Turvasu, Druhu, Anu and Puru were

the tribes who fought with Sudas on the banks of the Rāvi. They must be living to the North of the Rāvi. Calling Indra and Fire god from that region and holding Indus river in high esteem indicate that Kutsa Angiras, the singer lived in the region of Mohenjodaro and the country beyond the Eastern rivers, *i.e.*, Indus and the Saraswati might be Kalibangan. If the guess about the identity of Kalibangan is correct, then the first ruler might be Kutsa as appears from the verses of *Rigveda* 2.19.6 and *Rigveda* 6.31.3 where Kutsa is said to have been installed after defeating Kuyava. The name Betsu is found for this place from the verse of *Rigveda* 10.49.3-4. We cannot say at present the reasons for the founding of the city of Kalibangan except that it might be a second line of defence against the raiders who somehow sneaked into the area past Harappa, or as an administrative centre to collect tribute, to keep control over the area or as a trading centre.

We do not get any indication regarding Mohenjodaro in the *Vedas* where although a large number of kings are mentioned, some occasionally and some frequently and their names are sung in verses, yet except a solitary reference that a king Bhāvya was ruling on the river Indus[7] who belonged to the dynasty of Pajra, there is no other indication at all about it. *Purāṇās* are silent regarding the identity of Bhāvya and to which dynasty he belonged. Mohenjodaro must have been founded for the very reasons that Harappa was except that the raiders at that time must be the hillmen from Baluchistan's mountain ranges and hinterland was richer as is apparent from the excavations at Chanhudaro and such other places. We get a large number of frequent references to the cows being kept in the mountain caves. They may not be actually caves but small enclosures surrounded by mountains with difficult outlets in which the cows and other cattle were kept imprisoned by the raiders. If the surmise is correct that such references are actually to those raids from Baluchistan, then the founding of the garrison at Mohenjodaro is justified and we may also get the identity of the barbarians living there, the more important among them were the Panis.

Founding of the Cities

Cities of the Indus Valley excavated so far are not many. They are just a few and are at the periphery of the area of the main Indus Civilisation. As we have seen they were probably first set up as the garrison towns to protect the agricultural hinterland. However, when the barbarians were decisively beaten back and the danger became lesser and lesser the need was felt to set up a permanent place where not only the army could live and defend the hinterland but also the men who formed the machinery to collect the tribute and keep it safely, the priests who might keep the enemy at bay with their enchantment and also keep the sacred fire burning, the wives and children of the soldiers and officers as the station was to be a permanent one, the artisans who had to prepare the goods used in households, arms for the soldiers and sanitary staff. Hence, a plan for building such a city was drawn up and the city was built quickly followed up in the design by all the rest of the cities. Thus all the cities so far excavated, the Harappa, the Mohenjodaro, the Kalibangan, the Lothal have the same planning and almost the same layout and the same architecture. Nothing can at present be said about Dwārkā which is now submerged and where studies have been initiated in this regard. So far some finds belong to 15th century B.C. but nothing can be said definitely about its age whether it is an Indus Valley town or post-Indus and what was its layout and what was its architecture.

The notable thing about these towns is that they were first planned, the roads and drainage built and then the designs of the houses drawn up and they were built first before they were finally occupied.

The unique feature of the Indus town planning is that the roads of these cities are straight and almost parallel and they are criss-crossed by other straight and almost parallel streets crossing them at an angle of 90 degrees. They are broad even by modern standards being 60 feet wide. They have lanes 30 feet wide all straight and they in turn have lanes 15 feet wide. All along these roads are drains on both the sides. They are so laid that water passed through them and was not either spilled or stagnated. The houses are all double-storied and have the same design. They all have a courtyard, stairs to go up, a bath-room and a small well. They have the same construction of burnt bricks and the notable thing about their design is that none of the houses have either a door or window opening on the main road. The entrance is through the lanes by the side of every house. Why this attempt to prevent people looking on the main roads cannot be explained. The roads were paved with burnt bricks and could easily bear the weight of bullock carts, chariots or horses with riders. Looking to the monotonous similarity of the design and the constructions it appears that the houses were built simultaneously and when the city was completely built up only then the people moved in. It appears remote that the people were allotted the plots and they built the houses at their leisure or convenience piece-meal. The houses, it appears, were built as a whole and by the same persons and supervised by the same architect. When the city was fully constructed only then it appears that the houses were allotted by a single authority to persons according to their ranks or profession. Whether they were also furnished cannot be said for the only finds we can get are the things which cannot be destroyed by being buried, *i.e.*, burnt bricks, pottery, seals, fired toys and things made of stone or of shells. The rest of household goods or things of use of the menfolk in their profession were all destroyed by nature. We are, therefore, not in a position to identify the profession of the person or persons who lived in a particular house, whether he was a soldier or a scribe or a priest or an administrator. At the outskirts of the towns we do find the houses of artisans marked by hearths outside them or barrack-like houses meant for the menial workers.

The question of importance which arises is the structure of the household. The houses usually double-storied are so big that it is not possible that a single family will reside in a house. Some of the houses consist of even ten rooms, five in each storey. We have to consider whether there were other persons living in the house in addition to the family. It appears probable that some others also lived in addition to the family to help them in maintaining the house and running it properly. The house had to be kept clean, the water had to be drawn from the well inside the house or else it had to be brought, the fire had to be kept burning in the fire room, firewood for the cooking had to be brought, grain had to be ground and other jobs had to be done. No doubt some of the work like cooking and grinding of the grain could be done by the women of the household, but certainly all the jobs could not have been done by one or two women in the family. Hence, there must be other persons to do the jobs. Who were those people? We cannot imagine that at that early stage of civilisation there could be menial paid servants available. The society had not yet fully emerged from the tribal life and in the tribes the principle of equality and fraternity was generally accepted and there was the prospect of agriculture and animal husbandry in the villages. Why should one leave his village or tribe to become a menial servant in a far off land which were the cities at that time. Moreover, they were the garrison outposts at that time which consisted of armed men to protect the lands. Were they the slaves? Possibly. In the border skirmishes and fight with the barbarians probably only two options were available to them to end those raids: they could either exterminate them or capture them to make them slaves. They took recourse probably to both. In the *Rigveda* we find a mention of both. In the Dāshraj battle or the battle of the ten kings near Harappa and in the battle of Hariyupiā we find the description of massacres. In the former 66,066 men of the Druhyu and Anu clans were killed. A number of people of Anu clan were captured.[8] In the latter a hundred thousand Varchies were said to have been killed.[9] Similarly we find that the people of Turvasa clan were captured by the king Sranjaya.[10] Again we find in various Dan-statutis in the *Rigveda* that various kings had given male and female slaves along with the cows etc. to different persons. This amply points out the system of slavery in the Indus Valley times. Were they living in the same houses and serving the people? Probably. Otherwise how can we explain the unusually large double-storied houses.

To the west of those main towns were small fortified areas which, in addition to the living quarters, contained some special buildings also. The most notable among them were the bath at Mohenjodaro and some huge halls assumed to be granaries. The bath at Mohenjodaro was a small tank surrounded by a platform containing small rooms and a well. The other structure is a huge hall in each town in which there are platforms running wall to wall with spaces between them. It is assumed that they are granaries in which grain procured from the hinterland probably as a tribute, was stored. However, at Kalibangan we find that on one platform there are five fire-altars and besides them a well. It appears that after taking bath the 'fire' was worshipped.

Outside the town are again some more fire-altars in open and in addition we find that there was a special room in every house where fire was kept burning throughout the day and night. It appears that the large space in Kalibangan in the fortified area was meant for the public worship of fire meant for the free people and that outside the city for the slaves. If this is the finding in Kalibangan where excavations were done more carefully we are compelled to rethink whether the large halls in Mohenjodaro and Harappa may be, instead of granaries, places for worship of fire. The bath at Mohenjodaro is again intriguing. With such a large river as Indus nearby the bath cannot be meant for regular public bathing. It can only be meant for ceremonial bath. We are not in a position to find out the occasion for this ceremonial bath. It can be a bath on certain special days when after the bath the presiding deity of the city was placated. This special deity may be the fire, or the sun or the deity depicted on the Pashupatinath seal from Mohenjodaro. We are also reminded of the small tanks in the later republics or oligarchies of Vajji, Malla etc. of the 5th century B.C. where members of the oligarchy were required to take bath in those tanks before they were initiated and took their place among the rulers. Nothing can be said about the bath and its purpose at present in the present stage of our knowledge. The living quarters in those fortified areas were obviously meant for some special persons. They might be meant for the rulers or their priests. It is also probable that priests and the rulers might be the same persons. However, if we rely on the *Vedas* to be their histories, they should be different from the priests to be on a somewhat higher level than that of the temporal rulers.

The cities of the contemporary civilisations, Sumer and

Egypt were built around the temples or places of the gods. First the temples were built and around them grew the town without any plan. They had haphazard growth with streets and lanes not at all straight or planned without any drainage system or consideration of sanitation. The houses for the common people also appeared to have been built by the people themselves. Who was the genious who planned the towns of the Indus Valley Civilisation and designed the houses with a carefully thought-out drainage system and probably got it built? We do not get any indication of his name and it will probably be known only when the seals are read. In the ancient legends of India we get the names of two mythical persons said to be the designer of towns and their builders. Those two persons were Maya Dānava and Vishwakarmā. The former is said to have built the cities of Lanka and Indraprastha. The former was built for Kuber, the god of wealth and was later captured by Kuber's half brother Rāvana. The latter city of Indraprastha was built for the Pāndavās. Vishwakarmā built the cities of the gods. Can it be possible that either of them might be the planner of these towns, designer of the houses and their builder? The separation of the living area and the religious and the administrative quarters is also a unique feature of the town planning. In the contemporary towns of Sumer and Egypt the two were mingled. Not so in the Indus Valley towns. That was probably because those towns were primarily garrison towns where the camp of the armed men was at one place and they prayed together at another place outside the living area. The Town-Planner probably took that practice into account while planning. He, therefore, kept the living area separate from the place meant for the worship and administrative quarters. Again as we have seen probably the whole town was built first and probably with the same labour. They first laid the roads, built the drainage, built the lanes and then built the houses. Who built them, the labour hired or the slaves? We are at present not in a position to throw any light on it. But looking at the condition of the society at that time, it does not seem probable that they will get any labour on hire so far away from their homes nor will the armed defenders take to the building of the houses which requires a massive operation. Bricks will have to be baked which will mean that a lot of wood will have to be cut from the forests and brought to the respective sites. After baking they will have to be laid on the roads and in the houses at precise places at precise angles etc. In all probability that function was performed by the slaves captured in the wars. After doing that job those slaves were probably given to individual families for menial jobs in their homes. They did all those jobs under the supervision of the town planner and his associates whoever they might be. The planning and building of these towns is a unique achievement of the Indus Valley Civilisation unparalleled in the world till the 2nd millennium A.D. It is a tribute to their logical and systematic thinking and reveals their orderly mind. It also reveals that while the contemporary civilisations Sumer and Egypt were based principally on religion which was at the centre of their lives, Indus Valley Civilisation was based on necessity and reality and their religion was probably based on ethereal thought rather than being centred on material and physical manifestation expressed in stone in the shape of an idol or a Jiggurat.

Religion

Religious faith and religious practices of the Indus people are difficult to ascertain. We are not aware if they believed in a single deity or worshipped different deities and whether they observed the same religious rituals or different rituals. We do not know if there was uniformity in religious rituals or they differed from region to region. In order to understand the religious practices and beliefs of the Indus people we may have to look at the finds which we may think have a semblance of relation to religion or ritual. At Kalibangan we found a number of fire pits together with ash, bones and a well nearby; in Harappa and Mohenjodaro we found a large number of conical stones and ring stones almost similar to the linga and yoni of the modern times which today represent Shiv and Pārvati. We found from all the places terracotta figurines of women thought to be the figures of mother goddesses. Lastly we got seals. In a huge majority of them we had the figure of a one-horned animal named Unicorn (for convenience) along with a symbol said to be a sacrificial incense burner. In others, though fewer in number, are the figures of a tiger, a bull, a buffalo, a camel, an elephant, a tortoise, etc. There are a few seals still remaining which contain scenes which are thought to be religious and mythological scenes. We may study them one by one in order to understand their significance, and mythology behind them if there is any mythology at all. In order of priority we may start with fire pits and then seals for they are, it appears, to be the key to the whole.

We have already seen that there were fire pits found in Kalibangan. In the fort area outside the main city were found platforms in an enclosed area. In one platform found intact were five pits with plenty of ash in them along with a few bones. Nearby was a well with some space obviously meant to take bath. These were obviously fire altars meant for a public ritual in which animals were also sacrificed and offered to fire. This whole enclosed area might be the place full of fire altars. Outside the city again there were fire altars probably meant for the worship of fire by the lower classes or it might mean that the fire altars in the fort area might have been for worship either singly or in smaller groups, whereas those fire altars outside the town might be meant for worship by the whole population. It might be for some public festivals. In addition to these we also found at Kalibangan a room in every house where fire was kept burning, which might be also meant for worship by the individual households. Some scholars feel that the granaries identified at Mohenjodaro and Harappa might not be granaries at all. We might guess that they might be actually fire altars like that at Kalibangan. Fire, as we have seen, had changed the life of our primitive ancestors and it was fire alone which had initiated the progress into civilisation. However, the lighting of fire was a problem for the first men which they at first did not know and they solved it by keeping it burning throughout the year. That practice continued down the ages inspite of the discovery of the means of lighting it by rubbing two sticks together till they became hot enough to catch fire. For some time after that discovery the privilege of lighting the fire remained with some priests. We have in order to ensure that fire was regarded as deity, to find some additional proofs. If we look at the contemporary world, we find that there are a few festivals associated with fire. Parsees who belong to ancient Iran, a country associated with Indus Valley culture, still worship fire who is regarded as the son of their supreme deity Ahur Mazda. In modern times in our country there are two festivals associated with fire, Holi and Diwali which we have already described. We may, however, repeat that the Holi is celebrated on the last day of the Indian Lunar month of Falgun which also happens to be the last month of the Lunar year. In this festival at evening or morning whenever the full moon appears a huge fire is lit around which all the people of the village gather and then it is ritually worshipped. The obvious implication of this ritual is that on this day fire is regenerated and is given a new birth. A new fire is lighted in every home in the community every year. The next day is spent in great festivity and is celebrated with great abandon, obviously celebrating the birth of the new fire. The origin of Holi can be traced to this age and gives us the indication that fire was regarded as a deity in those times. Diwali is another festival connected with fire. On Diwali day at evening every household lights fire in a number of small earthen pots and keeps them in the open, outside the house and in the open courtyard inside the house.

We do not know if it was an attempt to create an illusion of the sky on earth, or to bring the sky on earth or something connected with fire itself. Sky is a deity in *Vedas* and moreover it is always treated as the father whereas Earth is treated as mother. Both together are treated as parents. It is possible that on the day of Diwali, Father Sky is brought down to join Mother Earth signifying the union of parents and birth of life or everything on earth or it may be the birth of a deity whom we might have forgotten. On the other hand if it is connected with fire, then the explanation is simple. As we had noticed the nomadic tribes during summer season when the vegetation in the semi-arid areas dried up used to come to those riverine places and stayed there during the rains. After the rains the time came when they must move again on their rounds which coincided with Diwali which occurs just after the rains. When they returned back they must take fire with them on their wanderings. That fire which they must take must be in earthen pots. It might be possible that in order to facilitate them in that task the villagers or town people lit the fire in numerous earthen pots and kept them outside their houses so that the nomads might pick them and keep those with them in their wanderings. We do not know which might be the real reason for the celebration of Diwali but it can be traced to these times and should be treated as connected with fire. We may thus see that one of the deities of the Indus Valley Civilisation was certainly fire.

The most important source of information regarding religious beliefs and religious rituals and practices are the seals unearthed in thousands in the Indus Valley. The study of these seals should have been interesting and should have yielded much material as they not only contain pictures but also some letters or their symbols engraved on them together. However, the study of the seals and their inscriptions, if they really are, got bogged down in the controversy over the language of the people of the Indus Valley. At the present time the controversy is confined to three languages—the Sanskrit, the Tamil and the Hittite. The protagonists of Tamil are Parpola and his associates of the Scandinavian group, the Soviet scholars and some of the Indian ones including Shri I. Mahadevan. The protagonist of the Hittite as the Indus language is Professor S.R. Rao, the excavator of Lothal. A number of scholars speak in favour of Vedic Sanskrit. Some prominent scholars among them are Shri Fateh Singh and Professor K.V.N. Rao. Each had fixed the idea of a particular language in mind and started to see in the symbols the language which they on their own rational thinking felt must be the language of the Indus people. The interpretations so far are not convincing to any body for no clear concept has emerged. What the scholars should have done is to study the symbols individually without caring for the language they may contain and then determine their message. This is so because some of the symbols are recognisable as standing for the Sun and should be treated as meant for the Sun whatever it is called in the different languages. Similarly the symbol for fish, river, etc. are recognisable. We may also understand that the language was probably evolving and had not taken a mature form like Vedic Sanskrit or else the symbols themselves might be evolving and what we find may be a jumble of symbols which may not give a precise sentence but a vague idea of the meaning of the seal. We may study the seals in this light before attempting to understand the language spoken in the Indus Valley Civilisation.[11]

The most important source of inspiration and at the same time of awe had been the natural forces and the phenomena, specially the Sun. The tribesmen had always been fascinated by the Sun, the Moon, the Wind, the Clouds, the Rain, the Sky, the Earth and Mountains, etc. Naturally all these objects of nature fascinated them, looked mysterious and inspired them to create legends and mythology around them. Among them the most mysterious had been the Sun and the Moon. The Sun was regarded as a deity everywhere and most of the ruling dynasties in ancient times in all countries traced their descent from the Sun. This was so from Egypt to Japan and had been so in India. The symbols of the Sun were always everywhere almost the same and included a wheel, a disk, a conch, a fish-hook, a drum and among the animals a lion. If we look at the seals and their inscriptions, we will be surprised to find those symbols in plenty often jumbled together. A peculiar symbol that we come across is of two circles, one almost overlapping the other along with three vertical lines. Probably the two circles, one overlapping the other, are meant to give the impression of a solar disk which is an important universal symbol of the Sun. It is found everywhere in the Indian Sub-continent including Maldive islands. It is found either singly or with three horizontal lines on either side denoting the Sun with wings. In course of time these horizontal lines became vertical and the solar disk with three vertical lines became the common symbol of the Sun. We may see these two circles almost overlapping each other along with three vertical lines with a fascinating frequency in the various seals. We may also note a pattern in these inscriptions. Towards the right the first sign is a solar symbol either a conch or the wheel or the solar disk. Towards the left is an apostrophe or two and then a few other signs. This should mean that the message had first named the Sun and wanted it to be understood that the rest of the writing is something in praise of the Sun. Sometimes the whole writing is almost full of the symbols of the Sun. In an interesting seal we find a solar disk, *i.e.*, two circles almost overlapping each other along with three vertical lines. In rest of the seal is engraved a lion and man with a drum. Thus even in pictures we find the symbols of a lion and a drum. Obviously the whole seal is dedicated to the Sun. We may thus assume that another deity most worshipped was the Sun to whom a fairly large number of seals were dedicated. Fire and Sun were the two important deities of the Indus people. Fire is still worshipped by the descendants of these people even today and we may also not forget that the temples of the Sun were the most numerous in those parts in later times.

Deity of the Pashupatinath Seal

We may now look at the most baffling problem of the Indus Valley Civilisation, the identity of the deity present in person in the seals, *i.e.*, engraved on the seals in a number of scenes depicting various incidents. It is baffling not because it is insoluble but because scholars hotly dispute its identity on the grounds based on their preconceived notions regarding the race of the Indus people, their language and religion. If studied in the perspective of the growth and development in the gradually emerging civilisation, the solution should not be difficult to find. We are fortunate in that the deity is shown in a number of seals in different settings which show the various incidents in his life. If we can find a mythology which contains these various incidents connected with the life of a figure who may be divine or mortal we may be able to identify him to some extent. This is so because mythology tends to mutate into new forms and tends to change the figure of the person from divine to mortal or vice versa, from benign to a malignant figure or vice versa. However the incidents in their basic element do not change. Instead of doing that scholars have first, identified the person and then tried to interpret the other seals. We find that some scholars believe that Aryans invaded India somewhere in the 12th century B.C., and exterminated the earlier race which was Dravidian, imposed their Vedic religion and language in Northern India.

Hence the early race must be the Dravidian and as Shiv was the principal deity of the Dravidians and as he is known as Pashupati, the lord of beasts, the deity of the seals must be Shiv. This view first propagated by Marshall is subscribed to by others among them Shri I. Mahadevan, the Scandinavian group of Mr. Parpola and his associates who are engaged in deciphering the Indus script on the basis that the language is Tamil. The Russian scholars are also deciphering the Indus Script on the same basis. There are others who do not believe that Aryan came to India but believe that they were the original settlers and that it was a Vedic civilisation. They, therefore, hold that the principal deity must be the principal god, *i.e.*, either Indra or Agni, the fire god. Protagonists of this belief include Dr. Fateh Singh, Prof. S.R. Rao and Prof. K.V.N. Rao. On the basis of their premiss they proceed to identify the deity and also attempt to decipher the Indus Script. It may be pointed out that on the basis of the extant mythologies neither Shiv, nor Indra nor Agni, the fire god had the remotest connection with any incident depicted on other seals nor the deciphered script as presented by them makes any reasonable meaning. Before attempting to prospect the great mine of various mythologies in search of one which may contain the various incidents shown in various scenes on the seals, we may look at the reasons and arguments regarding the various beliefs about the race and language of the Indus people.

The whole controversy revolves round the Aryan invasion of India during or after the time of the Indus Valley Civilisation. Those who hold that there was an invasion by Aryan tribes, also maintain that they were Sanskrit-speaking, believed in the Aryan gods like Indra, Varuna, Ashwini Twins, Fire etc. and that they simultaneously moved from their Central Asian homes in all directions. One group came into India, where they encountered dark-skinned, flat-nosed people who lived in cities. They subjugated those people who were Dravidians, destroyed their towns, made them slaves and imposed their own religion and language on them. Those who could escape fled to the South Indian peninsula where they gave birth to the Dravidian civilisation and created four languages, Tamil, Telugu, Kannada and Malayalam. According to them the religion of these Aryan invaders is preserved in the *Vedas* which also contain the references to the fight with the Indus people who are referred to as the Das or Asur. The others who do not believe that the Aryans ever invaded India naturally believe that the Indus Civilisation is the creation of the Aryans, that *Vedas* truly mirror the state of religion and society in those times and that Sanskrit of the *Vedas* was the language as spoken in those times. However, regarding the times when the *Vedas* were written there are still various schools of thought. While some maintain that they were written more than 4000 years before Christ that is before the Indus Valley Civilisation, some others believe that they were composed during a long period and recorded faithfully the religion of the Indus Valley. There is another group of scholars who hold that they were composed somewhere in the 12th century B.C. Those who believe that Aryans were invaders from the Central Asia also believe that the *Vedas* were actually composed in Central Asia itself and the reference to rivers, mountains, lakes, etc. are actually to those of Central Asia who were actually named accordingly and those names were subsequently transferred to their Indian counterparts.

Among these varied and mutually contradictory views we should find one which may stand the test of scrutiny and the touchstone of rationality. First we may examine the theory of migration of Aryans into India and also to other countries of Europe. It was a firm belief of Christians which is based on Bible also that after the Floods, as mentioned in the *Bible*, the Boat of Noah landed on Mt. Ararat in the Caucasian mountains.[12]. They settled there and the population grew. When they grew in population the God scattered them on the face of the earth.[13] Christians held that belief but they had no proof in support of that belief. Anything which supported that belief was accepted without much further investigation. Some English scholars who studied Sanskrit in the mid-nineteenth century found a more than ordinary similarity between the Greek, Latin, German and Sanskrit. After a comparative study of these languages scholars came to the conclusion that their similarity is due to the fact that they belong to a single group of languages. They felt that the original language might be a single one and out of it these various languages were evolved. The reason of this variation might be due to the fact that at some time the group who spoke the original language grew in population and various sections moved in all the directions. One section moved towards Greece and Europe, the other towards Iran and the third towards India. We may recollect that that was the time when the fact about the events of the history of ancient world were not known. Excavations had not made much progress and the great ancient pre-historic civilisations of Indus Valley, Sumer, Egypt and Minoan were not known. Actually it was believed that there was no history of India prior to 6th century B.C. and its history started with Gautam Buddha. Hence, it was assumed that the Aryan tribes must be having their original homeland in Caucasus in Central Asia. It was also thought reasonable to assume that they migrated in the 12th century B.C. *Vedas* were also thought to have been composed in 12th century B.C. It may be mentioned here that there is no physical evidence whatsoever of the migration of any tribe into India in those times. When tribes numbering millions carrying arms made of stones or metals and also carrying domestic goods including pottery and also animals, horses and other domesticated animals migrate they must leave massive evidence about this migration which in fact is not there. When the Indus Valley Civilisation was unearthed in the late twenties and early thirties of this century and its time was assessed by Marshall to be 3000 B.C. to 1700 B.C. the problem of the identity of the people who lived in the Indus Civilisation again arose. Marshall who thought about it came to the conclusion that the deity on the Pashupatinath seal is none other than Shiv. As Shiv is not referred to at all in the *Vedas*, the Vedic people cannot be the inhabitants of the Indus Valley Civilisation and as Shiv is the deity mentioned in the early Tamil literature, the people of the Indus Valley must be the worshipper of Shiv and hence Tamils or Dravidians, whom the invading Aryans drove to the South India. He found support from the presence of a small number of people living in Kirther Ranges of Baluchistan who speak a Dravidian dialect. This tribe called Brahui is living near the modern town of Quetta in Baluchistan who speak a language in which 90 per cent of the words are Baluchi words belonging to the language spoken in the province of Baluchistan and contain about 10 per cent words which can be called the derivatives of Dravidian languages. On this slender evidence rests the theory of the Indus people being Dravidian in origin, subsequently displaced by the invading Aryans. This evidence of the Brahuis being the original inhabitants of Indus Valley can be proved to be incorrect and misleading. As for the identity of the deity we will try to find out by delving deep into the mythological lore of India in accordance with the plan outlined above. We may first attempt to explain the presence of the Brahuis in Baluchistan. The presence of a people in any particular area can be due to either of the following causes. They might be the original inhabitants of the area since the stone age, they might be brought there as slaves, they might have been forced to migrate due to natural calamities in their original habitat like continuous drought or continuous civil strife or such thing or they might have been subjected to forced penal deportation by some conquering people. The extant records indicate all the above causes were practised even in the first and second millennium B.C. We find the Jews were subjected to penal deportation by the Assyrians from Palestine to Babylon. We find Darius, the Persian Achaemenid Emperor, deporting large tribes from one place to another as penal deportation, among them Greeks to the inhospitable region of Bactria. We find Romans populating Italy with slaves picked from the Mediterranean shores and in our own times negroes populating Southern United States as slaves. We find migration of Huns and other tribes from Central Asia due to desiccation of the region by continuous drought. We also find the migration of Shaka and Kushan tribes from Central Asia to Iran and India due to continuous strife by the incoming tribes from the North and East in their domains. India too indulged in that practice of deportation. Otherwise how can we explain the presence of gypsies in the Balkans and Europe speaking an Indian language, or of Kurds in Kurdistan at the junction of modern Iraq, Iran and Turkey speaking a language akin to Indian languages.

Due to paucity of records it is not possible to say how many such migrations took place in the South or from the

South India. We have only one recorded incident which affected some region of the South India. Emperor Ashoka in his 13th Rock Edict referred to the Kalinga War and noted regretfully that in that battle more than a hundred thousand people were killed and a hundred and fifty thousands were captured. He had not mentioned what he did with them. Had they been captured and then released subsequently the fact would not have troubled the conscience of the great emperor to have merited mention in the Edict. Probably they were subjected to penal deportation but we have no information as to where they were deported. It may be pertinent to remember that the kingdom of Kalinga was situated in the area which lies in the border of Orissa and the Dravidian region whose people were speaking a language of the Dravidian group or akin to Dravidian languages.

The kingdom of Kalinga also had, it is conjectured, both the groups, *i.e.*, Oriyas and Dravidians. Where were they taken when we know that only place in the North India where a language akin to Dravidian languages is spoken is the Brahui land in the Baluchistan and where one can approach easily through the sea from the Orissa coasts. Until and unless we know more about the Brahuis and their past it may not be possible to say with certainty that they were the original inhabitants of that area before the times of Indus Valley Civilisation.

We may now proceed to identify the deity of the Pashupatinath seal *Fig. 3.1*. But first of all we may analyse the various seals which contain scenes depicting either religious motives or historical ones. Pashupatinath[14] seal itself depicts a man in the nude sitting on a stool. It appears to have three faces, one in the front and two on either side and probably fourth on the back not visible in the picture. The faces are not of human being and are probably of a bull or as some people think of a buffalo. He is having a crown made of horns probably of a bull. His arms are full of bangles from wrist to shoulders and he appears to be wearing some such things in the upper part of the body which have close lines. He is sitting in a yogic posture which is called in India Padmāsan or lotus-seat. Surrounding him are four animals—a tiger, an elephant, a buffalo and a rhinoceros. There is a man

Fig. 3.1 : F.E.M. Pl. XCIV, No. 420

also with the animals. Some scholars thought that the animals are standing facing him before each face. However, if we look at the seal carefully, we will find that all the animals and the man are not stationary but are in motion. Three animals tiger, buffalo and the rhinoceros appear to face him while tiger is shown jumping. The fourth animal elephant is shown moving away from him. Actually the posture of the four animals show that they are moving in a circle round him along with the man. This movement in a circle round a man or a statue or idol called taking a Parikramā means showing deep reverence for the man or the deity and is still current in India. This also implies that these animals are not identifiable with some particular region or tribe as is thought by some but merely show that the deity was regarded as something special to every living creature on earth. Beneath the seat of the deity are shown two ibexes or goats. On the top is an inscription. The second seal, the seal no: 430[15] (3.7) from Mohenjodaro again has the same deity standing on one corner between two

Fig. 3.2: MIC Pl. CXVI, No. 29.

branches of a Pipal tree (*Fiscus indica*) both of whom are shown rising from the ground itself. The deity is again wearing the same crown of bull's horns. Before him is another person in the same dress and with the same crown of bull's horns kneeling before the deity. Besides him is standing facing the deity an animal who appears to be a goat but whose every limb is made of parts of different animals. Below are standing in a row seven persons as if watching the scene. On the top is an inscription identical with the one on the Pashupatinath seal. Another seal is a copy of this seal except that there is no inscription and the number of the persons standing in a row is five instead of seven. There is a third seal[16] (*Fig. 3.2*) in which the same deity is sitting on a stool and before him are kneeling two persons with some offering in conical vessels in their hands. Behind each person is standing a snake shown in such a way that it appears that they are associated with the persons in some benign or spiritual relationship. Another seal[17] shows a man sitting on a branch of a tree with a tiger below. Another motif shown is a tree near which is a three-headed beast as if guarding it and two ibexes or goats eating.[18] (*Fig. 3.3*) These motifs, a composite animal, a man on tree with a tiger below and three-headed beast guarding a tree are recurrent motifs shown in a number of seals and also in three-faced seals with other motifs including one in which the deity is shown standing between the branches of a tree with a devotee and a composite beast before him. This shows that the deity is intimately connected with the three-headed beast, the composite animal and a man on tree with the tiger below. In another seal[19] we see a boy standing

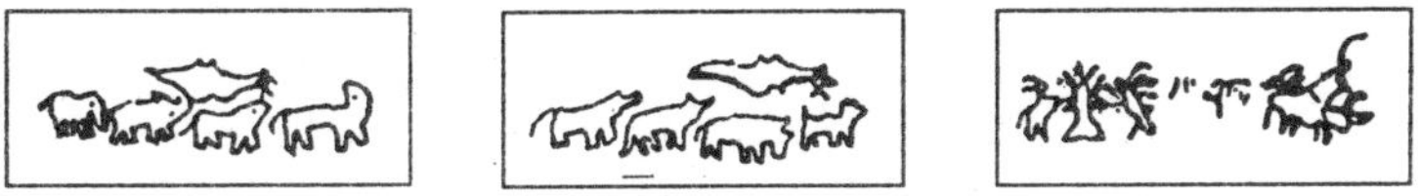

Fig. 3.3: FEM Pl. XCI, No. 4

with hands outstretched and two lions on either side. In another seal[20] (*Fig. 3.4*) is shown on one face of the seal a

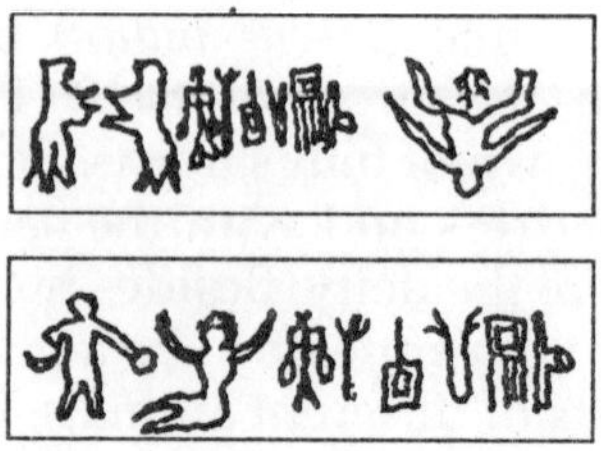

Fig. 3.4: E.H. Pl. XCIII, No. 304

woman wailing with a man with a sword standing near her and on the other the woman giving birth and two lions standing. These two seals also seem to have a connected mythological incident. In another two-faced seal[21] (*Fig. 3.5*), we find on one face a tree and before him a man kneeling offering him some thing in a conical vessel. On the second

Fig. 3.5: FEM Pl. XC, No. 24

face there is covered vessel, a man on tree with a tiger below and two men with parts of an uprooted plant or tree in their hands on either side of a person. This also indicates that the tree and the deity may have some relationship. Probably the tree represents the deity. Some seals have a file of animals all different going in one direction reverentially and in one[22] (*Fig. 3.6*) animals, among whom we find crocodiles with fish in their mouth, going somewhere giving

Fig. 3.6: FEM Pl. XC, No. 13

the impression that as fish cannot walk, crocodiles are carrying them or else the fish may be the offering they are taking. We have two seals[23] showing a figure whose upper half is that of a man and lower half of a lion. We have another seal[24] in which on one face deity is sitting with a man on tree on one side and a lion in an enclosure on the other. On the reverse is a bull tied to a tree, a man and a screen or a house. We also get the motif of a man killing a bull with a javelin[25] and two bulls fighting with their horns joined.[26]

If we can get any of the above incidents mentioned in any mythology of the ancient period, it will help us in advancing in the direction of the identification of the religious scene of the Indus Valley Civilisation. If we can get any scene connected with the deity in mythology then again we may get some idea of his identity. If, on the other hand, we can get a number of them connected with one person or deity, then we can be reasonably sure of the identity of the deity or of others. In this light we may scan the mine of mythologies of the ancient Hindu, Vedic, Jain and Buddha in the first instance. We may first look at the *Vedas, Rigveda, Yajurveda, Samveda* and the *Atharvaveda* as they are the oldest known scriptures in the world. Although they contain many descriptions of scenes, yet none of these scenes are found in the seals except one which itself may be doubtful and it may not be helpful. 'Purush Sukta' is one of the most famous of all the Suktas in the *Vedas* and interestingly enough it is repeated in all the four *Vedas* with some variations. The first two lines of the 'Purush Sukta' are as under:

> "Sahastra Shirsha Purush sahastraksha sahastrapat
> Sa bhumi vishvato vritavatyatishta dashangulam."[27]

Purush (man) has a thousand heads, a thousand eyes and a thousand feet. It encloses the earth though it is sitting in an area covered by ten fingers. Although many learned treatises had been written since thousands of years explaining that this indicates the omnipresent, omniscient and all powerful Supreme God, yet a simple reading of the two lines in their literary meaning tells us that this is a simple description of a banyan tree identified with Purush. Only a banyan tree has numerous branches standing for heads, numerous branches hanging and enrooted in the earth standing for feet and numerous small fruit called *'gooler'* in Hindi standing for eyes. Although covering a wide areas it stands on a very small area. We do not know to whom the singer refers as Purush but we find that Purush is identified with banyan tree and it is probably a banyan tree under whose branches the deity of the Indus Valley is standing and also the man who is offering something in a vessel to a tree is obviously identifying the deity with the tree. We also notice that a three-headed beast is guarding the tree in a number of seals but at the same time we notice that two goats are shown eating leaves nearby, probably the same two goats shown beneath the seat of the deity in the Pashupatinath seal. Again we find in couplets 6 to 10 of the same Purush Sukta that that Purush was sacrificed and out of it were born all the various animals in nature as well as the *Vedas* and other such things. We may remember that the animal standing before the deity along with a kneeling figure is a composite animal whose each limb is made of the limb of a different animal. Sacrificing this animal means that each limb took on the shape of the original animals. Thus Purush is again identified with the composite animal of the seals. Probably 'Purush Sukta' is describing this seal, seal No 430 from Mohenjodaro[28] (*Fig. 3.7*). The question arises as to who is this Purush and which deity it represents. We have at present no answer to it. It is possible that probably this particular Purush Sukta describes the scene depicted on the seal but as a matter of fact it does not lead us to anything.

We may now have to examine the Hindu mythology. Among all the deities deemed to be the figures of the Indus Valley, Shiv, Indra and Agni, besides others, there is no doubt that Shiv has the greatest resemblance to the Indus Valley

Fig. 3.7: FEM Pl. XCIV, No. 430

deity as judged by Marshall. If the Pashupatinath seal is seen in isolation, the figure sitting in a Yogic posture with a trident-like crown surrounded by animals can be said with confidence to be none but Shiv. However, as we have decided that unless a number of scenes on different seals are part of the same mythology identifying the figure with certainty we will not accept the identification. It is necessary to find out if any other seal contains any incident pertaining to the mythology of Shiv. None of the other seals contain any incident associated with Shiv except probably the composite animal. It is said that Vishnu assumed the form of Narsingh, a creature half lion and half man, and killed the demon Hiranyakashyap. After killing him his anger was not abated and Shiv on the request of gods assumed the form of Sharabh, a composite animal and pacified Vishnu. We have the composite animal in seals and at the same time we have two seals containing the creature whose upper half is that of a man and the lower half of a lion. But the two are not shown together. It is difficult on this solitary basis to accept the figure as Shiv. However, the possibility remains that though Shiv is a later figure in the mythology and religion, he might have taken to itself the figure and some of mystery of the Indus Valley figure. In that case we may also note that the composite animal might have been identified with the figure in the Indus Valley as it is in the case of Shiv and that it may also have some connection or relationship with the creature of half man and half lion. Indra and Agni too cannot be identified with this figure as none of the incidents in the seals are associated with them either in the *Vedas* or in the *Puranas*. So it is with Vishnu, except his doubtful presence in the shape of the creature of half man and half lion. We do not find any person identifiable with the figure in mythology of Buddhism.

We may have to analyse the mythology of the Jainism now. As compared to the mythology of the Hinduism and of Buddhism, mythology of Jainism is small in bulk and can be scanned thoroughly. However, as compared to both it was recorded very late, the first records prepared as late as 6th century A.D. The *Vedas* were composed in the 2nd millennium B.C. and as for *Purānās* some of them in the late first millennium B.C. Buddhist mythology was almost complete in the times of Emperor Ashok. We may have to analyse the Jain mythology carefully because it is likely that due to the passage of time the memory might have blurred, the descriptions of events by an addition of a word or change in a word might have been transformed and may not resemble the original. In that event we may have to recreate the original picture and get at the original story, narration or history, as the case may be. Most of the Jain mythology revolves round the lives of their Tirthankars, the preceptors of religion and its preachers, who are 24 in number. The life of the first Tirthankar and other Tirthankars is given in detail in *Mahapurān* by Acharya Jinsen and is the authentic *Puran* of Jains. However, nothing is said in the mythology about any of them except the first Tirthankar Rishabh and the last Mahavir. Of these Mahavir is said to be a historical figure and Rishabh probably mythical. Along with the lives of the Tirthankars the mythology contains histories of some of the emperors and heroes which is identical with that of Hindu *Purānās* with some variations. The only common feature in the lives of the Tirthankars is a certain mysterious dream which their mothers saw before their births. Again the mothers of emperors saw a part of the dream and the mothers of the heroes still a smaller part. As the dream has a great significance in Jain mythology we may have a look at it. It consists of 16 different objects including a few animals which do not have any connection with each other. However, the first objects are three animals—a bull, an elephant and a lion, whom we find in the Pashupatinath seal, *i.e.*, the bull-faced deity, the elephant and the lion along with a buffalo and a rhinoceros. As three things are common in the seal and in the dream, we may examine them more closely and try to see if the other two animals buffalo and rhinoceros are also discerned behind other objects which may be misnamed due to blurring of the memory during the transition of millenniums. If we can identify them and also find the meaning of other objects we may initially identify the deity and then try to see if the incidents in the life of that deity as mentioned in mythology are also shown in other seals. The dreams consist of 16 objects in one fixed order. However, there is a subtle difference between that seen by the mother of Rishabh and that seen by mothers of others. The difference lies in the order of first two animals. The dream seen by the mother of Rishabh consists of first object as a bull while the mothers of others saw an elephant as the first object. The sixteen objects of the dream[29] are bull, elephant, tiger, anointment, moon, sun, a pair of garlands, a pair of fish, pot, a tank full of lotus flowers, throne, ocean, a celestial aeroplane in the sky, palace of snake king, a heap of jewels and fire without smoke. As we have seen the first three animals are common to both and if we take the bull to imply the bull-faced man (Bull in Sanskrit is Rishabh and the name of the first Tirthankar is also Rishabh), then the two animals are the elephant and the tiger who are going round the deity. Next two animals in order are the buffalo and the rhinoceros respectively. Do the next two pictures anointing of a queen and moon respectively make out these animals? Anointing of a queen actually implies the picture of a queen and here queen should be meant. However, the word for queen in Sanskrit is 'Mahîshi' while the word for buffalo is 'Mahîsha'. It appears that during a transition period of more than two millenniums the word Mahîsha got confused with Mahîshi when Mahîsha is actually meant (Mahisha means buffalo) and the correct word and picture should be Mahîsha or buffalo of the Pashupatinath seal. The fourth animal is rhinoceros and the picture in the dream is of moon. Here the difficulty is not much because the Sanskrit word for both moon and rhinoceros is Khadaga or Khang. It was probably due to paucity of words in the ancient language that the same word is used for entirely different things. Thus khang or khadaga is used for both moon and rhinoceros while a similar word Khag means bird and in a few Jain works the word khaga meaning bird is used instead of moon. We can now be reasonably sure that the two words are 'mahisha' and 'khang' meaning buffalo and rhinoceros and this dream is actually a description of the Pashupatinath seal. Let us see what else we can make out from the other objects. We may examine the pair of two pictures, *i.e.*, a tank full of lotus flowers and a throne. As we have seen the deity is sitting in a yogic posture called 'Padmāsan', we may, therefore, take it that the first word actually means lotus called 'Padma' in Sanskrit and throne should mean a seat called Āsan in Sanskrit, the pair standing for the word 'Padmāsan' or lotus-seat, the yogic posture in which the deity is sitting in the seal. We may now consider the easily identifiable picture 'a heap of jewels'. In the old Sanskrit literature a heap of jewels always implies a sacred mountain. We may remember that the name of the mother of Rishabh, the first Tirthankar of Jains, was 'Meru' meaning mountain. Hence the picture 'a heap of jewels' appears to stand for Meru, his mother. Let us see if other pictures mean the names of his other ancestors. The last picture is 'fire without smoke'. In Sanskrit the picture is 'Nirdhum Agni', Agni meaning fire and nirdhum meaning smokeless. The name of Rishabh's grandfather, according to *Puranas,* is Agnirdhum, *i.e.*, the two words in reverse order. As the names of his mother and grandfather are among the objects of the dream, the name of his father which is Nābhi, according to *Puranas* and Jain mythology, should also be there. But among these rest of the pictures it is difficult to find out one which may denote it. 'Nabh' in Sanskrit means sky and Nābhi will mean son of sky. It is not possible to identify a being who can be a son of sky unless it may be the Sun. Hindu mythology does not regard Sun to be the son of sky nor does the Jain mythology. Sun, however, is identifiable among the pictures, where one is 'a celestial aeroplane in the sky'. Among the ancient Sanskrit literature the Sun is often alluded to as a bird in the sky or a kite in the sky. Hence, a celestial aeroplane in the sky may be the picture or word for the Sun. We have another picture of the two garlands which, as we have seen above also, was a symbol of the Sun. We cannot say anything about the other pictures. But as we have seen this dream actually describes the Pashupatinath seal and also tells us about his parents and grandfather, the other pictures must be connected with him. At this stage we can now confidently say that the dream actually describes the Pashupatinath seal and as we have been able to identify the names of the mother and grandfather, the deity is Rishabh. However in order to be certain that we have correctly identified him it will be necessary to see if the incidents in his life as given in mythology are depicted on other seals.

Life of Rishabh

Not much is known about the life of Rishabh. It is possible that even in the times of Indus Valley Civilisation he was a mythical figure and hence only a few incidents were associated with him or else much is forgotten during the passage of time. Even the original words of his teachings are not known. The incidents known through current available mythology can be briefly narrated. There is a slight difference in the versions of the Hindu mythology and of the Jain mythology but both together are complementary to each other and together give a composite picture. According to Hindu mythology he belonged to a dynasty founded by Manu. His parents had no child and hence they prayed to the Supreme God and made sacrifices. The Supreme God appeared before them and gave them the boon that he himself would be born as their son. According to Jain mythology also he belonged to the Ikshavaku dynasty, which ruled at Ayodhya and was also known in Hindu mythology as Solar dynasty. According to the Hindu mythology he descended[30] from Manu through his son Priyavrat, grandson Agnirdh and great grandson Nābhi who was his father. Both Hindu and Jain mythologies agree on Nabhi and Meru being his father and mother respectively. According to Jain mythology as soon as he was born he was anointed on Mount Sumer. When he attained age he was proclaimed as a king during the life-time of his father. At the time of his being crowned king Indra, the chief of the gods, performed a cosmic dance before him. When he ruled some years, he saw a dance performed by a girl which suddenly made him renounce the world. He appointed his son Bharat as king and retired to the forest to meditate. While he was meditating in the forest two snake princes came and kneeling before him worshipped him. As a reward of that worship they became king of two regions. After meditating for a few years Rishabh obtained Supreme Knowledge, which he wanted to impart to all the living beings of that world. Indra got constructed an audience hall called 'Samvashran' or 'Samsharan' whose literal meaning is cross roads. Every living being on earth, men, women, animals, birds came to that audience hall and sat together forgetting their enmity. Rishabh taught them the Supeme Knowledge and it is said that every living being including animals and birds understood it. After giving that discourse Rishabh took to the life of a mendicant never staying at one place for any length of time and getting food only when somebody offered him. It is said that once he fasted for a long time and then was given juice of sugarcane which highly gratified him. According to Hindu mythology he died in a jungle fire while Jain mythology holds that he finally went to live on Mount Kailash which, in Hindu mythology, is the abode of Shiv. Even when he was living on Mount Kailash, men, women, animals and birds continued to visit him in all humility and with all reverence. According to Jain mythology Rishabh in one of his past lives also lived and moved surrounded by four animals, the tiger, the bear, the mangoose and the monkey.[31] Bharat, the son of Rishabh became the sovereign ruler of the whole earth after a campaign of conquest in all the four directions. At the time of Rishabh, according to Hindu mythology, India was called Ajanābh but when Bharat became ruler it was named Bharat which is even today the name of the country. Bharat is credited with visiting his father on Mount Kailash and discussing with him various problems including his dreams. One of the most interesting dreams from our point of view is his dream of seeing two bulls fighting joining their horns, a scene we find on one of the seals. According to Hindu mythology Bharat married Panchjani, daughter of Vishwarup, the three-headed priest of Indra and son of Twastra, whose three heads were severed by Indra in anger.

Seals containing Incidents from the Life of Rishabh

We may now have a look at the seals to see if any of the incidents in the life of Rishabh are depicted on the seals. Surely enough we find some seals containing scenes which depict some incidents as mentioned above while some depict scenes which are not related to the available mythology concerning Rishabh. We may examine them one by one.

1. *Seal No. 29 from Mohenjodaro*[32]—In this seal the deity is shown sitting on a stool meditating. Before him are kneeling two men and offering him something in conical jars. Behind each is shown snakes standing on their tail and canopy of hood over their heads and the postures of the snakes show that they identified with the kneeling men. Are they two snake princes kneeling and worshipping Rishabh and who, as a reward, became kings of the two regions? It appears that this seal is faithfully depicting the legend.
2. *Seal No. 14 from Mohenjodaro*[33]—We may consider a three-faced seal. On one face is shown a tree with two ibexes or goats on either side eating its leaves with a three-headed beast in attendance. On the second face are shown four animals and a crocodile with fish in its mouth going in a file in one direction. On the third face again there are four animals different from the earlier ones going alongwith a crocodile with a fish in its mouth in a file. We thus find that there are eight animals and two crocodiles with fish in their mouth going in a file forgetting their mutual enmity. Crocodiles are carrying fish in their mouth simply because the fish cannot by themselves go and they must help them to go wherever they are going. It is obvious that they are going towards the tree shown in the third face. What does the tree stand for? It is apparent that this tree represents Rishabh. In the Jain mythology

every Tirthankar is identified with a tree and Rishabh is identified with a Banyan tree (*Nayagrodh*), just as in later times the Buddha was identified with a Pipal or Boddhi tree and was for long not represented in person but by Boddhi tree. In the Pashupatinath seal we find that two ibexes or goats are shown sitting beneath the stool on which the deity was sitting. The presence of the two ibexes or goats on either side of the tree shows that the tree is identical with the deity. We find on various seals trees surrounded by railings. We find in seal No. 29 from Mohenjodaro as pointed out above in item No. 1 snake princes offering something in conical jars, to the deity identified as Rishabh. In seal No. 24 from Mohenjodaro we find a devotee offering the same token to a tree. On the basis of the above we can say without hesitation that the tree is identified with Rishabh. The significance of the three-headed beast near the tree could not be explained.

3. *Seal No. 488 from Mohenjodaro*[34]—In this seal too are depicted four animals along with three crocodiles with fish in their mouth proceeding in a file in one direction accompanied by four birds flying and going in the same direction inside a forest symbolised by plants. These animals are going reverentially forgetting their enmity and crocodiles obliging the fish by carrying them in their mouth.
4. *Seal No. 13 from Mohenjodaro*[35]—A similar file of three animals can also be seen on one face of a three-faced seal. On the second face is the tree with two ibexes or goats on either side; there is another scene on this face in which a man and a woman are shown, man sitting on his knees and woman standing. It appears that either man is giving something to the woman or she is giving something to him. On the third face is shown a man sitting on a tree.

The seals at items 2, 3 and 4 show one thing that all the animals, birds and creatures who live in water are going towards the tree which is identified with Rishabh. They all gather for some, obviously a religious, purpose. This religious purpose can only be explained by the Jain tradition of a Samvashran addressed by Rishabh in which men, women, animals, birds and creatures of water gathered, to hear him forgetting their enmity. According to Jain mythology the gathering was headed by Bharat, his son and sovereign of the world, which may actually mean the Indus Valley.

5. *Seal No. 430 from Mohenjodaro*[36]—In this seal is shown a tree dividing itself into two branches from the ground itself. In the midst of the two branches is standing a figure who is having on his head the same crown of horns which are found worn by Rishabh in the Pashupatinath seal. In the middle of two horns is hanging behind his head in place of hair a twig. Before the figure some distance away is kneeling a devotee wearing the same crown of horns with a twig hanging behind his head. Behind him is standing a composite animal with different parts of its body made up of the parts of different animals, *i.e.*, the hind part is that of a tiger, the forelegs of a bull, the horns of a goat, etc. Below in a line are standing seven human figures covering the whole of the lower part of the seal. On the top is a legend slightly defaced but it is the same which is found in the Pashupatinath seal meaning thereby that the figure is the same as that in the Pashupatinath seal, *i.e.*, Rishabh. It is difficult to identify the kneeling figure but in all likelihood he might be Bharat, his son, who succeeded his father as king. The standing figures appear to be onlookers watching the scene. Similarly the significance of the composite figure is difficult to guess. One explanation can be that as every tribe in the Indus Valley must be having its own totem, composite animal is made of the parts of these totems to make it appear that the composite animal represents all and thus all the people. Second explanation can be that it was the scene described in the Purush Sukta of the *Vedas*, as discussed above. It describes the banyan tree identified with

Rishabh and describes the cosmic sacrifice of Purush from whose sacrifice all the different animals in the world took birth. If the Purush Sukta is a description of this scene, which it is more likely, then we can identify Purush with the composite animal and at the same time with Rishabh himself in terms of the Purush Sukta as well as with the *Banyan tree.* Purush is found mentioned a number of times in *Vedas,* the most notable of which is the Ayodhyā Sukta of the *Atharvaveda* where the city of Ayodhyā is said to be the city of Purush. We may note that according to Jain mythology Ayodhyā was the city of Rishabh.

6. *Seal No. 1 from Mohenjodaro*[37]—This is a seal similar to the seal No. 430 except that the composite animal is shown standing before the kneeling figure and there are five human figures instead of seven shown at the top of the seal. There is no inscription.
7. *Amulet No. 1 from Mohenjodaro*[38]—This is a three-faced one. On one face the same scene is shown but the standing human figures are missing.
8. *Seal No. 316 from Harappa*[39]—In this seal the same scene as above is shown but there are no human figures nor any inscription and instead of the tree dividing itself into two branches the tree is shown as if it is an arch and the deity is shown as if standing in a doorway.
9. *Seal No. 303 from Harappa*[40]—It is a two-faced seal. On one face we find a two-tiered structure, a person and a bull standing near a trident-headed pole. On the other side is a man on a tree with a tiger below, a person on a stool and a tiger or a goat. The man sitting on a tree with a tiger below probably symbolises the renunciation of life and a life in the forest. If this is so, then the whole sequence of the various scenes show the life of Rishabh. His life in a two-tiered palace, his renunciation of his worldly life and sojourn in the forest and ultimately his taking up meditation at one place, before his gaining the Supreme Knowledge.
10. *Seal No. 661 from Mohenjodaro*[41]—In this seal two bulls are shown fighting joining horns. Actually this scene is

a part of Rishabh mythology but its significance cannot be explained. According to mythology Rishabh who resided on Mount Kailash was once visited by his son, Bharat. Bharat had seen 23 dreams and he described these dreams to Rishabh. This scene depicts one of these dreams.

11. *Seal No. 24 from Mohenjodaro*[42]—This is a two-faced seal. On one face is shown two men uprooting a plant each shoulder high with a man in between. Alongside is a man sitting on a tree with a tiger below and nearby a jar with a lid. On the other face is shown drawing-like a filter on one end while on the other end is a man shown kneeling before a tree with a conical vessel in his hand. In between is an inscription. The plants which two men are uprooting appear to be the sugarcane plants which they were uprooting from a protected forest symbolised by a man on a tree and tiger below. The plants shown are one with shoulder-high thin stem and long leaves which only a sugarcane plant has. The jar shows that in it is sugarcane juice stored. The filter-like drawing indicates that the juice is filtered which the man is offering to the tree which symbolised Rishabh. We find in *Mahāpurān* in the life of Rishabh that when he was wandering as mendicant and had not eaten for some time he was offered sugarcane juice which highly gratified him.
12. *Seal from West Asia*[43] (Fig. 3.8)—This is a cylindrical seal. In the upper register from right is shown a person grappling with two animals, may be two tigers, a horned personage standing behind a pedestal and a tree. In the lower register from right is shown a bird in flight, over a unicorn; an antelope and two short-horned bulls facing each other. We may notice in the idols of Rishabh in the temples that two bulls facing each other are invariably shown. In fact it is only due to these two bulls that Rishabh is distinguished from other revered figures of the Jain religion. This must be the representation of Rishabh.

Fig. 3.8: Iraq: III (1936): p. 101, Fig. 1.

The above scenes are also shown in parts on various other seals and the total number is more than half of the seals containing scenes of religious significance. There are a number of scenes on other seals which do not seem to have any relation with the available mythology. Such scenes are that of a figure with his upper part that of a human being and the lower one of a tiger, a man with a snake near him identifying him as a snake prince fighting a bull with a javelin, a man with two tigers on either side, a wailing woman alongwith a man with a sword in his hand on one side of the seal while on the other is shown a woman giving birth to a child while two lions are standing as if to take the child in their protection, a snake reclining partly on a platform, etc. We do not know to which mythology they are indicating. It is possible that they might have been connected with Rishabh or with one of his associates or somebody else which we might have forgotten.

We thus find that all the incidents in the life of Rishabh are shown on the seals of the Indus Valley Civilisation which are so elaborately described in *Mahāpurān* and other works. We are told that renouncing the world he went to a forest and meditated there for a number of years. He is shown meditating while sitting in a yogic posture. We are told that while he was meditating two snake-princes came and knelt before him. One of the seals also depicts him meditating while two snake princes are kneeling. We are told that he was fond of sugarcane juice, and we are shown that sugarcane juice is offered to a tree representing him. We are told that when he gained Supreme Knowledge he gave a discourse to which all the living creatures on earth came to listen. We are shown that animals forgetting their enmity were rushing up to the place. Even birds are shown flying along with animals and fish are shown being carried by crocodiles. We are told that while wandering he came to the place where his son Bharat was ruling. He stopped in a garden where he was welcomed by the public and his son, king Bharat. One of the seals shows him standing between the branches of a tree while similarly crowned person is kneeling before him and seven or five figures are standing watching. May be two branches of a tree symbolise a garden and the crowned figure might be the son, and the figures standing watching might be representing public. Rishabh is symbolised even today by two bulls facing each other shown before him. We are shown this scene too. Finally we are told that Rishabh's mother as well as the mothers of other Tirthankars saw a particular dream with sixteen objects. These objects seen in the dream, it appears, are not separate ones but parts of an elaborate picture which, we find, is actually the famous 'Pashupatināth seal'. Thus the life of Rishabh is fully depicted on the seals and there should not be any doubt that the presiding deity of the Indus Valley Civilisation was none other than Rishabh. It was neither Shiv nor Agni or Indra. Rishabh means bull and the figure is bull-faced. We do not know if he was called in the Indus Valley Rishabh or by some other name. Who was Rishabh? Why he came to be worshipped by the people of the Indus Valley Civilisation? Who was Bharat, his son according to the mythology? To understand this we will have to go back to the *Vedas* and to the early tribal life in pre-Indus Valley Civilisation days. As was the normal feature of the early tribal life every tribe moved with his totem which was either an animal or bird. They identified themselves with that totem and regarded themselves as its children. However, as life advanced and they began to grasp the powers of nature they began to endow its powers upon their own totem which began to grow in stature. When they found the power of fire, they endowed their totem with that power though only mythically as having that power. They identified that totem with the god of fire. When they realised the power and qualities of the Sun, they similarly identified their totem with the Sun. When they realised that rain is bountiful they felt that if they have to worship the god who gives rain they must worship their own totem as representing that god too. Thus the totem came to mean for them the god who produces fire, the Sun-god, and the god who makes rain. We have ample references in the *Vedas* to Rishabh or the Bull as a God of Fire, as sun-god and as the god which produces rain. Rishabh or the bull is identified with all of them. So must have been the case with all other totems who were initially treated as equal to each other. We have seen that the animal mentioned in the early hymns of *Vedas* are actually totems representing the whole tribe as is amply seen in the case of Mudgal.[44]

Why the supremacy of the Bull over the other totems? Was it because the tribes treating the bull as their totem were more numerous? Or were they more powerful? It was not so, but only due to the historical role they were called on to play in the life of the Indus Valley Civilisation. What was the important role they played that their totem came to have a dominant influence in the whole area, and in its history? We had seen that the tribe which had bull as its totem and Mudgal as its chief had either invented the wooden club or first used it as a potent weapon and had defeated the other opposing tribes easily. We find that his descendant Sudas, as leader of the Bharat tribe, was ruling at Harappa and was the Guardian of the Frontiers at the Rāvi.[45] Whether the tribal Bharatas even in the times of Mudgal were actually living or roaming in the area between the Rāvi and Beās or they were entrusted with the job later on and shifted to that area is not known and may not be known. But the fact that they were the guardians of the northern frontier of the Indus Valley set them apart from other tribes. They now commanded a respect and trust and that must have been transferred to their totem, Bull. As the situation slowly changed in that they started having a sort of pre-eminence among the tribes being better armed and organised and also because of extracting tribute from others, their own totem Rishabh meaning Bull, became pre-eminent among the totems of other tribes. As the Bharatas became, in effect, rulers of the whole area as we find from the *Vedas*, the Bull or Rishabh became the chief figure.

We find that Sudas conquered various tribes and various areas.[46] We find that he assumed universal sovereignty by performing Horse Sacrifice or Ashwamedha Yagna.[47] Both these deeds made the people belonging to other tribes either instinctively regard Rishabh as outstanding among all other deities or were forced to do the same. We do not know the actual fact but our surmise is supported by the fact that the name of the figure remained Rishabh meaning bull and was not given any other name. It is still known only as Rishabh or Bull. Later on mythology began to be built around him and various scenes were depicted on the Indus Valley seals. No change is made in that mythology or any incident added to the mythology. Later when with the rise of the Hinduism, the cult of Vishnu became prominent and Vishnu gained the supreme position as the Creator, Rishabh was identified with him as one of his incarnations. The Tenth Chapter of *Bhāgwāt Purān* is devoted to Rishabh, as incarnation of Vishnu. This shows that we may not be far from the truth in assuming that *Vedas* identified Rishabh with Vishnu. However, in the *Vedas* Vishnu means the Sun which again supports our contention that the totems were identified with the Sun and became identified with Ādityās.

Who was Bharat treated as his son? Was he a real figure or a mythical one? Both *Bhāgwat Purān* and the *Mahāpurān* agree that Bharat was the son of Rishabh. However, the tribe headed by Sudās was named Bharatas. It appears that the tribe named as Bharatas naturally assumed that they were so named because they were the children of Bharat. They regarded Bharat as the common father and as Rishabh as the totem had also to be the father they made Bharat as his son. Bharat as a king is not mentioned in the *Vedas* nor even as a person. It is thus probable that he was a mythical figure. A whole chapter is devoted in *Bhāgwat Purān* to Bharat describing his rebirth as a deer and a second rebirth as Bharat, the sage. *Bhāgwat Purān* also mentions that Bharat married Panchjani, the daughter of Vishwarup, the three-headed priest of the gods. Is the three-headed beast so frequently shown on the seals actually Vishwarup? There are a people mentioned in the *Vedas* as Panchjanāh. They are variously described by different people as collection of persons or tribes or Varnas.

Can it be that they were actually the children of Panchjani and thus must be the tribe Bharat? Was the assumption about Bharat already made in the Indus Valley Civilisation times or is a later development? If made in those times is there any suggestion on the seals? *Bhāgwat Purān* treats him as mythical figure. So does *Mahāpurān*. *Mahāpurān* describes his conquest of all the known world in all the four directions. This may actually mean the conquest of the Indus Valley by the Bharat tribe. In the ancient *Purānās* three persons are found named as Bharat, the son of Rishabh, the son of Dashrath and brother of Ram and son of Dushyant and Shakuntalā mentioned in *Mahābharāt*. This last one, son of Shakuntalā, made so famous by Kālidās in his drama *Abhijnān Shākuntalam*, is relevant for our purpose. It is said about him that he was so fearless and brave that even in his childhood he used to play with lion cubs. We have four seals showing the lions. In three identical seals we find a boy on both sides of whom is standing a lion or a tiger.[48] In the other we find a woman giving birth to a boy and on its side are standing two lions.[49] Can it be that they are showing Bharat and this legend of his playing with lions was later transferred to the other Bharat, son of Shakuntalā and Dushyant of the lunar dynasty? Can it be possible that the tiger shown before Rishabh in the Pashupatinath seal might be representing the Bharat tribe or mythical Bharat himself?

Indus-Sumer Relations

When Indus civilisation became a fully developed area it was but natural that in addition to the trade within the area as well as with the undeveloped areas in the neighbourhood, it should have both trade and social relations with the contemporary developed civilisations of the world. The other contemporary civilisations so far unearthed were those of Sumer in modern day Iraq, Egypt and Minoan in the island of Crete near Greece. The nearest was Sumer and Egypt and Minoan was far distant beyond Sumer with the additional disadvantage of not being connected by water. We could not find any evidence of any relationship with Minoan but there are evidences of relationship with Sumer. The evidence of any relationship can be seen in a number of ways. There are ancient finds in each other territories of things which can be produced in the other country. Secondly, there may be a mention of the other country in the contemporary literature. Thirdly, there may be borrowing from the other country of many usages, *i.e.*, gods and goddesses, calendar, knowledge of stars and planets, etc. Fourthly, there is the evidence of the language. Let us examine each of these evidences.

Physical evidence of things which are perishable is not possible to be obtained after a period of five thousand years, hence such things are not available. The only things which can be available are things made of stone, or of fired clay or of metal, but they need be those which can be identifiable. We do not get any identifiable things produced in Sumer in the Indus Valley area except a few seals at Lothal and Dwārkā in Saurashtra similar to those found at Bahrein. In the Indus Valley proper there are none. However, the finds in Sumer are substantial. A very large number of seals belonging to the Indus Valley were found in various places in Sumer. These seals contain messages in the Indus script not so far deciphered. Among these seals a few are religious ones containing scenes from the Indus Valley. Among the most noteworthy is one which contains the deity of the Pashupatinath seal in the centre, on either side are the identical scene of a man standing between two lions and below are two identical file of animals led by bulls coming before the deity from opposite sides along with flying birds. We are not in a position to say whether the seals found in Sumer are commercial messages or votive offerings to local gods or goddesses sent along with goods. In case of the former it raises further questions. If those seals were made in India and sent to Sumer along with goods, then whether there were people who could have read them or whether there were Indus people living there. In case they were made in Sumer to be sent to India along with goods, then it implies that there were people living in Sumer who could have read them or else they might be Indus traders. We do not know and may, not know till the Indus script is read. As for the second source of evidence we may point out that in the absence of the knowledge of Indus script we are not in a position to say if the Indus records contain any reference to Sumer. However, in the records of Sumer there is a mention of two places which are Makan and Malluhā from where ships brought goods and part of the goods were offered to a goddess in Ur, an important town of Sumer. Though some of the goods do appear to belong to India, yet it cannot be said with certainty for these places may be anywhere on the coast of Indian Ocean from African coast to India or even Persia. As we are still in the dark about the then names of Harappa, Mohenjodaro, Lothal or Dwarka or other smaller towns we cannot say whether Makan or Malluha can be identified with any of the above towns. Again with regard to the third source, *i.e.*, the borrowing of the institutions or gods, in the absence of the knowledge of the Indus script it is not possible to say anything. The only common thing is the knowledge of the use of wheels which were found in both. The gods and goddesses in the extant mythology are certainly not common though there is one intriguing name found in both. The name of a goddess in Sumer is 'Istar' which is common word for woman in general in *Vedas* which are probably the religious and cultural history of Indus Civilisation. Sumerians, prior to the discovery of the Indus Valley Civilisation, were credited with the knowledge of stars and planets, with the seven-day week, with the annual calendar. Though the later day India has the same week, the annual calendar and the knowledge of planets, we cannot say whether the Indus people knew it and if they knew it whether it was borrowed from the Sumerians or vice-versa.

We may now look at the fourth type of evidence, *i.e.*, the evidence of the language. When two different civilisations with different languages come into contact through trade or even wars and develop social relationship, through them the impact on language is seen in two ways. Many of the words of one language are absorbed as a whole in the other language. We have seen above that the name of the goddess in Sumer, 'Istar' was taken in the language as the common word for woman, 'istri'. 'Ishaku' was the designation of the rulers of Ur in Sumer. It is the names of rulers of a dynasty in India, *i.e.*, 'Ikshwaku'. Either people borrowed it. No comparative study of the Sanskrit or an Indian language and the Sumeric or the Accadian words, it appears, had been made so far. If such a study is made, we may be sure that a number of words absorbed in the other language will be found. We may note that a very large number of Hindi words are found in Sumerian language. The other impact is seen in the formation of polyglottic words. Polyglottic words are those words which are formed by the combination of a word each from the two languages having identical meaning, and the word so formed also has the same meaning as that of its constituent words. An example can be seen in the Sanskrit word 'Karenu' meaning elephant. It is formed of two words 'Kari' and 'Anu' the former belonging to Sanskrit and the latter to Tamil both meaning in their turn elephant. That shows that when two languages come into contact, the result must be the formation of a few polyglottic words. If Sumer and Indus people came into contact, there must, of necessity, be the presence of polyglottic words in the two languages. Here too unfortunately due to absence of such a study it is not possible to point out such words. However, a few very common words come to our mind immediately. One such word is Kurukshetra. It is formed of two words 'Kuru' and 'Kshetra'. 'Kuru' in Sumerian means area, the same meaning as that of 'Kshetra' in Sanskrit. Together they mean the area, but in India it now means a particular area in the modern state of Haryana. A word can be 'matrabhumi' which is formed of two words 'Matra' and 'Bhumi'. The former appears to be actually the Accadian word 'Madu' meaning earth while the latter also means earth. The two together formed the polyglottic word at first 'Madubhumi' which later took on the form 'Matubhumi' meaning earth but as in Sanskrit matu means mother probably it was improved as 'matrabhumi' meaning mother earth. We do not know if after the formation of this word, that earth is known as 'mother earth'. If it is so, it will be interesting to study such other words which had an impact psychologically after their formation. It also appears that it was that polyglottic word which proceeded to Europe and Anatolia and introduced the notion of mother earth in every language. Another such word is 'Raksha-Bandhan' which is again made of two words 'Raksha' and 'Bandhan', former in Sumerian meaning "to tie" the same as the latter word which is in Sanskrit. Both together also mean the same thing. However, in modern day India it is the name of a particular ritual in which a thread is tied on the wrist of the brother by the sister. The presence of three such words in Sanskrit indicates that there must be a number of such other words and the matter requires an in-depth study. The absence of all the above three polyglottic words in *Vedas* creates a doubt if they were formed in the times of Indus Civilisation, but they certainly indicate that Sumerian-Accadian languages must have come into contact with Sanskrit and with Indians.[50]

We thus find that there are reasons to believe that the people of Sumer and Indus had contacts with each other and to some extent had influenced each other. The extent of their contacts and the influences on each other remain to be determined and require an extensive research.

REFERENCES

1. *Rigveda* 3.53.
2. *Rigveda* 6.47.21.
3. *Rigveda* 3.53.
4. *Rigveda* 1.104.4.
5. *Rigveda* 1.94-115.
6. *Rigveda* 1.108.8.
7. *Rigveda* 1.126.
8. *Rigveda* 7.18.12 to 14.
9. *Rigveda* 7.99.5.
10. *Rigveda* 6.27.7 and 8.
11. *See* Appendix D.
12. Bible Genesis 8.4.
13. Bible Genesis 11.8.
14. FEM Pl. XCIV, 420.
15. FEM Pl. XCIV 430.
16. MIC Pl. CXVI 29.
17. FEM Pl. XCVI 522.
18. FEM Pl. XCI 4.
19. FEM pl. LXXXIV, 75.
20. EH Pl. XCIII, 304.
21. FEM, Pl. XC 24.
22. FEM Pl. XCVI, 488.
23. FEM Pl. LXXXIX 347.
24. EM Pl. XCIII, 303.
25. NM 151.
26. FEM Pl. XCIX, 661.
27. *Rigveda* X. 90.
28. FEM Pl. XCIV, 430.
29. *Māhapuran* 12.104-119.
30. *Bhagwat Puran,* Book V—Chapter II, III.
31. *Māhapuran* Couplet 245.
32. MIC Pl. CXVI, 29.
33. MIC Pl. CXVI, 14.
34. FEM Pl. XCVI, 488.
35. FEM Pl. XC, 13.
36. FEM Pl. XCIV, 430.
37. MIC Pl. CXVI, 1.
38. FEM LXXXII, 1.
39. EH Pl. XCIII, 316.
40. EH Pl. XCIII, 303.
41. FEM PL. XCIX, 661.
42. FEM Pl. XC 24.
43. Iraq; III (1936): p 101 Fig. 1.
44. *Rigveda*. X. 102.
45. *Rigveda* VII. 18.
46. *Rigveda* VII. 18.
47. *Rigveda* VII. 53.
48. FEM Pl. LXXXIV, 75.
49. EH. Pl. XCIII, 304.
50. See Appendix D

4

POST-INDUS INTERREGNUM

Some time between 2000 to 1700 years B.C. the Indus people dispersed from the area. The next about a period of thousand years is a dark period in the history of India, dark not because it was a period of chaos and decadence but because of the non-availability of any contemporary record or some evidence of the type of civilisation prevalent in the country. In fact during this period the civilisation spread far and wide reaching every part of the country. It was a period of development in the field of religion and culture, of intense thought about the unknown and of speculations about things divine or inscrutable, as is evident from the ancient texts of *Brahmānas, Āranyakas, Upnishads* and the composition of literature just after that period, notable among which is the *Rāmāyan* and some of the the *Purānās*. We also know from references in the books of that period that an important branch of knowledge was history. There was a script in use during the Indus Valley times and after that period the first texts which were available were in the period of Emperor Ashok found either in the shape of inscriptions on the pillars or on the copper plate of Sahgaurā. But this script of Emperor Ashok appears to be widely in use and fully developed. Hence, it would not be wrong to assume that the writing was widely in use but somehow because of the fragile nature of the material used it was lost. The material for building houses, for writing and for other uses has all perished and we are left speculating about the history of the period and even if history began anew during that period, *i.e.*, whether the inhabitants of the Indus Valley were destroyed by the barbarian Aryans of Central Asia or whether those Aryans were the inhabitants of the Indus Valley who were forced to disperse, and who founded in their dispersal the civilisations of whole of the Aryan world. In fact if we had not prejudged the issue and taken for granted that it were the Aryans who destroyed the Indus-Dravidian people, and thought over the evidence dispassionately and in a rational manner we could have come to a proper conclusion. As the issue whether Aryans invaded India and destroyed the Indus Civilisation, or the Indus people were themselves Aryans and Sanskrit-speaking people is crucial to be determined first. Let us look at the facts first, and try to find out the truth if it can be found on the basis of the available facts. We have to determine who were the Aryans and whether the later civilisation was based on the Indus Civilisation or was an independent growth founded by the invading barbarian hordes.

Who were the Aryans?

If a civilisation is destroyed by invaders in midstream and the inhabitants exterminated or made slaves and forcibly converted to the invaders' religion, culture and way of life, then in the next phase of their civilisation we will not find any element of their religion, culture, beliefs and way of life. If, however, we find that even after a thousand years interregnum the same way of thinking, the same base of religion, the same beliefs, the same symbols of their expression and the same culture are the basis of their new life we can be sure that they were not annihilated by some invaders but had to disperse due to some natural calamity which has to be determined. We should study both the theories, their basis in this light and see if there is anything common in the Indus Civilisation and in the civilisation in the 6th century B.C., the earliest period about which something is known.

Common Features in Indus and Later Civilisation

Had the Indus script been deciphered to the satisfaction of

all and the language known, such a controversy would not have arisen. Attempts have been made to decipher it by various scholars and they saw different languages not even remotely connected. So far three languages are being scanned to find out their connection with the Indus language. These are Tamil, Hittite and Sanskrit. None is satisfied with the attempts. Hence, there is a need to compare the patterns and symbols of the Indus Civilisation and the civilisation of the known period, *i.e.*, 5th century B.C. onwards which marked Buddhist, Jain and later Hindu religions. We have only the seals containing scenes as well as script containing symbols in the Indus Valley to be compared with icons and mythology of the Buddhist, Jain and Hindu religions. We may begin with the scenes on the seals.

The most important seal for the purpose is inevitably the Pashupatinath seal. As we have seen above the deity is Rishabh. Rishabh continued down the ages along with the mythology noticed in the other seals, to be the deity for the Jains as their first Tirthankar. He was treated as such in the 5th century B.C. when Jain religion had a considerably large following both in the North India as well as in South India. He is still treated as such though the number of Jains has been reduced. Rishabh was later identified with Vishnu when with the rise of Hinduism the cult of Vishnu as the Supreme God became prominent. He is regarded as the first human incarnation of Vishnu, the earlier four incarnations being those of animals, *i.e.*, Fish, Tortoise, Boar and a being half man and half lion. Thus Rishabh is identified with the principal god of the Hindus. Although he is not identified with Shiv in person, yet if we look at the features of both and their mode of living, there should not be any doubt that Shiv had assumed all the features of Rishabh including their residence which is Mount Kailash. We may now have a look at the four animals moving around him in a circle, the lion, the elephant, the buffalo and the rhinoceros. This pattern of four animals surrounding the deity is a recurring feature in the later Indian Symbolism. Buddha is shown surrounded by four animals—the horse, the bull, the lion and the elephant—and all are shown on all the four sides on the pedestal. If we look at the temples of Krishna of the Pānchrātra concept of religion we find Krishna surrounded by his brother Balram, his son Pradumn and the great grandson Aniruddha who can be identified with a snake, a crocodile and a deer respectively. All the animals are shown along with those with whom they are identified. If we ignore the presence of men, the four animals surrounded on each side will be a snake, a crocodile, a deer and Garuda, the big bird in front. This pattern can be seen even on temples constructed as late as the end of the first millennium A.D. and the beginning of the second millennium. If we again analyse the mythology surrounding Earth as mother goddess, we find it being surrounded on four sides with four gods along with their mounts, *i.e.,* Indra with horse, Yama with buffalo, Kuber with elephant and Varuna with crocodile. All the gods are identified with their mounts and if we ignore the gods who appear to have been added later for there is no explanation of choosing these particular gods to surround the earth, we find the four animals, the horse, the buffalo, the elephant and the crocodile surrounding mother earth. If we examine Shiv along with his family which is usually shown in every temple we will find the same pattern, *i.e.,* Ganesh with his mount mouse, his second son Kumar with his mount peacock, Parvati with her mount the lion and bull the mount of Shiv himself. Thus these four animals which are mouse, bird, lion and bull are depicted surrounding him. If we have a look at Jain mythology we will find that they hold that Rishabh in his previous birth as Vajrajangh also moved surrounded by four animals, the mangoose, the tiger, the monkey and the boar. We should not be concerned here with the significance of each animal. What we should be concerned is the pattern and it is clear that in this matter the later Jain, Buddha and Hindu religions are following the pattern of the Indus Civilisation.

A notable feature of the seal is the pair of goats or ibexes beneath the stool on which Rishabh is sitting both facing each other. We may see the same pattern in the later religions. Jains claim 23 Tirthankars after Rishabh and in the statues of each are shown a pair of animals all different in case of each Tirthankar. These animals are shown sitting facing each other and in fact these pairs of animals are a distinguishing feature of the Tirthankars. We are familiar with the statues of Buddha with a pair of deer sitting facing each other beneath the stool of the Buddha. Among the Hindus we do not find a pair of animals associated with any god or goddess except Lakshmi. Her usual picture or statue is found with two elephants on either side holding in their trunks either two garlands or two pots as if they are annointing her. These elephants are shown with their trunks above her. However, the author has seen a statue of Lakshmi in a temple near the Gapsāgar Tank in Dungarpur in Southern Rajasthan in which Lakshmi is shown sitting on a lotus and the two elephants much smaller in size are shown below the lotus on either side of the stem. The pattern of the Indus valley having two animals beneath the seat of the deity continued in the later traditions of the Indian civilisation even after a thousand years and became a distinguishing feature of the traditions.

Another feature of the Indus Valley Civilisation seen on the seals is that of a tree identified with the deity and worshipped in place of him. If we look at the later religions we find the pattern repeated. Gautam Buddha was for long not shown in person on any statue or carving. Instead he was represented by the Pipal tree which became his symbol. Jains themselves regard the Banyan tree as identified with Rishabh and represents him. In fact in the later India and even today cutting of even a branch of either Pipal or Banyan tree is strictly forbidden. Jain mythology has identified a particular tree each with each Tirthankar. Among the Hindus Pipal tree is identified with Vishnu and it is worshipped even today. Among other seals we find a being half-man, half-lion standing as a protector of a child. He was not forgotten in later times and became Narsingh, a half-man and a half-lion, the incarnation of Vishnu, protecting Prahlād, a child. We find in a seal two snake princes worshipping Rishabh. These two snakes later became an ornament of Shiv. We again find a boy between two lions in a seal and on another we find the two lions present at the time of the birth of a boy. It is presumed that either that boy is Rishabh or his son Bharat. We are all familiar with the famous drama *Abhignān Shākuntalam* of Kālidas in which the young prince Bharat is shown playing with lions. Though this prince Bharat is different from Bharat, the son of Rishabh, yet it shows that the later Indians had not forgotten the tradition of a prince playing with lions who became his companions.

Let us now examine other finds from the Indus Valley which might have continued in the later day India. There are a large number of conical stones and ring stones varying in sizes from four feet to miniatures. They are said to have some religious significance and thought to represent Rishabh. These conical stones and ring stones continued their religious connections in the later religions and are representing Shiv in Hindu religion. Another interesting find is a toy cart. We can see the carts exactly like that cart used as bullock carts even in India of today.

Lastly we may study the symbols of the Indus Valley and whether they are found in the later period. The only extant symbols we get in the Indus Valley are to be found on the seals usually as part of the script. We will have to rely on them alone in our study. A feature universally observed is that in the tropical regions the most important deity worshipped is the Sun. There are numerous temples of the Sun in the tropics of which India too is a part and the orientation of the temples of the Sun is East to West. Further the direction is adjusted in such a way that when the Sun is highest on the particular day in the year, its rays fall on the idol of the Sun. Thus at the Tropic of Cancer the day will be in the month of June and at Equator it will be in the months of March and September. We find so in the whole of India including Maldives in the south. These temples of the Sun invariably have the symbols of the Sun in all their varieties and in every nook and corner. The symbols of the Sun usually found are the conch, the wheel, the lotus, the drum, the lion and a solar disk. The solar disk is shown as a plate on which a slightly smaller plate is superimposed and on either side or on one side are shown three lines either vertical or horizontal. Probably horizontal lines indicate that the Sun has wings or it flies in the sky and later to save space they became vertical. These symbols are found in the Sun Temples all over the world, not in India alone. We find these symbols in the Indus script with surprising frequency. Sometimes a few symbols are jumbled together. Seal No. 306[1] from Harappa consists of these symbols alone. In it we find the solar plate with two vertical lines, swastikas five in number, a lion and a man with a drum. Solar plates are shown in an ingenious way. Two circles are shown overlapping the other and two or three vertical lines. Overlapping circles are probably meant to convey that one is over the other and actually one plate is over the other. We have already seen above that the Sun was an important deity in Indus Valley and also probably the father of Rishabh. Hence, it may not be surprising to find a number of seals which contain inscriptions devoted to the Sun. However the point to be noted is that the symbols seen on the Indus script continued in the later religions. They may not have been associated in the Indus Valley with the Sun as they were in the later religions, but spirit behind it persisted and their form continued. We may now have a look at the crown of horns with a twig hanging behind the deity. If this crown along with the twig is turned at an angle of 90 degrees, we find that it takes the shape of the most sacred of the Hindu symbols 'OM'. It may not have meant the same in Indus Valley but the similarity is so striking and remarkable that we are forced to conclude that though the meaning might be or might not be the same in Indus Valley and later religions, the symbol continued to be used.

If we compare the alphabets of the early Brahmi script with those of the Indus script, we will notice that almost all the alphabets of the Brahmi script are to be seen in the Indus script. This similarity cannot be accidental. In fact this similarity has led some scholars to conclude that Brahmi script is derived from the Indus script. In their view when the Indians discovered the concept of alphabet they simply picked the words beginning with that alphabet from the Indus script itself and arranged them in order and started using them as alphabet. And they may not be wrong. However, one thing is clear that the form of the alphabets passed from the Indus script to that of the Brahmi.

When a people with a different religion and culture conquer another land and people with a different religion and culture the former either exterminate the latter or decimate them. As a result of this extermination or decimation there is usually no continuity and the old deities, old religious or cultural symbols, the language and the old script are changed and they are not allowed to continue. They just disappear from the scene and are forgotten. If, however, the people are merely enslaved and forced to adopt the language, religion or culture of the conquerors, then they are sure to reappear even after a millennium. This can be seen in the conquest of Islam and Christianity. In Sumer and Egypt after their conquest by Islam the language, the religion, the religious symbols and the culture just disappeared without leaving any trace. Similar is the case with the impact of Christianity in Europe and North America. However, in Central and South America where the natives were neither exterminated nor decimated, the old languages and the old religious symbols of the Mayas and the Aztecs and Incas are having a revival. Similarly in India of today even after 800 years of the rule of Islam and Christian powers, the Hindu religious symbols and the language can be seen everywhere. As there is a continuity after the demise of the Indus Civilisation which can be seen even after a thousand years there should be a reasonable doubt about the theory of Aryan invasion and extermination of the Indus people. We must submit the grounds on which the theory is based on the touchstone of sound evidence and rationality.

We have already discussed the theory of the Aryan invasion. We may, however, repeat some of the main points. Archaeological evidence unearthed so far does not support the invasion theory. None of the things the invaders could carry, *i.e.*, arms made of either stone or metal, pottery in which they could have carried grain, water or prepared food, clay toys for the children etc., were recovered on an any route coming towards India either through Afghanistan, or Iran or the more difficult route via the Pamirs. Similarly, archaeology does not support the massacre of Indus people by the invaders. Only a few skeletons in an obscure street in Mohenjodaro have been found. None are found in any other town of the Indus Valley. Just on the basis of a few skeletons in an obscure street of only one town, Mohenjodaro, it cannot be assumed that there was a general massacre, of the inhabitants, of the Indus Valley.

The presence of the Brāhui speaking a language akin to Dravidian languages in the Kirthar ranges near the modern town of Quetta and near the Indus town of Mohenjodaro is certainly puzzling. If there was no general massacre of the Indus people, then the Brāhuis cannot be the remnants of the Indus people running away from the attackers. As we saw above the massacre of Indus people is not at all proved and the presence of the Brāhuis should be attributed to other causes.

The other reason was the belief that the deity of the Indus Valley was Shiv and as he was regarded as primarily and originally the god of the Dravidians, the inhabitants must be Dravidians. We have already seen above that Shiv was not the deity of the Pashupatinath seal and of the Indus Valley. Hence, this reason cannot be accepted. It will be appropriate here to mention that Shiv was the deity of all Indians and not of originally the Dravidians. The first reference to Shiv as has been stated earlier, is found in a second century B.C. work, *Mahābhāshya,* a commentary on the grammar of Pānini, by Patanjali. He has made the reference in connection with the Mauryas, who, he stated, sold the images of Shiv, Skanda and Vishākha in order to earn money. The reference is very interesting and very important. If the images of Shiv were a source of revenue to the Maurya treasury, then the images made and sold must be in millions and billions or even more. A great Empire of the Mauryas, embracing the whole of North India and part of Southern India must be engaged in only that state activity regarding raising revenue, which brought sufficiently great amount of revenue. This cryptic remark of Patanjali indicates the immense popularity of the cult of Shiv and indicates that he must be a popular god even some centuries earlier. If he was popular god in the 5th and 6th centuries B.C. or even earlier it cannot be said that he was the god of the Dravidians originally and North India and the Aryans borrowed him from them. History of his worship is as old in the North as in the South India as far as the present state of our knowledge indicates.

We thus see that the theory of Aryan invasion of India resulting in the dispersal of the Indus people does not hold good on the strength of correct reasoning or on the basis of historical facts. There must be other reasons which compelled the Indus people to disperse and to leave behind the land where they created the Indus Civilisation. Let us see the reason which might have compelled them to migrate and if so to which place or places.

Probable Reason of the Migration of Indus People

For a period of about 6 to 7 centuries when the Indus Civilisation was at its zenith, it achieved a great prosperity. It resisted successfully the onslaught of the barbarian tribes both from the North and from the West. Some of tribes whom they repulsed at the battle of the ten kings on the banks of the Ravi, it appears, came progressively under their influence and were allowed to migrate and settle down in the hinterland. Probably some among them were taken prisoners and made slaves. They found that the life was probably better in the settled civilised area than hunting and searching for food in the forests. Inspired by them the tribes probably either migrated in bulk or were allowed to infiltrate. Notable among those who migrated and settled in the area were probably Yadus and Purus and among those who did not migrate were probably the Paktas. Yadus and Purus were probably allowed to settle on the banks of the Saraswati and its tributaries in the Eastern areas. It was probably somewhere in the 19th century B.C. that the catastrophe finally struck which compelled the Indus people to abandon their land and disperse.

A people abandon the land, the land of their ancestors either when another tribe stronger and better skilled in war forcibly evicts them or if a natural calamity of the magnitude of a disaster strikes them. We do not find the land to be settled by another tribe or people after that time and hence the reason for their dispersal must be some natural ecological disaster. We have reasons to believe that it was a natural catastrophe. A study reveals that sometimes in the 19th century B.C. the Saraswati river which was the mainstay of the civilisation became dry, its major tributaries, the Satluj and the Yamuna alongwith other minor ones changing their courses. The Satluj which was pouring its huge quantity of water in the Saraswati changed its course and moved to the North joining instead the Beās and similarly Yamuna changed its direction towards

East and joined the Gangā. A number of minor distributaries followed them and changing their courses joined either the Satluj or the Yamunā or else became dry. Their dry beds till date testify this. The reason of this change is simple. We know that once the Southern India was a separate entity from the Asian mainland but it started moving to the North. The South Indian plate struck the Asian mainland lifting a mass above it which became the Himalayas. This plate is still pushing into the mainland and the Himalayas are still rising. Whenever it lifts somewhere some area to such a height that some sort of imbalance is created, then in and around that areas some sort of upheaval takes place raising some areas and depressing other ones. Such happenings are witnessed periodically in the whole of North India. In living memory we witnessed the earthquakes in Quetta in Baluchistan, in Bihar and in Assam as recently as in 1947. In the 19th century B.C. or so the scene of such an upheaval must have been the area which was the course of both Satluj and the Yamunā which incidentally are close. Some area must have been elevated sufficiently to force both these rivers to change their ways, one to the North and the other to the East. Similar must have been the course with other minor tributaries who similarly joined either the Satluj or the Yamunā. The result was that the Saraswati, the most majestic, the most motherly, the Trishadhastā became dry and the land became a desert not in a position to sustain the civilisation, and the inhabitants. Probably the impact of the upheaval was sufficiently strong to make even the Ravi and the Beas too change their courses to the present ones, which are at some distance from the old ones of the Indus Valley times. If that too happened then Harappa was removed from the nearness of the two rivers which was its special feature and a reason of being a trading centre. Probably Indus also changed its course leaving Mohenjodaro dry. We are not in a position to say whether this catastrophe struck suddenly or came slowly. But when it finally came it destroyed the Indus Civilisation, changed the course of India and changed the history of the world.

Probably at the same time there was a lessening of rainfall in the whole area including the Saurashtra region. The whole area suddenly became unfit for agriculture and thus incapable of supporting the population of the rural as well as the urban areas. The Indus people who had resisted the earlier desiccation and created the Indus Civilisation might have resisted the idea of abandoning the area and in the belief that the river Saraswati might revive might have moved up the other tributaries still having water for some temporary period. However, when even that water might have started lessening and those tributaries themselves started drying up there was probably no alternative for them but to migrate to better areas with plenty of water and forests which were in the vicinity. Where did they migrate? Whether it was a planned migration by the Indus people as a whole? Whether they moved in a single region or in many regions? To which regions or region did they migrate? It is difficult to give any precise answer to the above questions in the absence of any records. However, on the basis of mythology, on the basis of epics, legends and the places where they were found it is possible to recreate their problems and how they solved them.

We get in the *Rigveda* a number of references to councils in which decisions were taken. It appears that the decisions were usually taken by the tribes in general councils. When a decision was taken to migrate scouts must have been sent to find out the proper and suitable area. After it was finally decided to migrate to that particular area the whole tribe might have migrated. We may visualise that they migrated to the nearest area in the neighbourhood either on the banks of the rivers or in the area between the two rivers, inevitably the major rivers. Thus the people of Harappa and the middle Saraswati might have migrated to the rivers of the Satluj, the Beās and the Ravi. The people in the Eastern area might have migrated to the area along the river Yamunā and the area between the Yamunā and the Gangā, while the inhabitants of the Saurashtra to the nearby Gujarat along the river Narbadā. We find from the excavations made so far that the late Harappan settlements were 130 in the modern state of Uttar Pradesh of which 70 alone were along the river Yamunā, 297 in the modern state of Haryana, 128 in the modern state of Punjab, 3 in Himachal Pradesh, 4 in Chandigarh, 1 in Delhi and 130 in the modern State of Gujarat, while there was none in the states of Sind, Baluchistan or North-West Frontier Province of Pakistan.

It appears that the Puru and Yadu tribes were the first to move and settle on the banks of the Yamunā. We find from the epic *Mahābhārat* that the Yadus settled on the banks of the Southern Yamunā near Mathurā and later founded the city while the Purus settled on the Northern banks of Yamunā and later founded the city of Hastināpur. *Mahābhārat* also informs us that the earlier settlement of the Puru tribe was in Kurukshetra on the banks of the Saraswati and they migrated to the Yamunā, the reason not being mentioned. From that time onwards the Purus and the Yadus played a leading role and their history was the history of India and was sung in epics and mythologies. The *Mahābhārat* is the history of the Purus and the Yadus and the *Purānās* too give them an important place. The Bharata and the Tritsu tribes were probably reluctant to give up the magnificent town of Harappa where they lived luxuriantly and only when life became impossible they were constrained to move to the adjacent areas of the Haryana and the Punjab but probably the better sites were occupied by other tribes who arrived earlier and had to be content with some poorer ones. They rapidly lost importance and were no more heard in history. Their memory is preserved only in the mythology of the Jains. We do not know much about the tribes who settled in Gujarat but from the epic *Mahābhārat* we find that a branch of the Yadus migrated to that region and established the sea-port of Dwārkā, becoming very powerful and playing a very prominent part in history. We also hear the names of two tribes Andhaks and Vrishnis but cannot say that they were branches of Yadu tribe or separate tribes of those parts who, combined with Yadus, became so powerful.

We have seen that the people of the three sides of the Indus Valley, Northern, Eastern and Southern had migrated to the neighbouring areas. But what about those living in the Western parts, in the city of Mohenjodaro and its hinterland in Sind along the Southern banks of the Saraswati? They could not have moved East because it was already a desert which, the tribe moving along with women and children together with their goods, could not have traversed safely. For the similar reason they could not have moved to North which too was a desert. In the South was either the sea or the marshes of the Rann of Cutch. They were fully conversant with the topography of the Baluchistan and the North-West Frontier Province of Pakistan and knew that it was unsuitable. We also do not find any late Indus sites in these parts. Were they frustrated and remained there to die? It was improbable for such enterprising people who successfully met the challenge of desiccation by creating the Indus Civilisation to be resigned to fate and remain there to die. Moreover, it is not supported by any historical evidence. It appears that they took far bolder course much greater than could be imagined. They had trade relations with Sumer as we know and probably it was both by sea and by land. They probably knew the land route and also might have known that in the Iran plateau they could have a home. It, therefore, appears that they moved *en masse* to the Iran plateau and settled there. We do not know whether they moved by sea or by land or by both. What we do know that at about that time a certain people were settled in Iran. They spoke a language which was akin to the Sanskrit of the *Vedas*, amply proved by the language of the Avestā, the sacred book of the Parsis and the most ancient text available from Iran. In the *Vedas* we find the name of a tribe Pārthian, which is said to have defeated the Varshikhs in the battle of Hariyupiā, and in the *Mahābhārat* a tribe Madra which played a prominent part in the *Mahābhārat* War. About a thousand years later in Iran, we find the tribe Medes, pronounced Mada, playing a vital role in the defeat of the Assyrians, and the Pārthians setting up an Empire two hundred years before Christ. Were these two tribes among those who migrated to the Iranian plateau from Mohenjodaro and its neighbouring parts when they were forced to leave their homes?

Settlement of Indus People in the New Homes

Indus people who moved in their new homes faced different situations in different climates. Those who moved in India found dense forests, perennial rivers and a salubrious climate. Those who went to Iran found the same semi-arid conditions they had in the Indus Valley but instead of the river Saraswati they found small streams. The Purus and the Yadus and other tribes who moved along the Yamunā and the area between the Yamunā and the Gangā cleared the forests either by burning vast stretches of forests or by felling trees. After clearing the forests they built the cities and started cultivation around them. This was unlike the Indus Valley where due to historical necessity they were cultivating the lands and later built the cities some distance away to guard the area from the raiders. After crossing the Yamunā with which they were already familiar and going East at some distance they found another river as majestic as the Saraswati. It was the Gangā. As the Saraswati, the motherly river had gone dry, they felt that this river to whom the Yamunā now joins in place of the Saraswati must be as motherly and as sacred as the Saraswati. They, therefore, transferred their reverence to that river and further to give it sanctity they imagined that the Saraswati too joined it at the same place as the Yamunā. Thus the Ganga became the most motherly, the most sacred and instead of 'Trishadhastā' which was the Saraswati, became 'Triveni' which means the same. They made their settlements prosperous and started educating the primitive tribes who populated the forests in their ways and culture. Whenever a settlement became too large and too populous some enterprising young men would move further East and settling there would propagate their belief and culture. In that way during the course of centuries the whole of India East of the Yamunā became settled and adopted the culture and the religion of the Indus people. A similar movement took place in the North of the Indus Valley and in the South India. In the movement to the South both the people, *i.e.*, those who moved from Saurashtra to Gujarat and those who moved to the Yamuna valley played their part. An indication of such a movement can be had in the later Sanskrit works, the *Brāhmanas*, the *Āranyaks* and the *Upṇishads*. We find in them the Rishis and seers engaged in religious discussions with others including kings and converting them to their point of view. The most notable were the discussions in the places now thought to be in modern Bihar, *i.e.*, Videh and Magadh.

There is no doubt that during their movement they must have encountered tribes with their own gods and goddesses which they might not have been prepared to give up. It appears that in such circumstances they must have identified them with their own gods and goddesses and convinced them that the gods and goddesses were the same with two different names. We find in the Indian mythology most of the gods and goddesses with multiple names, some even having names more than a thousand. This must be due to the identification of the gods of various tribes with one another. It is also possible that in their contacts with other people and their gods and goddesses, they added some to their own, identifying some of them with minor ones and thus making them much more important than they were previously. The cult of Vishnu, Shiv, Krishna-Vāsudev, Rām appears to have emerged in that period. Among the goddesses Durgā, Lakshmi, Annapurnā also arose at that time.

They must have taken quickly to the new life styles. In place of sun-baked or fire-baked bricks they might have found wood to be more suitable for their houses. Cultivation must have been easier yielding much more than in their old habitat and they must have found new things to cultivate. There must have been leisure enough to develop culture and to speculate regarding creation and the Creator. Though they must have initially followed the old religion and celebrated the old festivals, yet imperceptibly change was coming over with both of the religion and the doctrines which were getting more complicated and taking mysterious hue. During that millennium too the people must have first heard the stories and exploits of their ancestors and heroes and must have loved hearing them again and again. Those stories must have been later sung and songs composed which must have given rise to poets. We duly find that those songs and poems were later compiled either as *Purānās* or had become the great epics of *Mahābhārat* and *Rāmāyan*.

As civilisation spread far and wide, the number of settlements grew substantially, the people became richer and the trade must have developed considerably. It must have been helped by the huge rivers which provided easier waterways. That must have given rise to two classes, those who produced goods required for needs of the common people and also for the rich people and the class of merchants who transported and sold them. We have no knowledge whether they belonged to the same tribes or became one of a class due to expertise. But we know certainly that they were welcomed everywhere and rulers vied with one another in having them in their territories. These people too were not attached to a single territory or to a tribe but for them whole world was their territory and they moved wherever it suited them. They were probably more loyal to their interests and to their class than to the rulers.

Life in Iran

Those who went to the Iran plateau must have found that the climate was much the same but instead of a plain the land was undulating and partly hilly and partly plain. Instead of a major river the Saraswati, they found a large number of small rivers which must have pleased them. Tribes must have settled in different areas. They must have met the challenge of that undulating tract by successfully taming the small rivers for the irrigation and cultivation of various crops including the new ones which they must have found there. They must have coaxed the local tribes, they must have met, into adopting their own culture and religion. They could not move further West because though there was a major river, the Tigres, but beyond it was the ancient civilisation of Sumer, highly developed both culturally as well as in the art of war. There were also some of the most ferocious tribes known in history on the other side of the river, notably the Assyrians, whom as Asur they had often heard and mentioned in their religious poetry, *i.e.*, the *Vedas*. They kept clear of them for the time being. Later it were they who destroyed the Assyrians and overran the whole area.

When people had to leave their original homeland and had to move to a far away place, they are likely to stick to their religion and culture more jealously and tenaciously than those who move to the neighbouring area. We, therefore, find that the people who settled in Iran kept the purity of their religion and culture, while the people who moved into other parts of

India could not and their religion changed considerably with the addition of numerous gods and goddesses. The people in Iran remained confined to the worship of fire, of the Sun as Mitra and Varun, and Rishabh whom they kept in the form of the cult of the Bull. This was in the face of a highly developed civilisation with a religion like Sumer in the neighbourhood and of Egypt a little away to the West.

Vedas and Avesta

When people move out of their homes to other areas due to either natural causes or civil strife they tend to stick to their old religion and to the old rituals and festivals. However, after some time they are influenced by the new climate or new environment where they encounter new cults and rituals and their religion, the rituals and festivals tend to change under their influence. It is at this time that a tendency to conserve their past asserts and they try to collect all the old religious texts, folklore, and their history. Something similar happened with the Indus people in their new homes in the area to the East of Yamunā and in Iran. When they moved in their new homes the Indus people continued their religious practices, maintained their rituals and kept to their festivals. At the annual renewal of fire they continued with composing new hymns to the Fire, and to the other gods at different times as they did in the past. It was at that time too that they were trying to settle down to their new surroundings and creating new civilisation more glorious than the old. That must have taken them a few centuries. After a few centuries, some of their wise men might have realised that they were forgetting the older hymns and the older folklore which required to be preserved. It was in such circumstances that they might have deputed some of their more learned persons to collect them from various people. They must have moved about from tribe to tribe and from settlement to settlement and must have collected the old hymns and the old folklore. In India the hymns so collected became the *Vedas* and the folklore, the *Brāhmanas* and the *Āranyaks*. That mass of the hymns must have been then systematically arranged. The hymns so arranged were not only old but also included those composed in the new surroundings and therefore we find that the hymns are not only old ones which describe contemporary events, but also those which invariably embody the memory of those events at later times and are therefore new ones. The man credited with compiling them systematically is Ved Vyās. As stated earlier the *Vedas* are divided into four parts—*Rigveda, Samveda, Yajurveda* and *Atharvaveda*. These *Vedas* in turn are divided into various parts. Thus *Rigveda* is divided into Ashtaks, Chapters, Mandals and Anuvāks. None of them has any relation with each other and every one is independent. What may be the meaning of these divisions? Are they as per a composer or his descendants or as per a tribe or as per settlements? We cannot say anything except that eight out of ten Mandals belong to a family each. It may be that the Ashtaks, Adhyāyas and Anuvāks may be as per regions, tribes and settlements or else they can be according to some plan of the collector and arranger, Ved Vyās, now lost but known to people in earlier times. Some of the hymns are common to all the *Vedas* and may be that they were the most famous ones which had reached all the regions and therefore when they were collected settlement-wise, they had to find their place repeatedly in various *Vedas*.

A similar exercise must have been done by the Indus people in Iran. The collection of hymns is though much smaller, yet is quite significant. Known as Avestā it was arranged by Zarthustra. The language of the Avesta is very similar to the language of the *Vedas* and some of the hymns are very similar both in language, in imagery, in intent and in regard to the gods. We can, therefore, say that both the *Vedas* and the Avestā are parts of one whole. If we look at them closely, both of them give interesting reading in the omission of the contents of the other and in the parallel contents. We know that the people of the Eastern part of the Indus Valley including Harappa moved to different areas of India and the people of the Western part including Mohenjodaro moved to Iran. Hence, the things which are common in both Avestā and the *Vedas* must be common in all the regions of the Indus Valley. The things which are not found in one but found in the other must have been peculiar to that one region whether it may be the particular god or the particular place, or a particular ritual or festival. Thus hymns to Fire and to Soma, in Avesta Hoame, are common to both and therefore the worship of both must be a common feature of the Indus Valley. In the *Vedas* we find very few hymns to the two gods Mitra and Varun with the result that they appear to be minor gods. However, we find in the Avesta that these two gods have become the most important gods with Varun as the Ahur Mazdā, the Supreme God. We also do not find complimentary references to Indra and Ashwini Twins (Nāsatya). This indicates that whereas Indra and Ashwani Twins who are prominent gods in the *Vedas,* must be the deities held as important in the Eastern part of the Indus Valley including Harappa, the deities held in esteem in the Western part including Mohenjodaro must be Varun and Mitra, and they remained so in their new homes in Iran. Similar is the situation with historical references. We should not be surprised that we find ample references to the tribe of Bharatas and pointed reference with its exact geographical location to the city of Harappa where they ruled in the *Vedas.* Similar is the case with regards to Kutsa and to Kalibangan where he ruled. But we do not find any reference to Mohenjodaro, and to places in Saurāshtra. If we study Avesta in this light and the folklore preserved in the Pārsee religion we will find references to Mohenjodaro and to the places in Saurāshtra with the ruling dynasties. During their approximately 800 years sojourn in the Indus Valley area, it was but natural that there must have been differences and even prolonged wars between the two regions. It was, therefore, natural to find hostile references to the gods of the two areas and to the dynasties of the two areas ruling over them. We, therefore, find that Indian gods and kings extolled in the *Vedas, i.e.,* Indra, Ashwini Twins (Nāsatya), etc. are shown as demons and the people regarded as demons in the Hindu mythology are treated as pious people in the Pārsee mythology which is the mythology of the ancient Iran of the times when the Indus people settled there.

We may thus see that the *Vedas* and The Avesta are complement to each other and they together contain the spiritual history of the Indus Valley together with the glimpses of the historical incidents scattered in them. We are intrigued with the complete absence in them of the three gods of the Hindu trinity Brahma, Vishnu and Shiva who became so prominent later. We have already seen that the Indus people were scattered in all the directions and that a few gods were prominent in certain regions, *i.e.*, Mitra and Varun in the Western parts and Indra, Ashwini Twins in the Eastern parts along with some others. It may be possible that the gods of the trinity might have been the principal gods of those regions whose people went to remoter areas and whose hymns were not collected and they later became prominent when the tribes who regarded them as principal gods later became prominent in Indian life. The total absence of Rishabh is also intriguing. The explanation can be that the hymns were collected at that stage when his cult had lost its force due to decline of Bharatas or else he might be known in the Indus Valley period by some other name which might be Purush, Brahma or Vishnu with whom he was identified later. It is also possible that he was only worshipped as an ancestor of probably Bharatas tribe. He is still regarded as a human being. Human or ancestor is not mentioned in *Vedas*.

Contribution of Indus People to the Civilisation as a Whole

Although it is not a part of the Indian History, yet it will be appropriate to consider the part played by the Indus people who migrated to Iran, in the advancement of the civilisation. When they reached Iran plateau after the collapse of the Indus Valley Civilisation they settled in the areas outside the area of influence of the Sumerian Civilisation. In that undulating pleateau with its high mountains and small rivulets even the migrants from the Sumerian area would not have dared to move. We find that as per the Jews, when they left the city of Ur in Sumer in approximately 2000 years B.C. they preferred to take the route to Egypt and Palestine. Similarly other tribes from Sumer who migrated after the decline of Sumerian Civilisation migrated towards Egypt. The unattractive Iranian plateau was left to the Indus people. Here they carved out the territories according to the tribes and settled down in developing agriculture, in improving the land and in consolidating their civilisation based on the memory of their lost land. They had collected the hymns of their old land and named it Avestā. They might have traded with Sumer. We are not sure whether the seals with Indus script found in the Sumer lands belonged to them or to their old area in Mohenjodaro. Perhaps it may be possible to determine only when it is deciphered. They kept away from the political affairs of Sumer which was involved in internecine warfare with other people and with Egypt. Egypt had cast a spell, an undue fascination for the Sumerians, the Accadians and the Assyrians who, one after the other, conquered the land of Sumeria and always turned towards Egypt, sometimes fighting it and sometimes becoming friendly. Iran was too poor for their attraction. Indus people in Iran also wisely kept aloof from them and instead gave their attention to other areas to the North and East of that land. Memory of their recent disaster when they were forced to leave their land in India left them too civilised and sober to think of military conquest and replacing the local population by a wholesale massacre. They penetrated peacefully and converted the local populations to their religion and as their language was too primitive they gave them their own language. The first we hear about them in recorded history is in the middle of the 14th century B.C. This is a record of a treaty between the Hittite Empire and the Mittanians found at Khātusas now Bogaz Que in Central Turkey which was the capital of the Hittites and it mentions among the witnesses the gods who were Indra, Mitra, Varun and Nāsatya. All the four are no doubt Vedic and Avestan gods. But there is a difference. Mitra and Varun in the *Vedas* are minor gods and would not have been made a witness. Nāsatya in *Vedas* are twins and though they are invoked frequently, they were not worshipped and would not have been made a witness. Nāsatya is a single god in the Avesta. In India the gods are made witness in every ceremony whether it may be a marriage even today or any other ceremony are invariably the Fire and the Sun. Hence, if the Mittanians were under the influence of Indian branch, the witnesses would have been probably Indra, Agni, Surya and probably Maruts who were always invoked in wars. The fact that the witnesses were Indra, Mitra, Varun and Nāsatya as a single god indicates the influence of the Indus people in Iran. Again, as stated earlier, we find from Khatusas, a horse-treatise devoted to the training of horses by Kikkuli which uses Sanskrit terms. The names of the Mittanian rulers are too Indian names, *i.e.,* Dashrath. This indicates that the Mittanians were Sanskritised people. We do not know at present whether they were Indus people who migrated there or were converted to their religion and civilisation. Mittani was the country just South of the Turkish plateau and bounded by the Tigres and the Euphrates rivers. It may be possible that they were the Indus people who migrated there, settled there and set up a kingdom strong enough to face the Hittite Empire in war. The war itself was not a disaster as is indicated by the treaty according to which the King of the Mittanians married the daughter of the King of the Hittites. We also find at Yazili-Kāyā near Khātusās, in a rock sanctuary the carved figure of thirty-three gods and opposite them thirty-three goddesses. They are all shown standing on their respective mounts. The *Vedas* constantly refer to thirty-three gods. These thirty-three gods and goddesses with their mounts remind us of the Vedic gods. Their mounts are also similar. The most interesting among these gods and goddesses are those in the centre. The god in the centre is shown standing on his mount bull and also a symbolic mountain. Opposite him is the goddess on her mount, a lion and behind her is standing a boy. Interestingly enough the god is similar to Shiv and the goddess to Parvati, consort of Shiv, with her mount lion and a son, Karttikeya or Subramaniam, as known in the South India. The names of these gods and goddesses are either Hittite or as some scholars hold even pre-Hittite, Hurrian. The name of the god is given as Teshav, of the goddess as Hakat and of the boy as Shurrum or Kumarbi. How these thirty-three gods with their thirty-three consorts came to be etched on the wall of the rock sanctuary in Yazili-Kāyā in the centre of Turkey? How the central figures among the gods and goddesses came to be prototypes of Indian Shiv and Parvati? The question naturally arises is whether it was a coincidence or there is some connection between India and the figures at this rock sanctuary. In view of the matrimonial relations between the Hittite royal house and the Mittanians who might be Indus people or people converted to the Indus Civilisation there must be interchange between their people and a later regular interaction between them. Therefore it should not be a mere coincidence. Can it be possible that there was a peaceful penetration of the region by the Indus Civilisation in Iran prior to its adopting its language?

We may now examine the other borders of these Indus people in Iran. The other border is the Central Asia on both sides of the Caspian Sea. Archaeological excavations have not revealed any thing prior to this time. A solitary Indus seal was unearthed at Altyn-depe (tepe) in Southern Turkomania not far from the city of Ashkabad containing two Indus symbols and another seal made of silver in the shape of three-headed creature just as they were found in Mohenjodaro but with the difference that the heads of the creatures are a natural replacement of the Indus animals with locally found animals. The pottery too resembles those of the Indus Civilisation. These indicate that the Indus people in Iran had started influencing those people converting them to their civilisation and also teaching them their language. Though we have not yet found any evidence physically of their learning the language of the Indus people which may be Vedic Sanskrit, but comparative philology points out that in the region around the Black Sea in the remote past there dwelt tribes speaking the ancient Iranian languages. Even the old names of the regions of the Black Sea were similar to Indian names, *i.e.,* the locality near Khersones in the Crimea was called Dandaka corresponding to Indian Dandak. The Slav and the Indian mythologies had also a very close resemblance. It appears that Indus people in Iran had really influenced those people and through them the influence passed on to the Ukraine region of modern Russia and later to Greece, Baltic region and Europe. Thus we find a great similarity in the languages of Europe and Sanskrit as well as in religion with an almost similar pantheon of gods and other cultural influences. We do not know if the part of Indus people in Iran moved to these parts or only the cultural radiation reached them as well as the language which was given to them when they had no language of their own. But the fact remains that the influence of the Indus Civilisation reached Europe through the Iranian branch of the Indus people and not the unbelievable story of the Aryan migration from a common Central Asia home which has no proof at all. On the contrary the proof of the *Vedas* being the spiritual and secular history of the Indus people is for all to see. The Indus people in Iran had thus contributed immensely to the advancement of civilisation in the world. This was at the cost of both the Sumerian and the Egyptian civilisations which remained preoccupied in constant fights and attempts to annihilate their constituents as well as each other. They had failed to influence the world civilisation while the Indus civilisation did so through Iran via the Caucasus round the Black Sea and Caspian Sea into Greece from the North and Baltic region through the East. When during the Achaemenian Empire they again met the Greeks, it was the meeting of the old compatriots but with both the religion and the language slightly changed through the long journey.

Conclusion

We do not know much about the way the Indus people progressed after their dispersal from the Indus Valley area. But when we come to the historic period the time since when the recorded incidents are known which comes to somewhere in the 6th century B.C. in both India and in rest of the world we find them far advanced. In India their influence reached every nook and corner including Sri Lanka. This included the religious beliefs, the gods usually identified too with local deities, the language of course mutated with constant travel, and also the script mutated, too, to local variations. Some of the people might have also migrated but it appears that there was not a large scale migration but only the radiations of culture and religion which must have converted the people. A similar thing appears to have happened to the Indus people in Iran who too influenced an equally large area stretching from Iran to Greece going via round both the Black Sea and also probably the Caspian Sea and going upto Greece. From Greece it spread throughout the whole of Europe later. It, however, could not effect the region West of Sumer upto Egypt, where probably both the civilisations were too stubborn for it to conquer. Both these civilisations were too rigid to influence anybody else outside their territory and therefore were swept off leaving only archaeological remains just after a few centuries by Islam.

REFERENCE

1. E.H. Pl. XCIII.

5

THE AGE OF ENQUIRY AND THE RISE OF MONARCHY

When the Indus people had moved away from their homeland in the Indus Valley due to unforeseen natural calamity they truly settled down and converted the whole of India to their religion, their culture and their language. No doubt when they came into contact with the various tribes they successively met in their expansion over the land, probably not physically but through a cultural radiation, they themselves were changed. Their religion was effected, their culture was reinforced with new vigour as it absorbed some of the elements of the culture of the tribes with whom they had interacted and most important their language itself got changed. Though basically it remained at first Sanskrit but successively as they moved from the neighbourhood of the Indus Valley a greater and greater change was noticeable so much so that at the periphery of India it was not recognisable as Sanskrit at all. So much the interaction with the local tribal languages had effected it.

We may now first look at the state of the society at the beginning of the historical period, *i.e.*, 6th century B.C. It is indeed a relief to come to historical period after leaving the uncertainty of the dark period about which absolutely nothing is known and no records available. However, if we examine the available records of the period we again find that our relief is so shortlived. There are no records at all about this period also. Except for a copper plaque found at Sahgaura and the pillars on which there are some inscriptions attributed to Emperor Ashoka there are no contemporary records

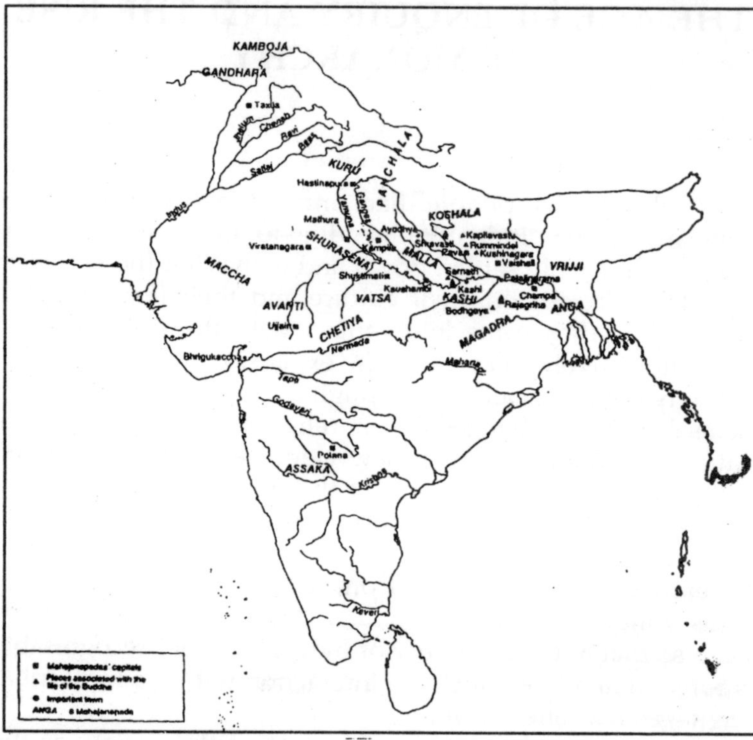

Map 4 : India in the Time of the Sixteen Mahajanapadas.

Source : Based on J.E. Schwarteberg ed. A Historical Atls of South Asia (Chicago 1978) p. 15

available. The records on which we rely are mainly Buddhist and Jain records. If we analyse the antiquity of Jain records, we find them dating to about a thousand years later and of the Buddhist records which again at least five centuries later. There are no doubt available a large number of other works on religion, literature and grammar but they singularly exclude historical study though they are contemporaneous.

We may first have a general idea of the political situation of India of those times in the beginning of the 6th century B.C. Buddhist texts mention 16 great republics 'Solasamahajanpada' which are Anga, Magadh, Kasi, Kosala, Vriji, Malla, Chedi, Vatsa, Kuru, Panchal, Matsya, Surseni, Asvaka or Asmak, Avanti, Gandhar, and Kamboja. These are per Vinaya text II 146; Niddesa II 37. Mahavatsu supports the above 1, 34, II 3, but it omits Gandhar and Kamboja and instead mentions Sivi and Dasharna. On the other hand Jain Bhagwati Sutra mentions Anga, Vanga, Magaha, Malaya, Malava, Achcha, Vachcha, Kachchha, Padha, Ladha, Bajji, Muli, Kasi, Kosala, Avaha, Sanbhittara. We thus find them giving separate lists many of whom are common. In fact seven are common and the rest nine are not. However, if we look at them closely, they mostly mention the republics East of the river Yamuna upto Bengal. In the Buddhist twelve belong to this region, *i.e.*, Anga, Magadh, Kasi, Kosala Vriji, Malla, Chedi, Vatsa, Kuru, Panchal, Suraseni, Asmak, while Matsya was contiguous to Suraseni. Avanti was in the Central India while Gandhar and Kamboja were beyond the Indus. If we take into account Mahavatsu's list, then instead of the republics beyond the Indus, *i.e.*, Gandhara and Kamboja, we find Sivi and Dashārna which were in the neighbourhood of Avanti. If we take into account the Jain Bhagwati Sutra we find all of them with the exception of Mālava lying in the region. Thus from the texts we get only the idea of the Gangetic region and a little of the area around Ujjain where the Buddhist texts mention Avanti and Jain Mālava. The difference can be due to the time lag between the composition of the texts. Buddhists claim these republics to be at the time shortly before the time of the Buddha while the Jain texts appear to be later. We do not get any idea of South of the Vindhyas, or East of Ujjain in the Central India. Similarly, we do not get any idea of North India and West of the Yamunā in modern Rajasthan, Sind and Baluchistan. We know that there were powerful republics in the North India, specially the Yaudheyas, Mālavas, Shivis, Kaths, Ksudraks, etc. We are also guessing probably correctly that Taxilā was an important centre of learning. Similarly Western India and Southern India too was equally politically and culturally advanced. We know from the traditions of Sri Lanka that Prince Vijaya from Gujarat had already established a flourishing kingdom in Sri Lanka, which speaks of the development in both Sri Lanka and in Gujarat which are omitted by the Buddhist and Jain texts. However, we may assume that the rest of India cannot be far behind the Eastern India if not equal to it or even surpass it. The only problem is that the records about it perished. We may never know much about them.

We may, however, take up first the area of which some records are available and they could survive because they were written late. It appears that somewhere about that time it was discovered that Bark of the Silver Birch or Bhojpatra was a good material which could be used as a writing material. Hence Bhojpatra and cloth became the standard writing material which unfortunately could not survive for long. In that area which now forms the states of Uttar Pradesh and Bihar and parts of Madhya Pradesh, there were a few republics and a few monarchies. Among the monarchies the ones known from literature and the Buddhist and Jain traditions, however late recorded, the most important appear to be Magadh with its capital at Rājgrih, Koshal, Vatsa and Avanti. Among the republics the prominent ones appear to be Vaishāli, Malla, Shākya, Koliya, etc. We do not know if they were republics and monarchies ruling over a well-defined area large enough or they were city states with a large number of villages surrounding them over which they exercised some sort of suzerainty. The author is of the view that in those times it was not possible to have a territorial loyalty and administration. The possibility appears to be that they were just city states and the surrounding villages accepted their suzerainty and paid them homage. The cultivators did not take part in the wars, nor were they affected by wars. They simply paid some nominal tax to the sovereign whoever he might be. However, the rise of monarchies was a development which began in that period which was to create a sense of territorial loyalty instead of a tribal one and was to affect the future course of society. However, the city states were living contentedly and in peace at the beginning of that period.

What was the constitution of those republics and monarchies? In the absence of any records it is not possible to say anything about it or about the people who were the ruling class or who were the serfs or proletariat. Whatever we know from the Buddhist or Jain records, however sketchy they may be, is that the republics were having a peculiar structure. Buddhists had given a greater detail of the Republic of Shākyas to which Gautam belonged, while Jains similarly gave details of Vaishāli Republic to which Mahāvir belonged. According to them the ruling class contained about 500 to 600 persons belonging to many families and called Rājās. They constituted the assembly which took decisions by majority votes and they also elected their chief. The usual designation of the Chief was Senāpati and we find the usual designation of the Head of the Republic as Senāpati in all other republics or oligarchies in other parts of India, *i.e.*, Mālava, Shivi, etc. Yaudheyas, however, designated their Chief as Mahārāj Senāpati probably due to their pre-eminence among contemporaries established earlier. The Rajas or the members of those assemblies were all related to each other by matrimonial ties and they were the leaders in war. The ministers were Brahmins. The cities were centres of trade and manufactures all of which were controlled by the Vaishyas, another caste.

If we look at it deeply and in a historical perspective and imagine their evolution the picture of the city-states or republics or *Janpadas* as they were called comes clearly before our mental eyes. We may trace their development from the dark ages when tribes started agriculture after clearing the forests and in that process lay the growth and consolidation of those states. In Bihar and Eastern Uttar Pradesh the area was criss-crossed by the major and minor rivers. Aided by them and with abundant rainfall the area was ripe for large-scale agriculture. The various tribes settled in marked areas, cleared forests and took to agriculture. As the area prospered with the abundant agricultural production, there came into existence certain class of people exclusively devoted to producing things other than food and included textiles, pottery, utensils, plough, bricks for building houses already known in the Indus Valley area from where either they themselves came or received the impetus. In short, class of artisans came into being. During the course of time the skill of the artisans came to be transmitted from father to son and continued in the families. These families lived together and started marrying among themselves to keep the skill and later formed separate castes, each according to the particular craft. As money was unknown and barter was the usual medium of sale and purchase, wherever the artisans lived people came to purchase bringing with them their agricultural surplus produce. Wherever a number of them lived it became a market and wherever the artisans of various articles required by the people congregated that became a trade centre. The various tribes invited these artisans in their areas so that their people might not have to go far to get those things. They gave them facilities and promised protection. Where they lived and when it became trade centre, came another class of people who specialised in being middlemen and thus merchants too came into being. With them came priests and warriors to give protection. But the supremacy of the original tribe that inhabited the areas and invited the people of the different classes remained intact and undisturbed. However, their leaders or Rajas shifted to growing towns where the artisans, merchants and priests resided. Thus the towns grew into big cities. Traders became wealthy, artisans got enough wealth, priests got their tithes and warriors their protection money, all out of the agricultural produce.

In times these warriors, the original 500 to 600 persons appointed to protect the tribe and artisans, became rulers, and their families the ruling families. As they were living in towns together they intermarried and formed a strong alliance. They, in course of time, decided that they, should have an assembly and one member of each family should be its member. After the death of father the eldest son would take his place. Thus the assemblies came into existence and when the necessity of the chief arose usually in times of war they selected the ablest among themselves as their chief. Since he usually belonged to warrior class and was selected to protect the tribe, naturally his designation was Senāpati. When the chiefship became permanent and even civic functions were entrusted to the chief the designation remained unchanged. The ruling families and those aspiring to join their ranks as new ruling families devoted themselves to the practice of martial arts and in other times to hunting to keep up their martial art. To maintain themselves in a style befitting their status taxes were instituted first as protection money and later as taxes both on agriculturists and traders, priests alone being excluded. In course of time more people other than the original tribe came to reside in the towns, their suzerainty enlarged and society became more complex. So also grew complexity in administration, in state policy, in relations with other states and rivalry generated by trade. Who was to look after that complex administration? The ruling families were not willing to bring other members of tribes into administration fearful that they might supplant them. They themselves were devoted only to the martial arts, hunting and enjoyment of the facilities which their position as rulers provided them. They were not willing to subject themselves to the drudgery of the administration. They, therefore, turned to that class of people who were supposed to have no interest in the mundane things of life, *i.e.*, the priestly class. They were scholars, learned in scriptures, had knowledge of everything from medicine to crafts, even the use of arms in times of wars. From times immemorial as far as our knowledge goes the ministers invariably were Brahmins who were also the priests. From the very inception they acted as teachers, as family priests and could keep records, issue instructions and give balanced advice. Actually the meaning of minister or Mantri is to give advice and in early days they were actually advisers only.

With growing complexities in administration on one hand and with the increasing wealth of the ruling families which turned them to pursuit of finer arts, in addition to martial arts, and fondness for the joys of the world, the administration passed into the hands of the priests completely. We thus find when the 6th century B.C. opened there were two sets of rulers. Peacetime rulers were the Brahmins who were administering the area in association with the mercantile classes and catering to certain whims of the ruling class of the Rājās. In times of war these Rājās under their chief, the Senāpati took over. If they were successful, then they became prosperous with the money and wealth of the vanquished taken either as part of the loot, or as ransom of the prisoners or in settlement of the conflict. If they lost, it were they who suffered most for the victors never touched the Brahmins or the artisans or the merchants. The Brahmins and the merchants who neither gained nor lost in the wars in course of time came to be loyal to their own caste wherever they might be whether in another state or in a distant area. They freely migrated to another state and took employment wherever they found it. Similarly the merchants or the artisans moved to that state where they found greater opportunity for the sale of goods. This can be seen in the legend of Varshkār, the Brahmin minister of Ajātshatru, the king of Magadha recorded in Buddhist annals. When he was expelled by Magadha, some imputed his expulsion to a conspiracy between him and Ajātashatru. He was welcomed in Vaishāli and became an important personage. As per legend he sabotaged the war effort of the Vaishāli against the Magadha empire and was responsible for its downfall.

The case with the monarchies was different. Although they are described as *Janpadas,* we find from the different legends that there were among the lists provided by the Jain and Buddhist texts at least four monarchies, Magadha, Koshala, Vats and Avanti. We cannot say whether they were the monarchies since the beginning, whether they were earlier janpadas on the lines of others and became monarchies later and if so when. However, when the 6th century B.C. began they were there. Legends do not mention when and how they came into being and who were the original monarchs and whether the earlier ones were elected or the succession was hereditary. We find that in such cities there was a greater prosperity and greater advancement. The population consisted of a greater number of artisans, traders and a greater middle class belonging to different tribes and peoples.

It appears at some stage of their development the populace heterogeneous in character combined under an able leader and overthrew the corrupt and interfering ruling oligarchy. That leader was established as ruler on the understanding that he would not discriminate among his subjects and would not put impediments in trade dear to merchants and to the devotion to knowledge and to religion, the pursuits of Brahmins. In times the succession became hereditary and if and when a weak ruler came on the throne, he was supplanted by another able ruler whose dynasty took over. They kept mercenary armies composed of all the different people not confined to one tribe and if victory was gained, it brought wealth and it was distributed. These measures made the people have a stake in the stability of the monarchical state. They helped the traders, threw their door open to every artisan and removed every obstacle to the movement of people or trade in their territory. They welcomed people who were either expelled or banished from the neighbouring republics and made the people committed to the ideal of a universal empire.

The co-existence of monarchies and the Janpadas or oligarchies became an anomaly. The area was an open society with the peasants indifferent to the rulers of the oligarchies and only desiring peace. The business class together with the artisans were free to trade, migrate and live in any city they liked. Moreover, they had trade relations with all cities. The administrative rulers were Brahmins who were more loyal to their counterparts in other cities whether *Janpadas* or monarchies. The only persons out of tune with the times were the Rājās in every oligarchy as they were called to play their role only at the time of war. Otherwise they kept themselves busy either in the practice of martial arts or more in worldly enjoyment of dances, wines and whoring. If the assembly ever interfered in administration it was to get more money for themselves which in reality meant more taxes and hindrance in trade and was highly irritating to one and all. They were ready to fight with one and all states for their selfish ends. They had not realised the menace which the monarchies were becoming to their very existence. Iron smelting was just discovered in Magadha region which had the biggest iron deposits in whole of India. Magadha armies were being equipped with arms made of iron which was considerably more strong as compared to the arms made of copper or brass. With its arms made of iron, and mercenary army better trained in manoeuvre and fight, Magadha was a real menace to all and sundry in the region whether Janpada or monarchy. When its policy became deliberately aggressive and a single-minded devotion to wiping off these anomalies in the shape of *Janpadas* or oligarchies, the stage was set for the Magadha empire. The Rajas or oligarchs of every republic and the other rulers of the monarchies were happily ignorant of these developments and persued their old anachronistic ways.

Situation in North-Western India

With regard to the recorded historical facts the situation in North Western India is no different from the situation in the East which has been described above. Here too there are no records. As for the situation in Eastern India we got some facts from the Buddhists and Jain records which, though written late, yet are not, it appears, entirely baseless. About the North Western India though considerable literature had been produced by the people who, it appears, belonged to that region and included Pānini, Katyāyan and Pātanjali, the grammarians, the writers of the *Upnishads, Āranyaks*, the *Rāmāyana, Mahābhārata* and *Purānās*, court poets of the Shak, Kushan and Bactrian kings who had their capitals in that region, yet no reference is to be found in these writings about the historical facts relating to that region. The only reference is found in the works of those who travelled in the train of Alexander and recorded his victories and absolutely omitted the defeats if any. We have to be careful about the writings of courtiers who write about the exploits of their patrons. In India since the earliest times court poets have written about the exploits of their patrons or their ancestors and in every case they are found to be unreliable. We find in them battles with uncertain outcome as victories and humiliating defeats as glorious triumphs. In this light we should test the writings of the people in the train of Alexander who tried to picture him as the one all conquering hero, generous to a fault and full of virtues.

According to the information provided by the Greek writers Alexander entered India and was welcomed by the King of Gāndhār Āmbhi at Taxilā who submitted to him. He then proceeded to Jhelum on whose banks he was opposed by Porus. At first he found it difficult to cross the river but somehow managed to cross it and in a fierce battle defeated King Porus. However, pleased at the courage and bravery of the King he restored his kingdom and proceeded to conquer the whole of India. However, on the banks of the Beās his soldiers who had heard of the formidable army of the King of Magadh, refused to go further and disappointed Alexander turned back. He also defeated a number of people who opposed him. Greeks had usually written the names with such spellings that the very pronunciation is changed and sometimes it is difficult to identify the correct name. Where the names persist, *i.e.*, in western history they continued down the ages and sometimes even the names given by them distorting the original is taken as the official name even today. Such were the names given by the Greeks to the names of the tribes, Malloi, Sibae, Aggalassoi, Oxydrakoi or Hydrakes, etc. However, taking their correct names they will include Mālavas, Sibi, Agraseni, Kshudraks, and Kaths. The Greeks had written Aggalassoi and some scholars feel that they meant Arjunayans. It is also mentioned that the Yaudheyas who had formed a confederation with the above tribes did not fight. Alexander also took away with him a hundred thousand persons from each tribe, as prisoners along with his returning troops. On the refusal of his troops to cross the Beās and proceed further he returned back along the Indus river, himself going by ship and his troops by a land route. It is said that on the way a number of people opposed him and he had to fight all the way. Greek chroniclers also mention that while he was in the camp, he was visited by Chandragupta Maurya who tried to persuade him that the King of Magadha was vulnerable and that Alexander would defeat him easily. Alexander somehow became angry with him and tried to keep him prisoner but Chandragupta Maurya somehow managed to escape from the camp.

The recent discoveries through archaeology and inscriptions, coins and legends give us some different places to which some of the tribes mentioned by the courtiers of Alexander, actually belonged. From the archaeological excavations conducted at Rairh a mound on the Dheel River in District Sawai Madhopur about 11 kilometers from the township of Bonli, revealed a site occupied by Mālava tribe in the 3rd century B.C. A seal was also found containing the name of 'Senapāti Vachchāg'. Seven other seals were found containing the word 'Vāpu'. Other seals and coins of Mālavas were also found from Nagar, a town in District Tonk not far from the site of Rairh. It appears that a belt along the river Chambal on the Western side in Eastern Rajasthan was the belt occupied by the Mālavas. In later times we find that the region East of the river Chambal was also populated by the Mālavas and came to be known as Malwā, *i.e.*, the land of Malavas even upto this day. Copper coins of about 200 B.C. recovered from Mādhyamikā near Chittor in Southern Rajasthan bear the legend 'Majhimakāya Sibi-Janapadassa' meaning the coins of the Sivi Janpada of Madhyamika. This indicates that the Sibi Janpada was powerful enough and prosperous enough to issue coins in the year near about 200 B.C. and that they were settled in an area in Southern Rajasthan near Chittor. Scholars have located Arjunāyans in the Eastern Rajasthan in the Bharatpur-Alwar area not far from the Mālavas and their coins found bear the legend Arjunāyanānām Jayāh on the pattern of the Mālavanām Jayāh of the Mālavas. We do not know whether the Aggalassoi of Greek writers mean Arjunāyans or the Agrasenis. However, the Agrasenis were settled in and around the ancient site of Agroha in Haryana state. The Yaudheyas with whom admittedly Alexander had not fought were living in the land to the South of the River Beās upto the Northern part of Rajasthan. Coin moulds of the Yaudheyas were discovered from Rohtak in the state of Haryānā and seals from the town of Ludhiana in Southern Punjab. Their area probably stretched from the Western Uttar Pradesh to Multan in Punjab, now in Pakistan. We know nothing about Kshudraks and Kaths.

If the Mālavas, Sibis, Arjunāyans or Agrasenis were living

at these places, far removed from the Punjab, how could they have fought Alexander somewhere between the Jhelum and the Beās? Could it be possible that they might have been living in the land between the Jhelum and the Beās and after their defeat might have migrated to those areas? It is improbable that they might have been living there. It is said that after their defeat singly, they were slaughtered and Alexander took about a hundred thousand to a hundred and fifty thousand from each as prisoners and took them away. Had it so happened, then the tribes would have been decimated to an extent that they would have ceased as an entity. They could not have been strong enough in a short span of a hundred years to have become so strong as to become a state and issued coins. Moreover, their coins would not have borne the legend 'Mālvānām Jayāh' or 'Arjunāyanānām Jayāh' meaning that their very name means victory. Had Alexander taken about five hundred thousand prisoners with him, he would have settled them somewhere and we would have known them and other contemporary historians would have mentioned their being settled in Iran or somewhere between Iran and Greece. Nobody had mentioned them being settled or being present anywhere. It does not appear to be correct that Alexander fought those people at all. They must have been settled in the 6th century B.C. in the very places where we find them in the 3rd century B.C.

We may also examine the event of Alexander defeating Porus on the banks of Jhelum and restoring to him his kingdom being pleased at his bravery and courage. Alexander, if we look at his campaign, was never found to be generous. Wherever, he was opposed the opposing armies were slaughtered, the inhabitants of those cities butchered and the cities razed to the ground. Witness burning by him of Persepolis, the capital of Persia. Looking to his nature and deeds in Persia where he had destroyed the capital of the empire he defeated it is not probable that he would treat a prince in that way when he wanted to conquer a country. His aim would be to terrorise others. Looking from that angle, it appears, that all the stories about his Indian adventure were concocted by Greek Chroniclers. His invasion was never mentioned or even alluded to in Indian records and literature simply because it was treated only as a border raid duly repulsed. Alexander might have been repulsed by Porus and as a result might have gone back defeated and broken hearted and because of that might have died. To avoid the news of his discomfiture, which would have triggered revolts everywhere from Iran to his kingdom in Macedonia, the above story of his victories and his inability to conquer due to the refusal of his army to proceed at the banks of the Beās, was concocted and sent to his empire. While concocting it they took into account whatever names they heard in India of mighty tribes, and kings. Among them thus figured Mālavas, Sibis, Arjunāyans or Agrasenis, who were far away while the Yaudheyas who were so near were not mentioned as fighting him. We may, therefore, take it that the stories of Alexander's invasion of India, according to his courtiers, cannot be relied upon unless corroborated by Indian records.

In the light of the above what was the state of the North-Western India in the 6th century B.C.? We simply cannot say anything. On the basis of the above and the archaeological excavations, it appears, that there were tribal Janpadas or republics in that part. From the chroniclers of Alexander, we learn that at the time of his invasion there was only a kingdom of Magadha beyond Yamuna and else there were only some tribes in between. We may, therefore, take it that in that part there were no monarchies and only Janpadas similar to those we encountered in the Gangā plains or the modern states of Uttar Pradesh and Bihar. They had probably an assembly and a head of the *Janpadas* called 'Senāpati' as can be seen from the later finds of seals and coins of Yaudheyas, Mālavas, Sibis, Rajanyas, etc. These Janpadas or republics or oligarchies, whatever they might have been, had their well-defined territorial areas. It appears that Yaudheyas were in the area between the river Beās upto the Northern part of the modern state of Rajasthan, Mālavas in Eastern Rajasthan on the banks of the river Chambal and spilling to the other side upto Ujjain, Sibis near Chittor, Matsya, Rajanya, Arjunāyans in the North-Eastern area of Rajasthan consisting of the Districts of Alwar and Bharatpur, Agrasenis in the modern State of Haryana near Agrohā, Avanti near Ujjain and Dashārna in Western Madhya Pradesh.

What was the condition in those parts not covered by the above, *i.e.*, in the area beyond the river Beās in the North and beyond the river Indus in what is now Sind province in Pakistan? According to Buddhist Vinaya text there were Gandhār and Kāmboja Janpadas in the area beyond the river Beās and those two might have been in the area now called North-West Frontier Province of Pākistān and Afghānistān. About the rest we have no information.

What was the social, cultural and religious condition in that area in the 6th century B.C.? We do not have any information in any record whether domestic or foreign. Presumably as far as language is concerned it might have been the Sanskrit as can be seen from its employment in the coins discovered in 2nd century B.C. in this area and the still later employment of Sanskrit as the state language and language of literature. Among contemporary writers and literature it cannot be said with certainty but probably *Brāhmanas, Āranyaks* and *Upnishads* were composed by that time. Among the writers of secular literature Yāska is said to be the earliest writer and it is thought that he belonged to 6th century B.C. or early 5th century B.C. He also probably belonged to that area. If so, then it points to an advancement in the study of language and the intellectual attainment of the people. Yāska wrote *Nirukta,* a book which dealt with the formation of Vedic words and the roots from which they were derived. Discussion of the formation and development of words and language, the distinction between various types of words and their proper uses, a subject dealt with in *Nirukta,* indicates that people had reached a stage of a great mental development where they started examining things in a critical way as well as in a systematic and scientific manner. If this was so in language, then the same could also be said about other aspects of life including culture, religion, medicine and science. We may assume that the people started speculating and philosophising things.

Placid though the life appeared to be in that area, yet the neighbouring area in the West in Iran and further West was in ferment. Asurs or Assyrians, as they were called by the Greeks, were having their brutal sway over the whole area from Iran to Egypt, soon to be overthrown by the Mada tribe or Medes, according to Greeks, who in turn were overthrown by Persians who had established an Empire under the Achaemenids. They invaded India and brought about the momentous changes here.

What was the condition of the Southern India South of the Vindhya mountain ranges? We know nothing about it. There are no records available whatsoever. However, as we know that the Indus people also went to the South at the time of their dispersal the condition of the South might not have been much different from the Eastern India or the North Western India.

We thus get some idea of the history of India upto the 6th century B.C. and some glimpses of the social, political and economic condition of the country at the time of the 6th century B.C. This is based on the fragmentary indications we get in texts based on folk memory. We also possess other literature mainly religious in the shape of *Purānās* but unfortunately the time when they were composed is not only not known but highly disputed. If they were written after the birth of Christ, then certainly we should not rely on them. If they were composed earlier but documented afterwards with some changes, then we can rely on them. India was developing out of its own forces set in motion by the various social, economic, cultural and political events and the ferment within. Later on with the changes wrought in its neighbourhood in Iran set in motion by their impact, those forces brought far-reaching changes in all aspects of life in India.

Rise of Monarchy in Eastern India

As we had seen there were a number of oligarchies and monarchies in Eastern India, specially in the modern states of Uttar Pradesh and Bihar. These oligarchies were also a sort of dual governments where the day-to-day administration was in the hands of Brahmin ministers and administrators while the army was composed solely of members of one tribe. The trade was in the hands of mercantile class who observed no state boundaries as far as their area of operation was concerned. For both the ministers and traders the oligarchies were a hindrance. In times of war the administration passed into the hands of the tribal leaders having the designation of Senāpati. The ministers and the traders had to cater to the demands of money by those rulers which must have irked them and made them desirous of an end to the small states and merger into the great empire which for the purposes of trade they already enjoyed. In the monarchies on the other hand there was comparative freedom and opportunities for advancement to any post. Though there might have been restrictions but not that type of despotism and unreasonable demands which they faced in the tribal oligarchies. In the records and stories available we have an instance of such a despotism in the Vaishali republic where a girl called Āmrapāli was forced to become a prostitute on the orders of the oligarchic council of the state.

As per the Buddhist records and later literature there were three monarchies in the area, Magadh, Koshal and Vatsa. In Ujjain then called Avanti which is in modern state of Madhya Pradesh not far from this area there was another monarchy. Though the rulers of the four monarchies were related with each other by marriage, yet they were fighting each other. This inter-relation gave rise to a number of romantic themes in the later drama and poetry. At the opening of the 6th century B.C. the kings in those monarchies were respectively Bimbisar of the Shishunag dynasty in Magadh, Prasenjit in Koshal, Udyan of the Pandava dynasty in Vats and Chand Pradyot in Avanti. Bimbisar was married to the daughter of the king of Koshal, Udyan to the daughter of Chanda Pradyot of Avanti and also to the daughter of the King of Magadh. But there was no love lost between these kings and they were prepared to fight the oligarchies too and even to obliterate them. It was also the time when Gautam, the Buddha and Mahavir, the Jain Tirthankar had started preaching and both belonged to the ruling oligarchies. Buddha was the son of the head of the Shakya oligarchy or may be a councillor as denoted by his title Raja, while Mahavir was the son of another Raja of Vaishali. The capital of Magadh was Rajgir, of Koshal Ayodhya or Saket and of Vats, Koshambi at the confluence of Gangā and Yamunā, the modern Allahabad.

The first friction began between the monarchy of Magadh

and the republic of Vaishali and the cause appears to be the right of toll of the trade passing through the Ganga. Bimbisār attacked the Vaishali republic but, it appears, that he was repulsed. He had his capital at Rajgir away from Ganga among the hills. He shifted his capital and founded a new one on the banks of the Ganga and named it Patliputra now called Patna. He also modernised his armies and equipped them with arms made of iron which was found plentiful in Magadh and which is so plentiful still that it is providing ore to modern India's steel mills. Iron as compared to brass is more strong and soon the fame of arms and swords made in Magadh spread. Bimbisār was later deposed by his son, Ajātshatru and kept prisoner. We are not sure whether it was Bimbisar or Ajatshatru who brought an end to the Vaishāli republic. But this time they used stratagem. A close confidant of the king, Varshkar who was his minister, was publicly humiliated and externed. He went to Vaishāli and was welcomed with open arms. He was given an important assignment and became very powerful. He engineered dissensions among the people of Vaishāli and isolated the ruling tribe from the people at large and encouraged various factions among the ruling clan. The war again broke out but at that time there was no unity and moreover, there was a sabotage. Dissensions weakened the Vaishalians and weaker arms made of brass were no match for the iron swords of the Magadh army. There was no support of the people and the ministers gave contradictory advice. Vaishālians under their Senāpati, Singh fought valiantly but were easily defeated and probably slaughtered. Vaishāli was merged into the empire and Varshkār resumed his earlier position in Magadh.

When Ajatshātru deposed his father Bimbisar and kept him prisoner dispute arose between Koshal and Magadh. The king of Koshal had given the city of Kāshi as dowry to Bimbisar on the marriage of his daughter to Bimbisar, a step mother of Ajatshātru. Koshal now wanted to take possession of that city which Ajātshatru was not willing to cede. Whether Prasenjit, the king was willing to let it remain with Magadh or there was some other cause for friction between father and son in Koshal we cannot say with certainty as the reference is vague in records. However, Vidudhabh, the son of the king of Koshal, too deposed his father Prasenjit. Prasenjit managed to escape and as a fugitive wandered and ultimately reached the gates of the capital of Magadh only to die there before entering the city. We are not given any indication whether it was Rajgir or Patliputra. It is said that when Prasenjit attacked Shākya republic and defeated them he wanted a princess of royal blood as his wife. Shākyas too proud of their superiority of blood but unable to refuse him passed on a slave girl as the princess of royal blood. Vidudhabh was the son of that girl. Later when the trick was discovered, Prasenjit who became fond of the girl, the mother of his only son, forgave the Shākyas but not so was the case with Vidudhabh. It is said that once he went to the house of his so-called maternal grandfather and was entertained royally. But when he was going back he forgot something in the house and sent a slave to fetch it. That slave found that the whole house was being washed and purified. On probing from another slave he was informed of the fact of his being the son of a slave and as he sat on a level with others the house had to be purified. He felt himself to be insulted but when he complained to his father who was fond of his mother, he forgave the Shākyas. The first act of Vidudhabh on seizing the kingdom was to invade the Shākyas. After defeating them he slaughtered every member of the Shākya clan and that too in the life time of that greatest of the Shākyas, the Buddha. However, it is said that Vidudhabh never reached his capital. Some say that he perished in the way being swept away by floods or died by natural calamity. Probably he was trapped by Ajātshatru and perished along with his army. The fact which emerges from the records is that Koshal was merged into Magadh. Magadh with that accretion of strength became formidable. It swallowed other minor republics which submitted without a fight. Probably they at first accepted its suzerainty and later were merged. We do not get any indication of their end either in Buddhist texts or in Jain version nor in the Puranas. We do not also get any idea when Vats was merged into the Magadh kingdom except that *Puranas* mention that Udyan was the last king of Vats. Hence, it will be pertinent to assume that Vats was incorporated into Magadh during the rule of Ajātshatru. We do not get any record which may indicate when other republics west of Vats came under Magadh or were merged into Magadh but in the later half of the 4th century B.C. when Alexander overthrew the Kingdom of Iran the boundaries of Magadh stretched upto the banks of Yamuna and was a unified state with a single unitary administration. Chroniclers of Alexander attribute the refusal of his army to advance due to the fear of that kingdom.

We have no information as to when the Shishunāg dynasty was brought down and who was the last king of the line. What we get amply supported by the *Purānās* is that a line of nine Nanda kings ruled over the kingdom. We cannot say whether they were brothers or descendants in the line. The most powerful according to the tradition, was Mahāpadmanand. *Purānās* mention that he exterminated the Kshatriyas and was a second Parshuram, who had exterminated the Kshatriyas twentyone times. We do not get much from the statement of the *Purānās* but if we go deeper into the implications they reveal much. Firstly that the Nandas were not Kshatriyas but, as the tradition mentions, were of low caste. Kshatriyas as per Hindu society were the rulers and warriors and in the then state of India they could only be the tribes of the oligarchies who were ruling over the different republics. It will be pertinent to assume that it was this Mahāpadmanand who conquered all the remaining republics East of Yamuna and merged them in the Magadha empire. His emulating Parshuram implies that he had slaughtered the tribes of the ruling oligarchies who were both rulers and warriors. After this time we do not hear of the names of the old ruling classes like the Vajjies, Mallas, Shaursenis, Rajanyas etc. As per *Purānās* he exterminated Aikshvakus, Panchalas, Kasis, Haihayas, Kalingas, Ashmaks, Sursenis, and Vithihotras in that region. So probably the Nandas eliminated the republics East of Yamunā, merged them in the empire and established a unitary form of government owing allegiance to Patliputra, the capital of the empire. The last of the Nandas was probably a morally degenerate person as well as effete that it was possible for Chandragupta Maurya to overthrow him easily in 321 B.C. Yet the administration was probably a good one and the ministers were capable and loyal. We find from later legends that Chandragupta Maurya and Chānakya, his preceptor and later minister tried to win back the able ministers of the Nandas and could persuade after great stratagem to bring back Rākshasa, the able minister of the Nandas back to administration as his minister.

India in the North-West

Situation in North-Western India, though different, is again entirely vague as no records are available. Whatever record is available is by the chroniclers in the court of Alexander which we have seen above cannot be relied upon and all available evidences are not authentic. However, the situation in the immediate neighbourhood in the West, *i.e.*, in Persia and Afghanistan was different and we could get facts from both Greek and Persian sources and to some extent they may be reliable. The situation in the west with a strong empire had affected the North-Western India considerably and itself made the tribal republics more warlike and having a different administrative structure than that in the Eastern India. We may, therefore, first examine the situation in Iran.

The dominant power in the area upto the end of the 7th century B.C. was the Asurs or the Assyrians as the Greeks called them. They were based in the area between the rivers Tigres and Euphrates in Iraq, the area where formerly Mittanians held sway. We cannot say if the Mittanians were the ancestors of the Asurs or Assyrians or were different. To the East were the Madas or Mads as they were called and near them were the Persians. Medes and the Persians were, as we had seen above, the people who migrated from the Indus Valley. Assyrians were probably the people who were the successors of the Sumerians. Asurs or Assyrians in their later times became extremely powerful and at the same time extremely brutal. They erased the whole cities and exterminated people whom they attacked and ruled from Egypt to the Indian border. At first, it appears, that Madas or Medes and Persians meekly submitted to them and were not much disturbed. But in course of time when the Asurs (Assyrians) became more demanding and aggressive and at the same time in the arrogance of power more hated and consequently getting weaker, the Madas (Medes) who were getting stronger and preparing to overthrow the Asurs, took up arms and destroyed the Asurs along with their empire. The Madas in their turn by 558 B.C. were overthrown by the Persians under Cyrus or Kurush as was his real name. But Kurush or Cyrus was careful enough to mollify the Madas and founded a joint Medo-Persian Empire. The dynasty was called Achaemenid dynasty after the founder of the family Achamani. Kurush or Cyrus consolidated the Empire and made conquests. From that time onwards the North-Western India had to live with the fact of such a strong empire on its Western borders and with attempts at conquests. Again as we do not have any indication in Indian records we would have to depend on the Persian and Greek records, however exaggerated they may be in favour of their patrons.

We get the statement of Arrian[1] that the Indians between the river Sindhu and Kabul (Cophen) "were in ancient times subject to the Assyrians, Medes, and finally, to the Persians under Cyrus to whom they paid tribute he imposed upon them". It indicates that probably there were raids on the borders of India since pretty long before the consolidation of the Persian empire in the 6th century B.C. After the consolidation of his empire Cyrus began his attempt to conquer India in which he probably did not succeed. We find a few scattered references in available Greek records. Ctesias[2] states that Cyrus or Kurush died of a wound inflicted in battle by an Indian, a battle which "the Indians were fighting on the side of Derbikes whom they supplied with elephant". We do not know who these Derbikes might have been. According to Xenophon[3] Cyrus (Kurush) "brought under his rule Bactrians and Indians" and extended his sway upto the Erythraen Sea, *i.e.*, the Indian Ocean. He further records[4] the despatch to Cyrus (Kurush) by an Indian king of an embassy conveying money probably in payment of tribute. The Greek writers on Alexander's campaign gave the glory of any conquest of any part of India only to Alexander and averred that none had ever conquered India. Thus Megasthenes states that "the Indians had never been engaged in foreign warfare, nor had they even been invaded and conquered by a foreign power except by Herakles and Dionysus and lately by the

Macedonians." He further states that "the Persians, although they hired mercenary troops from India, named the Hydrakes did not make an expedition into that country." Hydrakes are being identified with Oxydrakoi—Kshudrakas. Arrian[5] repeats the statement of Megasthenes that none before Alexander invaded India. According to Nearchus, as reported by Arrian[6], Cyrus came to grief in trying to invade India through the inhospitable desert of Gedrosia (Baluchistan) where the greater part of his army died." It appears from Herodotus, though not explicitly stated, that the early conquests of Kurush (Cyrus) included the Districts of Drangiana, Sattagydia and Gandiritis (Gandhar) which were located in the North Western region forming the boundary between India and Iran[7]. It appears from the above references that in the times of Cyrus (Kurush) attacks from the new established Persian Empire began in right earnest and though Kurush or Cyrus never could reach India and probably died fighting on the borders of India, yet the people in the North-West India felt threatened. They had also the bitter memories of attacks and raids by the Asurs or Assyrians and their brutality brought the name Asur permanently into the Indian vocabulary. They also watched and learned the weapons and methods of warfare by those invaders from the West. (Kurush 558-530 B.C.).

In the times of his successor Dayarvush or Darius as the Greeks called him (522-486 B.C.) we get both Persian and Greek references. While the Greek references include the writings of Herodotus, the Persian references are in the forms of inscriptions found in certain places in Iran. However like that of the Greek chroniclers the inscriptions were made by royal command and as such they are also not very reliable. We may analyse these references. The Behistun inscription (520-518 B.C.) lists twenty three provinces making up the Empire of Dāyarvush or Darius but does not include India as one of these. The inscription at Persepolis (518-515 B.C.) at Naksh-i-Rustam (515 B.C.) mentions Hidu as a part of the domain of Dāyaruvush. (Darius). Another inscription of Dāyarvush (Darius) known as Hamādan Gold and Silver Tablet inscription mentions Sindhu as a province of the empire. Herodotus (III, 94) states that India counted as the twentieth Satrapy of the empire of Darius (Dāyarvush). Herodotus also tells of a naval expedition despatched by Darius (Dāyarvush) in 517 B.C. under Scylax to explore the Sindhu[8]. He, it appears[9], excluded from Persian domination the region towards the South of Sindhu, the desert of Sindh and Rajasthan. The son and successor of Darius (Dāyarvush), Xerxes or Kshyārsh as was his real name maintained the parts of India as his domain as can be seen by the fact that he obtained the military service of an Indian contingent in his battle with the Greeks and they were named as Gandharians and Indians.

From the above scanty references not much can be known of the condition of the North-Western India in the period under reference, *i.e.*, from 6th century B.C. to the later half of the 4th century. However, it is clear that since early times there were raids by the Asurs or Assyrians and Madas or Medes and Persians. That must have made the people, living at least in the border regions of Afghanistan, North-western Frontier Province, Baluchistan, adjoining Iran and Sindh, know about the latest arms and battle techniques. They must have also acquired arms and must have become adept in their use and must have become somewhat sturdy warriors. When the Persian Empire came under the Achaemenians, it became a strong power conquering the whole of Middle East and measured swords with the Egyptians and the Greeks. That strong Persian army then turned towards Afghanistan and India but met resistance throughout so much so that the Persian Empire could not extend beyond probably the river Indus. Even in conquering that area they had to strive hard and in that process probably Cyrus (Kurush) lost his life. No doubt the hilly terrain helped the people considerably in their resistance but it also showed that they learned the latest techniques of war, innovated some of their own and acquired latest weapons. We may also assume that the Persians must have been raiding the interior and trying to conquer more territory as the Indian province was said to be the one contributing the most to the Persian treasury by way of tribute. The tribes or people on the East of Indus must have been constantly on their guard, constantly improving the art of war by learning and also that the internecine warfare so common during more peaceful times where there was no danger of foreign invasion, must have been absent from that area but a tendency to cooperate and achieve better cohesion must have been prevalent in that part of India.

Thus we find that on the borders of the North-Western India to the West were people including the dreaded Asurs or Assyrians who had been making incessant raids and from the middle of the 6th century B.C. a strong empire was determined to conquer it. On its Eastern border too was the Magadhan Empire trying to reach them in the early years of the 6th century B.C. and which indeed reached the Yamuna in a short span of time trying to conquer them. In between were the people of that area. We do not get much information about them from contemporary records but taking the records available from the 3rd century B.C. as the base we may try to make out their identity, their life and their administrative set-up. From the records available we find that here too were a number of Mahājanpadas mentioned in Buddhist and Jain sources. They are, according to a Buddhist text, Anguttara Nikaya, I, 213; IV 252, 256, 260, Matsya, Surseni, Avanti, Gandhara, Kāmboja. This is supported by Mahavatsu[10]. However, Vinaya text[11] omits Gandhara and Kamboj and instead mentions Sivi and Dasharna. The places of Kuru, Panchal, Chedi and Ashmak are not identified. Kurus might have been in the area still known as Kurushetra. Others might have been in Western Uttar Pradesh East of Yamuna or might be elsewhere. The Jain Bhagwati Sutra mentions Mālava which can be identified but for the others Anga, Malaya, Achchha, Padha, Avaha and Sambhittara it is not possible to establish the identity of their places of occupation. Pānini mentions in his Ashtadhyayi Yaudheyas along with Trigart as among Āyudhjivi Kshtriyas. Clay seals of Yaudheyas have been found in Ludhiana District of Punjab, while their coins have been found from Multan in Western Punjab to Saharanpur in Western U.P. Some coin-moulds of the tribe have been found in Rohtak in Haryana state. They, it appears, may have been occupying Eastern Punjab and adjoining tracts of Rajasthan. We also find from recent excavations that Matsya were the people settled in the North-Eastern Rajasthan in the Northern Jaipur District and parts of neighbouring Alwar. There was a Rājanya

Janpada in the area lying between Bharatpur and Mathura in Eastern Rajasthan with its coins bearing the Brahmi legend Rājanya Janpadasya. The copper coins of 200 B.C. recovered from Mādhyāmikā near Chittor in Southern Rajasthan bear the legend 'Majhimakāya Sibi Janpadassa', making this part as the seat of Sivi which is also supported by Patanjali in his *Mahābhasya* which mentions Mādhyāmikā. Excavations at Rairh in the District of Sawai Madhopur in Eastern Rajasthan near the river Chambal reveal that Mālavas were a flourishing tribe in the 3rd century B.C. and inhabiting an area on the banks of the river Chambal. We also get an indication that the Arjunāyans were occupying an area in between the Yaudheyas and Mālavas. The Agrasenis are traditionally regarded as occupying the territory in Haryana with their seat at Agrohā. Gandhāra is regarded traditionally as the area on the river Indus adjoining Afghanistan while Kambojas were in Eastern Afghanistan. The area between the Jhelum and the Ravi must have been occupied by other tribes and Mahābhārat gives an indication that probably it was occupied by the Madra tribe. The Sursenis were living in the area around Mathura on the banks of the Yamuna.

Thus we find this picture of various people and tribes and the republics in the 3rd century B.C. There is no evidence otherwise in excavations or in records like the *Purānās* or *Mahābharat* or in Pānini who was a keen observer of the migration of any people among the above from and to any place. In the absence of such an evidence of any migration, it will be reasonable to assume that those people were settled originally where they were found in later times, *i.e.*, where they settled after they were forced to migrate after the drying up of the river Saraswati and the end of the Indus Valley Civilisation. We may now have a look at their constitution and their internal administration keeping in view their peculiar position as being wedged between the two growing empires on either side, the Persian empire on the West and the Magadhan empire on the East. Both those empires were keen on bringing them under their subjugation and absorbing them in their empires.

The area they inhabited was not as fertile as the plain watered by the Yamunā and the Gangā. It was not a plain either as that it was a hilly tract and criss-crossed by huge rivers with patches of dense green forests in a vast brown desert and semi-arid areas where there might be small shrubs and low fertility. Yet in the absence of any other occupation they had to depend on cultivation. They could not keep herds of cattle fit for such arid conditions because of the threat of attacks from the two sides. Theirs was not a life of ease. In such an atmosphere where necessity demanded that the leader should be a man of ability they established republics where the ablest of them was elected as the head of the republic. We do not find any monarchies there with an assured dynastic succession in which not necessarily an able man might succeed the deceased monarch. From the later excavations and discovery of seals and some inscriptions on stones we get some glimpses of their constitutions. As stated earlier coins of a Rājanya Janpada have been discovered in the area lying between Bharatpur and Mathura. They bear the Brahmi legend, Rājanya Janpadasya. Copper coins of 200 B.C. recovered from Mādhyāmikā near Chittor in southern Rajasthan bear the Brahmi legend Majhimakāya Sibi Janapadassa. From excavations at Rairh a copper tablet of the 3rd century B.C. mentions Senāpati Vachhaga with the well-known Mālava symbols of Cross and Balls indicating the existence of Mālava republic. A group of seven coins have the legend "Vapu" in early Brahmi characters and ascribed to the period 250 B.C. to 200 B.C. Arjunayans probably lived in the Alwar-Bharatpur area of North-East Rajasthan. Their coins bear the legend Arjunāyananām Jayah corresponding to the Mālvanām Jayah of the Mālava people. Yaudheyas were probably the strongest people in North-Western India. They were mentioned in Panini's *Ashtādhyayi* and were classed with the Trigarttas and other people among the 'ayudhjivi kshtriyas'. Clay seals of the Yaudheyas have been discovered in the Ludhiana district of Haryana and their coins in the area extending from Saharanpur in Western Uttar Pradesh to Multan in Western Punjab. Some coins moulds of the tribe have come from Rohtak. The Yaudheya territory may be the Eastern Punjab and adjoining territory of Uttar Pradesh and Rajasthan. The tutelary deity of the Yaudheyas was Kārttikeya or Brahamanyadeva. They may be identified with the

Mattamayuraks of Rohitaka (modern Rohtak) which is described in the *Mahābhārat* as a place specially favoured by the god Kārttikeya. The clay seal from Ludhiana bears the legend 'Yaudheyānām Jayanām-tradharanam', *i.e.*, the seal of Yaudheyas who are in possession of victory charm. The coins of Yaudheyas of a later date have on one side the figure of Kārttikeya and on the obverse of a goddess with six heads who can only be Devasenā or Shashthi, the consort of Kārttikeya. These coins are believed to be issued in 2nd or 3rd centuries A.D. The full legend on them appears to be 'Swamino Brahmanyadevasya Kumarasya Yaudheyānām'. The earliest coins attributed to the end of the 1st century B.C. bear the legend 'Bahudhānake Yaudheyanam', meaning Yaudheyas of Bahudhanyaka. In the Junagarh inscription of Rudradaman with whom they came in conflict and ascribed to 150 A.D., they are described as 'untameable on account of their pride, resulting from the ascription of the title 'hero' to them amongst all Kshtriyas'. The Bijaygarh (2 miles from Bayana in Bharatpur District of Rajasthan) inscription of the 3rd century B.C. speaks of a Mahārāj-Senāpati, the title given to their chief and appointed to the post by the Yaudheya republic (Yāudheya-gana-purushkrita). We may remember that the title Senāpati was the title of the head of the republic of Vaishāli, of the head of the Mālavas. It appears that the title 'Senāpati' might have been the title of the head of the republics all over Northern India. Yaudheyas, we thus find, were in the area now divided between Punjab, Uttar Pradesh and Rajasthan and their immediate neighbours were Arjunāyans, a fact also mentioned in *Brihat Samhita* though a late text. Another neighbours were the Mālavas.

What does the title 'Senāpati' mean? And what does the title 'Mahārāj-Senāpati' mean? These two words are mentioned in connection with the events of later times and their correct meaning may explain some events. Does the word 'Senāpati' mean the commander-in-chief of the armed forces or head of a republic? When Pushya-Mitra killed the last Maurya king was he the commander-in-chief of the Mauryan army or was he the head of a republican tribe? Similarly what does the term 'Maharaj-Senapati' mean? Does it mean that the holder of the title was 'Senapati' of a republican tribe and at the same time ruler of other territories? Or does it mean that he was elected head of a number of republican tribes with their own 'Senāpatis'? We may remember that in Kalidas's *Malvikāgnimitra,* drama about the times of the Sunga dynasty, Pushyamitra was called 'Senāpati' by his Mālava compatriots and as Emperor by others. Can it be the explanation of the title 'Mahāraj-Senāpati'? Bijayagarh inscription is said to date in the 3rd or 2nd century B.C., the time when the Mauryas were holding sway over whole of Northern India and parts of the South India and certainly over the territory occupied by the Yaudheyas, to whose head the title was given. If Kalidas belonged to the 2nd century or 1st century B.C. as is believed by some scholars, then he was too close to the period not to understand the peculiarities and niceties of the situation and could not have missed the significance. If Kalidas is correct, then should we not presume that the Mauryan Emperor stood in some such position with the Yaudheyas as did Pushyamitra with his Mālava tribe? Similarly, Kalidas has described Kārttikeya as Senāpati of the gods. What does it mean? Was he the commander-in-chief of the gods or head of the gods in a republican type of constitution? More of this later.

We may now again recapitulate the whole scenario of the North-West India. Physically a more varied area may not be seen in India. From the snow-covered ranges of the Hindukush mountains in modern Afghanistan upto the river Indus it is one long uneven area criss-crossed by deep valleys, mountain rivers or rivulets with some rare passes connecting the Indian portion with Iran, the more notable being the Khaiber and the Bolan. After the Indus river upto the Jhelum and later the Chenāb it is a plain and in those times must have been full of forests. Between the Chenāb and the Rāvi the area becomes semi-arid. To the South of the Ravi and to the East of the river Indus in the Southern portion is now a big long desert, the desert of Thar. Only a little area between the Yamuna and the desert is semi-arid. In the South of this desert where the Aravalli ranges bisect the modern Rajasthan is again a semi-arid area which is also uneven and where dwelt the tribes of Sibi and the Mālavas. Only in the semi-arid regions was some agriculture possible. In the rest of the area the only economic activity possible was rearing of cattle, sheep, goats, etc.

Politically we have seen that there were small independent tribes living in that area with little economic activity. On both sides of that area, *i.e.*, East of Yamuna river and to the West of Hindukush mountains in Iran were well-established and rich communities, a natural temptation to those tribesmen for plunder. On both sides were, however, mighty empires ready to bring them within their fold with force. On the West was just the Achaemenian Empire established by Kurush (Cyrus) and on the East was the growing empire of the Magadh. We had seen that Bimbisār and Ajātshatru had extended the empire beyond Koshal and the Nandas upto the river Yamuna. That must have taken a small time of that period and might have been achieved fairly early. The two mighty empires must not be looking at those small independent republics with equanimity and must be trying to conquer them. In fact we find that Kurush (Cyrus) tried to pierce the mountain ranges separating India and Iran but met with fierce resistance. We also learn that he died fighting on those mountains. His successor Dāyarvush I (Darius I) only succeeded in bringing the area upto the river Indus in North West Frontier Province of Pakiṣtan under his control. Beyond that his writ did not run. Similarly, the Magadh Emperors must have tried to subjugate them.

A people who were ready to plunder the rich and prosperous area and might have already made forays into those two mighty empires suddenly found themselves to be preyed upon instead. In that probably lay the conditions which made them what they became. A people who were already called 'Ayudh-jivi', *i.e.*, living by arms alone, must have been raiding far and wide and sometimes fighting the other tribes had now to defend their own homes, their wives and children. That must have bred in them a fierce sense of independence. They must be prepared to fight Imperial armies on both sides. As they could not fight well-organised armies, they must have taken to resisting them by raids and hiding themselves on the approach of the armies. Those hit and run tactics, guerilla tactics of the modern times, must have saved their independence. However, it did not allow them a settled life. But as they were living in semi-arid areas with little agriculture, it probably did not matter. We do not find any big town of those times in those areas now being excavated. They must be all armed, moving around on horse-backs or camel-backs and whenever there was some peace they settled down for some agriculture in small hamlets.

When there is a prosperous empire which is peaceful and quiet and has on its borders armed tribesmen, then this empire has a sinister fascination for the tribesmen. These people armed to the teeth covet the riches, the luxuries of life in those parts but do not want to undergo the hardships required to earn them. Why should they? They can get them by their arms when they get opportunities in the shape of thinning or weakening of the border guards. Thus they always remain on the lookout and leaving their womenfolk to look after the other activities. We, therefore, find them idling themselves while their women look after the house, agriculture or rearing of sheep. The young men sometimes join only those activities in the neighbouring empire which provide the skill in arms. Thus they will join the armies or border guards, a thing which the empire too finds useful for it reduces the raids or chances of raids. However, this policy has a dubious utility for although it restrains these tribesmen temporarily from raids, it also gives them knowledge of new weapons, new uses of other weapons and of the war strategy. When the imperial armies march against their tribes, they leave the royal employment and join their compatriots with knowledge of the tactics to be employed by the armies and also equipped with latest arms which they had acquired during their employment. Whenever the empire weakens, they can pounce upon it and destroy it. In that part of India they had an additional advantage. They were faced with two hostile empires, *i.e.*, the Achaemenian and the Magadhan on either side. They, therefore, learned the art of war from both the empires which were manifestly different and at the same time acquired arms used by both the different empires and thus became a formidable war machine. When the times came, they were ready to destroy both the empires and to prey on their carcass. They could not do it in the West for when the time came they lagged behind and the prize was taken by the Greeks who sat over that carcass and did not allow them to get any share. However, their greater problem was with the Eastern empire of Magadh and we will see some time later what they made of dying body politico of that empire.

However, in the beginning of the period both the empires were just in the making and full of energy and vigour. Both were a danger to the tribal republics in between and these tribal republics were a danger to each of the two empires. That was the situation in which we find the republics. They were in a way the frontiers of the two empires and were constantly at war with them and among themselves. They could not settle down and take to agriculture. They had not made any large city. At the beginning of the period they were not properly organised. They were probably only settling down to the functioning of state just like their counterparts in the Eastern India, in the Gangetic Valley. But unlike them they had two major handicaps. Firstly the physical features of the area were not conducive to agricultural life. Secondly they had to face the threat from the two empires. Let us first examine their growth after the dispersal from the Indus Valley, somewhere in the 17th century B.C.

When the river Saraswati dried up and the rivers Satluj and Beās changed their courses going North the whole of the Saraswati valley became unsuitable for living and the people had to move to more habitable areas. Thus the people to the East moved to the areas further East into the Yamuna and Ganga valleys where they created the new civilisation. But the people along the river Satluj and Beās had to move North to the area along the new beds of those rivers and in the area between them and the Rāvi. With Rāvi also moving away Harappa was left high and dry without the life saving waters of the two rivers, the Rāvi and the Beās which also protected them from the enemies. The people had to abandon it and move along with the rest of the people to the new areas. The people who moved must be the Bharat and Tritsu tribes whom we found inhabiting the town of Harappa and its neighbourhood. What were the other tribes which inhabited that area and found mentioned in the *Vedas* doing and whither they settled? Excepting a few we do not find the names of other tribes among those found in that area. Perhaps as they moved they might have changed their names or they just merged with others and evolved a joint new name. However, we cannot be certain of which tribe joined which one and their new name.

The people or tribes mentioned in the *Vedas* are Bharat, Tritsu. Both might have been the two names of a single people as Sudās is alternately said to be the leader of them; Yadu, Turvasu, Dhrahyu, Anu and Puru all the five are always mentioned together. Yakshu, Brigu, Pakta, Bhalan, Vishanan, Shiva, all of them were defeated by Sudas in the battle of ten kings. Who were Kavash, Shruta, Vridha, Shigra, Aja, Varchi and many others? In later times we find that the Yadus were settled around Mathura on the banks of the Yamunā in modern Uttar Pradesh and in the Saurashtra peninsula which was a part of the Indus Valley Civilisation. Purus were settled in South-Eastern Punjab and in West Uttar Pradesh on the banks of Gangā in Meerut District. Paktas regarded as modern Pakhtoons were settled in modern Afghanistan and in the North-Western Frontier Province of Pakistan and are even now known as Afghans and Pathans. Shiva might be the people known as Shivis who settled in the area around modern Chittor in Southern Rajasthan and became a powerful people. Pakhtoons are a large people and consist of a large number of tribes with different names. Yusufzai tribe had their own name, Asip or Isap which appears to be the colloquial form of the Sanskrit word Ashvak, the name of a famous people. It is possible that others might have also become part of a larger tribe, losing their identity under the name of the larger tribe. We do not know which people from that migrating mass formed the tribes settled in this region, and now identified as the Yaudheyas, Agrasenis, Arjunayans etc. But it is they who peopled this area. By the 6th century B.C. they were the people who predominated over that part with Mālavas and Shibis in the South. They could not find any iron in that area which made the people of Magadh prosperous and powerful. They were living in a semi-arid region which did not allow them to be settled and become prosperous. But adverse climatic conditions made them hardy, innovative and jealous of their independence.

When the 6th century B.C. opened, the tribal republics or Janpadas as they were called suddenly faced danger. Two empires in East and West took shape. One was the Achaemenian Empire in Iran and the other in Magadh, in modern Bihar. These two empires rapidly expanded and soon reached the borders of that region, Achaemenian empire upto the Hindukush ranges in Afghanistan and the Magadh upto the banks of the river Yamunā. It must not be long when those two empires tried to bring those people under their sway. We find that even the first Achaemenian emperor Kurush (Cyrus) attempted to conquer that area and attacked with a large army in person in which he lost his life. However, the republics of that region were alert to the danger and took all precautions to guard their independence for we find that for the next centuries they remained independent. To meet the threats of the two empires the leaders of those republics must have devised some special ways to protect their lives and to preserve their administration, their means of livelihood and their fighting techniques, etc. In the absence of any records we can only visualise what they might have devised and done. It appears that they entered into some sort of informal contacts with their neighbours and might have given up wars among themselves. They might have entered into some sort of alliance and might have decided to have a single chief in times of emergencies. The Bijayagarh inscription of the 3rd or 2nd century B.C. mentioning that the chief of the Yaudheyas was elected by the whole people as the 'Mahārāj-Senāpati' might have been the last of a practice begun in those perilous times of the people. On that basis we may safely assume that such a practice might have started in the beginning of the 6th century B.C. In addition to the alliance the republics might have posted some sort of watchmen along the borders to report any invasion or troop movements so that they might get alerted and prepare to face the threat. They might have so trained their people that all the able-bodied people might be ready to fight if need be so. They had a larger national body of soldiers as against the mercenaries in the imperial forces. They must have become a highly mobile force usually mounted as we find the appellation of Ashvak or Ashmak used by the tribesmen in the border areas mentioned in the

Buddhist and Jain records of tribes. The name of those times continues even today as the Pushto name Asip or Isap of the Yusufzai tribe. Moreover, they might have seen that no permanent habitation in the shape of cities should be built so that the forces of the empire might not have any chance to ravage their homes and disable them. On the approach of the army they could just disappear. We have not been able to find any signs of cities of this area of that period inspite of extensive excavations. Whatever we get is either of the Indus Valley Civilisation times or of a time after this period. As for war they might not be having a face to face battle with the trained troops of the empires. After a few initial battles they might have learned and decided to use only hit-and-run tactics or what is now called guerrilla tactics. In this way it appears that they defied the empires allowing their armies to pass without submitting and so harassing them that they ceased attacking them. On the other hand they themselves attacked them at their own convenience after surprising them. It may be that in later times the representatives of empires in the border posts might be giving them some sort of peace-keeping money to keep them away. They might also be recruiting their young men in their border forces to pacify them but at the same time giving them valuable training in arms and battle techniques, giving them an added opportunity of procuring latest superior arms for themselves and for other members of their republics. They thus learnt the use of arms of the two empires which must be different, the different battle techniques and must have known the strengths and weaknesses of the two empires.

In the circumstances we can easily imagine the type of internal administration those republics must be having. They cannot have much of industry or commerce necessitating the presence of the merchants among them. Nor can they have the dominance of the priests or Brahmins as it was essentially an atmosphere of constant preparedness for war. They must essentially have the supreme ruler in the shape of 'Senāpati', a real commander-in-chief. He must, of necessity, be an able person and that too a younger not an elder one. Under such a chief the decisions were to be taken promptly and only in times of some grave crisis advice from elders or of the full council was to be sought. The priests or the Brahmin class had not much role which they had in the republics in the Eastern India. They were essentially one people and one caste and not that multiple caste system where the power passed from the oligarchs to the Brahmins and the merchants. In times of war or emergencies they had one chief for the whole area. Necessarily their laws and social system must be simple easily understood by the people and easily obeyed too.

We do not know much about Southern India. There is no record about South and also no legends prevalent about its state of affairs. The only legends we get are about Sri Lanka. As per the legends recorded in the Ceylonese or Lankan chronicles Mahāvansatikā and Dipvanshatikā about the beginning of the 6th century B.C. a prince Vijaya calling himself the son of a lion came from India along with 700 of his followers and settled down in Lanka and made it prosperous. There are disputes about the part from which he came. Some think that it was Bengal while some regard it to be the coast of Gujarat. There are legends prevalent in Maldive Islands off the coast of Lanka that a large number of ladies came in ancient times to those islands unaccompanied by men and settled down in those islands. It is thought that Prince Vijaya started from his home accompanied with both men and women and that the boat carrying men landed in Lanka while the boat carrying women separated and drifted to Maldive Islands and hence was unaccompanied by men. If it is so the likelihood is that they came from the Gujarat coast. This is also supported by the fact that lion is mostly found in Gujarat and hence can be appropriately be regarded as the progenitor of the race in Lanka still known as the Singhalis and that the language of the Maldives Divehi is more akin to the Gujarati language. We do not know anything else about the conditions in Southern India though the Lankan chronicles refer to prosperous kingdoms in the South Kerala State of India.

REFERENCES

1. Indica I, 1-3.
2. Fragment 37-ed. Gilmore.
3. Cyropaedia I, 1-4.
4. Cyropaedia VI, 2, i-ii.
5. Indica IX, 10.
6. Anab. VI, 24, 2-3.
7. Herodotus I, 153, 177.
8. Herodotus IV, 44.
9. Herodotus, III, 98, 102.
10. I, 34; II 3.
11. II 146, Niddess II 37.

6

THE AGE OF REASON

How is it that in the life of a people stretching upto millenniums there suddenly descends on them either an age of romanticism or an age of reason? Usually the life of the people goes on in their usual way for centuries but suddenly a time comes when the imagination of the people runs riot and they start imagining all sorts of things, composing songs, taking to painting or carving sculptures. In short, they want to express themselves in all sorts of ways. Simultaneously they want to achieve the unattainable things of life leading them from one adventure to another. At another times all sorts of romantic fancies are banished and rational thoughts take predominance leading man to find out the rational basis of things and to find hidden meaning in all sorts of phenomena. What are the causes of this sudden spurt of either the activity of the heart and imagination or the activity of mind in the nation as a whole? If we can find the answer, then we may be able to explain the age of reason which descended on the people of India as a whole. No doubt that in this age from the high mountains of Hindukush in Afghanistan to the Bay of Bengal people started questioning everything and started trying to find the reasons and hidden rules thereto not known in every thing on earth. We find people critically examining religion, language, administration, aim of life, the basis of mythologies, and sciences like metallurgy, manufacture of goods as well as arms etc. There was no doubt about the variations in stress on the different aspects in different regions depending on the social factors then prevailing but the trend was the same, the desire to find the rational basis of everything. Among them as usual with mankind the predominant accent was on religion and we find religious thoughts taking a new leap.

Religion

The state of religion in the various regions of India was different. In the area nearest to the Indus Valley Civilisation area the religion must be the one based on the gods and goddesses found in the *Vedas* but among the people to whom it was transmitted, *i.e.*, among the people of the East it was different. In the immediate vicinity of the Indus Valley which is the North-Western India the people believed in the hymns of the *Vedas*. They subsequently collected the old hymns and probably newly created ones by their ancestors after their dispersal from the Indus Valley. This we can say on the basis of the presence of Asurs in some of them. Asurs or Assyrians as Greeks called them rose only later and it appears that those hymns were created at that time of their predominance and their barbarity. We even find the mention of the country Asuryā, the land of the Asurs (Assyrians) in the 40th Mandal of the *Yajurveda* which subsequently became the *Ishāvasyo Upnishad*. The hymns of the *Vedas* are addressed to various gods, the prominent among them being Agni (Fire), Indra, Varun, Mitra, Sun, Ashwini Twins, Vishnu, Rudra and that mysterious thing Soma. Soma in Sanskrit stands for moon as well as the drink for the gods. We do not know why it is given so much prominence in the *Vedas* where a very large number of hymns are devoted to gods and an entire Mandal is devoted to the hymns to Soma in the *Rigveda* which is something unusual. These *Vedas* are divided into four parts—*Rigveda, Yajurveda, Samveda,* and *Atharvaveda*—of whom the *Rigveda* is undoubtedly the oldest. However, it too consists of hymns which are very old and some undoubtedly much later and probably formed after their dispersal from the Indus Valley Civilisation area. We also find that a number of hymns which are considerable are common to the *Vedas* or have some minor variations. Why this is so cannot be explained. The hymns too contained references to a large number of kings, saints or rishis, various other people and to incidents in the lives of people, the deeds of gods to help them. They also contained references to various beliefs about the gods, the Supreme God, the Creator, and the belief about the life. The people who collected the hymns had not much of ideas about them. Hence, in later times various speculations began about the reality and identity of the various references. We find that first the *Brāhmanas* were written to explain those references and sometimes later the *Āranyaks*. *Brāhmanas* and *Āranyaks* were written for each *Veda*. We do not know when they were written. They could have been written prior to the 6th century B.C. as it is presumed but they could have been written at the beginning of the 6th century B.C. when enquiry into the old things began. There must be a gap of a generation or two between the consolidation of what is known earlier and the critical enquiry into their contents, sifting of what is believable and what is not, and appearance of new beliefs.

Consolidation of old texts, specially the *Vedas*, their study, explanation of obscure references and critical examination of the texts were probably undertaken simultaneously, though not the critical examination of beliefs. The only extant evidence of such an exercise is the *Nighantu* and *Nirukta* of Yāska. Although Yāska refers to a number of other writers and other texts preceding him, yet that is the only and the only one extant. *Nighantu* is a list of words used in the *Vedas* and is divided into five chapters. In some of them there are words which have the same meaning, in some are words which have different meanings and some contain the names of gods appearing in the *Vedas* which are again divided into gods of the sky, gods of the air and gods of the earth. *Nirukta* is actually a study of the etymology of these words and Yāska tries to derive their meaning by identifying their roots. While doing so he gives examples and gives his own view of a number of references in the *Vedas* and also of various aspects of social life, of geographical aspects, of evolution of language, of grammar and above all of current thinking about the things mentioned in the *Vedas* which reveals that the blind beliefs in the things mentioned in them were being discarded even in his times. *Nighantu* and the commentary on it, *Nirukta* by Yāska is an interesting study. *Nighantu* is said to be a separate book and is said to be existing prior to Yāska. Some scholars do hold that it was also prepared by Yāska but the majority do not subscribe to that view. However, it does not appeal to reason why a list of different words should be prepared and circulated when it does not contain all the words used in the *Vedas* and appears to be an arbitrary selection of words to be studied etymologically. The author is of the view that list or *Nighantu* must be the creation of Yāska who embarked on a study of etymology of certain words. The period of Yāska is not known. It is assumed that he lived sometimes between the 9th and 7th centuries B.C. But the assumption is not based on any study of references or on any evidence. Whatever it may be *Nirukta* was prepared at that critical period when the two ages met and it explains many aspects of the earlier ages preceding it and many directions the society was about to take.

It will be interesting to have a look at some of the more important statements in the *Nirukta* made by Yāska and their implications. Yāska had made an interesting statement that sometimes the words in *Vedas* were formed from the words of Bhasha (language) and sometimes the words of Bhasha were formed from the words in *Vedas*[1]. We do not know what he means by Bhasha (language). Pānini much later in his book *Ashtadhyayi* says that Bhasha (language) means Sanskrit. But during the time of Yāska it might not have been so. Bhasha (language) obviously means the language spoken currently and it may not be the Sanskrit of the time of Pānini who lived a few centuries later. It implies that there was a spoken language earlier and words of *Vedas* were formed out of it and that later when again the spoken language was being enriched some words were again taken out from the *Vedas* and used. This may imply that the *Vedas* were not composed in the spoken language and that the language of the hymns might have been later changed to their present form, which is still preserved. This also implies that the original hymns composed in the times of Indus Valley may have been in a simpler but immature language, later enriched with new words and new additions. We get an example in the use of the word Asur. Asur throughout the *Vedas* is used in the sense of demons who opposed gods. But we know that Asurs (Assyrians) were a historical though a remote race. They only came into prominence much later and at that time some of the hymns must have been transliterated. The statement also implies that the language was growing and changing taking a different form with the addition of a large number of Vedic words. Yāska has written the *Nirukta* with the sole aim to study the etymology of words and to find the roots from which they were formed. But the interesting thing is that he had failed to find a single root for a fairly large number of words. A number of words had more than one meaning and he points out that the word may have been formed by more than two roots, something which is not possible. No doubt the word contains those roots from which it may be formed but languages are not formed that way. It is possible that originally the word was used by the primitive man and due to paucity of words it was used for two or more than two meanings. Later to systematise the language and due to the need to evolve more words in view of the growing complexity of civilisation the idea of finding roots came up. This was attempted by a large number of people whom Yāska referred to in *Nirukta* and continued much after Yāska or Pānini, Kātyāyan and Pātanjali. No doubt it helped in coining new words but the fact is revealed in *Nirukta* that words were formed in Bhasha or language earlier and attempts were made to find roots from which they were made much later. All the *Vedas* abound with the references and sometimes even description of Indra's epic struggle with Vritra. Yāska in the *Nirukta* plainly says that Vritra means cloud. If Vritra is just a cloud, then there was no such epic struggle and Indra whose importance in the *Vedas* is only due to the victory over Vritra loses all importance. Thus by the time of Yāska Indra and other gods had probably lost their importance. The stories in the *Vedas* were probably not taken seriously and the way was clear for an enquiry into the religion and regarding the Creator. We find this in *Upnishads* and in the philosophy of Buddha and Mahavir.

Yaska has mentioned *Upnishads* in the *Nirukta* though he had not named any. Hence, it is certain that the writing of *Upnishads* had already begun prior to him. But it is also probable that *Upnishads* continued to be composed later. *Upnishads* are usually discussions between a teacher and his disciples or between a learned one and the disciples or a discussion in some assembly of learned men. Hence, it had to be based on logic. Therefore they are a rational enquiry into the meaning of god, religion, life or duty of man. Today we have about a thousand *Upnishads* but the more important ones are few. Some of them must be the product of that time. The *Upnishads* do not mention minor gods at all but concentrate only on the supreme creator, an illusive and mysterious Brahma as distinct from Brahmā, one of the later trinity of Hindu gods and also regarded as the creator of the world. The *Upnishads* also point out that it is not possible to understand Brahma but only to realise him. It also maintains that to realise him one has to lead a good life. Based on logical discussions the *Upnishads* come to the conclusion that the Brahma is the supreme creator, though it is not possible to understand him and that one must lead a good life to realise him. What the type of life one must lead? This question too is widely discussed in all its aspects.

Brahma is declared to be the all powerful, creator, and present everywhere though unseen. He is also regarded as the creator of even gods. With this conception the importance of all gods mentioned in the *Vedas* was almost obliterated. That especially hurt Indra. Indra's importance was solely because he defeated the demons, the most important being Vritra, Shambar and Shushna and also that he rescued the cows from the Panis. However, we find from Yaska that Vritra, Shambar and Shushna were the names for the clouds and that Panis were merchants. So Indra was not only downgraded but was also shown defeated by other local deities who sprang up in the vacuum created by the exit of the Vedic gods. We find from Pānini during that period that a number of deities unheard of in the *Vedas* were worshipped whose names he mentioned while giving examples of words formed from roots of Sanskrit. The prominent among those, he mentioned, were Vāsudev, Arjun, Sankarshan and Pātanjali who was a contemporary of Pushya Mitra of Shunga dynasty, mentioned that the cult of Shiv, Skanda and Vishākha was prevalent in the times of Mauryas so much so that they sold images of those gods and got considerable revenue out of the sale. There may be more of cult figures not mentioned in any contemporary literature or record.

Who were Vāsudev, Arjun, Sankarshan, Shiv, Skand or Vishākha? None of them is mentioned in the *Vedas*. We simply cannot say who were they and how they sprang up into prominence. However, it appears that when the tribes who were worshipping the Vedic gods or held them in high esteem, were prominent in the social and political life of the Indus Valley Civilisation, they composed hymns and when they dispersed those hymns were collected and formed the *Vedas*. When in later times these tribes lost their importance, and either disappeared by disintegrating and merging with some other prominent tribes or migrating to Iran then the gods they worshipped lost their importance too. Evidence of this can be had from Iran where the cult of Agni, Varun and Mitra continued well after that period indicating that the tribes who regarded them as their gods migrated to Iran and had not lost importance there. It also appears that the other tribes who came into prominence in that period and formed the *Janpadas* or republican states in the area had their own gods and it were those gods who now became the new gods worshipped and sung and also who were regarded to have defeated the old Vedic gods, specially Indra. We find confirmation in the Arjunāyans who, as the name indicates, were the followers of Arjun and of Yaudheyas who were the worshippers of Skanda. We do not know which tribe regarded Vāsudev as its god but as per tradition he was the god of Shurseni tribe who lived near Mathura. However, when the epigraphic records of the 2nd century B.C. indicate that he was worshipped in as distant places as Ghosundi near Chittor in Southern Rajasthan and Vidisha in Madhya Pradesh we are left wondering as to whether a number of tribes worshipped him or the people who thus worshipped him were in fact part of a single people earlier. Ghosundi inscription mentions the erection of a Pujā-Shilā-Prākār or a stone wall meant for worship in honour of Vāsūdev and Sankarshana and Besnagar inscription mentions the erection of a pillar in honour of Vāsudev, the god of gods. Vishākha who is now regarded as another form of Skanda might have been worshipped by some allied tribe of Yaudheyas which might have later merged with them.

Each of these gods had their legends which later took the form of mythology. We find that they are stated to have defeated Indra thus downgrading the Vedic gods completely with the single exception of Vishnu whom we later find to be identified with the illusive and mysterious Brahma by the 1st century B.C. Why this is so we cannot say. But we also find that by that time Vāsudev, Sankarshana and even Arjun were identified with Vishnu in fact as his incarnations. We do not know the mythology about Skand in this time but we find later in the 2nd century B.C. or 1st century B.C. that he was designated as the 'Senāpati' of the gods when Indra was defeated by a demon Tārak. Later mythology not understanding the earlier meaning of the term 'Senāpati' thought that Indra was the king of gods and Skanda as the commander-in-chief. However, as we know that there was no king in the North-Western India and that 'Senāpati' was the designation of the head of the Janpadas or republican states all over India, it should be safe to assume that Skanda was the head of the gods in a republican constitution. We find the narration of the birth of Skanda and his nomination as the 'Senāpati' of the gods in the immortal classic *Kumār Sambhava* by Kalidas who wrote that poem in the 2nd or 1st century B.C. during the reign of Shung dynasty.

Can we stop the growth and development of mythology when it takes wings? We cannot even if it becomes intricate and assumes unrealistic forms. Usually the myths of different gods tend to make them supreme individually and place them in adversary relationships. However, in that region when there was threat from two growing empires, *i.e.*, Achaemenid in Iran and Magadh in Eastern India and the *Janpadas* or republican states in the region were coming together they could be adversaries but had to be friendly and cooperative against those two empires. It was but natural that the various gods of those tribes had to cooperate and an integrated mythology of that cooperation had to emerge. Such an integrated mythology indeed emerged in the shape of the story of *Mahābhārat*. No doubt the story of *Mahābhārat* took shape and was composed as an outcome of that integrated mythology for we find Pānini not only mentions the name of *Mahābhārat* in his book *Ashtādhyāyi* but also gives the names of all the heroes of the epic. However, we are not certain of the form. *Mahābhārat* in its present form consists of more than a hundred thousand shlokas or couplets but as per tradition originally only ten thousand shlokas or couplets were there and it is believed that as later continuous additions were made that it took its present form. What was the original story we do not know. But the main theme of the present story which must have been that of the old one is the fight against the rulers of Magadh and Iran. We find in the story that on one side the heroes had killed the king of Magadh, Jarasandh and his allies Kansa and Shishupal etc. and on the other they defeated the combined strength of Kuru and Madra tribes along with their allies. Who were the Kurus and Madras? Madras were those whom the Greeks call Medes but are named in ancient Iranian literature as Mada which is an obviously either a colloquial form of Madra or Madra itself might be the Sanskritised form of Mada. Founder of the Achaemenian dynasty was Cyrus, but the correct name is Kurush meaning head of the Kurus. Either the makers of the mythology were ignorant of the name and assumed it to be address of the head of the Kuru tribe or the word Kuru might be connected with the tribe to which the ruling dynasty belonged. We may thus see that the adversaries in this epic, *i.e.*, the Kurus and Madras were actually the people of the western empire. It is further interesting to note that the allies of the Pāndavas were invariably the people of that area and also those dispossessed by the two empires, *viz.*, the Matsya, Panchal, Shursenis or Yadus, the king of Kashi who was ousted by Magadh, the people of Dwarka stated to be situated in Saurashtra or Gujarat coast, and such other people. The allies of the Kurus and Madras were similarly the people of the Magadhan empire and those subordinate to it upto the modern state of Assam or of those allied to the Iranian empire, *viz.*, King of Prag-Jyotishpur in Assam, king of Sindhu-Sauvir, King Shalva etc. Bhishma, the son of the river Gangā, though respected and regarded as patriarch by both sides more so by the Pāndavas, had to be in adversary relationship with Pāndavas because the river itself flows inside the Magadh empire. All the gods with the sole exception of Sun are with Pāndavas. Sun or Mitra was an Iranian deity and as such had to favour the Kurus and thus his son Karna fought on their behalf and was killed in battle. The other gods were Pāndavas who included Yama in his incarnation as Yudhister, Bhim, the son of Wind god, Nakul and Sahdev, the sons of Ashwini Twins along with Arjun. Arjun and Vāsudev were actually the heroes killing most of the opponents and winning victories. Agni, the fire god equipped both Arjun and Vāsudev with divine weapons, Arjun with his bow and arrows, chariot and horses, Krishna with that mighty weapon Sudarshan Chakra or wheel and a conch. Even Shiv gave Arjun his arrow. We thus find the mythology created in such a way that it reflected the reality on the ground, around them. The gods of various tribes including the gods of the *Vedas* were juxtaposed in family relationship so that nobody might have been offended. To that arrangement which was the base of the epic *Mahābhārat* and all the mythology was added bits of philosophy and religious thought with all the later additions it became an all comprehensive book regarded as even more important than the *Vedas* and containing the immortal *Gitā*, the greatest religio-philosophical poem of the Hindus.

Religion in Eastern India

If we move to Eastern India, the state of religion is entirely different. In the beginning of the 6th century B.C. the area produced two great world teachers, the Mahāvir and the Buddha and two world religions, Jainism and Buddhism which are based on their teachings. Jainism denies the existence of God while Buddhism neither affirms nor denies. In the respective mythologies of the two religions which although compiled many centuries afterwards, Buddhism a few centuries and Jainism about a thousand years, there is no mention of Vedic gods or even other gods. There is a vague reference to Indra in the *Jātak* stories of Buddhism which tells the stories of the Buddha's previous births and in Jain stories of the lives of their Tirthankars, *i.e.*, world teachers, but his role is just subservient to that of the Tirthankars or of the

Buddha. It is as if it was an afterthought to bring those mythologies in line with that of the other parts of India and to make them acceptable to those people who believed in the gods living in other parts of India. In Kautilya's *Arthshāstra* which might have been written towards the end of that period there is no mention of Vedic gods. Instead he had mentioned the worship in temples (Koshthas) of gods and goddesses like Aparājita, Apratihata, Jayanta, Vaijayanta, Siva, Vaisravana, Asvin, and Sri (Lakshmi), Deities of Vatsu (Site) and Dik (quarters)[2]. To ward off natural calamities or to obtain natural benefits people made offerings and oblations and incantation of peace, worshipping Fire, Rivers, Indra, Ganga, Seashore, Forests (Vanaga), Mountains and Caityas of Rakshasas[3]. Naga-pratimas or Snake images and Dhvajapratimas or flagstaffs standing for some deities were objects of worship. Persons who practised inferior magical arts invoked Bali, Sambara, Vairochana, presiding deities of several Narakas, sages like Nārada, Devala, Savarni and Gālava, Manu, Devas and Devalokas, Vedic scholars, Siddhas, Tapasas, Brahma, Brahmani Paulomi, Tantukaccha, a great Asur and others of his class.[4] We thus find that there is no mention of the important Vedic gods which were worshipped in the Western India. Although Indra, Agni (Fire) and Aswins do find mention but they are among a host of other gods and goddesses, they lost the importance given to them in the *Vedas* and might have been there due to the late incursion in the area or might have just sneaked in with some people. On the other hand there are a host of other deities benevolent or malevolent worshipped there. However, if the later records are to be relied upon, the importance was given to the Universal Teachers like the Buddha and Mahāvir. They were respected by both the common people and by the heads of states including Kings and Senāpatis. We may also remember that according to Jain and Bauddha traditions they themselves were successors to a long line of Universal Teachers. The Buddha was the twenty-third and Mahavir the twenty-fourth in their respective lines. According to Jain and Buddhist traditions there were a number of other teachers who were contemporaries of the Buddha and Mahāvir, who were held in equal esteem and whom their followers claimed to be Universal Teachers, the most prominent among them was Makhli Ghosal. Other notable among them were Purana Kassapa, Pakudha Kaccayana, Ajit Kesa-Kambala, Sanjaya Belatthi-putta. The followers of Makhali Ghosala were called Ājivakas and of Mahavir were called Nigantha.

Why the religious scene was different in the two parts of India? It is rather difficult to give a precise answer based on facts simply because we do not have any records pertaining to the period. However, there can be one possible explanation. As stated earlier we know that when the Indus Valley grew arid and the people dispersed somewhere in the 17th century B.C. they migrated to nearby places. The people who thus migrated continued to worship their deities who were the Vedic deities and special to their tribes. However, the culture and religion of the Indus Valley continued to influence people far and wide. Those people who were other than the Indus people came under the influence of that culture and religion through radiation which left much of the minor details behind. Bihar, as we know, was almost the last outpost of India and it too received the religion through that radiation. In the process they either did not receive or give up the minor deities as supreme gods and instead received the figure of the person known to us as the Pashupatinath of the Indus seals, as the worshipful one. That figure was probably not the god but a sage, who knows all, is a Universal Teacher and had guided people in their lives. That figure the Jains called Rishabh. The Buddhists too regarded him as their first Buddha. Hence, this tradition of a Universal Teacher who takes birth for the salvation of mankind became the most important aspect of religion in those parts. They did not care for the God, the supreme god or the creator. They cared for the Teacher who will teach them the main elements of life on this earth.

Confirmation of this can be had from the Jain traditions. They had accepted the figure on the Pashupatinath seal as their first Tirthankar. They had accepted that figure along with all the four animals surrounding him and preserved that tradition in their 'Dream of Merudevi', the dream seen by the mother of every Tirthankar. We had seen above that this dream describes the figure and the four animals in the Pashupatinath seal. They called him Rishabh. We do not know what he was called in the Indus Valley but they might have called him Rishabh because of his bull-like face for Rishabh means Bull or else it might have been his name. However, instead of two ibexes or goats beneath his seat they put two bulls instead. However, we might recall that in the cylinder seal of the figure recovered in Iraq two bulls are shown beneath his seat. Jain traditions also mention that Rishabh in his previous birth as Vajrajangh moved with four animals surrounding him, *viz.*, monkey, mangoose, tiger and boar[5]. Jains, therefore, hold the figure of the Indus Valley as their first Universal Teacher and what is more have preserved the tradition of four animals surrounding him in this birth as well as surrounding him in his previous births. They have also maintained the tradition of having two animals beneath the seat of each of their Tirthankar or Universal Teacher, the animals being different in each case. This is the tradition they derived from the Indus Valley Civilisation. Further as they had seen the figure in the seal to be standing between the branches of a tree, they had maintained that every Universal Teacher had received his knowledge beneath a tree and the names of trees are inevitably associated with that of the Tirthankars. This marks them out as the successors of the Indus Valley Civilisation. In case of the Buddha we find this tradition in actual iconographic representations. In the Lion Capital at Sarnath we have four lions standing back to back carrying on their back a wheel. On the abacus of the Sarnath capital are shown four animals in different sides, a lion, an elephant, a horse and a bull. The wheel should not be taken to be the wheel of religion as is commonly thought but should be treated as representing the Buddha himself. We find that throughout the period the Buddha was never shown in person but was represented by either his seat or a tree or it appears by the wheel. In later times when the images of the Buddha were actually prepared we will find these animals surrounding him on those statues. We also find in later times Buddha shown having a pair of deer beneath his seat just as we find different animals beneath the seats of various Thirthankars and a pair of goats or ibexes beneath the figure in the Pashupatinath seal of the Indus Valley. This makes out the Buddha also to be the successor of the Indus Valley holy figure.

How is it that believing in the traditions of the Indus Valley we suddenly have a number of the Universal Teachers in this age? It appears that upto that period there was a single tradition of the Universal Teacher and people believed in a simple way of life which they called Dharma or religion. The spirit was in the air as soon as the age began. Both the Buddha and Mahāvir were scions of the oligarchic families of two Janpadas or republics, Shākya and Vaishāli. The old order was changing and the days of the *Janpadas* or republics were coming to an end as we had seen above. With their sharpened and accentuated sensibilities they understood that their order was coming to an end and that a new era was to begin which would change everything and life had to be redefined. In fact even during their own lifetimes the Vaishāli and Shākya republics were defeated and destroyed and what was worse the Shākyas were massacred to a man. With the old order passing away and the spirit of enquiry in the air they both reflected on the meaning of life in the new age. They read deeply, thought deeply and after years of meditation in the forests came to some conclusions about life, religion and the way of life one should pursue. Along with them a number of other persons thought too and came to some conclusions. These they taught to people and soon each had his followers who believed in their teachings, thought that they had given new meaning to their religion, and regarded them as the true successors to the old line of teachers they had always believed. They called them Tathāgat and Arihant. In later times the followers of those teachers merged and only two currents of religious thought remained in the form, the Jainism and Buddhism. There is not much of difference in their teachings. Both the Buddha and Mahavir taught the people to speak truth, believe in religion and have compassion to all living beings to an extent that they should not kill any living being even if it may be an insect but should have compassion for it. So was taught by other teachers. The difference was in fact only in the personality of those teachers and their followers aggravated the differences in minor details to maintain their identity. We may regard this phenomenon as a split in the old religion based only on personalities of the Buddha and Mahāvir. Soon their followers built up mythologies around them and their sect. Both built up stories giving their lives in previous births. *Jātaka* stories give us the previous births of the Buddha in which he is said to have done good deeds and sacrificed his life in the cause of others. Similar too are the previous births of Mahāvir. Miracles were attributed to the births of both in this life too. Jains declared that they had twenty-four Tirthankars, Mahāvir being the last, and the figure of the Indus Valley Civilisation to be the first. All of them also had previous births and instead of enjoying life in heaven deciding to be born in this world to guide and help Mankind. Buddhists too believed that there would be the twenty-four Buddhas, the Buddha Siddharth Gautam being the twenty-third with the twenty-fourth Buddha still to come. Why this number of twenty-four for both? When we remember that Hindus too believe that Vishnu had twenty-three incarnations with the twenty-fourth still to come some deep mystery and significance seem to have been attached to this number. What is that mystery? In the present state of our knowledge we are unable even to guess. Thus the two religions, Jainism and Buddhism, both tracing their lineage from the Indus Valley Civilisation, took firm roots in the soil of Bihar. In a few centuries Buddhism swept through Asia and is today the religion of whole of East Asia and South-East Asia along with Burma and Sri Lanka. When Hindus accepted the Buddha as one of the incarnations of Vishnu and accepted most of its doctrines Buddhism lost its hold and became a mere memory. Jainsim survived perhaps through Rishabh who was accepted as one of the incarnations of Vishnu but Mahāvir was not, and this made a difference to his followers. Moreover, Jainism had not swept India as Buddhism did and its adherents remained small though staunch followers to this day.

If Buddhism and Jainism were the dominating religions of Bihar, were they also the dominating religions East of Yamuna which included the modern state of Uttar Pradesh? Was the Vedic religion non-existent in that area? When we know that the people of the Indus Valley Civilisation moved

Plate 1: Buddha

to the banks of the Yamuna and beyond after their dispersal, it was but natural that the Vedic religion must be present there. In that age like the people of North-Western India the religion was the same but like them the gods were different and new gods emerged to take their position among the people. Mathurā became the new habitat of the Yadu tribe and Yadus regarded their chief to be Vāsudev who was later named Krishna. We find a cult built around him and he was mentioned by Pānini and regarded as the god of gods. We also find the cult of Rām who was regarded as Prince of Koshal, an area around the river Saryu in Eastern Uttar Pradesh. Before long his cult became the dominating one in Uttar Pradesh rivalling Krishna and became the subject matter of the epic *Rāmāyana* written in that period. It may also not be assumed that even in Bihar there were no adherents of the Vedic gods. The teaching centre at Taxila was famous in that time and according to Jain and Buddhist traditions a number of boys were sent to that centre for learning and they must have brought back those gods. With reference to the role of Indra in their traditions we may take it that among the Brahmins and the ruling classes Vedic gods may be having adherents.

About the Southern India we do not have any information whatsoever.

Shiv and His Family

Who was Shiv? What was his origin and in which place? Inspite of not being mentioned in *Vedas* and other Hindu scriptures how he gained such an importance that he came to be recognised as a universal god fairly early? What were his attributes? How he gathered round him his enigmatic but equally popular family? Shiv is the most enigmatic figure among the Hindu gods. His position as the most popular among the Hindu gods appears to have been established fairly early, in fact even in 3rd century B.C. Patanjali in his *Mahābhāshya* mentions that the Mauryas sold images of Shiv, Skand and Vishākha in order to raise money. If the Mauryas could sell their images and make it a source of revenue, it implies that these three must have been the most popular among all the gods. In the 2nd century B.C. Kālidās, who, it appears was a contemporary of Pushya-Mitra and Agnimitra of the Shunga dynasty, composed his famous poem *Kumār-Sambhava* which revolved round Shiv and his consort Pārvati and depicted the birth of Skanda, their son. If Shiv was so popular in the 3rd century B.C., his cult must have originated fairly early even prior to that period and though Yāska had not mentioned it, yet it might have preceded even Yāska.

Attributes of Shiv are numerous. He is said to live on Mountain Kailāsh in the Himalayas along with his family consisting of his consort Pārvati also known as Durgā, his sons Skand and Ganesh along with numerous attendants who are said to be ghosts, demons and such spirits. He is said to be all knowing and knowing all the arts. He taught the people dance, music, the knowledge of use of arms, use of bow and arrows, the language, grammar, script is said to have come out of his musical instrument called 'damru', a kind of small drum, and he also taught religion. In fact the image one gets of him is that of a Universal Teacher. His adherents regard him as the supreme god, the creator as well as the destroyer. Now he is regarded as one of the Hindu Trinity. How and why he is regarded as one associated only with destruction now-a-days cannot be explained.

What is the historical origin of Shiv? In the absence of any historical evidence it is difficult to say anything but an attempt can be made. We do not have any iconographic representation of Shiv of the earlier times. The first might have been those prepared and sold by the Mauryas but which could not be found now. They might have been destroyed being made from a perishable material or are not yet unearthed. The first prototype might be seen in Turkey if it is a prototype of Shiv. Bogāz Que was the capital of the Khatti (Hittite) Empire in the centre of Turkey in the 13th and 14th centuries B.C. In Bogaz Que was also found a treaty between the Khatti (Hittite) King and the Mittanians in which the Vedic gods Indra, Varun, Mitra and the Ashwini Twins were sited as witnesses. From Bogaz Que was also recovered a 'Horse treatise' by one Kikkuli in which terms in Sanskrit for the training of horses were used. Some distance away from Bogaz

Que in Yazilikaya in a cave were found the statues of 33 gods and opposite to them of 33 goddesses. We may remember that the *Vedas* also frequently mention 33 gods. It may be a coincidence that there are 33 gods in Yazilikaya too but if it is a coincidence it is odd. In the centre is a god who is standing on his mount Bull. All the gods and goddesses are shown standing on their mounts. This god is also standing on a symbolic mountain. Opposite to this god is the goddess standing on her mount, a lion, and behind her is a boy. The names of these gods and goddesses are also given. The name of this god is Teshab, of goddess Hekat and of the boy Shurrum or Kumarbi. The names, the historians believe, are not in the language of Khattis or Hittites as they are known but are in Hurrian, the language of the people who preceded Khattis in this region. The question arises as to whether this god, goddess and the boy are prototypes of Shiv, his consort Pārvati or Durgā and his son Skand. The resemblance is striking. The mount of Shiv is bull and he is said to live on a mountain, the mount of his consort Parvati is lion and their son is of course Skand.

Language and Literature

Just prior to the 6th century B.C. the language was in a way stagnant. Throughout the Indus period and later in the Vedic period when the *Vedas* were compiled, the growth of the language was painfully slow. There was a paucity of vocabulary and a single word denoted a number of meanings. As an example the word 'khang' may be cited which means a sword, a moon and rhinoceros and if the nasal sound is removed means bird. Probably the sign of bird in the Indus script denotes all the four and could be expressed only by putting determinatives before or after them. The paucity of vocabulary plagued the thinkers and in effect prevented new writings and new literature. Another word, for example, can be 'Shundhyu' which means Sun, bird and water. In fact as Yāska points out in the *Nirukta* that the fourth chapter of *Nighantu* which contains two hundred and seventy-nine words, gives those words which have more than one meaning and he had given the different meanings of each in chapters

4th to 6th in his *Nirukta.* The people faced the problem of the paucity of vocabulary and tried to increase it in view of need for more words due to the increasing complexity of life which required them. Again in the matter of script they were faced with a tedious and unexpressive script. As we find in the Indus script there was a sign for one word but the word in many cases would mean different things. They probably solved it by putting determinatives before or after them. Most of such signs were crude pictures of the things expressed by one of the meanings. As an example the word 'Khag' for bird could be expressed by a crude picture of a bird. For the other words 'Khang' expressing different meanings they could be shown by a determinative. By putting the picture of a fish beside it the indication may be of an amphibious animal and may mean rhinoceros. In fact this appears to be the intention in the Indus script as can be seen in the identical seals Nos. 10, 11 and 13 from Mohenjodaro[6] in which we find a rhinoceros on the left and facing him on the right is bird and fish within a bracket. It may mean that the bird and fish together stand for rhinoceros. Such a script was a tedious one and so inexpressive that it might be difficult to write new words coined by adding prefixes and suffixes only. The solution to both the problems came and the solutions were simple but audacious and they revolutionised the whole language and script and made the society cope with the challenges of the growing complexity of life. Who were the people who proposed the solutions to the two problems? We do not know their names nor the places to which they belonged, nor the time when they lived, but whoever they might be, they made a signal service to the people and must be immortalised.

Fig 6.1: MIC Vol. III, Pl. CXVI, No: 10

We may first see the reform in the field of increasing vocabulary for it might have preceded the reform of the script. The idea of coining new words and the way they might be coined was simple enough. It was suggested that the basic sound of a word already in use might be found out and isolated and then by adding certain prefixes or suffixes new words could be coined. The meaning of each suffix and prefix might be fixed and rules laid down regarding the new meaning of the word to which the suffix or prefix was attached. In some cases two such roots might be conjoined to form a new word which might express the combined meaning of the two roots. The existing conjoint words in the then language might have been examined and principles derived from them. Those together with new rules formed the new principles for the joining of two such roots or even words and later more than two words or roots were joined together to form new words. In this way vocabulary could grow. The idea must have appealed to scholars and after some discussion must have been accepted. Soon there must have been a large number of scholars analysing the roots of words, the way the word was formed, the rules of the formation of words from roots, the formation of words by adding prefixes and suffixes to the roots and the rules for joining two or more words to form new words. There must have been discussions and heated arguments over the different interpretations of such rules, over correct rules and over the choice of root in a particular word. Schools might have developed sound scholars who might have collected words from the existing literature which invariably must mean the *Vedas* and who might have analysed the words, found their roots and have laid down rules. Soon learned treatises must have been circulated both by word of mouth and probably in script as well. Among such scholars was Yāska who probably composed the *Nighantu* in which words from the *Vedas* were arranged and classified in different chapters. In the first three chapters are the collection of words which denote the same thing or have the same meaning, *viz.*, 21 words meaning earth or 12 words meaning many. The number of words collected in the three chapters are 1341. In the fourth chapter of *Nighantu* are words many of which have more than one meaning but they could not be classified, the number of words being 278. In the fifth chapter are the names of gods and other deities. *Nirukta* makes an analysis of some of the other words and many others not given in the *Nighantu*. The total number of words which Yaska had studied and found their roots and the rules under which they could be formed is 1298. We get in *Nirukta* a glimpse of the discussions and arguments for Yāska has quoted the opinions of his contemporaries refuting them and giving his own reasons for the derivation of words from the roots. It is unfortunate that we do not have the works of his contemporaries but at the same time fortunately we got his work in its entirety. Soon we had new industries, new way of life, new republics and monarchies, and an empire embracing whole of India and beyond with complexities of administration and diplomacy, new thinking about religions which developed shortly into world religions and development of medicines, sciences and fine arts. All these required coining of new words. We had a succession of great grammarians, Pānini, Varruchi Kātyāyan, Katya, Vyādi and lastly Patanjali. They met the challenges and made the Sanskrit language rich and fully expressive. Pānini laid down very elaborate rules for the formation of words and helped in the full development of the language which were only elaborated by Varruchi Kātyāyan and later by Patanjali. Soon a dictionary *Amarkosh* also came into being. Among the above grammarians, if *Brahatkathā* is to be believed, Pānini and Varruchi Kātyāyan were the contemporaries of the Nanda king, Pānini probably a generation older to Varruchi Kātyāyan.

An interesting development in the language also took place not through the grammarians but through the people themselves. This was the formation of polyglottic words or what others call 'translation compounds'. When two people speaking different languages interact, then sometimes words having the same meaning in both combine to give a single word having the common meaning. Thus 'Kari' of Sanskrit and 'anu' of Tamil both meaning elephant became a single word 'karenu' meaning elephant. Austric Shali and gutra-hotra of unknown origin from which we get the word ghota both meaning horse became Shalihotra of Sanskrit. We had that phenomenon in Sanskrit since very early times. 'Kuru' of Sumerian and 'Kshetra' of Sanskrit meaning area joined together to become Kurushetra though it came to indicate a particular area and its residents became Kaurava of the *Mahābhārat*. 'Madu' in Accadian and 'Bhumi' in Sanskrit both meaning earth became Madubhumi and later Matubhumi denoting earth which later became Mātrabhumi meaning mother earth. Why such phenomenon took place? It appears that when two people speaking different languages interact with not much fluency in each other's language, then they speak the two words combining them to be more precise and to be more clearly understood. Such a word then sticks and becomes a part of the language. If we can trace such words and the time when they were first used, we can find the precise period when the two people came into contact. Incidentally such an interaction also makes the people take into their language a number of words from other languages. Sanskrit thus came to have a large number of Greek and Iranian words, *viz.*, mudra, dipi or lipi, nipista, asavari, kshatrapa, karsha, dramma from Greek drakhme, suranga from surinks or syrinx, and other astronomical terms. Similarly from China we had the words chīna, kīchaka, a kind of bamboo, etc.

The second major and revolutionary reform was in the script. We had seen that the Indus script was a very cumbersome and inexpressive script and when new words began to be coined, then it became a problem to write them in the Indus script. While scholars pondered over it, somebody came with a simple and audacious proposal. When people were analysing the roots of the words, they must have come to have an important finding of different sounds from which words began and from which they were composed. Each word was found to be formed of different sounds. They must have analysed them and classified them, identified them and tabulated them as distinct sounds. The proposal must have been to assign a different symbol to each of the sounds thus identified. The assigning of symbols was not a difficult proposition for the Indus script must be having sufficient number of words which began with those sounds and it was just to pick up an appropriate word whose symbol was to become the symbol of that sound and which began with that sound. This must not have been difficult and soon the alphabet with a sign for each sound or letter was proposed. This must have appealed to scholars and soon the alphabets came into being appropriately named Brāhmi alphabets. In this alphabet the symbols are exclusively from the Indus script and though we do not know the original word but looking at the sense it conveys we can make a guess. In the script we find a symbol resembling a spider which is called 'Asthtapād' meaning a spider and also is a name for Mountain Kailash. This symbol appropriately modified becomes the letter 'a' of the Brahmi alphabet. The sign showing the foot of a man called 'Charan' in Sanskrit becomes the letter for 'cha', a fish-hook called Vadisham becomes letter 'va'; a hill called giri in Sanskrit becomes letter for 'ga'; raindrops symbolised by three dots, one above and two below, called 'Indu' becomes the letter for 'i'. In this way the alphabet was suggested and must have been enthusiastically received. It might have taken a century or two for the alphabet to become a universally accepted one but universally accepted it was. We do not know the timing of the move and the period when it was first proposed and when it was first accepted. The earliest records of this script we have are on the Ashokan pillars and Ashokan edicts engraved on rocks. A slightly earlier one may be the Sahgaura plate. We do not know the kind of paper or material which was used for writing. If it was a perishable material like cloth or wood, then naturally they must have been destroyed. The bhojpatra leaves also could have been used but they too are a perishable material. Hence, it is not possible to ascertain when actually that script came into use. But looking at the mass of literature which was produced in that period and also looking at the fact that by the time of Ashoka the script could be read throughout the length and breadth of the country it might not be wrong to guess that it must have been evolved prior to the 6th century B.C. and increasingly coming into use.

When the script came into use, it was but natural that the older script must have been also in use. However, with the universal acceptance of the new script it was also natural that the existing books in the older script must be rewritten into the new one. But this always presents a problem of rewriting the whole mass of books or some selected books. Naturally those books alone which had obtained universal recognition would be rewritten in the new script. Those which failed to get general acceptance and failed to get rewritten in the new script were doomed to extinction. A time would come when the people who could read the older script would pass away and such books would remain a puzzle and would be destroyed deliberately or by time. An interesting example had survived to this day. The books secular in nature and non-religious would be rewritten immediately. To that effort we may ascribe the survival of *Nirukta* of Yāska while those by his contemporaries perished. Similar must have been the fate of other books which are referred to in other books but are not available. The strictly religious books whose very script must also be sacred must have been left untouched but when it might have been felt that for want of being rewritten they would also become unreadable, then they would have been rewritten in the new but universally accepted script. Such religious books must be the last and among them naturally will be the *Vedas*. The *Vedas* reveal to us, among other things, the attempt to rewrite them in the new script and the portions where the attempt failed. The *Vedas, Rigveda, Samveda, Yajurveda* and *Atharvaveda* have their importance in that order and they must have been rewritten in that order. We find the first three *Vedas* and the earlier portions of the fourth *Atharvaveda* to be intelligible and properly written. But when we come to the later part of *Atharvaveda,* we find an abrupt change. The last thirteen Suktas of the *Atharvaveda* from Sukta No. 129 of the last Mandal No. 20 fall into this category. They are not at all intelligible and coherent and in fact the seven Suktas from Sukta No. 129 to Sukta No. 136 are just a blabber of a tongue. These Suktas known as 'Kuntābh Suktas' convey nothing. They are only a list of words put together without any order or method and have such words like three names of a camel, growing horns, arrows in the possession, two boys, etc. Are they there without a method or order? No. The order and method appears to be there. They all appear to be random pictures and may actually be the symbol of Indus script. It also appears that when that last portion of the *Atharvaveda* was being rewritten in the new script there were only very few persons left who could have read the old script and may be that when the person who was rewriting it came to the Sukta No 129 of the 20th Mandal or the 'Kuntabh Sukta' there might have been something which prevented him to read it. The one who succeeded him and was asked to read and write could not do so and probably none was available who could have done so. Hence, he wrote down what he saw describing the symbols as best he could without being able to assign any meaning to them. We thus have this last portion unexplained. However, it gives us an interesting example of the change in script and the failure to re-write something in the new script, in spite of ardent desire of everybody to get it done.

We had seen the development of Sanskrit language in these parts but that does not mean that it was the spoken language and language of common conversation of all the people in North-Western India. Because of the prestige of Sanskrit it remained the language of aristocracy and of religion and books continued to be written in it, yet it can be conjectured that the language of common conversation must have started deviating from it and after some time must have differed considerably. However, the new words and enlarged vocabulary must have become the common property of the newly-developed languages. We, however, do not have any written record of such languages surviving. Probably they were not written. Whatever religious or scholarly was written was in Sanskrit. We see a similar situation in Europe where in spite of having well-developed languages books on religion and scholarly treatises continued to be written in Latin till very late.

When we come to Eastern India where it was not inhibited by the prestige of Sanskrit, the local languages had their day. Had the empire been based in some such area like Mathura or Western Uttar Pradesh where the Indus people settled, the language might have been Sanskrit. But as we know that the influence of Indus Civilisation reached there by radiation which gave them ideas but the language did not form a part of it and it allowed the local languages to be used in all transactions and in religion. We, therefore, find the religious teachers teaching in the local languages. The Buddha and Mahāvir, we find, taught in the languages spoken by them and the people. Both belonged to places lying north of the river Gangā and north Bihar. They, therefore, preached in their respective dialects which are now designated as Ardha-Magadhi. Not only their teachings but the mythology which grew around them and the religion they preached as well as the scholarly discussions on their teachings were composed in those languages. However, it appears that they were not written as those people till then had no script and as such they had not survived. But the works though small continued till the time of the Mauryas. We have seen that whenever the people establish a universal state even in some alien land, they impose their own language as the language of administration and other scholarly works. The Mauryas imposed Pāli which became the language of administration and consequently of other works. With Ashoka's patronage of Buddhism the teachings of the Buddha were rewritten in Pāli and in Pāli they came to us. His original words are forgotten and lost. Pāli being the language of the empire can be seen from the Ashoka's edicts engraved on rocks and pillars which go far to tell us about the language in whole India which people were supposed to understand and learn. All subsequent works on Buddhism were then composed in Pāli and as the Brāhmi script was adopted by the Mauryas they were also written and survived. Taking a clue from Buddhism the Jain literature also came to be written in Pāli but the words of Mahāvir himself came to us in original Ardha-Magadhi.

How the administration and commerce were carried out in such an undeveloped language like Magadhi and Ardha-Magadhi which were the languages of the republican states in Bihar? This was a problem to be faced by the republican States but it was probably solved by borrowing the newly coined words in Sanskrit. Buddhist traditions tell us that the young people were sent to the teaching centres in North-Western India, specially to Taxilā to learn and study medicine, philosophy, martial arts, science and even religion. They mention that even Singh, the Senāpati of Vaishali at the time of attack on the kingdom by Ajātshatru studied in Taxilā.

So the scholars who came back from Taxilā introduced the new words and their new forms in the local dialects. We get a preponderance of Sanskrit words in the local languages, specially Pāli but the words due to the impact of local languages slightly changed their forms. Harsh sounds were dropped or softened. As an example 'r' is dropped and 'sh' becomes 'ha'. Pāli is in fact almost Sanskrit without the harsh sounds. In addition to the scholars who went there to study we find the tradition of scholars coming to these parts either being invited or otherwise. Traditions hold that scholars like Pānini, Varruchi Kātyāyan etc were associated with the Nandas and probably Kātyāyan was a minister under him. Traditions also hold that even Chānakya was invited to his court but because of his dark colour and ungainly features was turned out which made him take a vow to remove the Nanda king, a vow he carried out with the help of Chandragupta Maurya. Thus this interchange of scholars enriched the local languages and enabled them to rise to the occasion. However, none of the works if written in those languages survived except the teachings of the Buddha and Mahavir and the mythologies around them and even they in another dialect.

We do not know anything about the languages of the South. But removed from the influence of Sanskrit and any effective intercourse and interaction with the North they must be having an independent development. Whatever records we get is in the 3rd century A.D. when we find them rich and developed.

Sanskrit Literature

It was in Sanskrit literature that the genius of the age blazed forth and produced massive works in every sphere whether they may be religious works or works on dramatic arts, philosophy, economics and administration, grammar, or pure poetry. Unfortunately a large portion of it is lost. We get an inkling into the works by getting references to them in later works on those subjects. Among the extant works which were created during that period the most enduring are the religious works and those which later acquired the religious overtones like the *Rāmāyana* and *Mahābhārata*. However, works purely religious or even of grammar, in addition to the matter they contain, are fine pieces of literature. We find that during the period the *Upnishads* and some of the *Purānās* were composed. *Upnishads* as we had seen above enquire into the nature of supreme god and take us a stage further higher in religious thought. In addition, *Grahya Sutras* and *Dharma Sutras* were also created, some at least if not all. They deal with the duties of man and rituals. It was during that period that the celebrated mystical work. *Brahma Sutra* was created which deals with the concept of the formless god, an audacious thought for all the times. We have already seen the works of the great grammarians of whom the most important was Pānini. The others of note were Varruchi Kātyāyan, Katya, Vyadi, and some of those referred to by Patanjali, such as Bharadvāj, Sunag, Krōshta etc. as his predecessors. Some of the *Prātisākhyas* must also have been written during that period. *Prātisākhyas* are a class of works designed to preserve Vedic texts correctly as handed down in their several branches or group of branches. Among them *Vājasaneyi Prātisākhya* is attributed to Kātyāyan and certainly belonged to that period. Whatever may be the date of the present text of *Nātya Shāstra* of Bharat, it incorporates within itself and cites passages and verses handed down to him from the past. Therefore there must have been works on drama and dramatic art or the art of actors. We do not know the age of Kautilya's *Arthashastra* for although tradition ascribes it to Chānakya, yet some scholars attribute it a later age. In my view looking to the language, text etc. it must have been written by Chānakya and that too before he engaged himself in overthrowing the Nanda king and helping Chandragupta Maurya to become emperor. He wrote it when he must have been engaged in teaching and developing his ideas about administration and public finance. Thus this work must also be counted among the great works of this period. It is interesting to note that Kautilya refers to his own work as a critical compendium based on *Arthashāstras* prevalent in his time and refers to works of about a dozen writers Bhāradvāja (Kaninka), Vishālākshā (Shiv), Parashara, Piśuna (Narada), Kaunapadanta (Bhishma),

Vātavyādhi (Uddhava), Bāhudantiputra (Indra), the Mānavas, the Bārhaspatyas, Aushanasas and Āmbhiyas. This indicates that there were a large number of works of polity probably inspired by the intense political activity of the times which were full of Janpadas, Sanghas of different descriptions and numerous small monarchies. Chānakya probably saw the danger of these numerous small free states, communities and kingships, specially in view of threat to India from the West because of his association with Taxila, and set forth the scheme of the detailed working of a huge centralised authority in a new empire embracing whole of India in his *Arthashāstra* and later set about bringing to reality his dream of the empire in which he was eminently successful with the help of Chandragupta Maurya.

Among the pure literature the works which had survived are the two great epics, the *Rāmāyana* and the *Mahābhārata*, the finest and immortal creations in Sanskrit. As per tradition *Rāmāyana* has continued to be available in the form in which it was originally created. Not so with *Mahābhārata* which tradition ascribes to being a smaller work and the present work is said to be about ten times its original length. It is unfortunate that the original work is not available nor we have any idea of its contents. Had it been so, we would have got an insight into the social and political conditions of the times. For it has all the elements of religion, philosophy, history and above all the ethics and theories of polity. It has become such a complete work that it is taken as a religious book, specially with the *Gitā* forming a part of it, and stands above the *Upnishads* and the *Brāhmanas.* It is taken to be at par with the *Vedas* and in fact is regarded as the fifth *Veda.* This is due not to the contents of the *Vedas* but mostly due to the sanctity attached to them. *Rāmāyana* is the story of Rām, the prince of Ayodhyā in Koshal lying in Eastern Uttar Pradesh who took to exile and rid the country of Rākshasas, an evil people and solely revolves round him and his deeds. *Mahābhārata* on the other hand is the story of Vāsudev Krishna and Arjun who rid the world of evil with their mighty deeds and tagged with them is the evil nature of man seen through the eyes of Yama, the god of death during his ordeal in the real life. What were the contents of original *Mahābhārata*? It is regretted that we do not know but a guess can be legitimately made which we will see presently.

Looking to the richness of the language, subtle weaving of the plot and the flight of imagination together with the insight into the nature of man, society and reflection on polity and ethics in both these epics which had left a deep and enduring imprint on the consciousness of the people it can be safely said that they were not the first works of the kind but were the culmination of a mass of similar works undertaken in the previous centuries. What were those works and where are they? It appears that they are all lost and we have at present no knowledge of the works which might have been created, prior to the two epics. If we look at the two epics, we find that the story of *Rāmāyana* is built round the adventures of the Ram and Lakshman and of *Mahābhārata* round the adventures of Arjun, Vāsudev Krishna, and the Pandav brothers. We know about Arjun and Vāsudev to be cult figures from Pānini and one may guess that others too were cult figures in their own right or else a large number of ballads must not have been in circulation celebrating their adventures and deeds. They must have been sung in gatherings, in festivals and special days associated with them. It must have been the genius of the two authors that they collected the ballads, wove them into a story and narrated them in an incomparable language and a coherent and fine plot. What will not one give to get some of those ballads. It is probable that some of those ballads might have been incorporated into the epics in their entirety in relevant places. Some parts of polity, works on ethics or philosophy which might have been composed earlier might also have been incorporated in their entirety. Among such pieces is the *Gitā* which, it is conjectured, was composed much earlier but was incorporated in the *Mahābhārata* either as it was composed earlier or with some slight modifications to suit the purpose.

As per tradition *Rāmāyana* was composed earlier and *Mahābhārata* later. The former was composed by Bālmiki and the later by Veda Vyās. Ved Vyās appears to be mythical for he is also credited with arranging the *Vedas* into four, writing of *Purānās* and other works in addition to *Mahābhārata* and at the same time being himself the real grandfather of the

Pāndavas and Kauravas. Notwithstanding anything these two epics are the most precious gifts of Sanskrit and of the age which continues to mould the thinking of Hindus in India and of the people of South-East Asia including Indonesia, Thailand, Cambodia and Malaysia where inspite of the people not remaining Hindus they still continue to be their national epics.

In view of the threat to the region from East and West, *i.e.*, from the Magdhan empire and the Achaemenid empire and occasional attacks from them, it is amazing that such a plethora of creative literature was produced. It is also amazing that they had enquired into every aspect of life, be it the study of language and its forms, polity, ethics, religion or philosophy. It is understandable that in view of the threats poems or ballads celebrating the mighty deeds of warriors and heroes might have been composed, but not on the other aspects of life which require tranquillity and peace. We can only pay our humble tribute to the genius of the people that they achieved so much in times such as they faced. What they created remains unmatched to this day and was indeed a golden period of India's creative activity.

REFERENCES

1. *Nirukta* 2.2.
2. *Arthashastra* II. 4.
3. *Ibid*, IV. 3.
4. *Ibid* XIV. 1.
5. Jinsen—*Mahapuran* 8. 245.
6. Marshall—*Mohenjadaro and Indus Civilisaton*—Vol. III, Plate CXVI.

7

THE MAURYAN AGE

The new age which began just after the withdrawal of Alexander from India completely transformed India. It began with a suddenness and force. Events followed upon events with such a rapidity that it left everybody breathless. Within a couple of years after the withdrawal of Alexander in 323 B.C. in fact by about 321 B.C. or 320 B.C. the whole of Northern India was united under a strong and vigorous government which was so strong that when after about fifteen years the successors of the Achaemenid empire, the Greeks under Seleucus Nikator attacked India to regain the part of the empire lost during the interval, the area comprising Sind and North Western Frontier Province of modern Pakistan they were decisively defeated ceding a large part of their empire consisting of modern Afghanistan and some parts of the Central Asia. What was more Seleucus had to give a daughter too to maintain a permanent peace.

Who brought about this unified empire? Probably it were the Nandas who conquered the North-Western India. Probably the republican tribes and republican states fearing the establishment of a strong Government in Iran in place of weak and effeminate Achaemenids decided to submit to the Nandas to save themselves. Nothing of the sort happened for Nandas were the first to be swept away and were consigned to the dustbin of history. They, who united the whole of Eastern India, gave it a strong government and were patrons of letters, were from now onwards decried and reviled as no other dynasty ever was. The first Nanda was declared to belonging to a low caste, who became a paramour of the queen of the last Shishunag king, who killed his master and usurped the throne. The later Nandas were said to be greedy, miser, and took great pleasure in insulting the men of learning. If the Nandas had not united the country, then surely it must have been some subordinate king or head of some tribe in the empire who taking advantage of the weakness of the empire, consolidated his army and overthrowing the Nandas conquered the republican states of North-Western India? Had he been some subordinate king or noble, he must have required some time to overthrow the Emperor and surely the republican states who had defied both the Nandas and the Achaemenids simultaneously could not have been subdued so easily and within a period of a year or two. It could not have been a subordinate one who could have come to the throne of Magadh. It must be one who simultaneously commanded the trust and confidence of the states of North Western India. Who was he? He was Chandragupta Maurya. More we do not know except that his grandson was Ashoka and his successors ruled over India for 150 years.

Chandragupta

Who were the Mauryas? They, it appears, came as if from nowhere. We have got a lot of surviving literature and there is a greater notice of historical events including that of Greeks. Greeks mention nothing about the ancestry of Chandragupta Maurya nor the place from where his ancestors came or to which they belonged. The Buddhist literature is full of panegyrics and praise of Ashoka but they too are silent about Chandragupta or his ancestry. Jain literature though compiled much later does mention Chandragupta but not of his life prior to his getting the throne. The Hindu *Purānās* do mention the Mauryas and even give their genealogy but their genealogy differs from that given by the Bauddha Divyavadān and do not mention anything about the origin of the Mauryas. Ashoka had left a large number of inscriptions, fourteen *rock* edicts and a host of other minor inscriptions. But in none of them he had revealed anything about his great ancestor or even about himself. Everywhere he was described only as 'Devānāmpiya Piyadasi lajā', in one 'Piyadasi lājā

Magadhe.[1] Only in Maski record he called himself as 'Devānāmpiyas Ashokas'. This alone identified Ashoka as the king who gave us inscriptions. But this is not sufficient to find about the origin of the Mauryas. May be the people in those times knew about the family and its origin and therefore did not find it worthwhile to write about it in the books they composed or other writings they left us. It is also possible that the books which contained the details of the dynasty had not survived. However, inspite of the absence of any record of their origin and their deeds, there are a number of references to Chandragupta Maurya, both contemporary and later, both present in the books of India as well as of the foreign authors, which may help us in forming some ideas of their origin as well as the method they adopted which brought the first Maurya to the throne. Are those references complementary? No, they are not. They are in fact contradictory at least some of them, yet taking into consideration the evolution of the social and political condition of the people as seen above, they may help us in finding out the reality and in answering our question.

Who were the Mauryas? Let us look at all the references to the Mauryas and also references to any thing which might be connected with them. As stated earlier Pātanjali, the grammarian, in his *Mahābhāshya,* the commentary on Panini's *Ashtādhyāyi* has a reference to 'Chandragupta Sabha'[2] and also that the Mauryas sold images of Shiv, Skand and Vishākha to earn money—Mauryaīr hiraṇyārthibhir arcāḥ prakalpitāḥ. Patanjali was a contemporary of Pushyamitra Sunga and must have lived during the age of Māuryas and about hundred years after Chandragupta Maurya. In *Milind Panha* (the questions of king Menander) it is mentioned that Chandragupta had a fight with Nanda army led by Bhaddasala and the slaughter caused in that army by Chandragupta. In *Mudra-Rakshasa,* an 8th century drama, the story revolves round the capture of power but it makes Chānakya, the hero who by his intrigues brings about the rule of Chandragupta. Among other things it mentions the epithets of Chandragupta, Chanda Siri, Piadamsana and Vrishala. It also mentions that he was a son of Nanda king. *Brihat-katha* also mentions Chandragupta to be the son of

Nanda king but Kshemendra, the author also mentions that Ashoka was born in the Solar Race in the 'Avandānakalpalatā'. Jain tradition recorded in the 'Parisishtaparvan' mentions that Chandragupta was born of the daughter of a peacock-tamer (Mayurposhaka) who lived in an obscure village. The Buddhist traditions as per the Ceylonese text, 'Mahāvanso' mentions him to be born to the queen consort of Moriyanagar when the last king was killed and she took shelter in Pātāliputra and he was reared by a herdsman and a hunter. Ceylonese text 'Mahāvansh Tikā' mentions the repeated attacks of Chandragupta on the Magadh kingdom and their failure and also the lessons in strategy he learnt from a village woman while in flight. It is said that when after the failure of his attack he sought shelter in a cottage in disguise he was given food, a semi-liquid vegetable on a bread and as he started eating the liquid started flowing out of bread. The woman scolding him told him not to behave like Chandragupta by attacking on all sides at once but attack from one side only. He learnt his lesson and won his last battle. About the clan name Maurya some connect him with the 'Moriyas' who were mentioned as a kshatriya clan in Mahāparinibhāna Sutta, where it is said that they were the cosharers of the ashes of the Buddha at his death and that they belonged to Pippalivan, but the location of Pippalivan is not known. The Jains claim that Chandragupta was a Jain and that he renounced his throne and went to South near Mysore along with the Jain monk Bhadra-Bāhu and died on Chandragiri named after him. The symbols on the coins of Mauryas are generally 'hill and crescent' and 'Peacock'.

We may now have a look at the notices taken by the Greeks. Megasthenes came to India as the Ambassador of Greek King of the Babylonian empire which succeeded the Achaemenids and wrote a detailed account of the conditions in India in the time of Chandragupta and his son. Unfortunately most of it is lost. The only surviving fragments of it are those incorporated in the works of other succeeding writers. However, the surviving fragments do not contain any account or even the reference to the origin of the Mauryas and their ascension to power. Among the train of Alexander were a number of people who wrote about Alexander's campaign and its history. The works of all are lost but due to references to them in later writings it is possible to identify a few. First is Nearchus who commanded the fleet while the Greeks returned. His memoirs are now lost but Strabo and Arrian made copious extracts from it. Onesieritus, who was chief pilot of the Nearchus fleet wrote the life of Alexander which is now lost. Aristobulus who accompanied Alexander wrote a history of the wars and it is one of the principal sources used by Arrian in his *Anabasis* and by Plutarch in his life of Alexander. Kleitarchus who also accompanied Alexander also wrote a history of the expedition of Alexander. However, all are now lost. The subsequent histories which were written must have been based on the works of these people and we may be sure that they must be incorporating the events described in the above. We will have to depend, therefore, on these subsequent histories and specially on Plutarch and on Justin who draws on the history of Trogus who in his turn has based it on that of Nearchus. Both Justin and Plutarch record that sometime in 326-25 B.C. Chandragupta met Alexander and probably acquainted him with the conditions in Eastern India. According to Plutarch Chandragupta is reported to have said in later times "Alexander narrowly missed making himself master of the country since its king was hated and despised by his subjects for the weakness of his disposition and meanness of his origin"[3]. We are told by Justin that the tone of Chandragupta gave offence to Alexander who gave orders to kill him. However, he sought safety by a speedy flight[4]. Justin also gives the impression that Chandragupta after his escape from the camp of Alexander went to forest and gathered a body of armed men and attempted to overthrow the government. These are all the references which we possess. Do we have some other facts which may help us in answering our question? Is there some place specially favoured by the Mauryas which may indicate their place of origin? We can not say for certain because no surviving records of the period or the succeeding period mention anything regarding this aspect. What about the inscriptions? Do not their locations indicate something? Pillars inscriptions and rock-edicts are found in all corners and in every place of some importance. However, in one instance we do find some indication of the place being favoured. At Bairāt in Jaipur District of Rajasthan South-West of Delhi we find a rock-edict, a rock inscription of rather a personal nature and fragments of two pillars, Ashokan pillars. What is the rock- edict of a personal nature? It is the Bairāt- Bhābhru rock-edict now in Calcutta Museum in which Ashoka had mentioned the parts of the Buddhist scripture which he liked and in which he had exhorted the Bhikkus residing there to study them and to meditate on them. Why this concentration of four inscriptions, two rock-edicts and two pillars in one place? Is it because it was connected with the original place of the Mauryas or may be it was a religious place? It can be probably either. Bairāt, according to some scholars, is corrupt form of the name Pāriyātra, which was sacred mountain, in fact one of the seven mentioned frequently by the *Purānās*. It was mentioned by the Chinese traveller Huen Tsang also. The Vihar and the monastery there was an important one and probably contained the relics of some important Buddha personage. However, on the other hand it can have some personal connection also. We may remember that the place is mentioned in *Mahābhārata* as the capital of king Virāt of the Matasya and its importance lay precisely in the fact that his daughter gave birth to Parikshit who was a grandson of Arjun and succeeded Yudhister as the Emperor of India. Was this episode inserted in *Mahābhārata* precisely because it could have been a place to which the mother of Chandragupta, the emperor might have belonged? Or probably his father. Otherwise why such an obscure place should find a place in the great epic. Was it a tribute to the Mauryas and also did it reveal their identity? We may have to examine this in detail but meanwhile we may not forget that the place lies in the territory of the Yaudheyas.

If we look at the *Mudrā-Rākashas, Brihat-Katha* and the *Purānās* together we find that a peculiar story was current since the early centuries of the era about the coming to the throne of Chandragupta. The story is full of romance but fails to give any details. In brief it is said that the last Nanda king had among his ministers a brilliant man named Shaktāl. The fickle king once enraged put Shaktāl along with his wife, his children and rest of the family into prison and starved them with a view to killing them all. All perished except Shaktāl who vowed to destroy him and because of that determination survived. Once the king remembering his brilliant mind repented and put him back into favour. However, Shaktāl had not forgotten his family and his vow. He himself could not do anything but once when he was passing through a forest he found a man digging 'kusha', a dry hard grass over a big patch as if determined to destroy even the roots. On enquiry he was told that the grass had pricked his foot and therefore he was determined to destroy even the roots. Seeing the determination of the man and also finding that he was a great scholar, Shaktāl felt that if he could make that man an opponent of the king, his aim might be realised. He also knew that the king had an aversion to ugly persons and that man who was a Brahmin was ugly too. He invited him to a feast given by the king and made him sit on a prominent place. That man known to history was Chāṇakya. What Shaktāl anticipated had come true. The king on seeing Chāṇakya seated on a high pedestal was enraged and asked his people to turn him out. He in turn loosened the hairs on his head and vowed to destroy the king. While looking for a suitable person who could replace the Nanda king he came across Chandragupta who was a bastard of the king by a woman of barber caste Mura and found him suitable for his design. He got the king killed on day of Holi festival when the town was busy in celebrations and installed Chandragupta on the throne. All the nobility and ministers refused to acknowledge Chandragupta and deserted him. Then followed intrigues by Chāṇakya. With his efficient network of spies he got all information about the activities of the dissidents. Using that information and using intrigues coupled with threats and blackmail, he brought all of them to acknowledge Chandragupta. Some of the opponents were destroyed by dubious means. Bringing round of Rākshas, the most important of Nanda's minister to Chandragupta, is the theme of the drama *Mudrā Rākshas* by Vishakhadatt while the subtle intrigues and remorseless conduct are the main elements on the part of

Chāṇakya and simplicity and compassion along with loyalty to friends on the part of Rakshas.

Will the nobility of the Magadh empire accept Chandragupta being a bastard by a low caste woman Murā, howsoever he may belong to royal line, after a patricide? Will the army and the bureaucracy accept him? Will the people of the vast realm accept him without a protest or probably revolt? Will not the local chieftains with their independent armies try to revolt and become independent or even to capture the empire? Will not there be anarchy after such a sudden murder of the king and how was order restored in such a short time? How was he able to secure the allegiance and submission to him of the republican states of the North-Western India who had not submitted and had defied the Achaemenid Empire on the one hand and the Magadhan Empire on the other? To each of the above questions we will have to give an emphatic No. Only a strong force with a generalship of a high order could have secured an empire. When Alexander overthrew the Achaemenid Empire he could do it with a superior force and even when he established that he had an unbeatable force, yet still as the provinces of the Persian Empire refused to acknowledge him he had to undertake expeditions to subjugate them. In a vast empire with a diverse and caste-conscious population Chandragupta could not have been acknowledged as king even though he might have been a bastard son. Empires are not won simply by intrigues and assassinations. He must be having a strong force to achieve his aim, must have been endowed with a generalship of a high order and might have fought many battles. He could not have such a force in the empire itself for his activities must have become known almost immediately, and put down by the still loyal people. Loyalty of the army can be secured by a great leader alone, who has to be a great commander as well. Hence, Chandragupta could not have become a king only by intrigues of Chāṇakya coupled with the assassination of the king. No body says that he was an army commander of the Nandas and as such could not have secured their loyalty. He has to be one with a very strong force, stronger than the Nanda army, a great general and one with unimpeachable ancestory to have won the allegiance of the people.

Who was Chandragupta Maurya then? Let us see what are the accounts of his contemporaries among the Greeks recorded by Plutarch and Justin. We are told that Chandragupta, a mere stipling, met Alexander sometimes in 326-325 B.C. and invited him to attack the emperor Nanda who was "hated and despised by his subjects for the weakness of his disposition and meanness of his origin". Why should Chandragupta go to meet Alexander and invite him to attack Nanda king? More, why should he be admitted to the presence of Alexander? We know from the contemporary accounts that Alexander was intolerant of bold tongue and should be deemed to be haughty and ill-tempered. Moreover, he was a mighty monarch who had just defeated the mighty Achaemenid Emperor of Persia and ruled over an area said to comprise almost the whole of earth. Why should he admit an unknown person to his presence who was neither a king submitting himself to him or a leader of people with strength behind him? Certainly he would not. Only a subordinate king of the Persian Empire who had come to submit himself and his kingdom would be admitted to his presence. A leader of the republican state or of a tribe too would be admitted if he came there to submit to his rule. Would not a leader with a strong force behind him be also admitted to his presence if he had come to offer his help in conquering further territories in India and specially to conquer the Eastern Magadh Empire of whom he had heard so much? Certainly such a person would be admitted to his presence and Alexander would certainly talk to him. To which of those categories Chandragupta belonged? He was certainly not a king. Otherwise that must have been mentioned by the Greeks and later Indian writers. He was not a leader of a republican state or of a republican tribe going there to make submission. Had it been so, he would not have given offence by tone of his speech. It would have been meek and submissive, pleading for mercy. Chandragupta could only belong to the third category, the leader of a strong force or a strong tribe offering help to Alexande: in overthrowing the Nanda king. Probably when Alexander asked him to make submission first, he flatly refused offering only a safe passage and help. That tone must have annoyed Alexander who had his own design of conquering the whole of India and not leaving any part independent. He must have, therefore, ordered his arrest. Chandragupta must have thought of that eventuality and must have already laid his plans to escape which he did. That must have inspired that episode in *Mahābhārat* when Krishna came as ambassador of Pāndavas to the court of Kauravas and when Duryodhan tried to arrest him, he managed to escape. The method of Krishna's escape is not given in *Mahābhārat* and so also the way Chandragupta escaped from the armies of Alexander. Did Chandragupta belong to some republican tribe of North-Western India? Was he its leader? Probably he was. Probably when he saw that of the two empires which they feared, Alexander had defeated and destroyed one, the Achaemenid Empire of Persia, he thought that it would be a good idea to induce Alexander to destroy the other and thus be rid of the twin danger. With that idea he went to Alexander and asked him to destroy the second. He probably found that Alexander had other ideas and that he wanted to rule over them without committing himself to destroy the Nandas. They who had defied the two empires could not bear to submit to a third one and hence probably he refused to submit. Did he notice the Greek army and learn something? He certainly did. He must have noticed the disposition of the Greek army, their method of warfare, the startling innovation in fighting technique which had swept an empire so easily. The innovation of the fighting technique by the Greeks, specially by Alexander's father Phillip who was to lead the army, was almost revolutionary. Formerly the fight between the armies was frontal and in lines facing each other. He introduced a solid phalanx composed of cavalry armed with long lances. The cavalry charge aimed at the centre almost always destroyed the opposing army and got them near the opposing king. Chandragupta must have learnt that technique and must have trained his forces which so easily destroyed the Nandas later.

To which tribe, if any, did he belong? None of the contemporary records mention his tribe or place to which he belonged. Do we not have some other evidence from the long rule of the dynasty which might reveal their origin? Do the coins give some indication? The coins issued by the Mauryas give two pictures, one is a hill and a crescent and the other is a peacock. What does peacock signify? Do we have any other indication of the importance given by the Mauryas to the peacock? On the gates of the Sarnath Stupa we find peacocks shown on high pedestals. Peacocks must have some significance for the Mauryas. We cannot say anything at present about the motif of hill and a crescent on the coins. Does it indicate the home of the Mauryas? Translated from the sign language it means only Chandra for cresent and giri for the hill, together Chandragiri. We are told by the Jain traditions that Chandragupta died on a hill in the South called after him Chandragiri. Does this motif indicate the hill on which Chandragupta died? Or does it indicate in some way the name of Chandragupta? Or does it indicate the original home of the Mauryas? Peacock on the other hand must indicate the tribe or republic to which he belonged? Is not Maurya derived from the word Mayur, the name of peacock in Sanskrit and reduced in local languages as Mor. Peacock was a sacred bird for the Yaudheyas, who, because of their feeling for the peacock, were also sometimes called 'Matta Mayuraks'. They also worshipped Skanda, the Hindu god of war, whose mount was peacock. How did the Mauryas regard Skanda? Do we have any indication of any respect shown by the Mauryas for Skanda? We have. We may recall that Patanjali, the great grammarian, had mentioned in his great work *Mahābhāshya,* that the Mauryas sold the images of Shiv, Skanda, and Vishākha in order to raise money. Shiv is regarded as father of Skanda and Vishākha is but another form of Skanda. Patanjali is said to be a contemporary of Pushyamitra Sung, who succeeded the Mauryas and might have spent his early life during the rule of Mauryas and his reference to Mauryas must be regarded as authentic. They are not mentioned as selling the images of any other god. What light does this symbol of peacock on their coins and their selling the images of Shiv, Skanda and Vishākha, throw on their origin? There can be only one inference and that is that they were Yaudheyas, who worshipped Skanda and regarded his mount peacock as sacred. In fact even today killing of a peacock is regarded as a crime. In this connection the Jain account in their book *Parishishta Parvan* that Chandragupta was the son of the daughter of a 'Mayurposhak' or one who tames or takes care of peacock assumes significance and corroborates that the Mauryas were Yaudheyas. For a people who worship Skanda and regard his mount peacock as sacred, there must be priests who might be conducting the worship of Skanda and also a class of people who must be looking after the peacocks, their feeding and well-being. If Chandragupta was the son of the daughter of a Mayurposhaka, he must be a Yaudheya. We may also recall the Edict of Ashoka in which he had mentioned that he had prohibited the killing of peacock in his kitchen, and where a thousand peacocks were killed daily, he had reduced them to just three. Why that fascination for peacock and Skanda? This points towards only one thing that the family worshipped Skanda and regarded peacock as the symbol of Skanda and sacred and they took pride in the fact. This means only that Chandragupta was a Yaudheya, as Yaudheyas were the only people who worshipped Skanda and regarded peacock as sacred.

If Chandragupta was a Yaudheya, then what about the story in Hindu *Purānās* alluding him to be the son of the Nanda king and supported by the drama *Mudrā-Rākshas*? This appears to be wrong. Had it been so, the Greeks would have referred it and the Buddhist accounts would have mentioned it and called him the son of a king. None had ever alluded it. Hence, the story appears to be incorrect. What connection he might be having with the Moriyas of Pippalivan? Were the Moriyas of Pippalivan and Yaudheyas were the same people? Moriyas of Pippalivan are just mentioned only once and that in *Mahāparinibban Sutta* of the Buddhists in which it is mentioned that when the Buddha died and was cremated, there was a quarrel among the tribes who claimed to be kshatriyas desiring to have his ashes. When it was decided to distribute the ashes among the tribes, the Moriyas too came forward to demand a share claiming themselves as kshatriyas and akin to the Buddha. They were given a share. If the Yaudheyas are to be identified with the Moriyas, then the ashes of the Buddha must have been enshrined somewhere in the Yaudheya territory or near it? Is there a place where the ashes of the Buddha could have been kept, inside or near the Yaudheya area? There is one place in the area where there was a prominent Buddhist monastery and that place is Bairāt in North-Eastern Rajasthan. As we had seen above Bairāt received a special attention of Ashoka. Here were found two rock edicts and two Ashokan pillars. There are two small hills in Bairat, one called Bhimji-ki-Dungari and the other known as Bijak-ki-Pahāri. The rock edicts are found in each. On Bijak-ki-Pahāri was the Buddhist monastery from where the rock edict known as Bairāt-Bhābhru was recovered. As we know it is surmised that Bairāt is the colloquial name of Pāriyātra, which is described as one of the seven sacred mountains of the Hindus mentioned in the *Purānās* as 'Kul- parvats'. Bairat was also noted by the Chinese pilgrim Huen Tsang and mentioned in his travels. Which of the two hills is the mountain Pāriyātra? We are not in a position to say. It can be either. The mountain Pāriyātra must have been sacred to all the tribes living in the vicinity. If the Moriyas received the ashes of the Buddha and are suspected to be the Yaudheyas, then where they would keep the ashes. Naturally they would keep and enshrine in the mountain Pāriyātra or in its vicinity. What is the evidence that the ashes of the Buddha were kept in Bairāt? The places where the ashes of the Buddha were kept are nowhere mentioned. We are only informed that they were buried at many places and monasteries sprang up in those places. At Bairāt too excavations were conducted in the fourth decade of this century by Dayaram Sahni, one of the excavators of the Indus Valley Civilisation. He found that on this small hill of Bijak-ki-Pahāri there was a Buddhist monastery. On top of the hill is a small tank with a giant circular rock over it, raised on small pillars. This rock is now broken into two. A little below this tank on one side of the hill is a small platform and further below this small platform is a big circular plain which is facing the platform and the small tank above. On this plain are long circular benches where monks used to sit facing the platform. On all sides of the hill were small rooms where monks used to live. When Dayaram Sahni excavated the platform he found that it was already dug before and pilfered. When enquiries were made from local people he was informed that some years ago the platform was dug by a local official and a casket made of gold was dug out and that official took it away. The contents were probably thrown and the gold used in ornaments. Further enquiries elicited no further information.[5] What was in that casket before which the Buddhist monks meditated? The casket must have contained the relics of some great personage of the religion of the Buddha. Were they of the Buddha himself? They may be but in the absence of any further confirmation we are not in a position to say anything definitely. But we may keep in mind that the rock-edict at the gate is the only rock-edict in which Ashoka gave out his personal view of the Buddhist religion, named those portions of the Buddha scriptures which he personally liked and enjoined the monks to specially study them and meditate on them. It was also mentioned by Ashoka in another Edict that he lived as a lay person in one of the monasteries for one year. Was this the place where he lived? We should regard it as a possibility that the ashes of the Buddha might have been enshrined here. We do not know where Pippalivan was for the local name of the area does not correspond in any way even remotely with Pippalivan. Yet still if the ashes of the Buddha were enshrined here, then it is a possibility that the Moriyas of Pippalivan and the Yaudheyas were the same people and Maurya might have been only a Sanskrit adaptation of the name Moriya. We may also note a very interesting thing about this monastery and that is its architectural pattern which has been copied all over India. If we look at the older temples and even modern ones designed after them we will find that they are a copy of this portion of this monastery. In the temples we find that there is a mandap or a place where people sit or stand to worship. Before them on a raised platform is the idol or a symbol of the deity like a linga or stone and on the top is a pot called Kalash covered by a betel leaf and a coconut. This corresponds with the circular plain of the monastery where monks sat in front of the raised platform containing the ashes of the Buddha or an important personage of Buddhist religion, and on the top is the tank containing water covered by a circular rock. Was this copy of the design of this monastery deliberate or just coincidence? We may not forget that at this stage Buddhism, Jainism or Hinduism were not regarded as separate religions. There was only one religion and people were free to follow the teachings of any great man and the Buddha was respected as a great man, revered by all. If the pattern is adopted for the temples from that particular monastery, then we may just wonder at the great importance given to that monastery by the people and we are left just to wonder at the reason of its uniqueness.

Why did Chandragupta, even if he was a Yaudheya, go and meet Alexander? How could he, a mere stripling as the Greek writers call him, gain admittance into Alexander's presence? What authority, if any did he carry with him to negotiate with Alexander? In whose behalf he was negotiating with Alexander? In the absence of any reference to the answer to these questions in the accounts of his contemporaries or in later traditions we can but reconstruct what must have happened. As we do not get any reference to his father, it appears that he was brought up by his maternal grandfather who was a keeper of peacock. We do not know what position he occupied in the community but it appears that it must have been a prestigious one. He at least gave Chandragupta a very good education. In view of the tradition of a very close relationship of Chandragupta with Chāṇakya in founding of the Empire and even afterwards in administering India, it is possible that one of his teachers might have been Chāṇakya himself. Those were extraordinary times. In ordinary times the seniormost person would in natural course be the executive head or what was called Senāpati and the advisers or councillors would be senior persons and the voice of the young was not likely to matter much. But in extraordinary times age loses its importance. What assumes importance is the man with novel ideas, man of ability who may be a man of destiny. We had seen above that the republican states of the region were threatened by Empires from both sides. As far as living memory went they were threatened and they had fought both, though not able to defeat them decisively. They now heard with delight that another oppressed people from Ionia whom later Indian literature termed as Yavans had not only attacked the Achaemenid Empire in Iran but had destroyed it and had even captured its capital. A surge of sympathy must have filled them. Then they heard that the Ionian army led by a young man, one called Alexander, had entered India to destroy what they thought the garrisons of the old empire. They might have admired their boldness and thoroughness. They might have thought that enemy of their enemy must be their friend, a precept later embodied in *Arthashāstra,* a treatise on polity by Chāṇakya. The simple people as they were they thought that if Alexander could be persuaded to join his forces with them they might destroy the other empire which menaced them, *i.e.,* the Magadh Empire of the Nandas. They knew its weakness but required some help as they felt that they alone could not accomplish that feat. It is possible that menaced by the two empires they always had consultations among the leaders of all the republican states and might have even formed a consultative council or even a confederacy. We get some indications from the Greek writers that when Alexander was returning from India, he had to fight a confederacy of the republican tribes. This was just three years after he entered India. So the formation of that confederacy must have been there or might have been formed at that time. For inviting Alexander they required one who might be able to talk to him in his language, which was an alien tongue, must be educated, must be able to guage the strength of the army, the method of warfare with which Alexander had destroyed the mighty Iranians, and must be able to deal with the situation which might arise unexpectedly. Such a man they found in Chandragupta. It is possible that Chāṇakya might have played a part in the selection of Chandragupta and who must have known of his extraordinary ability. So Chandragupta went to the camp of Alexander accompanied probably with some other men and possibly Chāṇakya who might have remained in the background to advise him if need be. As representative of the Yaudheyas or of the confederacy he must have gained a ready entry into the presence of Alexander and must have been amused to find the leader of the Ionians a few years elder to him. That must have given thought to him and to the other representatives of the republican tribes including his own who had accompanied him. Alexander too must have been surprised to find that young man a few years junior to him talking as an equal. He who must have thought that he had come to him to offer submission, found that instead of submission he was asking him help as an equal partner in ousting the Magadh king. Chandragupta must have soon realised that Alexander had come to conquer India, to destroy their power and to rule over them and not to help them in maintaining their independence and was a more dangerous adversary than the Achaemenid emperors. He might have told Alexander with spirit that if he thought that he could subdue them, he was mistaken and that he would be fought at every place. As the Greek writers mention that Alexander was annoyed at the tone of Chandragupta, it was possible that he might have asked him to stay and think it over and must have instructed his staff to kill Chandragupta if he did not submit. Chandragupta, however, made his escape. We do not know how. However, he must have noticed the Greek army, their arms, their method of warfare, specially the formation of phalanx, their main method of war and the Greek organisation. He must have also thought of countering the impending Greek invasion, the way to counter the attack of the phalanx and also of the means by which the Greeks could have been defeated. On return he must have explained it to the elders of his tribe and the members of the confederacy. He must have explained the intentions of Alexander, which must have alarmed the elders of the tribe. But Chandragupta must have explained that there was no need of despondency, that they must be more firmly united, that there were ways in which Alexander could be prevented to advance and that he could be defeated and must have explained the ways in which if they trained their armies that could be achieved. Encouraged and feeling confident and at the same time impressed by his wisdom and knowledge they must have elected him as their new chief designated as Senāpati. He must have also been elected as the chief of the confederacy as probably Yaudheyas were the pre-eminent among them. The representatives of other tribes must have been impressed by him too. We find from the Bijaygarh inscription near Bharatpur dated just about two hundred years after that their chief was appointed to the post by Yaudheya gana and given the title of Mahāraj-Senāpati. It appears that the Chief of the Yaudheyas bore the title of Senāpati and probably when he was appointed the Chief of the confederacy he might have been given the title of Mahāraj-Senāpati so that he might treat on equal footing other monarchies and might get the allegiance of people liberated from the empires. Was Chandragupta the first Mahāraj-Senāpati? Probably he was.

Chandragupta on becoming the chief of the Yaudheyas and the head of the confederacy which probably included the Mālava republic, the Arjunayans, the Agrasenis or Agglasians etc., set with zeal to organise them to oppose Alexander and his army. He trained the army probably on the pattern of the army of Alexander with innovations of his own including the use of elephants and the archers which Alexander lacked. When Alexander reached the banks of the Jhelum, he was ready to fight. Probably information was passed on to Puru on the impending attack of Alexander. Committing the sin of repetition, it will be pertinent to say that even according to the historians accompanying Alexander the last battle which Alexander fought while advancing into India was at Jhelum. Afterwards according to them there were a few minor skirmishes and on the banks of the Beās not far from Jhelum, his army refused to advance further due to the fear of the might of Nandas. Can this be true when the Nandas were far away? This cannot be true and the fear which might have made the army refuse to go further must have been the strength of the confederacy led by Chandragupta and it might not have been the banks of the Beās but the banks of the Jhelum. We do not know whether Puru or Porus was the name of a king or the name of a tribe. We know from the *Vedas* and other books that there was a tribe of the name of Puru in olden times. Can this be the same tribe? It can be. For the Greek historians also refer to another Porus, a younger one. We also do not know if it was an advance guard of the confederacy which opposed Alexander or Porus or Puru themselves. Whatever it might be there was a bitter fight, something like it was not fought by the Greeks at all. Whether they were victorious or the battle was drawn neither side gaining victory, the advance of Alexander was stopped and he decided to withdraw from India by river down to the ocean and from there to Babylon via the Persian Gulf. Even on his return journey he was constantly harassed by attacks by people of different republican tribes. That must have been the work of Chandragupta who thus ensured that for a long time to come no Greek forces would dare to attack India. It was during that return voyage that, we are informed by Greek writers, that they had come to know of a confederacy of the tribes. The Mālava and Sibi soldiers who fought them must have been the part of the confederacy forces deployed against the Greeks. But at the same time that could have been a myth created by the Greek writers to glorify Alexander. Whatever it might be Alexander's attack against India was reduced merely to an adventure and that too only a minor raid not found worth mentioning by the writers of the age and of the ages succeeding it. We do not find even allusions to it in the *Purānās,* in Buddhist accounts, in Jain accounts, in Patanjali's works or in that of other writers.

What Chandragupta did after Alexander's exit from India? Chandragupta knew that Alexander would not sit back calmly but would again attack India with a bigger force. He must have strengthened the army. He must have made arms matching those of the Greeks along with those required after his own innovations and must have been busy training his army. They must have learned much after the skirmishes with them and included the lessons learnt. Then he must have heard after about a year that Alexander had died and that there was a quarrel among his generals about the succession and that the Empire was going to be divided among them. He would have realised that the Greek invasion was put off for a long time to come. Now he thought that it was a time to remove the danger from the other empire from the East, whose weakness he knew so well. So was his expedition towards Magadh and Patliputra. Was the Magadh Empire defeated in the first attack by the forces led by Chandragupta? According to Ceylonese chronicles Chandragupta made a number of attacks and in them he was worsted. It is also said, as mentioned earlier, that once after a rout he took refuge in the cottage of an old woman who offered him food probably rice on a leaf. Chandragupta started eating from middle and thus liquid rice soup started spilling in all directions. The old woman scolded him giving him the example of himself that just as Chandragupta was spoiling his wars by attacking directly in the middle he was allowing the food to spill by eating from the middle. Chandragupta, according to the chronicler, learnt his lesson and moved towards the Magadh capital conquering the territory as he moved forward. The *Milind Panha,* the book composed in Northern India, mentions that Chandragupta had a fight with the Magadhan forces led by Bhaddasal and there was a terrible slaughter of the Magadhan army by him. Both could be true but we are not apt to believe the Ceylonese chronicles not only because they were written in Ceylon which could only mention myths but also because if we believe in it the final defeat of Nanḍa king would have taken a number of years even decades when we find that he overthrew Nanda within a few years of Alexander's withdrawal. According to some it may be only a couple of years. It appears that with his newly organised forces on the pattern of the Greek army and the new technique of the phalanx and a cavalry charge it was a small matter to defeat the Nanda army. So he must have struck directly at the capital Pātliputra of course marching all the way. He must have been opposed by the Nanda army which must have been no match for him. There must have been not a fight but a slaughter. And Nandas were dumped into history.

Chandragupta was crowned king after the overthrow of the Nandas. But was he accepted as such by the republican states of the North-West India? He must have been for he was already recognised as the executive head of the republican states in the confederacy and those who were not in the confederacy must have speedily done that for fear of reprisals and losing the loaves of office. The posts in the empire must have been liberally given to his partners. Here the principal role must have been of Chānakya. According to the tradition he was the principal organiser of the polity of the empire and brought it to a sound basis, so sound that it endured for 150 years. We already have a glimpse of his work in the drama *Mudrā-Rākshas* by Vishākhdatt. Though it is a late drama, yet there must have been an enduring tradition which it brings forth. According to the drama after the defeat of the Nanda king a large number of officials loyal to him refused to serve under Chandragupta and even were determined to oust him. It was necessary that they should be brought back to work for the new empire so that the business of government might not suffer and continue smoothly as the empire without the support of the leaders of Magadh and of Eastern India would not have lasted. Chāṇakya set about to bring them into the service of Chandragupta and to bring about a lasting alliance. By stratagem, by manoeuvre, by creating such situations that they had to submit he brought all the old guards to owe allegiance to Chandragupta and to work for the new empire. It is possible that lure of office and riches musts have also played their part in the attempt. We are told in the drama of his efforts to specially entice the able minister of Nanda, Rākshas to his fold and he succeeded. It must have been the work of Chāṇakya to integrate the republics too into the empire. This too he must have done by stratagem and lure of important offices as well as riches to the leaders of different republican states. So India, at least the Northern India from the Indus to Bengal, was integrated into one polity. We do not know the extent of Chandragupta's Empire into the South. However, Gujarat and Saurashtra appeared to be within his domain. We find in the Girnar inscription of Rudradāman (150 A.D.) the reference to construction of lake Sudarshan by the Rāshtriya Vaisya Pushyagupta in the reign of Maurya Chandragupta. We do not know of the other extent of the empire in the South, whether it was conquered or simply submitted to Chandragupta or to Bindusār, his son for by the time of Ashoka they were part of the empire except the extreme South. If we go by the Ashokan inscriptions, the empire at least in his time was stretched upto parts of modern Karnataka and Andhra Pradesh. The lasting contribution of Chāṇakya appears to be the political structure and the rule of law firmly established which sustained the empire and discouraged any mutiny or rebellion for a hundred years. This must have been backed by the generalship of Chandragupta and the strong army. This must have been largely composed of the victorious members of the confederacy and must have left the rank and file contented.

Had the threat from the West lessened with the consolidation of Northern India into one state? It had not. Chandragupta must have been watching the situation in Iran and the Greek Empire. He must have known that with the death of Alexander, the empire which he built was partitioned among his generals and that the whole of Western Asia had fallen to the lot of Seleucus, one of his able generals and whom Chandragupta must have met when he had visited the camp of Alexander. He must have been watching the activities of Seleucus while consolidating the empire and his forces. Seleucus too must have been surprised at the success of a boy whom he had not thought of much and probably did not think much later. He must be thinking of the conquest of India which even Alexander could not achieve. He must be preparing for it while consolidating his position and his empire. When both sides were preparing for war, it could not be delayed. The war, according to Greek chronicles, was fought in 305 B.C. while it is not even referred to in Indian chronicles or literature. Who took the initiative in attack? We do not know of any reference to it in the surviving Indian literature. According to the Greek writer Appian[6] Seleucus crossed the Indus where he was met by Chandragupta leading his troops in person. According to him the fight went on "until they (*i.e.*, the Syrian and the Indian kings) came to an understanding with each other and contracted a marriage relationship". The understanding was that Seleucus would cede large tracts of territory and give a daughter in marriage while Chandragupta gave 500 elephants. It is fairly obvious that Seleucus lost and ceded the whole of his Indian possessions and the whole of modern Afghanistan and some portions of the Iranian territory. Strabo in his Geography[7] mentions that "the Indians held much of Ariana having received it from the Macedonians". Large portions of the territory beyond Afghanistan seemed to have been given to Chandragupta. Thus fortified the Mauryan Empire stretched from beyond Afghanistan to Bengal and probably Assam in the East. It also probably included the Bactria and Khotan in the area beyond Afghanistan.

The Empire with its victory over Seleucus acquired prestige considerably and became supreme in India. Its neighbours, the kings of the Western Asia, held it in high esteem and never did they venture against India. They had friendly relations with Bindusar and Ashoka, successors to Chandragupta. Their ambassadors resided in their courts, the most famous was Magasthenes.

Tradition assigns the rule of Chandragupta to only 24 years and that of his son Bindusar to 25 years according to *Purānās* and 27 and 28 years according to the Burmese and the Ceylonese chroniclers. Ashoka ascended the throne in about 269 B.C. This implies that Chandragupta left the throne sometimes about 301 B.C. or a couple of years just after. When we find from the Greek historians that he was a mere stripling when he met Alexander in 326 B.C. he must not be even 50 years of age when he ceased to rule. How his rule came to an end? We have no knowledge about it and this is a question which will not be satisfactorily answered. Whether he died or whether he abdicated? This too is not certain. In normal course it will be assumed that he died but the Jain work *Parisishtaparvan*[8] affirms that he was converted as a Jain towards the end of his rule and when a famine continued over Magadh for twelve years he abdicated in favour of a son named Singhsena and retired to Sravana-Belgolā in Mysore with saint Bhadrabāhu. There he starved himself to death (*Parisishtaparvan* VIII 444). He is said to have died on a hill named after him as Chandragiri. Was the name Chandragiri adopted from the sign of a hill and crescent found in the Mauryan coins? It is just possible that it may be so. Surely the Mauryan rulers will not adopt the symbol in memory of Chandragupta dying on a hill. It must have been the symbol of something else, something sacred. Similarly could a person who had devoted his life to building of an empire, setting up an administrative system, dedicated to the good of the empire he created, would run away after a famine leaving his people to take care of themselves. Moreover, since the Jain story is written after a very long time, so it appears to be less credible than even the Ceylonese chronicles. The story is not believable, specially when none else had referred to it. It appears that after an extremely busy and hectic life involving extreme exertions Chandragupta's health had given way. He probably died and was succeeded by his son Bindusār or Amitraghāt as the Greeks called him. There is no mention of Singhsena alluded to by the Jain book *Parisishtaparvan* which too makes the story incredible.

Chandragupta was the most outstanding figure India had ever known. He removed a corrupt government in Magadh giving it a sound administration and uniting whole of at least Northern India, if not Central and Southern India, too and removed the threat of Greeks from Iran for ever. He gave a new administration based on the appropriate polity with greater centralised control. The administration was so sound and efficient and army so strong that the government established by him endured for more than a hundred years without any external attack or internal rebellion leaving his successors to devote themselves to the well-being of the people, both material and spiritual. And they did with his grandson Ashoka leaving a name as the most benevolent monarch in the annals of the world. Only two other emperors in India could achieve similar to him, Samudragupta and Harsh, but while the former left a legacy and a dynasty which also lasted for a similar period, empire founded by Harsh disintegrated after his death. The creation of a sound administration almost from scratch, in large part of which it was not existent at all, which could be utilised to the good of the people was the greatest achievement of Chandragupta. Equally important was his removal of internal dissensions and squabbles among the people, uniting them and giving them a national identity. Chandragupta and his deeds and achievements had not received as much attention from historians as he deserved.

So Bindusar ascended the throne sometime after 300 B.C. What were his achievements? We simply do not know. There is no reference found about his rule anywhere. The Greek Ambassador, Megasthenes who was accredited to his court could have thrown a flood of light on him. But unfortunately the surviving fragments of his work do not have any reference to him. We are not aware if he added to the dominion of the

Empire left by Chandragupta or made any innovations to the administration, nor whether he had to face any opposition or rebellion. The only assumption can be that he maintained the Empire intact and the administrative structure as vigorous as it was. Probably he made the administration responsive to the public good, something which under his son and successor Ashoka was converted into a benevolent administration. With the kings of West Asia, it appears, that he was on good terms. We find from the Greek references that ambassadors from the courts of Greek kings of Syria and Egypt came to the court of Bindusār referred by the Greeks as Amitraghāt, mentioned as Amitrochades or Allitrochades. There is a story mentioned by Athenaeus, a third century writer, on the authority of Hegesander, that Amitraghāt wrote to Antiochus (I of Syria) asking him to buy and send him sweet wine, dried fig and a sophist. The Syrian king replied that he would send him figs and wine but the laws forbade the sophist to be sold. We do not know how much credibility is to be placed in this story. It only indicates that he had good relations with the Greeks and had some curiosity on ethical and religious questions. The fact that the Greek kings respected him indicates also that they were impressed with the might shown by Chandragupta and that they still realised that the army of Bindusār was not to be trifled with.

Ashoka

Ashoka, a most complex personality, succeeded Bindusār as the Emperor. His was a complex personality sensitive to the people, to the trends of the society, to the various events which were happening either due to the changing society or due to some steps he had taken. By a peculiar chance it was the times when the society was changing, it was in a flux. The certain measures he had taken had their impact on the changing society and these changes sensitive as he was to them made him take further measures which in their turn had their influence on the society. This interaction between Ashoka and the people during his long rule so moulded the people and their thinking that the society which emerged was entirely different from what we found at the beginning of the career of his grandfather, Chandragupta Maurya. The society which emerged was certainly highly developed and energised in every respect and had its fixture which remained for the next centuries. Ashoka himself was a different personality. This interaction caused such contradiction in his personality which is notable and cannot otherwise be explained. Every action of his was contradictory. At one time we find him very brutal who mercilessly killed people, attacked a weak people of Kalinga, killing in his own admission a hundred thousand people and deporting a hundred and fifty thousand people to distant lands and on the other regretting his action and subsequently banning the killing of small animals and even insects. He became a follower of the Buddha, one of whose creeds was that that they neither affirmed nor denied the existence of God but he believed in his family deity Skanda and got built innumerable images of Skanda, Vishākha (a form of Skanda) and Shiv and induced people all over India to purchase them and thus installed Shiv as a universal god. He was generous to every religion giving grants to the followers of the Buddha, to the followers of the Jain Tirthankar Mahāvir, to the followers of Jain Tirthankar Pārshwanāth, to the Parivrājaks and to the Brahmins but in the Buddhist religion he became a bigot; he got a creed for the followers prescribed and anybody transgressing it was expelled from the Buddhist Sangha or organisation. This consolidation and enforcement of a particular creed not only made Buddhism a distinct religion from Hinduism but sowed the seed for its future splits giving birth to various sects like the Mahāyān, Hinyān or Vajrayān. It was this action of Ashoka which, instead of making people follow the precepts of any religious person they liked within the folds of a single religion, brought into existence different religions and subsequent religious conflicts in India, conflicts between Buddhism and Hinduism, in the Hinduism among the followers of different gods and among the different sects of Buddhism. All these took place because of his complex nature and because of his interaction with the changing society, changes accelerated by a century of Mauryan peace.

The information about Ashoka is, as was usual with his predecessors, very meagre. There are 14 rock Edicts engraved

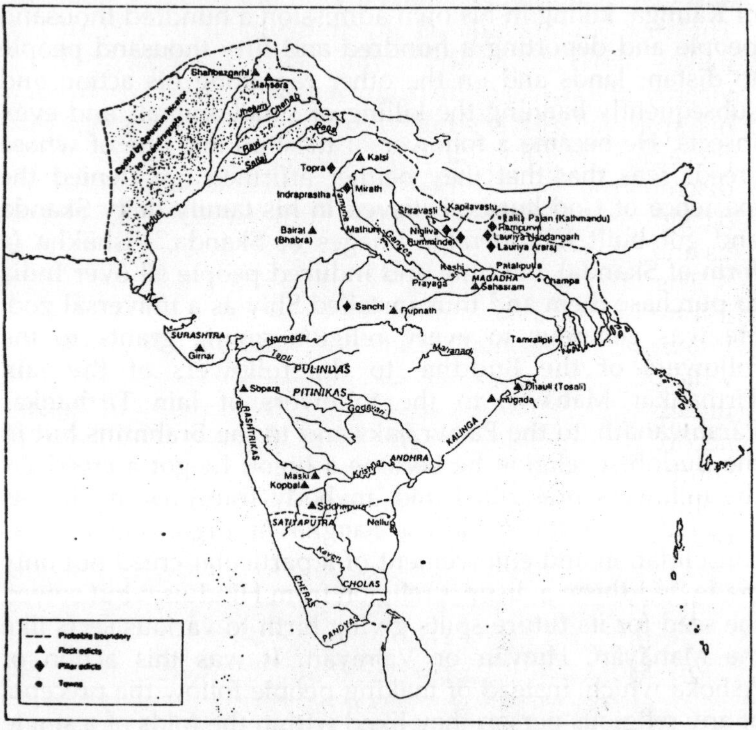

Map 5: Ashoka's Empire and the Places where his Edicts were found.
Source : Based on C.D. Davies. A Historical Atlas of the Indian Peninsual, (Oxford, 1965) p. 13

on the rocks in various parts of the country, all the Edicts one after the other and pillar inscriptions similarly engraved in all the parts of the country. They usually do not mention any name and for long it was uncertain that they were inscribed by Ashoka. Only one Edict at Maski mentions name of Ashoka. There are the Pali chronicles, Ceylon Dipvansa and Mahāvansa of the 4th and 5th centuries A.D. and Avadāns, the Buddhist chronicles, which glorify the Buddhist religion and give the account which are highly coloured and biased. The historical details as given by them vary. Mahāvansa makes him viceroy at Ujjayini, while Avadāns makes him viceroy at Taksilā. Similarly one makes Tissā Mogāliputra as his spiritual guide while the other makes Upgupta as his preceptor. Nothing definite can be said in view of such discrepancies but we may look at some of the details in the background of political, social and religious affairs known to us and try to find out the events which must have happened.

The facts about the life of Ashoka and his rule as can be inferred from his inscriptions are very meagre, but whatever little information that we get is very important as something which actually happened and is not a hearsay and help us in understanding his life and rule. The inscriptions are dated according to the year of coronation, something which continued down the ages upto at least the 6th century A.D. Following are the inscriptions so far discovered as per the order according to the year of the coronation, issued by him:

1. Two Barābar cave inscriptions recording gifts of caves to Ājivaks in the twelfth year.
2. Minor Rock Edicts found in slightly different versions at Bairāt (Jaipur), Sahasrām (Bihar), Rupnāth (M.P.) in Northern India; Maski, Pālkigundu, Gāvīmath, Brahmagiri, Siddāpura, Jatinga Rāmeshwara and Yerraguḍi (Kurnool district) in the South, issued in the 13th year.
3. Calcutta-Bairat (Jaipur) Edict addressed to the Buddhist Sangh in the 13th year.
4. The Fourteen Rock Edicts found at seven places at Girnar, Kalsi, Shabhāzgarhi, Mānsehrā, Dhauli, Jaugada and Yerragudi. A small fragment of eighth

rock Edict was found in Sopāra and others in Laghman. These were issued about the fourteenth year.

5. The two Kalinga Edicts at Dhauli and Jaugada meant only for Kalinga and taking the place of the eleventh to the thirteenth Edicts in other collections and issued either along with others or soon after.
6. The third Barābar cave inscription in the nineteenth year.
7. The Rummindeī and Nigālī pillar inscriptions in the twentieth year.
8. The Seven Pillar Edicts found in six places, Delhi-Mirath, Lauriya-Arārāj, Lauriya Nandangarh, Rampurvā, Allahabad-Kosam and Delhi Topra. The first six contain only the first six Edicts. The sixth one at Allahabad-Kosam has in addition two short inscriptions 'Queen's edict' and 'Kausāmbī Edict' on Sanghabheda. The seventh Edict, the longest is found on the seventh pillar at Delhi-Topra along with others. They were issued in the 26th and 27th year.
9. The minor Pillar Edict at Sānchī and Sārnāth issued towards the end of his reign.

Thus there are thirty-three inscriptions of varying length and importance in the language being Māgdhī and the script Brahmi except in Shābazgarhī and Mansehrā which are in Kharosthī and at the end of the Mysore inscriptions the word lipikarena is in Kharosthī. The important historical references are the Kalinga war, his conversion to the doctrine of the Buddha, his taking care of his brothers and their families, reference to the Queen Kaluvāki and son Tivar, the names of some contemporary kings in the Western Asia and above all a mysterious number 256 mentioned at the end of the first Minor Rock inscription without any context and whose exact significance is not known. On the basis of these references in the Edicts and inscriptions which are authentic ones and the Buddhist records, the *Purānās* and the Ceylonese chronicles let us try to delineate the life of Ashoka and the history of his rule. Contradictory though much of it is yet in the background of political and religious trends some concrete picture may emerge.

Purānās call him Ashokavardhan while the Buddhist

records mention him as Ashoka. In the Edicts the name given is usually as 'devānampiya piyadasi lājā', except in the Maskī record where he is called 'devānāmpiyas Ashokas' and in the Calcutta-Bairāt Edict where he calls himself 'Piyadasi lājā māgadhe'. Are we justified in regarding Ashoka as the author of all the inscriptions on the basis of a single mention of his name in the Maski records? When we look at the mention of the contemporary kings and the support in the legends in the Buddhist and Ceylonese chronicles to the main events which are also found in the inscriptions we are justified in regarding his name as Ashoka.

Not much is known of the birth and early life of Ashoka. The only tradition recorded is by the Divyāvadān and Ashokavadān supposed to be written in the 1st century A.D. According to the above his mother was a beautiful daughter of a Brahim from Champā and was married to Bindusār. According to one version her name was Janpadakalyāni and according to another her name was Subhadrangī. The other queens alarmed at her beauty intrigued against her and managed to keep her out of sight of her husband. Ultimately undertaking to do some menial work for him which she did to perfection and winning his confidence she confided to him that she was his wife. Bindusār on getting it confirmed restored her to her status and she bore him two sons Ashoka and Vitāshoka (Vigatashoka). Can we believe in the above story? There is no evidence regarding veracity of this story. Can the kings or even emperors in those remote early times have such a large harem full of queens that they may not even recognise them? If we look at the literature of those times still existing among them *Ramāyān* and *Mahābhārat* we find that the number of queens were very few not exceeding three and the ideal stressed was to have only one queen. In the circumstances such a large number of queens in the household of Bindusār that he may not recognise one raises doubt. In addition the name of the lady is said to be Janpadakalyāni, a strange one indeed. What do we understand by the name Janpadakalyāni? The meaning of the word is that the lady who does good to the Janpada. Janpada, as we know, were the so called republics or oligarchies such as, Vaishāli, Malla, Videha, Shākya, Mālava, Yaudheya *et al.*

We know from tradition recorded later that the most eligible and beautiful girl among the tribe was elected by the Rājās or the electors or members of the oligarchy as Janpadakalyāni. Was the mother of Ashoka the Janpadakalyāni of some republic? Was she Janpadakalyāni of Yaudheya republic? The name gives us the indication that she was. However, it is not possible to say if she really belonged to the Yaudheya republic. But if she was, then it is not difficult to understand the succession of Ashoka to the throne even if he was a much younger son. We should not exclude the possibility of her being a Yaudheya, the king's tribe and of her being Janpadakalyāni of the Yaudheya republic duly elected by the tribe to that position. And if that was so, Bindusār could not have ignored her and we would be justified in doubting the story as in any way based on facts. Even if she was not a Yadhueya, the story in itself was incredible, on the ground that a man whatever he might be could not fail to recognise his own wife. Her beauty being acknowledged by Divyāvadān and Ashokavādan, the mention of her name as Janpadakalyāni which was actually a designation indicated that she was not the daughter of a Brahmin from Champā but belonged to the King's own tribe and that she was duly elected as Janpadakalyāni of the Yaudheya republic by the tribe itself and as such married to the Emperor. Her own name could have been Subhadrāngī.

Tradition associates Ashoka with the viceroyalty at different places. From his inscriptions (Separate Rock Edict) it appears that the viceroyalty of Taxilā and Ujjain were held by the princes of the royal family. It might be true of the period under his father Bindusār. According to Mahāvansa he was viceroy of Ujjayani and according to Avadān, of Taxilā. Which of them is the fact? There should not be any dispute for both can be true and Ashoka might have been Viceroy of both Ujjayanī and Taxila by turn. Ashoka had a long apprenticeship under his father as Viceroy and could have gone to various places in that capacity or even in any other capacity. This can be seen from the age of his son Mahindra who according to Dipvansa[9] was twenty years of age in the sixth year after the coronation of Ashoka and taking aside the period of four years which took in preparation for his coronation Mahindra must have been born at least ten years before the accession of Ashoka. As Mahindra was born when Ashoka was Viceroy of Ujjayanī he served as Viceroy for at least a period of ten years which must have included both the places. Who was Mahindra and what we know about him? Mahindra along with Sanghamitrā were the son and daughter of Ashoka. It is said that when Ashoka on his way to Ujjayanī to take over as Viceroy stopped as Vidishā he met Devi, the daughter of a merchant, falling in love with her he married her and had a son and daughter, Mahindra and Sanghmitrā. Mahindra and Sanghmitrā when they grew up took to the religion of the Buddha, renounced the world and went to Ceylon (now Sri Lanka), Sanghmitrā carrying a branch of the Bodhi tree which they planted there. They are celebrated as the persons who converted Ceylon to Buddhism and are mentioned both in Mahāvansa and Divyāvadān.[10] However, Hiuen Tsang states that Mahindra was a brother and not son of Ashoka. Why was it that Mahindra had not succeeded Ashoka as the king and during his life time was not asked to take the duties of administration either as viceroy or in other capacity? We should not lose sight of the fact that the reign of the Mauryas was the rule of the Yaudheya clan in alliance with other republican clans like the Mālavas and only the son of a Yaudheya woman as queen could have succeeded to the throne. That must have been known to Ashoka and also might have been made plain to him before he married their mother. Probably Mahindra and his mother knew that. This was probably the reason that Mahindra could not have been brought into the administration and given duties. Ashoka and Mahindra both must be knowing that if Mahindra had taken up the duties in the administration of the Empire even if he was not ambitious he was likely to lose his life at the hands of the person who would have succeeded Ashoka even if he might have been his brother. Nobody would like to let a person remain alive who might be a danger to him. Both Ashoka and his wife who was not a Yaudheya woman but the daughter of a merchant of Vidisha probably decided that the best and safer course for Mahindra would be to become a Buddhist monk and if possible leave India. So Mahindra renounced the world, became a Bauddha

Bikkhu, went to Sri Lankā (Ceylon) and there preached Buddhism. His sister Sanghmitrā accompanied him and both became celebrities as the king's children who renounced the world for the sake of religion.

After the death of Bindusār Ashoka succeeded to the throne. Was it a smooth succession? What the evidence says however slender it may be? There are different statements in the Ceylonese chronicles and in Divyāvadān and within the Ceylonese chronicles too there are different versions. One version is that Ashoka killed ninety nine of his brothers born of different mothers before he could become emperor[11] and the other is that he killed his elder brother after his father's death and became sovereign. According to Divyāvadān and Ashokāvadān Bindusār had 500 ministers and they decided earlier that Ashoka and not his elder brother Sushim should succeed. The reason as indicated was that Sushim was not respectful even towards venerable ministers and was arrogant and playful. Having decided on Ashoka they began manipulating his succession. When the king wanted to send Ashoka to distant Taxila, they persuaded him to stay. When nearing his deathbed Bindusar wanted to call Sushim who was in Taxilā, they did not allow the message to be sent and when Bindusār believing Sushim to be in the capital called him to be present before him so that he might annoint him himself, they presented Ashoka instead and Bindusar getting enraged died. The ministers immediately enthroned him and proclaimed him emperor. The one fact which emerges from these conflicting versions is that the succession was not undisputed and unchallenged and that Ashoka was not the eldest one and that he killed some of his brothers. Why Ashoka, a younger son succeeded Bindusar? How he got the full support of the army and administration without which he could not have succeeded? Who were the 500 ministers who decided that he should be the emperor? Did they have the authority to overturn the succession even against the wishes of the emperor? Should we not have a look at the political and social background of the regime to find an answer to the above questions? We have seen above that it were the Yaudheyas who in alliance with other republican tribes Mālavas and others had seized the Government of

Magadh and built an empire overmastering the whole of Northern India. The army must have been totally manned by Yaudheyas and their republican allies. For administration too Chandragupta Maurya must have drafted the Yaudheya nobility mainly the Rajas and must have appointed them to important posts equivalent to ministers. Yaudheyas must have been keen to see that the government did not slip out of their hands. They must have seen that the successor was always a Yaudheya and must have kept the selection in their hands. For confirmation we should look at the Bijoygarh inscription of the Yaudheyas belonging to the 2nd century B.C., a period not far from the time of Ashoka himself. In the inscription they proudly claimed that their chief the Mahārāj-Senāpati was appointed to the post by the Yaudheya-gana (Yaudheya-gana-puraskṛta). So it is they who elect or appoint their Mahārāj or king. Chandragupta in his own life time saw that his son Bindusar was selected as his successor. However, Burmese legends mention that the mother of Bindusar was of Mauryan lineage. Probably he was an only son. But with Bindusar the things were different. He married a number of women from different places and different mothers and the son of the Yaudheya Janpadkalyanī was a younger son. Bindusār wanted to appoint his eldest son whose mother might not have been a Yaudheya. Had he done so, the power so far enjoyed by the Yaudheyas and Mālavas along with their allies might have passed on to the clan of the eldest son's mother or at least they would have shared it. That might not have been acceptable to the Yaudheyas, Mālavas and other republican allies. Hence, the Yaudheya nobles or the Rajas who were the ministers intervened and selected Ashoka to be the successor. The number of 500 ministers appear to be figurative and must have meant the whole electoral college of the Yaudheya clan or their number might have been actually approximately 500. They must have confronted Bindusār with their choice, who though getting enraged but feeling helpless must have acquiesced. After Bindusar's death the people hostile to Yaudheyas and Mālavas must have challenged the succession of Ashoka and they might have grouped around the clan to which his elder brother Sushim's mother belonged. Other clans too in different parts of the empire taking advantage of the dispute in succession and the wars that must have entailed, might have risen in revolt. The army manned exclusively by the Yaudheyas and Mālavas must have defeated Sushim and his supporters putting them to death. They must have suppressed the other revolts with a heavy hand. To remove any further disputes regarding succession which the clans of the different mothers of Ashoka might have raised all his brothers belonging to different step-mothers must also have been executed. Any person who might have been suspected of sympathy towards Sushim or his other brothers killed or of antipathy towards Ashoka or the Yaudheyas and their allies must also have been put to death. That might have taken him four years the time lag between his succession and his coronation and that too must have earned him the sobriquet of Chandāshoka meaning 'cruel Ashoka' so frequently mentioned in Buddhist literature. This bitter experience must have prompted Ashoka to persuade his eldest and beloved son Mahindra to renounce the world and to move away from India itself and go to Sri Lanka, a safer place. The stories in the Ceylonese chronicles and the Buddhist literature no doubt give us the facts but they try to so colour them that it may appear as a miracle of Buddhism. Looking to his later life it is doubtful if Ashoka was a willing participant in those brutalities but probably there was no choice for him and probably his power to intervene was also limited in those troublesome times when his clansmen to save their power and him undertook the task of securing the throne for him. No date for his succession and his coronation can be given with certainty. Divyāvadān claims it to be 100 years after Buddha's Nirvān which cannot be correct. Dipvansa, the Ceylonese chronicle, mentions the accession in 214 A.B. and coronation in 218 A.B. The problem would be to fix the real date of Buddha's Nirvān which is in dispute. However, according to Ceylonese chronicles the date may be 543 B.C. or 483 B.C. If we take the later date, the date of coronation comes to 265 B.C. and accession to 269 B.C. The earlier date would be too soon. Do we get any confirmation of this date? Rock Edict XIII gives the names of contemporary Hellenic monarchs, 'the Yona King Antiyoka and beyond him four kings, *viz.*, Turumaya, Antekina, Maka and Alikasudara'. These kings are now identified respectively with Antiochus II Theos of Syria (261-246 B.C.), Ptolemy II Philadelphus of Egypt (285-247), Antigonus Gonatas of Macedonia (276-239), Magas of Cyrene (300- 250) and Alexander of Corinth (252-247). The only years which are common to all who were living at the time of the Edict which was written thirteen years after his coronation is 252 and 250 B.C. and therefore the year of his coronation must lie between 265 and 263 B.C. and his accession between 269 and 267 B.C. Thus as the two coincide we may take it to be the years of his accession and coronation. But what about the mysterious number 256 at the end of the first Minor Rock Edict? The Figure 256 mentioned in the Edict must have some deep significance either to the empire or to Ashoka and it must be either a religious or a political event. It is difficult to visualise as to what might have happened to which the records either do not pertain or they might do. Adding to the year 252 B.C. when the Edict was issued It comes to 508 B.C. and in the period of vague memories anything could have happened. It was at about that period that the capital of the empire Patliputra was founded. It was somewhere at about the date that the Buddha got his enlightenment and it could have been that at that date the Yaudheya republic came into existence, something which the Yaudheyas might have calculated and Ashoka might have taken care to mention. Is there any reason to believe that the Yaudheya or as a matter of fact any other people were thus maintaining exact records from some religious or political event? Although from the available records of the age there is no indication that people had maintained such records from some religious or political event, yet we find from China and contemporary Sri Lanka (Ceylon) that the people were maintaining such calculations. If we look at the later period, just two centuries later, we find the period of eras among them Vikrami Samvat and Shak Varsh and later Vallabhi era, which started from some religious event of great significance. May be that either the family of Ashoka, or the Yaudheyas or the Magadh Empire might be maintaining such records dating from either a political event or a religious one. As a matter of fact we cannot say whether the figure 256 indicates a period of time at all. It may signify something else too about which we are just ignorant. The practice of writing figures in numerals only began in 5th century A.D. They must be written in words in Brahmi script on these inscriptions. Can it be that something else was meant and they were misinterpreted.

For the events after his coronation we can depend on the inscriptions which indicate, however, obliquely the main events of his reign though there may be some self glorification too. The first historical event of his reign was the conquest of Kalinga. In the thirteenth Rock Edict he says that he brought about the conquest of Kalinga eight years after his coronation and affirms that 100,000 men were killed in battle, 150,000 men were deported and many times that number died. He regrets the injury to the beloved ones of the Brahmins and the Shramans. Why Ashoka attacked Kalinga and undertook slaughter and deportation on such a large scale? Rock Edicts are just silent and not much light is thrown by the Buddhist literature or Ceylonese chronicles. Where these deported persons were taken and rehabilitated? To the question too no light is thrown by any record. Not even by the Kalinga inscriptions of Khārvel. As the Kalinga war had an abiding and deep influence on Ashoka and the Mauryan polity it is necessary that we understand the background of the war and its subsequent effects. Kalinga was situated in the modern state of Orissa and probably towards the South of the state overlapping parts of modern Andhra Pradesh. Its people might have been partly Oriyas and partly Dravidians and some might have been speaking a mixture of the two languages as is always the case when two different language areas overlap each other. It is also on the main route to the South from the capital of Magadh, Pātliputra. We do not know if they refused to recognise the sovereignty of Magadh, or if they might have repulsed even Bindusār, had he tried to capture them or whether they revolted on the accession of Ashoka. Any of the three reasons could have been possible. They must have been a big state territorially and might have thought themselves too strong which they were not as indicated by the outcome of the war. They might have made even attacks on Magadha which could not have been tolerated in those times. Ashoka probably led a strong force in person. Better arms made of iron which was available in plenty in Magadh and the new technique of cavalry charges brought the ruin of the Kalinga army and probably it was a slaughter which Ashoka was unable to prevent for his battle hungry troops and over 100,000 soldiers were killed. Probably to teach them and other people who might conspire to revolt and achieve independence his ministers and the army chiefs must have prevailed upon him to deport the rest of the population exception being made in the case of the Brahmins and Sharmans for their persons were always regarded as inviolate. Why it was thought to inflict such a severe punishment like deportation? To those living near the borders of North-Western India the idea of penal deportation was not new. They knew that the Jews who became a thorn in the sides of the Assyrians were uprooted and deported *en masse* far away from their original home in Palestine. Later during the regime of Achaemenids in Iran in the times of Darius I (Dāyarvush) when the various tribes including the Medes (Mada) tribe revolted against him and refused to acknowledge his succession, he defeated them and deported them to far away places. That had totally suppressed the militancy of the Jews in the times of the Assyrians and of the Medes and other tribes in the times of Darius I so much so that they became a pacific people. Those incidents had happened just a short time before. The Yaudheya chieftains who formed the bulk of his armies must have remembered the penal deportation and must have decided to inflict the same punishment on the people of Kalinga at least on that section of population which might have been the more militant. Hence, the deportation. Where those people were taken? On the analogy of the precedents in the West Asia, they must have been taken far away probably in the West. Wherever they were taken we are to find the language of their original home still spoken or if they had merged with the local population some words including the Dravidian words were still spoken. We do not find such alien people anywhere in India except in the hills of Baluchistān, the Brahui people. Although they now speak a language spoken by the people of Baluchistan, yet on an estimate about 10 per cent of the words in their language are Dravidian which indicate them to be alien to the population. These words are spoken only by the Brahuis among the population. Are Brahuis the people whom Ashoka deported? The Yaudheya chieftains must have known about the inaccessible Baluchistan hills and must have thought that they would lose their martial ardour once they were sent there from where there was no way back. How they were sent there? We do not get any indication from the folk stories of the intervening land or in any other record of their migration by land. The most convenient course would be to transport them by sea round Sri Lanka up to the Arabian Sea coast and going up the Indus river from where the Baluchistan hills are within sight. Hence, they might have been deported through sea. As we had seen above, the Brahuis could not have been the Dravida-speaking original inhabitants of the Indus Valley Civilisation times. They were certainly brought there. Except Ashoka's confession in the Rock Edicts there is no indication anywhere that such a penalty was inflicted on any people. They must have been the original inhabitants of Kalinga.

The conquest of Kalinga and the carnage together with the penalty imposed must have a terrific impact on the rest of India. We do not know if the conquest of rest of India upto the far South was effected by Chandragupta or by Bindusar. But by the time of Ashoka the whole of India upto far South was within his dominions. The extent of his empire is not given in any record nor it is mentioned by any chronicle either Ceylonese or Buddhist. But if we presume that the inscriptions were installed within his dominions then we would find that they were spread over practically all over India including Afghanistan excluding the extreme South where there were the independent states of Chola, Pāndya, Satiyaputra and Keralaputra. The territory should include the whole of modern state of Karnataka and at least half of modern state of Andhra Pradesh. There are no inscriptions or Ashokan monuments in Assam as well but it is difficult to believe that Assam so near to the capital might not have been under his rule. If Bindusār or Chandragupta did not conquer them and Ashoka too did not bring them under his rule how they came to be part of his empire? We cannot be sure if they were not conquered by his predecessors. But if they were not conquered, then probably terrorised by the example of Kalinga the rulers and the people must have surrendered themselves without his armies coming to conquer them.

What was the effect of Kalinga war on Ashoka himself? The effect is found referred to by Ashoka himself in his inscriptions. He fully subdued Kalinga in the ninth or tenth year after his coronation (256 B.C.) and in the eleventh year on account of his remorse at the thought of the holocaust of the Kalinga war he adopted the teachings of the Buddha as his creed. It appears that for over a year he must have been tormented by the thought of the carnage he witnessed and must have been studying the teachings of religious teachers including those of Mahāvir, the Buddha and other teachers. He must have finally found solace in the teachings of the Buddha and adopted them as his guide. In the opening sections of the Minor Rock Edict he says that for over a year after he had openly proclaimed himself a Buddha-Shākya (Maski) he was not very much zealous. Then after a year he paid a visit to the Sangh, received instructions, became more zealous in the cause of the Dhamma and began to lead a life of a celibate. He also gave up the time-honoured practice of going out on hunting or pleasure tours. He caused a record of his experiences to be made along with an exhortation to all to exert themselves likewise in the good cause (Minor Rock Edict). About the same time (253 B.C.) he disclosed his mind to the Sangh in an inscription at Bairāt in Rajasthan. In this inscription he says that his faith in the Buddha, Dhamma and Sangh is well known to the Monks and cites the names of seven texts from the Buddhist scriptures which he desires that the monks and nuns should hear frequently expounded and should meditate upon; this in his opinion will secure the long duration of the true Dhamma. (Calcultta-Bhābhru-Bairāt Edict). At the same time he presented to Ājivaka monks two caves in the Barābar hills in South Bihar. We thus find that the Kalinga War made Ashoka remorseful, deeply religious, tolerant, sensitive to the suffering of the people or as a matter of fact of any living being including animals, devoted to the welfare of the people and following the teachings of the

Buddha which he adopted almost as the creed of the State. Ashoka was a completely changed man after the War and the finer instincts came to the fore in him which led him to instruct the people and to raise the level of their worldly and spiritual life.

How and by whom was Ashoka converted to the creed of the Buddha? As mentioned in his inscriptions that he spent some time in the Sangh and received instructions, where did he spend the time? Inscriptions are silent about the person who first taught the principles of the creed of the Buddha to him. Nor do they mention the place where he spent the time in the Sangh. It is certain that immediately after the Kalinga war Ashoka devoted considerable time in understanding the religions as taught by various religious leaders. Among them must have been some monk of Buddhist faith. Legends mention Tissā Mogāliputra or Upgupta. It may be either of the two. The other version of the *Divyāvadān* that he saw miracles performed by Samudra, a Bauddha Bikkhu who entered a prison where persons were tortured and that he escaped by disappearing from the prison appears to be imaginary. Similarly the *Deepvansa* and *Mahāvansa* story that Ashoka once saw Sumana, the posthumous son of his elder brother whom he had got killed, as a Buddhist monk, felt attracted towards him, invited him and hearing his sermons got converted, appears to be unbelievable. If the story is to be believed, then that must have happened in the fifteenth year after his accession or the death of his brother. This makes Sumana to be only fourteen years of age and at that age his teaching about the Buddhist faith appears to be doubtful for he himself might not have learnt it completely. We may not know in the present state of our knowledge who gave him first convincing reasons for converting him to the Buddhist creed. All the chronicles are similarly silent on the place where he spent his time in the Sangh. No doubt he spent as per the indications about a year and we could only guess where he might have spent the time. We have already stated that among all the Buddhist monasteries the one which received a special attention appears to be at Bairāt near Jaipur in Rajasthan. It has the special honour of having an inscription by Ashoka indicating his religious thinking and the names of the religious texts which specially appealed to him (Calcuttā-Bhābhru- Bairāt Edict). That Edict was engraved on the entrance of the monastery on the top of a small hill. The excavations conducted here revealed that on the top of this small hill is a small monastery together with a small place for meditations. All around this place were the dwellings of monks. The place of meditation is a three-tiered place; at the bottom is a big circular open place with benches for monks all arranged in a horseshoe fashion. Facing this assembly is a small platform in which excavations and local legends confirm was buried a casket made of gold containing the relics of somebody. On the top of the hill a little above the platform was a small tank covering which was a circular rock raised on two raised stones. This is a typical architectural plan of a Hindu temple. There is a Mandapam in a Hindu temple where people can sit on the floor; before the Madapam on a slightly raised platform are the idols or a single idol or a representation of Hindu gods or in ancient times of the Buddha as well. Above the idol on the top is always a pot covered by either a coconut or a betel-leaf or both. Did the place for worship and meditation at the monastery at Bairat serve as a model for the temple architecture in India? Probably it did. Firstly, it must have served as model for other places of meditation in the Buddha monasteries. Later when temples of the Buddha began to be constructed then the same model with suitable modifications was adopted. It continued to be a model when the Jains and the Hindus began constructing temples. In addition to this inscription there is one more Minor Rock Edict in Bairāt at the foot of another hill nearby called Bhimji-ki-Dungari. Pieces of two Ashokan pillars were also found in Bairāt. What was the reason for this special attention of Ashoka to that monastery? If we look at the location of Bairat, we will find that it is situated in ancient Yaudheya territory. Can this be the only reason for this special attention? This should not be the only reason. Why did Ashoka choose to single out that monastery for expressing his view of Dhamma? This may be that he stayed there for some time and received the instruction in scriptures and left the record of what appealed to him for the benefit of the pupils who might come later. It may be a commemorative inscription though its language does not indicate it. The number of his inscriptions do point out this special regard for the place and it may be due to his stay there. Why did he choose to come here instead of another monastery? We do not know whose relics were contained in the casket of gold which was unfortunately taken out a few years before the excavations and could not be traced. They might have contained the relics of some important personage of Buddhist religion or they might have contained the relics of the Buddha himself given to the Moriyas who might have buried them on the hill. The name Bairāt is said to be a local variation of the original name 'Pāriyātra' which is considered as one among the seven sacred mountains of the Hindus described in the *Purānās* and supposed to be somewhere here. Thus the Moriyas probably buried the relics of the Buddha on the sacred mountain and made the place doubly holy. It is also possible that the teacher who first showed him the true creed might have lived in that monastery. Because of any or all of these reasons it appears that Ashoka himself lived there for about a year.

A year after his sojourn in the Sangh (253 B.C.) Ashoka issued the Minor Rock Edicts found in several places. They were issued in the 13th year after his coronation *i.e.,* in 252 B.C. approximately. In the thirteenth and the fourteenth year of his reign *i.e.,* 252-251 B.C. he issued the Fourteen Rock Edicts, the most important set of proclamations for the whole reign. In these Rock Edicts which are engraved at different places all over the Empire he set forth the principles of the Dhamma which he wished to inculcate upon his officials and on the people and the steps he took to secure the observance of those principles within his empire and to propagate them in foreign lands. In these Rock Edicts at Dhauli and Jaugaḍa which are situated in Kalinga territories the eleventh to the thirteenth Edicts are replaced by two edicts called Kalinga Edicts which concern the administration of those conquered territories. Ashoka began his efforts to improve Buddhist monuments from that period onwards. He undertook pilgrimage to all the Buddhist sites, improving the Stupas and building new ones. It is said that he broke open the old stupas containing the relics of the Buddha, subdivided them and again interred them in new ones in different parts of the country. Divyāvadān's claim that he constructed 84,000 stupas appears to be highly exaggerated. He again in the 26th and 27th year of his coronation issued the Seven Pillar Edicts. They contained further elaboration of the principles of the Dhamma and the administrative measures calculated to secure their voluntary observance by the people and their enforcement by the officials of the Government. (238 B.C.). A year later in 237 B.C. the seventh Edict was added on one pillar making a more or less systematic review of all the steps taken by Ashoka for the promotion of the Dhamma and the motives which prompted them. This is found on the Delhi-Topra pillar. Throughout his long reign after the Kalinga War Ashoka did everything possible to propagate the creed of the Buddha and to make people live according to those precepts.

What was the effect of the conversion of the Emperor to the creed of the Buddha on the people? What was its effect on the people believing in other gods and other creeds? Did they become junior citizens, lose their privileges and feel discriminated? Before answering this question we may ask a counter question. What do we mean by religious conversion? Does it mean a religious conversion in the same sense as it is done in the Semitic religions such as, in Islam and Christianity where the person converted is an outcaste from his family and clan, becomes a member of another community and treats the former members of his family and clan as strangers? In India before the advent of Islam in the 7th century the conversion never meant what it was understood in Islam and Christianity. Belief in creed and god was a personal affair of a person. The unit in the then Indian society and now the Hindu society was the tribe or clan called the caste. People had to marry within the caste and at the time of family rituals like birth, death, marriage *etc.* the whole clan or caste living in that particular area had to gather and every member of the caste had his privileges and obligations to the caste equally. In this gathering of the clan belief in a particular god or in a particular creed had no place. People believing in different gods like Shiv, Vishnu, Brahma, Indra, Skanda, Krishna, Arjun, etc. or believing in the creed of the Buddha or of Mahāvir or in Ājivaks, Parivrājaks will gather in such rituals with equal privilege and equal obligation. Even if one changes his personal god and starts believing in another god and also changes belief to another creed, he will continue to remain the member of the same caste. He will continue to marry within his caste without taking into account the personal god or the creed of the wife or the husband as the case may be. So it happens that a man may have a personal god and may believe in one teacher, but his son may change his belief in some other god and in some other teacher, sometimes under the influence of his mother or wife or sometimes by himself without his standing in the caste being impaired. Belief in a god and belief in a creed were always regarded as something personal to a man in the Hindu society and it is regarded so even today. We find even in India of today among Hindus following the same tradition. People marry within the caste and we find Hindus marrying Jains, Sikhs and vice versa. We find people believing in idol worship marrying people having faith in Arya Samaj which forbids the idol worship. So it happened in the times of Ashoka. Jains claim that his grandfather Chandragupta was a believer in Jain religion while Ashoka was a believer in the Buddha and his teachings and we are also told that his own grandson Samprati was a devotee of Jainism. Because of this resilience in the society that we find the rulers of ancient India changing their faith often, the various rulers in a dynasty belonging to the different faiths without in anyway weakening the society or injuring the body politics of the state. In such a state of affairs where one sees a number of his family members believing in different gods and different creeds he may start believing in more than one god and in different creeds simultaneously. Even in the case of Ashoka himself we find him believing in the teachings of the Buddha, propagating them, renovating the Stupas of the Buddha but at the same time getting the images of his clan deity Skanda, his other form Vishākha and his father Shiv made in innumerable numbers and selling them to the people as pointed out by Patanjali and also having the images of Peacock, the mount of Skanda on his coins. Neither he nor the people found any incongruity in that. Hence, the conversion in Hindu society in those times as at present meant nothing injurious to the society or to the state. The conversion of the Emperor only meant that the attention of the people was drawn to the teachings of the Buddha and a large number started believing in them too. When another great teacher like the Ādi Shankarāchārya arrived on the scene and impressed them they began to believe in his teachings without any adverse effect on the caste or the state. Nor the people believing in other gods and following other teachers became junior or less favoured citizens. However, because of the Emperor's conversion and his actively propagating the creed of the Buddha a very large number of people started studying the teachings of Buddha and began to follow them.

What was the ultimate effect of such a large number of people accepting the Buddhist philosophy and creed on the creed and the state? When a very large number of people accepted the Buddhist creed, it naturally followed that a very large amount of wealth was donated by the people to the Sangh, a pretty large number of people even renounced the world and joined the Sangh as Bikkhus or monks and nuns. The Sangh unlike other creeds like Jains was a centrally controlled and well organised Sangh. It became wealthy and at the same time unwieldy. The monks and nuns who were studying the teachings of the Buddha had their own interpretations of the teachings. The teachings of the Buddha were given in the local dialect of North Bihar and were easily understood by the people. In case of the areas of other dialects they were slightly changed to conform to those dialects. Prominent among those was the dialect known as Pāli spoken around Western Uttar Pradesh and North Madhya Pradesh near the Yaudheya territory and the Buddhist scriptures are preserved in that dialect. That easy understanding of the teachings was one of the factors for the spread of the creed. But different interpretations by the learned monks and nuns and different derivations of the intentions of the Buddha led to conflicts among different monasteries and even within the monasteries between different teachers. These conflicts many times led to heated discussions, violent language and sometimes even violence among the adherents of the various teachers. It also might have happened that unscrupulous people joined the Sangh with an eye on its wealth and instead of studying the teachings deeply and earnestly must be working with superficial knowledge. That state of affairs in the Sangh must have worried Ashoka for it would have caused schisms in the Sangh and he took steps to bring order in the Sangh. According to Ceylonese chronicles *Deepvansh* and *Mahāvansh*[12] he convened a Buddhist Council, the third one, after Buddha's death. It was presided over by Tissā Moggāliputta and comprised over one thousand of the best Arhats attended by the Emperor himself and lasting nine months. It systematised the scriptures, gave correct interpretations to the teachings, and set forth the treatise belonging to the Abhidhamma which is called Kathāvatthu. It also set rules to be followed in every monastery. It also expelled those who did not agree to what the Council decreed, unfrocked them, and compelled them to put on white robes. Although the Edicts do not mention the Third Council, but the Allahabad-Kosam pillar contains the Edict known as Koshāmbi Edict on Sanghbheda. This Edict confirms the holding of the Council. According to that Edict an order was issued to the Mahāmātras that the monk or nun who caused schism in the Sangh should be punished by expulsion, and he or she was decreed to wear white robes and live outside the Vihāra in a place not fit for the members of the Sangh to live in. This order was to be properly circulated among monks and nuns and lay worshippers and officials and lay worshippers were to assist in carrying out that instruction by attending service on every uposatha day. That harsh measures probably ended the quarrels among the Sangh and formalised the Buddhist religious literature and the interpretations of the teachings of the Buddha.

Why did Ashoka lend the power and majesty of the Empire to suppress the schism in the Buddhist Sangh? Was it solely due to his devotion to the creed of the Buddha or could it be inspired by other reasons of the state? When the various interpretations of a the teachings of a religious nature or belief that are actually different prevail, then it encourages the formation of sects. When the sects become powerful and the beliefs of the people take concrete forms according to the sects, then it is likely to rouse tempers and create bad blood among the adherents and even provoke them to violence. We have witnessed throughout the ages that such schisms tear apart the social fabric of the masses and disturbances of a violent nature bring anarchy resulting in the destabilisation of the state. So it happened with Christianity and with Islam. Probably it must have been happening with the sects in Buddhism and their growing power and the roused zeal of the people must be tending to create disorders. Sensing that Ashoka must have thought out the plan of convoking a council to be attended by all the eminent teachers and presided over by the most revered one to systematise and formalise the creed of the Buddha. He must have taken care to attend it personally so that the formalised creed might be according to his wishes and according to requirements of the state. He was eminently successful for the set of teachings and the creed was agreed upon and circulated among the Sangh and the people as the authoritarian version of the creed. The Sangh and the people must have accepted them gladly and with the expulsion of the dissenters order must have been restored.

What must have been the effect of this formalisation of the creed? The first effect was that the religion for the time had authorised scriptures in which the other gods had no place. However, the *Jātak Kathas* and other mythology grew up rapidly raising the Buddha to divinity with a distinct mythology of their own. It had a form of a new and complete religion and so it became a distinct religion. Fundamentalists insisted that the other Hindu gods should not be considered at all. Thus for the first time there was a new and distinct religion apart from Hinduism, though it must not have affected the caste structure. After some time the Jains followed suit and there was another distinct religion i.e. that of Jains. However, the Jains retained the other gods though in another capacity which did not separate them from the Hindus completely. Did not the Buddhism still contain dissenters and what about the old expelled ones? When different versions once come into picture then it is not possible to erase them. Some of the dissenters must have recanted and must have managed to remain in the Sangh. Moreover, the differences must have cropped up over the new mythology created round the Buddha in which some had raised him to divinity while others might not have thought so. Hence, the dissent must have continued for a time under the surface and later when the Empire was no longer supporter of the Buddhist religion, it came into the open. The dissenters must have united with their own version or their own variation or their belief in their version of mythology. We find that almost two hundred years later during the rule of Kushan Kanishka there were again an open split and dissensions when taking the leaf out of doings of Ashoka Kanishka convoked a new Buddhist Council. But this time the dissenters were neither a handful nor powerless. They were vocal and articulated their views aggressively. With heated arguments and roused passions the Buddhist religion split into two. The majority with their belief in the divinity of the Buddhist and his exaltation into the greatest of gods became the Mahāyān or the Great Vehicle, while the others believing in the strict following of his teachings and not the mythology regarding his exaltation as a god became the Hīnyān or the Lesser Vehicle. Almost at about the same time Jainism also faced a similar split into two sects, the Digambar and the Swetambar sects. Thus we had in the time of Ashoka a distinct religion, the Buddhism and some time later another distinct one, the Jainism. Both about two hundred years later split into further two sects each. However, it may be emphasised that due to the peculiar structure of the caste system of India they could not split the caste according to religious lines. People continued to have marital relations with the persons of the different faiths and their children were tolerant of the religion of their mother or father as the case may be and when some other great teacher like Ādi Shankarāchārya arrived on the scene and when they were impressed with him they easily accepted his doctrines forgetting the old ones. Buddhism or Jainism did not disappear from India, Buddhism completely and Jainism leaving a remnant, by any state suppression or by forcible conversion. Because of the resilience of the caste system people just switched over to new doctrines.

Ashoka devoted all his life to the spread of the Buddhist religion in India as well as abroad. He sent Buddhist missions to as much of the world as possible. In the thirteenth Rock

Edict he gives the places where he sent his missionaries. Among the most interesting ones are the Greek rulers of Iran and the Middle East, to the Western territories of his empire which he named as among the Kambojas and Yonas and to the South to the kingdom ruled over by the Pandyas as far as Tāmbparni. Yonas mentioned in the Edict must have been the Greeks living among the territories of the North-West India which must be those later known as the Bactrians (or the Bākhtris their real name) and the Kambojas who probably lived to the North of Kashmir around Pamir. The missionaries did not probably succeed in Iran and the Middle East but they certainly did convert the people of his North-Western territories, the Kambojas and the Bactrians as far as Khotan in Central Asia which was a part of his Empire. From this place it entered China and in its Mahāyān version spread over the whole of the far East. His son Mahindra and daughter Sanghmitra are credited to going to Ceylon (Sri Lanka) and converting the people and the king who became a good friend of Ashoka. Within India itself he sent missionaries to every part. For himself he took certain measures to mould his administration in conformity with the tenets of Buddhism. Killing of a large number of animals was totally banned and the long list included even birds and ants. He also prescribed certain holy days when no animal or bird would be killed. Even in his own kitchen he reduced the slaughter of animals and in time totally stopped it. This banning of a large number of animals might also be due to reasons of state. We may not forget that in those times the people were just emerging from an earlier society which believed in totems and that list might have included the totems of the new emerging tribes who were mingling with people in urban areas or in areas where people with different totems were living and some of the animals were again mounts of newly emerging and newly recognised gods and thus revered by people. That list might have been issued with twin motives of compassion according to the creed and in accordance with interest of state to preserve peace among people with reverence towards certain animals or birds.

Ashoka was one of the greatest emperors India ever had. He was great not because he ruled over the largest area to come under one sovereignty, but because during his reign he established most of the traditions and shaped the society and polity in such a manner that it became worthy of emulation for future India. When he became king, India as one state had been in being only for about 50 years. The society was in flux under the impact of this oneness and absence of wars among states which had ceased to exist. Ashoka himself was a sensitive man, more sensitive to the mood of the people. Hence, when after the Kalinga War and the brutal suppression of the people, there was a revulsion of feeling against wars, Ashoka too felt repelled and took to the Buddhist doctrine of non-violence. When people started moving about throughout the country, to facilitate the movement he got constructed the roads and provided trees on both sides for shelter. As a consequence when people started intermingling, started living together but probably each having his own totem as sacred and consequently creating tension, Ashoka swiftly banned the killing of a large number of living beings, to protect them and to ease the tension. Probably to make the people having diverse beliefs live amicably, he got the basic essence of good living inscribed on rocks and pillars without mentioning any religion or god and declared that all the monks of any belief were revered alike for him. All the traditions established by him continued in India down the ages even upto the present time. This ensures Ashoka a lasting place in Indian history.

Successors of Ashoka

Not much is known of the successors of Ashoka as no epigraphical record is available pertaining to them. Nor do we know the precise year when they succeeded him. We can only deduce the period when he relinquished power. The Pillar Edicts began to be issued in 238 B.C. when six edicts were issued. The second Edict was issued a year later. This can be said because they were dated from the year of coronation. He continued to reign for about ten years after this seventh Edict. Thus he must have relinquished power by about 227 B.C. The Mauryan Dynasty was overturned by about 185 B.C. Thus his successors ruled only for a period of 43 years. But who were they? The *Purāṇās*, the Buddhist

Avadans, the Jain accounts, and the writings of later authors like Kalhan of Kashmir and Taranath of Tibet all have differing versions. No two lists agree and it is difficult to accept one as authentic. Added to it is the fact that Tivar, the only son of Ashoka mentioned in the inscriptions, does not figure in the lists nor is he heard of even. The only name which is confirmed by epigraphy is that of Dashrath, whose dedicatory inscriptions bestowing the Ajivakas caves in Nagarjuni hills near Barabar hills in Bihar resemble those of Ashoka and were inscribed immediately after his coronation. But Dashrath is ignored by Buddhist and Jain accounts.

According to *Purānās* nine or ten kings succeeded Ashoka. They are Kunāl, Bandhupālita, Indrapālita, Dashona, Dashratha, Samprati, Sālisūka, Devadharman, Satadhanus, Brahdratha, all ruling for a total period of 85 years which as we had seen is not possible. According to Divyāvadān the successors are Kunal, Sampadi, Brahaspati, Vṛshasena and Pushyadharman and Pushyamitra. According to Tāranāth the successors are Kunal, Vigatāshoka and Virasena. Kalhana, the historian of Kashmir, mentions the story of Jalauka, a son of Ashoka as his successors in Kashmir. We do not know who were the real successors or whether the names mentioned were of the same persons who were merely called differently by different authors. It is also possible that the contemporary accounts had perished and those which survived were written after the considerable period and thus the real situation was made obscure. We may not forget that even the accounts regarding Chandragupta Maurya, Bindusār, and Ashoka are irritatingly sparse. We know about Chandragupta Maurya from Greeks and about Ashoka from the Buddhists' accounts and both are not very accurate. Some modern writers have advanced the view that probably the empire was divided among his sons and therefore there are differing accounts. This cannot be accepted in view of the fact that Pushyamitra who overturned the Mauryas held sway over the whole of India upto at least the Indus. He succeeded to the whole empire and was not credited to have reconquered the new territories.

What might have happened in the choosing of successors to Ashoka? The coalition of Yaudheyas, Mālavas and other tribes must have continued even after Ashoka's death with the chief of the Yaudheyas as the head. The choosing of the new head of Yaudheyas and hence the new emperor must have been left to the Yaudheyas and they must have chosen the son from a Yaudheya woman. Thus was Ashoka chosen in preference to his brothers though older and the same convention must have continued even after. Thus Mahendra, the eldest of his sons, Tivar, son of his queen Charuvaki, mentioned in his own inscriptions, were ignored. Mahendra became a Buddhist monk and we have no knowledge about the fate of Tivar. It is possible that the successors might have proved to be incompetent or might have shortlived. It is also possible that the last one was not the son of a Yaudheya mother and somehow became king but was not approved by the Yaudheya clan, who allowed the Mālavas their coalition partners, who had monopolised the army since the time the coalition was formed to take over the kingship by virtue of their chief being the Senapāti of Mālavas. That may be one of the reasons why the transition was so peaceful and bloodless. The last Maurya king was killed in the sight of the whole army without a protest. That might have happened due to the fact the army itself might not have been willing to accept one as emperor whose mother did not belong to any of the tribes of the coalition partners and who therefore had no right to be the king.

REFERENCES

1. Bairat-Bhabhru Edict.
2. *Mahābhāshya* I. 1.9.
3. Plutarch, p. 403.
4. Inv. Alex. p. 327
5. Archaeological Remains and Excavations at Bairat—Daya Ram Sahni, Department of Archaeological and Historical Research, Jaipur State—not dated.
6. *Roman History*, Vol II—Loeb Library—Syr. XI. 9.55.
7. Loeb. Library—translated by H.L. Jones. XV. 2.9, page 143.
8. Jacobi, 2nd ed., P. lxxix, VIII. 415 ff.
9. DV. VI 21 2; VII 21-2 24
10. Mahāvansa XIII 8-11; Divyāvadān VI 15-17
11. Mahāvansa V 20; Dipvansa VI 21-2.
12. Deepvansh—7.34-59; Mahavansh 5.282-88

8

PEOPLE AND SOCIETY IN THE MAURYAN AGE

From the accession of Chandragupta Maurya to the death of Ashoka, India witnessed a century of peace and prosperity. During these hundred years of peace, spurred on by the movement generated during the years of first consolidation under the Nandas, it was but natural that the society must take a definite shape, generate new movement which would take it to new paths and bring about a new awakening and sensibility. Unfortunately no record of those times is available except in later accounts recorded by the Hindu and Buddhist works. They were recorded after such a lapse of times that no credence could be placed on them. It could not have been that nothing was written in those times for they were the times of peace and much must have been written. But unfortunately nothing has been survived. Why is it so? The reason appears to have been the change in script. We had seen earlier that when the Indus script gave way to Brahmi script which was alphabetical, the whole literature written in Indus script was lost. Only some important works essentially of a religious nature survived because people had re-written them in the Brahmi script. Even this rewriting became difficult as could be seen in the last few hymns of *Atharvaveda.* The Brahmi, an alphabetical script easy to write became the prevalent script in the Mauryan times. The script probably continued for two or three centuries and then became so metamorphosed that Brahmi itself became unrecognisable. Faced with that problem the people tried to recapitulate what was written earlier in the Indus script and the Brahmi and the works so produced were called *Smrities*, but probably they differed materially from the original works and embodied the prevalent notions. An example is the *Manu Smriti.* The *Manu Smriti* is the code of social and political laws. Among other things it denies the daughter any inheritance on the death of father. However, we find in the *Nirukta* of Yāska, a work attributed to at least 7th century B.C. a statement that the inheritance of daughter and son is equal[1]. This indicates the chaos introduced by the changes in script. The older material which could have been written only on cloth or Bhojpatra, the bark of Silver Birch, could not survive. Hence, to understand the times we would have to depend on the few inscriptions, the secular literature, *i.e.,* the grammatical works which by its very nature and constant use in those times survived intact and some later works strived to fit themselves into those times. The grammatical works which survived are *Nirukta* of Yāska, *Ashtādhyāyi* of Pānini and *Mahābhāshya* of Pātanjali.

Administration

The study of the administrative structure has to be undertaken first in order to study the people and the society simply because the unified administration and removal of restrictions on intra-regional movement played its part in its evolution. Chandragupta Maurya established a unified administration for the whole of North India. To be more precise he extended the administration of the Magadh and its structure to the whole of India. Probably if there was an administration, it was in Magadh and both Chandragupta and Chāṇakya must have known it and its capabilities. The very late work *Mudrā Rākshas* attempts to portray the efforts of Chāṇakya to get the minister of the late king of Magadh, the Nanda king to declare his allegiance to Chandragupta Maurya and to work towards administering the dominions. It may be a fancy or it may reflect an ongoing tradition that the Mauryas did their best to re-establish the administrative structure already there, to improve its efficiency, and to extend it to the whole of India. This was probably what they did. They extended that set-up to the whole of India under their control. In that process they also in order to provide top officials loyal to them drafted the nobility of the Yaudheyas and Mālavas from their original homes to head the administrative units in various areas. They also probably abolished various checks and controls on inter-regional movements, encouraged the movement of people and probably established military camps and colonised certain areas, by clearance of forests.

Religion

The period of the rule of Emperor Ashoka is said to be the period of the growth of the religion preached by the Buddha. But were other religions devoted to other gods declining in relation to Buddhism or becoming static? Probably not. What was then, the state of other religions, i.e., Jainism and the one which later became Hinduism? Were they too static or in a state of decline? Again the answer is to be probably in negative. For we find that at the end of the rule of the Mauryas the Hindu religion rose to be a major religion, the religion of the Buddha declined in the land of its birth, and became extinct in India except in some mountain fringes in the north. The reason may lie either in the state of society, in the policies of Ashoka or even in beliefs, mythologies or even in the philosophy they taught. The evidence in written records available is too scanty. However, taking it all into account it appears that though the society was religious, yet their beliefs, mythologies and the philosophies were in a state of growth and their interactions led to their further growth and also probably decline of some beliefs which lost their value in the estimation of people in this contest. We may first look at the facts available so far and then draw appropriate conclusions. Among some of the conclusions we would like to mention the role and intervention of the state under Emperor Ashoka which too played its part.

Religion Prior to the Mauryas

Religion prior to the establishment of a great empire

comprising whole of India was probably tribal or confined to special regions. The only evidence we find is confined to the only surviving contemporary work which surprisingly enough is not religious but secular which is the Grammar of Pānini, *Ashtādhyāi.* It points out a large number of deities whom people worshipped, among them Vāsudev, Arjun, Sun, Indra, Fire, etc. Tradition records that the Yaudheyas had Kumār Karttikeya or Brahamanya as their god, whose mount peacock was found on the Mauryan coins giving us the first clue to their identity. Megasthenes who lived as the Ambassador of Seleucus at the court of Chandragupta Maurya and his son Bindusar had mentioned that the people around Mathura held 'Heracles' and 'Dionysus' in special esteem. We do not know whom he meant by Heracles" and "Dionysus" who were *Greek gods* but it is surmised that he might be alluding to Krishna and Balrām, the two deities of the Shurseni tribe living there. These are the evidences we have of the deities worshipped in various regions of India during the period immediately preceding the Mauryas and in the earlier part of their reign. But looking to their existence and the later phenomenon of the Hindu religion we may safely assume that all the gods who are mentioned today or in the ancient *Purānās* were worshipped in some region or the other, and were probably localised among some tribes. They must be having their own legends about their deities and must be devoted to them, propitiating them and turning to them in the times of their needs or difficulties.

There were two or rather three other religions entirely different from the above regional religions devoted to certain deities. Those were the religion preached by the Buddha, known as Buddhism, the Jainism preached by Mahāvir and a third one preached by Makhaliputra Goshāl. We get the indication of the first one, *i.e.,* Buddhism in the inscriptions of Ashoka, specially the Bairāt-Bhābhru Edict and about the other two from later records and stories mentioned about them in their accounts.

Both these types of religions changed beyond recognition by the impact of the establishment of the Mauryan Empire embracing the whole of India and more powerful than the powers beyond the frontiers of India known to the people of this country. We may try to understand the types to which these two categories of religions belonged, the nature of impact and the transformation which they had undergone. We may like to call the religions based on the worship of local deities as the religion of the living god and the second type, *i.e.,* Buddhism, Jainism and the preaching of Makkhliputra Goshāl as revealed religion for they did not have a living god.

Religions of the Living God

The religions of the living gods probably came out of the primitive tribes who had their primitive worship of a deity, their totems and their taboos. They propitiated their gods while going on a hunt, while taking the first step in agricultural operations and any other undertaking in connection with the tribe as a whole or their personal affairs. When in dread of some calamity they again approached them and believed that the calamities were due to their breaking some taboo or due to the wrath of the gods. The god was their personal friend, philosopher or guide and was there to help them. Such a god is a living being for them. That is why it is a living god. When the tribes grew and their area of living expanded, so did the area of the god. Probably in the case of conflicts among the tribes if a tribe was successful over the other tribe consistently, their god became the god of the defeated one too and thus the particular god took over as a regional deity. Such regional deities were found all over the country and we may include among them Vāsudev, Arjun, Shiv, Kumār Kārttikeya or Brahamanya, Ram, Vishnu, Ganesh, Sun, Moon, Balrām, and the various mother goddesses, be they Pārvati, Lakshmi, Durgā, Bhawāni, or those known today as the sixty-four *Yoginis.* They were all local deities known by their local names, and were worshipped in their respective regions by the tribes living there.

What happens when two regions come into conflict? That must have happened frequently in the past. It must be that if a less advanced tribe comes into contact with a more advanced tribe and is attracted to its ways, then no matter which one is a more advanced or which is a less advanced, the less advanced one will adopt the gods of the other one as a manifestation of its own one. In other words the two gods will tend to be identified. If they are not charmed or attracted then a war of attrition between the two gods may ensue in the souls of the men and in the creation of mythologies antagonistic to each other in which one is shown as a demon and the other as the benign one. This must be behind the growth of mythologies and legends. And that must have happened in India before the Mauryan age and might have even an earlier beginning.

What happens when civilisation advances to an extent that there is such an economic activity that it involves movement of people like traders, artisans, migrant tribes to newly colonised areas and people believing in various regional gods and various rituals and various totems and various taboos mingle with each other on equal terms? In such a situation there must have been a free exchange of ideas, exchange of notes about their deities, their origin, way of life, behaviour, dress etc. And if many of the attributes appear to be common, then the gods are identified as one and the same and the two names given by respective people to their version of god are treated as two names of the same god. The identification and the names go on adding together so that we now have a thousand names of Vishnu, a thousand names of Shiv, or a thousand names of Sun. If the god was treated as a human being, then he naturally becomes an incarnation of the other god like Vāsudev Krishna, Rām or the Buddha as the incarnation of Vishnu. In some cases they may become associated with each other in personal relationships like brothers as in the case of Vāsudev Krishna and Balrām or Rām and Lakshman, or else as friends like Vāsudev Krishna and Arjun. In cases the friendly people believing in different gods live for a considerable time together respecting each other's gods then their gods are tended to be allied together in family relationships. The most obvious manifestation of it is in the Shiv family, *i.e.*, Shiv, his consort Pārvati or Durgā with Kumār Karttikeya and Ganesh as their children when in every case they are even today worshipped singly in different regions. It so happened in ancient Sumerian Civilisation with the identification of Marduk and Bel and in ancient Egyptian Civilisation. Even today we find the same identification going on. About a thousand years earlier wars were fought between Allah of the Muslims on the one side and gods of Hindus on the other, and Allah on one side and God of the Christians on the other. But today people regard the God, the Creator as one and Allah, God, Ram or Krishna as one and the same. However, they are called by different names in various languages.

This process of identification was not completed by the time of the Mauryas. There were still regional gods in the regional territories. However, the intermingling of people must have started in the 6th century B.C. when Kings of Magadh of the Shishunag dynasty Bimbisār and Ajātshatru started on their conquest of the area comprised in modern state of Bihar and Eastern Uttar Pradesh. They brought that whole area under one rule and the relative peace brought about the movement of traders, artisans, soldiers of fortunes in search of lucrative employment, stationing of garrisons in various places in the conquered territories, and the establishment of guilds of people with similar interests among traders and artisans. The process must have been carried forward by the succeeding Nandās who conquered the area upto the Yamunā dividing it from the rest of the Western India, beyond which were the warlike tribes of Yaudheyas, Arjunāyans, Mālavas, etc. who did not allow the Nandās to rule over them.

What must happen when the various tribes with their gods having a territorial jurisdiction coterminus with the extent of the tribes' own territory are brought under the ambit of an empire having a larger area under its rule? The extension of the rule of a big power with an earthly king ruling over a much larger area than their god must have been psychologically profound. Can an earthly ruler be greater than their god? Certainly not. He must be greater than the earthly man. Their horizon of vision must have become broader and the territorial jurisdiction of their god must now embrace the known world. In substance he must become god of the world. Various gods worshipped within the empire must be the manifestation of either one and the same god or must be in relationship with one another. In the process some must be relegated as of no consequence in direct relationship with the fortunes of its worshippers and its attributes. This process must have started in the times of Nandās. Priests of various gods must have started thinking on those lines. There must have been free interplay of religious thoughts, of mythologies, various merits of gods, the purpose of religion, of creation, of man's duties and obligations towards gods and towards state.

Towards the end of the 4th century B.C. and the 3rd century B.C. within the life span of a single generation momentous changes had taken place. By 323 B.C., as we know from the Greek historians about the condition in India that there were numerous states in India with Nandā as the most powerful. However, by 321 B.C. Chandragupta Maurya appearing as if from nowhere overthrew the Nandās, subjugated all other small states and established a unitary Universal state comprising the whole of Northern India north of the Vindhya mountains and that also included parts of modern Afghanistan. He consolidated the Empire by remodelling the bureaucracy, by removing all the internal barriers bringing India into a sort of monetary union and also modernising the army. By 305 B.C. he became so powerful that he defeated the Greek king Seleucus Nikator who invaded India to incorporate it into his Empire. Seleucus, the successor of the conqueror Alexander who just 30 years earlier had defeated the mighty Persian Empire, conceded defeat, ceded a large part of the territory under his control and in addition gave his daughter in marriage to the Mauryan Emperor. Just half a century later his grandson Ashok completed his feat by establishing the Empire throughout India excepting a tip of the Indian peninsula whose kings were friendly with him. There was a universal state in India and the kings of certain known countries who were less powerful than him held him in high esteem.

What was the effect of that spectacle of such a powerful universal state on the psyche and vision of people? Their god who uptill then was identified with the territory of the state or at the most of the known world must be now regarded as more potent and powerful than a merely human being who might be the universal monarch. How can he be regarded as more potent? In the growing imagination and fancy of the people he must be the creator of the universe including the Sun, Moon and stars and as well as the elements. That was the form in which every god earlier worshipped in a region must have been thus regarded.

Can there not be an influence of the *Vedas* and subsequent literature like *Brāhmanas* and *Āranyaks, Upnishads* on the development of this religion of living gods? Probably not. The concept was there in the tribal stage, which gradually expanded to region, to the territory governed by the king and to the universe. It was simply a movement of the belief among the common people or among those who were the most ignorant. It is true that the concept of the ultimate Creator of the universe and the identification of such an ultimate creator with their particular god might have been helped by the knowledge of the *Vedas* and other scriptures. But we may note that none of the gods mentioned in the *Vedas* were in that age worshipped by the common people as we gather from the available contemporary literature. On the other hand we find in the legends and mythologies that these popular gods and goddesses are said to have worsted the gods of the *Vedas*. Ideology of the *Vedas* whose conception of the Creator is crystallised in the Sukta 129 of the tenth Mandal of *Rigveda* and known as the hymn of Creation could not have been accepted by the people for that 'Creator' of the *Vedas* was remote whom neither the gods nor the rishis had known. But people could not do without a living god who had to be at hand, overlooking all their actions and punishing them when they deviated from the righteous path but also helping them in the times of need, and who they could be sure was certainly near at hand. Their god became a formless god who was present everywhere, a concept new as well unique which makes Hinduism so different from other religions of the world including Islam and Christianity. This thought was not and could not be the gift of the *Vedas*. The author is of the view that the logical culmination of the growth of the religion of the *Vedas* was in Jainism and the religion of the Buddha. The major help which these religions of the living gods derived from the *Vedas* was in the formulation of the mythologies which grew with abandon during that time which invariably depicted the pitiable position of the gods mentioned in the *Vedas* and who were helped and saved by their gods or goddesses.

Philosophical Religions or Revealed Religions

Philosophical religions were two in India, Buddhism and Jainism prior to the times of Mauryas and probably during the rule of Nandas and their predecessors, the kings of the Shishunāg dynasty,Bimbisār and Ajātshatru. There was a third one also that preached by Makhhliputra Goshāl but whose records are not available.

Buddhism and Jainism do not believe in the existence of God. Jains flatly deny his existence while Buddhism neither denies nor affirms it. Thus for the followers of Buddhism and Jainism there is no living God who can help them in their problems, whose propitiation before starting some work would ensure its success and their salvation would depend on their own actions, to release them from the cycle of rebirth. Their salvation depends upon following the righteous path realised and preached by their prophets. In case of the people believing in a living God, who built up their doctrine of behaviour on the tribal life, their conduct was governed by the original taboos and customs as practised in their tribal life by their ancestors. They might have been changed by the changing times, by the urbanisation, by the urban-tribal-rural mix, by coming into contact with different tribal structures of other people having their own taboos and customs. This code of righteous conduct as taught by these preceptors may be easily compared with the Ten Commandments of Moses in Judaism later adopted by Christianity and in the verses interspersed in the *Korān* of Islam. They all preach a righteous conduct. Another eminent Prophet, Confucious of China also preached righteous conduct and according to him too there is no living god who may help the people.

Buddha and Mahāvir are said to have been born in the 6th century B.C. during the times of the first king known in history, Bimbisār. It is said that Mahāvir was the 24th and last Tirthankar or their prophet in the line with 23 predecessors while Buddha is said to be the 23rd Buddha with the twenty-fourth Buddha, Maitreya still to come. We do not know anything about any of them. The Jain scriptures mention their names, parentage, place of birth and some other details about their previous birth and a few possible or impossible incidents from their lives. The Buddhists do not give any information about the predecessors of the Buddha. The books about the Buddha and the Buddhism were written about 500 years after him and about the Jainism and Mahāvir about 1000 years after his death. But surely after such a lapse of time people might have forgotten much about them? On the contrary it is likely that after such a long time when it was first written people must have added many imaginary and supernatural events to lives of predecessors of the Buddha and Mahāvir as they did to those of Buddha and Mahāvir. Probably they were a myth.

Were Buddha and Mahāvir also myth? Did they belong to the age to which they are attributed? Both Buddha and Mahāvir are said to have belonged to the time of Bimbisār, the first known king who exercised sovereignty over a large number of other states and established an empire which lasted for long. We do not know of any other king who ever exercised such a domination earlier than him. He is the first known historical figure and probably was so when people started writing the life of Buddha and Mahāvir in the early centuries of the Christian era. So it is just possible that both Buddha and Mahāvir were associated with him and his times in order to give the stories and legends greater credibility. We may see the respective Jain and Buddhist chronicles in this regard. Both Buddha and Mahāvir were thus contemporaries and were continuously moving and preaching in a limited area i.e. the modern state of Bihar and Eastern Uttar Pradesh. As ascetics they had to move not staying for more than a few days at one place except during the rainy season when they stayed for a period of four months. But the chronicles of both do not mention the name of the other as if they had no knowledge of their existence, what to say of meeting each other. If they were contemporaries, it is just not possible that they had neither heard of nor had met each other during their wandering life and to have abstained from commenting on each other's preaching. Probably they do not belong to the time of Bimbisār and their real period is therefore either later or earlier than is generally assumed. Also both may not be contemporaries. A similar misplacing of a religious figure happened in the case of Zarathustra, the great preacher of Zoroastrianism, the ancient religion of Persia. His place of birth and time is not known and thus he too must belong to the age of the first great king Vistasp of Persia. He lived certainly much earlier. No secular literature of the period mentions either Mahāvir or Buddha nor that in succeeding times till the beginning of the Christian era. Were they a myth? We cannot say. They may have existed; they may be a myth created to give credence to the creed accepted by the learned of the period, by a sect or by the preachers of a religion. They are not alone in doing so for we had the same phenomenon in the *Upnishads* where the preaching is given by a teacher who certainly is a mythical figure. Jewish accounts of their great prophets of their earlier period is more honest in that they either do not give any name of the king or the country which they have visited or in which they have settled briefly or they give some strange names which are not found in history of their adjoining region, the Fertile Crescent, which is much more known.

If supposing they were a myth, from where did we get the creed which they are supposed to give to the people? The earlier known religious literature and creeds prior to both Buddha and Mahāvir whatever may be their age, are the *Vedas*. What we find in *Vedas* is nothing but either a propitiation of the gods to help them in their duties or an exhortation to people for righteous conduct. In certain hymns they appeal to Indra to help them fight their enemies; in other ones they exhort the Ashwini Twins (Nasatya) to help them if they are ill or in distress; they appeal to Agni (Fire god) to help them and thus to other gods including the Soma, the Divine Drink, or Varun, for maintenance of *Rit*, the cosmic order. In none of them do we find the gods to be addressed or even regarded as the creator of the universe. They have their own work assigned to them and only to those are the hymns addressed. In fact in the numerous hymns of the four *Vedas* there are just a few which can even be counted on fingers, which mention that there may be a Creator. The most clear statement is in the Hymn No. 129 of the Tenth Mandal (Book) of the *Rigveda*. In this it is stated that before there was a universe there was nothing but He and afterwards He created the universe and established the cosmic order. Gods and the Rishis (learned men) were created long afterwards and as such even they do not know Him. How the world was created is known to Him or even He may not know. This Hymn known as the Hymn of Creation is the only one which mentions that there may be a Creator of the Universe and also that it is futile to speculate about Him as even the Gods and Rishis do not know anything about Him. The other few hymns are not this much clear. Did the Buddha have knowledge of this Hymn when he said that he can neither affirm nor deny the existence of God? Or did this hymn bring about such a statement in their creed? This must be so. The Jains, as we had seen earlier, deny the existence of God while the Buddhists neither affirm nor deny His existence. Their sole preaching is the code of righteous conduct which man must pursue if he has to escape the cycle of rebirth. In fact the creeds of both Jainism and Buddhism are very similar and they may be taken as just a schism in a system due to clash of personalities of their religious heads. So the *Vedas* preach the righteous conduct and the same is taught by the Jains and Buddhists or by Mahāvir and the Buddha. The preachings are almost similar. We find in the *Vedas* a very interesting Hymn. The Hymn[2] mentions that the learned man had established seven limits within which a man must remain. These limits or *Maryāda* as *Vedas* call it, are just not clarified in the *Vedas* but the details about these limits are given by Yāska in his book of etymology *Nirukta*[3] while explaining the etymology of the word 'Anhur'. They are: One should not steal, should not have sexual intercourse with other women except his own, not to kill a priest or learned man, not to help abortion, not to drink wine, not to do a bad deed, and not to tell a lie to conceal his bad deed. What is a bad deed is not clarified. This is something like the Ten Commandments of the Jews and the Christians. The Vedic exhortation is for a righteous conduct while the Jains and Buddhists also advocate the same. Both do not believe in God and if according to them there is

One, no body can know anything about Him including the gods and learned men. It appears that the beliefs which began in the Vedic times culminated in the creeds of Jainism and Buddhism duly modified and cleansed of inessential things during the long period in keeping with the changing times and thoughts of men. The gods like Indra who in the *Vedas* were assigned particular task in the Cosmic order and were all powerful were now subordinated to a Jain Tirthankar or a Buddha doing everything necessary to help them in accomplishing their task.

Did not the Indus Valley Civilisation have some impact on the emergence of the creed or of mythology? It certainly had the influence which it must have inevitably for the *Vedas* were a part of it and mythology had to associate Indus Valley Civilisation for its projection. We have much greater evidence of the influence of Indus Valley Civilisation on the Jain mythology than on Buddhism. As we have seen earlier the figure known as Rishabh on seal No. 420 from Mohenjodaro is taken over by Jains in their mythology and they regard him as their first Tirthankar. In this seal there are two goats beneath the stool on which the figure is shown sitting. Both the goats or may be ibexes are sitting. However, in another seal obviously Indus seal but found in Iraq, there are shown two bulls facing each other before the figure who is the same as that in the Indus seal.[4] Jains had the bulls in front instead of two goats or ibexes. May be the Buddhists did the same and took the deer and placed them below the figure of Buddha in various representations. We may remember that Rishabh was a mythical figure in Indus Valley times as well. In addition we may note another fact and that of the map of Bharatvarsh according to the Jain mythology. The map is that of heartland of Indus Valley Civilisation, the portion between the Saraswati and the Beās as it then flowed parallel to each other with two-third of the Indus Valley sites lying in between. This map is actually having East on the top. Both the Jain and the Buddhist mythologies speak of large beautiful cities with fine houses and the prosperity and high level of culture of its inhabitants. Probably they were not wrong for they were describing the Indus Valley towns of Mohenjodaro, Harappa and Kalibangan. As far as the names of their kings in both mythologies are concerned we are not in a position to say anything till the Indus script is deciphered and the names of kings found if they are there.

Why was it that the Buddhism and Jainism started and flourished in the area comprised in the modern state of Bihar at first? Probably because the area comprised a large number of oligarchies which were not only well-organised but were also well-armed and warlike. They had been fighting each other continuously over a long time. There was no peace between them and with the growing power of the armed forces the public at large was oppressed. In such a troubled time the people were not interested in religious mythologies but longed for a man of peace. We may remember that during the life time of both Buddha and Mahāvir there were fights exceeding all savagery and brutality between Magadh and Vaishali in which Vaishali was all but destroyed and its people either killed or utterly humbled and humiliated. Similarly in the fight between Koshal and Kapilvastu, the city from which Buddha himself came, the Shakya clan, the clan of Buddha himself was killed to a man during the life time of Buddha himself. People were terror stricken, fearful of anything they possessed, their family and society, and were tired of such unpleasant and degrading affairs. They could not think of a god who might have been their saviour. In such an atmosphere if anyone preached peace, non-violence to every living being, a righteous conduct which may lead to salvation, is more likely to be heard than at any other time. So people listened to the utterances of the teachers. They respected them and believed in what they taught. Moreover, they were not teaching something new. It was the essence of the old religion which was already there since long. In addition to improve the deteriorating atmosphere what the great contribution of the Buddha was that he gave the religion a unique framework, made it into an organisation and also created an hierarchy. In order to sustain the organisation and the structure he founded monasteries in various parts of the area. They were known as Ashrams or more popularly as Ārams and Vihārs. These Vihārs came to be so multiplied that the name of the area came to be called in later times Bihar, which is still retained as the name of the state. These monasteries had a number of Shramans or monks permanently living there and they were supervised by an higher hierarchical authority in turn controlled by a still higher and ultimately by a single chief. In the monastery itself there were hierarchies. These monasteries taught new converts and gave them good secular education as well. They were in addition giving secular education to the children of their devotees as well as giving them the basics of their religion and making them fit for their secular life as well. This spread of education combined with a kinship due to belonging to a common faith was one of the major factors for the entrenchment of the Buddhist religion in the area. It is due to the growth of Empire and the growing complexities of administration the bureaucracy proliferated and the recruits to the bureaucracy came mainly from the ex-students of those monasteries. The centre of empire being in Magadh the monastery-trained students who formed the bureaucracy controlled it.

Why it had not spread to such an extent to other areas where too these monasteries were established? In the rest of the country mainly in the Northern India there were also tribal republics. They were in North-Western India and in West Uttar Pradesh. However, the tribal republics in these areas could not afford to fight each other. As we have seen earlier Iran was united under the powerful dynasty of Achaemenids and by 6th century the Iranian or Persian Empire under Darius I (Dāyarwush) extended its hegemony upto the river Indus in India and became a threat to the other tribal republics not only bordering the Indus but even in the heart of the country upto the river Yamuna. The threat was real and it prompted the republics to be united in a defensive alliance. Because of that alliance the Persian Empire could not advance much further for the area was criss-crossed with gigantic rivers like Jhelum, Chenab, Ravi, Beās, Sutluj and their tributaries. It was also under a dense forest and the terrain was thus favourable to the tribes and a hindrance to the armies of the Persian Empire. The persistent attempts by the Persian Empire to conquer the land and the resistance it evoked united the republics and also hardened them in war. However, the most important result was the attempt to unite their gods into relationships either as friends as seen in the case of Krishna and Arjun or in relationships like Shiv, Skand, and Durgā etc or in identifying various gods as incarnations of one and the same universal God. Similar was the case with the republics and people in the western part of the area now the modern state of Uttar Pradesh. These republics came very early under the rule of kings of Magadh. It is said that the Nanda kings exterminated the kshatriyas. It probably meant that they conquered the whole territory upto the river Yamunā and killed the members of the oligarchical families leaving the other people unharmed and established peace. The people had no reason to give up their gods and to accept Buddhism or Jainism as their creed for the salvation of their souls after giving up their gods. They retained their gods after making them as great as universal gods. They must be having good relations with the people across the river Yamunā who were able to defy the Persians on one side and the kings of Magadh on the other. There must have been admiration for them too and so the intermingling of the gods must have taken place and new relationships established among them. Their imagination running riot, they must have expected their god to destroy the abominable and tyrant Magadh kings. We find among the Shursenis, the followers of Krishna, that they made the Magadh King a powerful one but it was Krishna who ultimately destroyed the Magadh King with the help of Arjun and Bhim, the deities from the other side of the river Yamunā. That probably signified their yearning which became a reality when the Mauryas destroyed and replaced the Magadh kings in real life. There were monasteries of Buddhism already in the area and they played their parts in giving secular education to the people, making them familiar with the tenets of Buddhism, taught them the common newly evolved script which was phonetic thus giving fillip to reading and writing, but failed to shake people from the belief in their gods. The part played by the Buddhist monasteries in educating the people was commendable but their role in influencing their religious beliefs was probably negligible. That was also probably a reason that Buddhism could not make much headway in those parts.

We may study the state of religion in the time of early

Mauryas and in time of Ashoka. The ease and rapidity with which Chandragupta Maurya had replaced the Nanda dynasty and established a universal state in Northern India must have come as a great shock which must have left a dazed population and a stunned bureaucracy in Magadh. It must have been similar to that which the people of Persia must have felt when their ruler was overthrown by Greeks under Alexander. However, the difference was that Alexander and the Greeks were aliens while Chandragupta Maurya and his army were Indians and their culture was also the same. We also know that the bureaucracy which was dazed reconciled to that change. The efforts of Chāṇakya in persuading the bureaucracy and other elements to extend their support to Chandragupta Maurya and to serve him ably, succeeded and even the ministers of Nandas continued to serve him as before. However, the establishment of a Universal State in the eyes of the people had a totally different impact on the people in so far as the status of their gods was concerned. Hitherto they were their regional gods but having a greater area than that of the state. Now the gods must be greater than the Universe or in other words must be omnipresent, omniscient, omnipotent and eventually Creator of the Universe. Thus the status of the gods was enhanced and thinking on the lines must have begun among the religious thinkers. The conflicts among the people had ceased and so must be the conflicts among the gods. They must be either identified with one another or made related to each other.

How much the state played its part in this religious renaissance? We do not know anything about the actions or thoughts or steps taken by either Chandragupta Maurya or his son Bindusār. The only thing we know about Chandragupta Maurya is that the coins issued by the Mauryas contained the image of peacock on them which gave us a clue to his identity for peacock is the mount of Skand or Kārttikeya or Brahmanya or Kumar (all are his different names), who was the deity worshipped by Yaudheyas. Mauryas, therefore, proclaimed their faith in Skand. The other facts known to us is that Chandragupta Maurya got images of Skanda, Vishākha another form of Skanda and of Shiv made and got them sold throughout the empire which incidentally brought revenue to the state as mentioned by Patanjali. Probably coercion was also used to make people buy them. This must have been done in order to impose his own god on the people. We are not in a position to say about the people's reaction towards that coercion. His son Bindusar maintained the tradition of his father of having the image of peacock on his coins and the selling of the images or statues of Shiv, Skand and Vishākha. We do not have any other information about Bindusār except that he once wrote to Antiocus I, son of Seleucus, king of Syria to send him among other things a sophist. Antiocus I wrote back that it was not lawful in Greece to send a sophist. Probably Bindusar was interested in knowing more about different creeds to establish a single one in the Empire and hence wanted to know about the Greek creed. By declining to send one Antiocus I lost an opportunity of making Bindusār aware of the creed of Greeks and may be of influencing Indian thought.

The rule of Ashoka had a great influence on the religions of the various regions and of India as a whole. Ashoka, it appears, really tried to reconcile to people to have love and friendship among themselves and wanted to remove every excuse for friction among different regions and people. Probably one of the reasons for such a conflict might have been the slaughter of the animal or a bird which might have been a totem of another man's tribe. Ashoka began by forbidding the slaughter and sacrifice in the kingdom in the first Rock-Edict. He himself stopped such slaughter of animals in his kitchen. In the fifth Pillar-Edict the gave a long list of birds and animals whose slaughter was absolutely prohibited. She-goats, ewes and sows with young ones in milk were not to be killed. Evidently that might have been due to his benign nature or it might have been policy to remove all kinds of things causing friction. Prohibition of killing of totems of different tribes might have been one.

However, Ashoka was converted to Buddhism in the eleventh year of his reign. He had conquered Kalinga just an year earlier. It is believed that it was due to remorse at the killing and deportation of a large number of persons in the war. This he has himself admitted in the thirteenth

Rock-Edict. It is possible that there were a large number of people in Bihar who believed in tenets of Buddhism and Bihār was the seat of Government and also of Ashoka. The bureaucracy too must be belonging to Buddhism and of Jainism and they must have used the opportunity provided by their close contact with the Emperor in converting him to Buddhism. He was also probably made to feel remorse at that killing too. After being converted and having studied the tenets of the religion he must have noticed that belief in this religion does not interfere with other religions. He must have, therefore, decided to stick to it and to try to make people accept it so that they might have a uniform religious belief binding them together. Hence, the adoption of Buddhism as a state religion.

The adoption of Buddhism as a state religion had a great and profound influence on the growth of other religions, the regional religions which formed a part of Hinduism and Buddhism as well as Jainism. We may first study its effect on Buddhism. The effect on Buddhism of its adoption as a state religion was similar to the effect on Christianity of its adoption as state religion by Constantine. First it flourished but later it was subjected to numerous schisms, all because of state support to it originally. By becoming a state religion and the religion of the Emperor it suddenly got all the facilities and privileges which it could get. It got a large number of wealthy persons among its adherents and thus was not short of funds. It also got money from state. In addition its wishes could not be ignored by the officials. The adherence of the Emperor and the pomp and prestige which accompanied it had enhanced its stature to attract a far large number of people to it than it would have been possible otherwise.

Buddhism prospered as never before. However, the state patronage had its drawbacks too for a religion which is a philosophy as well. Just as in the Roman Empire based at Constantinople where the Head of the Orthodox Church became an Under Secretary of State, similarly the Head of the Buddhist hierarchy became a Minister of Empire who was looking after all the religious affairs as well as affairs of the social welfare and had not only vast financial resources at his disposal but had a say in all the affairs of state. That position gave him so much importance that like his Christian counterpart he wielded authority even on the purely religious matters including the interpretation of canon as well. Those not agreeing with his views were to be branded as dissidents and accordingly punished. That unfortunately happened in the lifetime of Ashoka himself.

The founders of religions, in addition to giving elaborate pronouncements on their doctrines, have a tendency of speaking in aphorisms or even in parables. These always are interpreted in different ways by different people leading to disputes, mainly theological. If there is no arrogance at the top, then they are later on either reconciled or tolerated and there is no schism. This happened with Hinduism. But if there is arrogance at the top backed with state power as happened with Buddhism and Christianity, then dissidence, schism and expulsions are bound to occur. Moreover, when the founder of the religion dies, the important disciples or even all the disciples gather and try to collect all his sayings given to different persons and organise them into a canon. Even then there must be some persons, even laymen who might have heard the prophet in person and who might give a different version which might not be accepted by the disciples or might not be known to them.

This must have happened with Buddhism. It is said that when the Buddha died, his disciples and all the elders of the Buddhist organisation gathered together in Council and after a great deal of discussing the matter collected the sayings of the Buddha. As there was no phonetic alphabet at that time, they pronounced the sayings of the Buddha as they remembered and asked Anand, the Chief disciple and a constant companion of the Buddha to confirm them. After he confirmed them they pronounced it as the Buddhist Canon. However, it is more than probable that there were a large number of persons who must have heard the Buddha in person, must have even conversed with him and might have different versions of his sayings with them. These might not have found the way into the canon but might have been current. Secondly, the aphorisms might have been interpreted differently by different religious persons who might have sincerely believed in them. With a sudden large influx of persons in the faith due to state patronage, and among them a large number of educated persons and scholars of various shades of theology this was to be expected. Had there been no state patronage, these mainly theological disputes might have been discussed in public and disputes amicably solved and if no solution was found out at least tolerated. But as Minister of State, Head of the Buddhist hierarchy, could not afford to be proved wrong in any of his interpretations. Such an attitude was surely to undermine his position. Hence, a *rigidity* in the attitude of the State-backed organisation was bound to appear. Rigidity in every type or order when backed by state authority assumes horrible proportions which makes even the head of the religious denomination helpless when a particular view having gained the adherence of fanatic coterie becomes formidable as once happened in a Buddhistic order that the head of the monastery had to exhort the lay disciple to quietly quit the monastery, though his view-point on the topic of discussion was correct. We have to speculate on what must have happened for there are no records and whatever are there were recorded much later and have to be one-sided. But what appears to be facts are that there was much dissidence and probably schismatic fights leading to violence. There also appears to be the possibility that because the monasteries had huge funds at their disposal and they had considerable influence in the state, a large number of unscrupulous persons had managed to enter the order and managed important positions or may be the existing ones might have become corrupt. The real dedicated persons who were true followers of the order might have resented it and opposed them leading to discontent. Whatever might have been the causes the schisms continued unchecked and there must have been frequent disorders.

Such disorders must have reached such a stage that the words of the chief of the Buddhist order and the senior monks might have lost conviction and Emperor Ashok himself might have some doubts. Hence, as pointed out earlier, he convened a Council, the Third Buddhist Council under the presidency of Moggaliputta Tissa, a venerable monk living in solitary retreat.[5] This Council decided about the true principles of Buddhism discarding all the false doctrines as they saw it and established doctrines belonging to Abhidhamma and called them Kathāvatthu. The Council also took the extraordinary step of expelling all the adherents of what they saw as false doctrines, unfrocked them and compelled them to put on white robes. That, according to Mahāvansa, took place in the seventeenth year of the reign of Ashoka. However, the Buddhist order so reorganised still could not or dared not stand on its own feet and used the royal authority to establish themselves. They induced Ashok to issue an Edict against schism called Sanghabheda and ordered the officials of the civil administration to see that within their respective jurisdictions all schismatic monks were expelled from the Sangh, compelled to wear white robes and driven to live in places not suited for the residence of the monks. Obviously the Buddhist organisation did not find itself capable of purging of undesirable elements from it and establishing a pure organisation and had to invoke the civil authority of the state to get rid of such elements and the people so purged in that way were those who might have been indicted by the monks in authority. It might have also been possible that the people in authority might have been unscrupulous persons and might have expelled the true disciples. It is also possible that a large number of people might not have agreed with the view of the Buddhist Council. However, the schism continued to plague Buddhism for long. Such a strong support to the Buddhist organisation by the state and the Third Buddhist Council had a disastrous consequences on the Buddhist religion and on India as such. Having enjoyed such a strong support from the civil government to the extent of getting their opponents on matters which are theocratic, punished, the Buddhist hierarchy became not only dependent on state support but tried to manoeuvre in such a way that the control might remain in its hands or at least in its favour. It enjoyed this privilege during the life time of Ashok but only about forty-five years after his death when the state came under the rule of a non-Buddhist dynasty, the Buddhist hierarchy lost its ground and felt helpless. It started, as tradition holds, hatching up conspiracies to get the ruler substituted by another more favourable one. They got into contact with other kingdoms within the country and later with those outside the country. Tradition holds them responsible for inviting a succession of foreign invaders including Shaks, Kushān and Bactrians. The second consequence of their being out of power was the improvement in the position of those who were expelled from the organisation and from monasteries by the civil power during the rule of Ashok. They were in a better position to challenge the official Buddhist hierarchy in theological matters. There was no state now to punish them and there were people ready to listen to them. Being deprived of living in monasteries and of power they were probably ascetics who thought about the spiritual and theocratic matters deeply and also having come into contact with the rising Hindu religion had reconciled to certain attributes of Hindu religion, specially their faith in a living god. They could not raise Buddha to the status of a living god for people knew that he had died and that he himself never claimed to be either a god or even an angel. They, therefore, invented Bodhisattva, the compassionate one who refused to get Nirvān or salvation but full of compassion tried to help all in trouble. With this ideology they confronted the old organisation.

The Third Buddhist Council which after long deliberations standardised the Buddhist beliefs according to them had produced a document *Kathāvatthu* embodying all their beliefs in it. When an Ecumenical organisation of a religion convenes a council of its elders to consider the dogmas of the religion under challenge from others, it has to take into account the fact that any deviation from what the master has said will be challenged and the deliberations discredited. They are compelled to be on a safe side agreeing to accept ones not likely to be challenged and specially when the audience includes the Emperor well-versed in their faith. That happened in Christianity too when it had to deliberate on points in a world council convened by Roman Emperor to standardise the faith. The schism in the Christianity followed. The *Katthāvatthu* presented the Buddhist religion a dry and sterile one, such a thing none among the lay men facing a mundane life was likely to be attracted with. Subsequently Buddhist organisation declined in popular esteem though it retained an organisation, its monasteries, and its adherents in bureaucracy which was conspiring with foreign powers to displace a king who was not controlled by them. When the organisation was again challenged by those who were expelled earlier and presented with a new compassionate Bodhisattva they refused to accept him and rejected him outright. The matter was subsequently decided before another Buddhist Council. This Council was convened during the period of Kushan rule by the king Kanishk where the majority opinion favoured the new view with a Bodhisattva, Buddha in a former life, who refused to accept Nirvān, salvation, in order to help people in distress due to his compassion. The minority opinion continued to believe in the old dogmas. The majority opinion called themselves as belonging to Mahāyān (Great Chariot) and called those belonging to minority opinion as belonging to Hinyān or Lesser Chariot. The two could not reconcile and thus the Buddhist religion split into two sects of Mahāyān and Hinyān. That conflict between the two ruined Buddhism in India. People who were already attached to their own gods who were living gods refused to do anything with such a dry religion. Even though they subsequently produced Bodhisattva, the Compassionate One, yet he was no match for a living god like Vishnu or Shiv or his incarnation Vāsudev who was a Creator as well. Buddhism declined and totally disappeared from India. Mahāyān under the patronage of Kushāns who ruled on both sides of the Hindukush made its way to Central Asia and from there to China and Far East where it became the dominant faith. Hinyān remained on the fringes of India, Sri Lankā, Myanmar (Burma), Thailand, Malaysia and parts of Southern Vietnam and Philippines. In some of them it was later replaced by Islam and Christianity. The date of that meeting of the Buddhist Council appears to be important for from that time one of the Indian Calendars, Shak Samvat appears to have been born. It is presumed that it was named after the King Kanishk but it is wrong for Kanishk was a Kushan who replaced Shaka rulers and secondly, none of the existing calendars of the world were named after kings or earthly rulers. They invariably date from some significant event in the progress of the religion whose adherents first observed the calendar. So it was with Gregorian Calendar, the most widely used in the world today which is dated from the supposed time of the birth of Christ, Hijri from the arrival of Prophet Mohammad in Medina from Mecca, Vikrami Samvat from the time of a gathering of prominent Hindu saints who at a sacrifice named Vishnu also called Tri-Vikrama or Vikrama as the ruler of the world. Similarly Shaka Samvat must be dated from that meeting which proclaimed Shākya Muni, a name of Buddha as the Compassionate One in the form of Bodhisattva.

We may now examine the position of other religions in the times of Ashoka. The Jain religion containing an equally dry and sterile philosophy could not make any headway in Northern India and a doubtful one in South India. Jain tradition claims that towards the later part of the rule of Chandragupta Maurya the Jain monks migrated to South India due to a long famine and that Chandragupta Maurya too renouncing throne joined them. The latter's claim appears to be far-fetched. They did migrate but whether it was self-willed or whether they were expelled cannot be said in the present state of our knowledge. King Khārvel of Kalinga in modern state of Orissa claims in one of his inscriptions that he defeated a king of Magadh and brought back some Jain images taken away by the Nanda kings. It is possible that the Nandas might have been Jains and because of support of Jains they might have been expelled by Mauryas. May be due to state support of Buddhism and the enthusiasm it aroused due to the conversion of Emperor Ashoka, and the two philosophies being almost similar the adherents of Jainism joined the Buddhist order. The rest of the true believers finding their life insecure in Magadh empire might have migrated to areas beyond their rule. Whatever may be the cause the Jain religion did not prosper in India and remained confined only to select groups.

We may now examine the progress of other religions formerly confined to tribes and regions. Those cults or regional religions devoted to particular gods were neither given state patronage nor they faced any hostility from the state. As there was peace everywhere, specially between various tribes and regions under the Mauryas there was no cause of hostility among various gods. All the gods attained ecumenical status as the Creator. As due to mobility of people they came into contact with each other and a sort of affinity too developed among the various gods. In that mingling certain gods attained a wider area of influence while some lost ground. We find from inscriptions belonging to 2nd century B.C. just after the times of the Mauryas that Vāsudev Krishna was regarded as a supreme god over a much larger area. He was traditionally the god of the Shurseni tribe near Mathura in Western Uttar Pradesh, but the inscriptions are found in as wide an area as Ghosundi near Chittor in South-West Rajasthan, at Besnagar near Vidishā in Central India and in the caves at Nānāghāt. We find the cult of Shiv all over India probably was spread by the Mauryas themselves, due to their selling the images of Shiv. However, the cult of Skanda and Vishākh did not spread so widely though Mauryas also sold their images. However, due to reconciliation among the various gods new equations arose among them. A larger number of gods were regarded as equally reverential and came to be regarded as one and the same as the incarnation of the supreme deity, while others were joined together in a family relationship. Among the first group come the incarnations of Vishnu and among the second the family of Shiv. A large number of deities, twenty-four in number both men, animals and half man-half-animal were regarded as incarnations of Vishnu and thus of equal power and prestige. Among the second group were Shiv, Pārvati, the mother goddess, Skanda and Ganesh. What had happened to the large number of mother goddesses worshipped throughout India? All the mother goddesses including Durgā, Kāli, Bhawāni, the Yoginis, etc. were identified as only a form of Pārvati and thus the consort of Shiv. There was no conflict between the two groups and they are shown as having great respect for each other to the extent of each worshipping the other. We may note an interesting fact in this identification. Both Buddha and Rishabh, the first Tirthankar of Jains are treated as incarnations of Vishnu, thus eliminating any hostility among the adherents of Jainism and Buddhism. At the same time Shiv is shown having all the attributes and form of Rishabh, the deity of the Indus Valley Civilisation as seen earlier. We have a new composite religion. Mystics were not far behind in evolving mythology integrating all of the gods into one harmonious whole. This new mystic religion became the religion of the masses. They had still to worship their old tribal god whom they had worshipped since times immemorial as the omnipotent, omniscient Creator and who what was more was a living god full of compassion ready to help in distress. They had the interesting, romantic, full of supernatural stories as mythology whom both they and their children liked to hear again and again. Both Buddhism and Jainism with their philosophies sans god were unable to meet with the challenge of such a god, or gods. Even the newly-created Budhisattva, the Compassionate One was unable to displace the Hindu gods so created. Buddhism as creed ceased to influence the people almost with the end of Mauryas. Jainism was never revived in Northern India.

When should we regard Hinduism to be formally recognised? Normally Hinduism came to be a single unified religion during the time of Ashoka and the succeeding dynasty of Sungas with Pushyamitra as the first king. But if a formal date is to be searched, then it should be some time later. Was there some formal ceremony to inaugurate it? There appears to be a formal function when it was proclaimed or actually the Supreme God was proclaimed as the ruler of earth. This date should be the date when King Vikramaditya was proclaimed as the King of Kings and the Samvat known as the Vikrami Samvat came into being. Was he not a small king of Ujjain after whom such a Samvat was named? Probably not. There is no evidence that a king of the name of Vikramāditya ever ruled Ujjain at such a period. Nor any calendars named after even mighty monarchs survived for long. We may see the fate of Gupta Samvat named after the Gupta kings which began from their rule. Calendars which survived invariably began from some date associated with some significant events of a religion or a religious prophet. The calendars of Islam and Christianity serve as examples. What are the evidences which may attribute Vikrami Samvat to be named after Vikramāditya and who was Vikramāditya? Vikṛami Samvat was first known as Krita Samvat and inscriptions having this name are found. Some historians thought that Krita might have been some chief. As it was also sometimes called Mālava Samvat, they thought he might have been some Mālava chief. Krita means a Yagya or sacrifice and we should look at such sacrifice which is recorded in religious literature and is significant. Secondly, we may analyse the name Vikramāditya and try to understand its meaning. Vikramāditya is made of two words Vikrama and Āditya. Literary meaning of Vikrama is bravery and that of Aditya Sun. Joined together it may mean a Sun of Valour. However, we should try to see its meaning in terms of mythology. Here it takes another meaning. Āditya means the sons of Aditi, the mother of Gods. She had twelve sons who were all called Ādityas, among them are Indra, Sun and Vishnu. Vishnu had an appellation commonly used in *Vedas,* Tri-Vikram. So Vikramāditya could be Vishnu. Why should we regard Vishnu to be the ruler of the world? If we look at the *Purānās,* the stories of those times we find one theme current in all. There was a time when the gods under Indra were defeated by Bali, the king of Asurs and Bali became the king of Heaven. He was so powerful and had been given boons which made him invincible that the gods despaired. They were told that only Vishnu alone could save them. Vishnu was born as the twelfth child of Āditi and was a dwarf. Bali was holding a sacrifice when Vishnu in the shape of the dwarf approached him to grant him some land.

On Bali enquiring the extent of land he demanded, Vishnu said only three steps. When the demand was granted and Vishnu asked to measure it he assumed enormous proportions and in one step measured the earth, in the second the heaven and demanded where he might place the third one. Stunned Bali offered his own body and by placing the third step on his head Bali was made his slave. He restored the earth and heaven to Indra and sent Bali to live in the underworld under his protection. The gods were happy and it was decreed that while Indra would be nominal ruler of heaven, Vishnu would be the real Ruler of Earth. This Vishnu or Vikramāditya is the ruler of earth, the King of Kings whose praises are sung in Sanskrit poetry with such raptures and whose deeds of three steps are mentioned in *Rigveda* often and in others as well. We do not know what the seers who created the hymns of *Rigveda* actually had in mind, but this is how the people later interpreted and absorbed it in the mythology. Thus Vikramāditya is not a ruler of petty kingdom after whom the Samvat is named but is Vishnu, the Supreme God himself. We have evidence of the name Vikrama being used even earlier. Kalidas in his drama *Vikramorvashi* written in the 2nd century B.C. had used the name Vikrama for the king but the king in that case was Pururvā not Vishnu. Moreover, the deeds of Vikramāditya as sung in poetry are indeed supernatural as we find in *Vaitāl Pachisi* and *Singhāsan Batisi*. King Vikramank of Tamil literature also appears to be none other than Vikramāditya. We may now search for the Krita or Yagya or sacrifice where he was proclaimed as the King of kings. The only sacrifice from which our warrior clans also claim descent appears to be the sacrifice by the seers under the guidance of Vashist and was performed at Abu in Rajasthan. We may take it that it was at some such sacrifice Vikramāditya was proclaimed as the King of kings and as it was essentially a religious event of great importance it was remembered. People at first started estimating the time from the date of that yagya or kritu and called it Krita Samvat and later called it Vikrami Samvat. Why it was for some time called Mālava Samvat we do not know and cannot explain it in the present state of our knowledge.

Thus we find that the foundations of the new Hindu religion were laid in the times of Mauryas and the seeds of demise of Buddhism and Jainism were also sown in that time, especially during the reign of Ashoka. It can be stated, however, that the above analysis is purely based on logic. There is no historical evidence whatsoever. The traditions are contradictory. There is so much paucity of evidence that we cannot be sure even to the identity of Devānām Priyadasi of the Edicts both on Pillar, and on Rock. In only one the name is mentioned, *i.e.,* in the one at Maski. However, in *Mudrārāksasa,* a seventh century Sanskrit play about Chandragupta Maurya it is an appellation of Chandragupta Maurya. If it was an appellation of Chandragupta Maurya too, then it might have been the appellation or official name of kings of Maurya dynasty and we may not know as to who had issued Edicts. It is possible that some of the earlier ones might have been those issued by Chandragupta Maurya himself.

Language and Literature

In every part of the world the languages spoken by the people vary after a small distance and are usually coterminus with the economic and social intercourse of the people. However, when the area of the economic and social intercourse enlarges a common speech must necessarily evolve, and this speech becomes the *lingua-franca.* When a large Empire is formed then what is likely to be the *lingua-franca?* In such a case some peculiar circumstances work together to select a particular region whose spoken language must necessarily be treated as the language of the empire and its *lingua-franca.* It is usually the language of the capital region of the empire. It may be so for two reasons. Firstly, the bureaucracy which resides there has necessarily to be conversant with the local spoken speech if they have to meet the necessities of life from the local market and if they are coming from different regions, then to converse with each other. Secondly, the bureaucracy is usually recruited from the local population and thus finds itself able to work easily in that language. Historically too when a strong government comes into being which is to make a bid for power, for world dominion it locates its capital in its homeland and recruits the bureaucracy from amongst its people. So the language of the capital region becomes the *lingua-franca* and when the dynasty is supplanted by another one from a different one, the *lingua-franca* remains the same. What happens when the capital is shifted to some other place? Then for the same reasons as given above the *lingua-franca* rapidly becomes the speech of the new region where the capital is located. We may see the example of the first in English spoken in and around London as the language of British Empire, of English spoken in Washington-New York area as the language of U.S.A., of language spoken around Paris as that dialect of French which is the official language of France and so on. The examples of the second can be seen in India itself. When the capital of the Slave Dynasty which came to power in India in 1205 A.D. was located in Delhi, the language spoken around in Delhi region became the *lingua-franca* though not the official language which remained

Persian. We see some examples of it in the writings of Amir Khusro which survive today. However, the Lodi kings shifted the capital to Āgrā and we suddenly find that the *lingua-franca* became the dialect spoken in and around Āgrā as the language of intercourse between the different people. We find the examples in the contemporary poetry in which even nobles of court like Abdur Rahim Khānkhānā wrote. However, during the times of Aurangzeb when somewhere about 1660 A.D. the capital was again shifted to Delhi the *lingua-franca* again became the language spoken around Delhi called Khari-Boli. Delhi ceased to be the capital of India during British Rule and hence the language of these parts declined. However, when again in 1918 A.D. the capital was shifted to Delhi the language not the official Hindi but spoken in and around Delhi became the language of the land. The literature which we have in Hindi came to be produced only after this period.

The same must have happened in the Empire founded by the Shishunag Dynasty whose successors were the Mauryas. The original capital of the Dynasty founded by Bimbisār was Rājgrah but it was soon shifted to Pātliputra, the modern Patna by Bimbisār himself. The speech of Patliputra region became the *lingua-franca.* It must have been the language of the Empire also. The efforts of the Mauryan Empire were directed towards making that dialect the language of the whole of the territory of the Empire and probably beyond it as well. It must have been understood by common people as well due to the necessity of communications to and from officials in remote parts of empire and the capital. During the times of Ashok the territory of the Empire extended to cover almost the whole of India and the whole of India became the area of that language where it was understood. The adoption of Buddhism as the state religion and its propagation in a language which might be understood everywhere made the language of Patliputra, the Ardha-Māgadhi dialect, the language of Buddhism and Jainism also. Thus the language also known as Pāli became the official language, the language of Buddhism, the language of Jainism and hence the *lingua-franca.* When the Emperor wanted to communicate something to the people he had to take recourse to that language.

What are other factors that facilitated the spread of language and learning? The spread of language requires a script and the propagation of a suitable script was the greatest contribution of Mauryas, specially Ashok. That script was the phonetic Brahmi script. We do not know when it was discovered and who was the genius who discovered its use. But whoever he was had given something unique to the world. And its widespread use and acceptance was due to Ashok. None of the written records prior to the inscriptions on Pillars and rocks attributed to Ashok is found except the Indus Valley seals belonging to the Indus Valley period two thousand years earlier and possible one plaque known as Shahgaura plaque which may be a little older. We have no evidence of what transpired between the Indus Valley period which ended by 16th century B.C. and period of Ashoka in the 3rd century B.C. as far as development of script is concerned. Earlier when the Indus Valley Civilisation was not unearthed and people thought that India's history began in the 6th century B.C. with Buddha it was presumed that the Brahmi script was originally invented by the Phoenicians and brought to India. But when in the thirties of this century Indus Valley Civilisation was discovered and the symbols of Indus Valley script were found to have a strikingly close resemblance with the letters of the Brahmi script it began to be surmised that the Brahmi script may actually have the origin in this country and from Indus script. The messages conveyed through that script, the spread of religious literature made possible through state grants and state support and the ever present Inscriptions on Rock and Pillars made the script well known and universally used in India and the surrounding areas. This popularisation and making it the vehicle of the use of written word is the greatest contribution of Mauryas, specially Ashoka. The great failure, however, lay in their inability to find a medium on which it might have been written and might have been preserved for succeeding ages. Though the writing something on clay and burning it into fire had been known in the Indus Valley Civilisation, yet it was not used in later times. The only written record of those times and those prior to it are the Rock and Pillar inscriptions and a solitary copper Sahgaura plaque. Again we have the same inscriptions on stone which are found in the succeeding ages. What tradition says about the medium on which people and state might have been writing their messages or compositions? According to tradition the people used the bark of the Silver Birch known in India as Bhojpatra, an extremely fragile thing for composition. For sending of messages probably cloth was used. Since the slaughter of the animals was prohibited by the state, the skin which is more durable was not used for that purpose. However; looking to the availability of vast volumes of religious literature composed prior to the Mauryan age including the epics *Mahābhārat* and *Rāmāyan* there must have been some such medium which was enduring for a fairly long period. What it was we are in the dark.

Was there any literature produced during the period of Ashoka? The literature produced during the period had not survived as nothing has been found so far. But we find in the next century, *i.e.,* 2nd century B.C. a fairly good quantity of literature, among them the Grammar of Patanjali, his *Yoga-Shatak,* and most important of all the works of Kālidas who must have written them in the times of either Agnimitra or Vasumitra of the Shung Dynasty which succeeded the Mauryas. Looking to the brilliance of Kalidas's poetry it is just apparent that a lot of literature, good and mediocre, must have been produced in the preceding generations to be able to bring such a poetical genius to flower. But due to the fragile nature of the material on which it was written it perished.

Was literature produced in all the various languages of India? We do not know much. The only literature which survived can be categorised. First, we have the literature of Buddhism. The core portion containing the sayings of the Buddha and his teachings is in Pali, a language used by the administration and by Ashok. Rest of the work which was the product of the Buddhist Councils was also in Pali. However, the later commentaries were in Sanskrit. On the other hand the religious literature pertaining to the Hindu religion, the *Brāhmanas, Āranyaks* and *Upnishads, Brahma Sutra,* the *Grahya Sutras* if they were written during that period were in Sanskrit. Some of the *Purānās* also which were produced during that period were in Sanskrit. The regional religious literature is simply not available and we do not know if they were in local language or not. But the hymns dedicated to their regional gods must have been in the local dialects but they are not available. They might be still existing in tribal lore in an amended and modernised form. But we have no knowledge about it. Similar is the position regarding the languages of the other regions of India. We have to be content with just guessing the extent of such literature and its fate.

Were the two scripts, the phonetic Brahmi script and the old Indus script or its later form, used simultaneously during that period? We may say that this is a more probable one. Both the scripts must have been in use. The Brahmi script being easier must have been liked more by new writers but the older religious writings and writings by conservative writers must have been using the older script. However, when a script is changed and substituted by another script then it usually happens that the books written in the older script are no longer read. What the succeeding generation likes most is usually rewritten in the new phonetic script but those which are not liked or appreciated by the people are not rewritten in the new script and after a while they fall into disuse and perish. That must have happened and a whole lot of books just perished. We simply get in the surviving books the names of various authors but they are just names and the books are not extant. In *Nirukta* of Yāska we get a large number of names of scholars and grammarians whom he had either agreed or disagreed with but we are not aware of the works which they might have produced. It is simply because *Nirukta* of Yāska was thought important but his predecessors were not considered so. Hence, the work by Yāska survived because it was rewritten in the new script while his predecessors' works perished because they were not so rewritten. It was also because of that factor that the works produced during the Mauryan age and the age of Nandas had not survived. The contemporaries of Shunga kings might not have either dared or thought it prudent to rewrite the books praising the Nanda or Mauryan kings.

What other problems might have arisen due to the change of script? The change of script might have created at least two types of problems. One might be the rewriting of sacred books. Such books are usually kept in the original form wherever it is possible. Thus the *Vedas* might have been kept in the old form and script. However, when it might have been noticed that the script was going out of use or might have gone out of use and if not rewritten in the new script a time might come when nobody would be able to read it at all, people might have decided to rewrite the *Vedas* in that new script. Hence, the *Vedas* were written in that script and were thus preserved. However, as we may notice in the last few hymns of *Atharvaveda, i.e.,* from hymn 129 onwards in the last Mandal, the hums so written are unintelligible. Somebody not knowing the script had hastily put down what he might have read without caring if it made any sense. And really it does not make any sense. Such a fate might have fallen to many a book. The second problem is created when a word in a book is rewritten but its meaning is disputed. If the book is a religious one, then a whole lot is written in trying to explain its meaning by different persons differently. An example may be given of a controversy about the form of sacrifice, whether it is grain or it is animal. The word is *Aj* meaning both a grain or a goat. Probably in the original script it might have been shown as an animal followed by a determinative. The former might have been a symbol of an animal and the latter might have denoted it to be a grain or something eatable both denoting grain. This as we have seen above is quite likely for the original vocubulary was a limited one—one word being used for a number of things quite different and the determinative clarifying the meaning. But during that time since the meanings in old script had become obscure, the controversy started regarding the real meaning. A whole lot was written about the real meaning. Authorities were quoted in favour of each and supernatural elements introduced in resolving the problem. This was an outcome of the change in script and the people not familiar with the old one saw the symbol of animal while not realising the meaning of determinative. But this also indicates that the controversy was largely academic, the practice of sacrifice not being in vogue at that time as it is not in vogue today. Similar are other such theological disputes on the meaning of words. We should be cautious of such disputes and try to see its real meaning in the old discarded script. Such were the problems created by the change of script. We had to pay the penalty in the loss of much of old literature, both secular and religious. While a good portion of religious literature survived because of sanctity and because some had memorised it, most of the secular literature has been lost, a priceless loss indeed. We had gained in easy writings, easier understanding of written word and easier and quicker communication all over the country. There were both loss and gain but the Mauryan age, specially that of Ashoka, was a watershed in the literary history of India, because of new medium of writing, *i.e.*, the new script whose use nationwide was made possible by the patronage of the Mauryas.

REFERENCES

1. *Yāska-Nirukta*, III, 4
2. *Rigveda* 10.5.6
3. *Nirukta* 6. 111
4. *Iraq* : III (1936) : p. 101, Fig. 1
5. *Dipvansa* 7.34-59; *Mahāvansa* 5. 288

APPENDICES

APPENDIX-A

MAHĀBHĀRATA—HISTORICAL AND POLITICAL CONTEXT

The original name of *Mahābhārata* was according to tradition *Jai Bhārat* and was much smaller probably about ten thousand couplets as against more than ten times its present length. If we study it, we will find that three stories are woven together to form the present epic and those can be independent stories. The question will naturally arise regarding the one which was the theme of *Jai Bhārat*. This can be answered only when we examine the *Mahābhārata* in its present form in its historical and political setting. The three stories are the ordeal and education of Yama, the god of justice and death, the story of Vāsudev Krishna and the story of Arjun or Nar. The story of the ordeal and education of Yama has been given quite an important place in the present *Mahābhārata* and involves his incarnation as Yudhister, the eldest Pandava. As per the story Māndavya was a great saint with considerable supernatural powers. He was once given a punishment by a king due to some misunderstanding of a torturous death by forcing a needle—like stick into his anus which would pass through the body and cause a miserable death. The saint was pained and angered and knowing that the punishment was in reality decreed by Yama he summoned him. On coming before the saint and being asked the reason for this punishment, Yama informed him that in his childhood the saint had killed an insect by a needle. The saint told him that Yama had forgotten the reality on earth that he should not punish for deeds done in innocence and that in order that Yama should understand the reality of life on earth in which man is sometimes forced to do things he does not intend, he cursed Yama to be born on earth and live for a hundred years. Yama took birth first as Vidur and had his first experience of life. As per the story King Vichitravirya of Hastinapur died issueless. He had two queens. Her mother in order to get an heir summoned her eldest son Ved Vyas, an illegitimate one but a great saint himself, to beget sons by the two widows. However, in the palace of the queens he met three girls and all the three became pregnant. Obviously one among them was a slave. Even after persistent questioning they refused to divulge who was slave and who were princesses. As the time for delivery approached the matter of deciding the queens and slave became urgent for on it depended the decision about the prince and a slave. In the face of their refusal it was felt that only test which could determine the queen and a slave would be heredity and they should be subjected to some test which would reveal the heredity. The three girls were made to come before them nude. The one feeling ashamed closed her eyes, the second draped a very fine piece of yellow cloth but the third came before them without indicating any shame and that third one was declared as the slave because of her shamelessness. Yama was the son of that third one and was named Vidur. Because his mother was declared to be a slave he was born a slave and was insulted and humiliated all his life. The son of one who closed her eyes was born blind and named Dhritrāshtra while that of the girl who draped a cloth round her was a sickly child named Pandu and remained sickly all his life. As the blind could not become the king, the sickly one occupied the throne. Yama had his first experience of life. For no fault of his he became a slave all his life. His mother might have been in reality a princess and one of the other princesses might have been a slave, but by a risky and doubtful decision Yama had to toil as a slave. He again took birth as Yudhister, the eldest son of Pandu, the king of Hastinapur, and was destined to succeed him as king. Misfortunes and accidents of life stalked him. His father died a few years after leaving behind five sons and a widow, Kunti, mother of Yudhister. They had to fall back on the mercy and hospitality of their uncle, the blind Dhritarāshtra who was now crowned king with Yudhister as the crown prince. There too attempts were made on the lives of the brothers by their covetous and envious cousin Duryodhan who wanted to kill him so that he might become the king. They were helped and supported by their grand uncle Bhishma and uncle Vidur, the slave. After they had completed their education they were sent to a far away place ostensibly to watch a festival but in reality to be killed for they were made to stay in a house made of inflammatory material and the plan was to set fire to the house. Forewarned they made their escape and facing dangers in the way, they reached the capital of king Drupad where a function was in progress in which the most skilful archer was to gain the hands of the princess of Panchal, the daughter of the king Drupad. His youngest brother Arjun won the princess. Here a tenet of religion, obedience to the words of the parents, much upheld by the God of Justice faced him. The Pandava brothers when they reached the house along with the princess in their jubilation told their mother from outside their house that they won a beautiful prize. The mother in that unguarded moment without looking at the prize told them to share it. Parental command was more important to Yudhister and true to the tenet of Yama to obey the parental command, he forced his brothers to marry her altogether in a sort of polyandrous marriage. Backed by the might of Drupad, the king of Panchal, they returned to Hastinapur and demanded the kingdom as its rightful heir. However, the crafty blind uncle, in his love for his son Duryodhan decided to divide the kingdom and persuaded his court to agree to it and later so divided it that the portion Yudhister got was only forest without any habitation. Yudhister accepted and built a mighty empire. His envious cousins persuaded his uncle to order Yudhister to have a bout of gambling with his son. Yudhister lost the gambling by fraud knowing it full well and lost everything including the freedom of himself, his brothers and what was worse his wife too, for he gave up as slaves. His wife and queen, the beautiful Draupadi was dragged to the court and insulted. That somehow roused the conscience of Gandhari, their aunt, who asked her husband, the blind king to restore the freedom and kingdom back to them but the crafty old man again under pressure from his son made Yudhister to play again. True to the creed that one should obey the elders Yudhister played again and lost. As per the stakes he had to give up his kingdom and go to the forest alongwith his brothers for twelve years and spend one year in concealment during which if they were discovered, they would have to wander again for twelve more years and one more year of concealment and so on. After that only their kingdom would be restored. He went in exile along with his brothers and wife and for twelve years wandered from forest to forest meeting with hardships, dangers and was continuously insulted by his cousins. He also spent one year in concealment as a courtier in the court of king Virat of the Matsya. His brothers too served the king in various capacities, Bhim as a cook, Nakul and Sahdev as keepers of cows and horses, his wife as a maid-servant and what was worse his brother Arjun, the finest archer in the world, an unconquerably warrior had to disguise himself as an eunuch teaching music and dance to the king's daughter. He probably could not be concealed except in the women's apartments. The year was spent in humiliations being heaped upon their heads and dangers of exposure lurking everywhere as well as dangers to their wife. He endured it and was surprised when after the expiry of the periods his cousins refused to give back his kingdom. True to the creed of kshatriyas that they must fight to get their right, much against his will he had to fight and the celebrated *Mahābhārata* war was fought in Kurukshetra. The battle lasting eighteen days was another lesson in the ways of the world. He found that he could not win without taking recourse to stratagem involving deceit and fraud. He had to accept the hard realities of life and three people, his grand-uncle Bhishma and his teacher Drona whom he revered and his cousin Duryodhan were felled by deceit. He who had not taken up arms and had not killed a single being, man or animal, had to take up arms and kill his uncle Shalya, the king of Madras, who was fighting in the ranks of his enemies. Why he alone was required to kill Shalya? No reasons are assigned and no explanations are given. Any other warrior including Bhim or Arjun could have been asked to fight him. Was there some compulsion in that fight? Probably there was. Shalya was wise, very accomplished in every art and was virtuous. According to religious beliefs if a person was very virtuous and had not committed any sin, Yama, the God of Death, himself had to come and take his soul to heaven. In Hindu mythology there is only one instance when Yama had himself arrived to take away the soul and that is in the case of Satyavan, the husband of the celerbated Savitri. Was it in the case of Shalya too that only Yama could have killed him, because of his virtues and purity? He had also to face a last ordeal. In his last days when leaving the earth he was going up the mountains on his way to heaven, a dog became deeply attached to him. He could not take it to heaven for it was supposed to be a dirty beast. But could he leave a dog who loved him in life? He decided that he could not go without the dog. The last scene was a hilarious and comic one but was made to appear solemn. When he reached his abode he found an anarchy in heaven. People he knew to be sinners were enjoying in heaven while those he knew to be virtuous were suffering in hell.

The second story is that of Vāsudev Krishna. The role of Krishna in *Mahābhārata* is a limited one. He acts as a friend, philosopher and guide to Ārjun. He did not take up arms and everytime acted as a charioteer of Ārjun. His contribution was that whenever Arjun required any guidance or advice he gave it as his charioteer and small help whenever needed. His main contribution was when Arjun before the start of the *Mahābhārata* war, in the field of battle was assailed by self-doubt about the wisdom of killing his elders and relations whom he revered or loved, he gave him a religious discourse which removed his doubts and enabled him to fight. That religious discourse now known as the *Bhagwat Gita* has become so important a book that it has replaced all other religious books including the *Vedas* as the principal religious book of the Hindus. However, the story of Vāsudev who was also a cult figure of those times was a large and extensive one, the glimpses of which can be seen throughout the *Mahābhārata* and we are reminded of it at every stage of the story. His story is given in detail in the *Bhāgwat Purān* and *Harivansh Purān.* He belonged to Yadu tribe which settled down after their dispersion from Indus Valley near about Mathura and came to be called Shurseni tribe consisting of a coalition of two tribes, Andhak and Vrishni. As we know that

Plate 2: Krishna teaching *Gita* to Arjuna

the threat to the tribe was not from the Western Achaemenid empire but from the Eastern Magadhan empire and hence the whole story of Krishna was devoted to the destruction of first the allies of Magadh and then the king of Magadh. His maternal uncle Kansa was described as son-in-law of the king of Magadh and also his Senāpati or commander-in-chief. It appears that this description of him being the Senapati of the king of Magadh was due to a later misunderstanding of the meaning of the term Senapati. Probably he was the head of the republic of the Shursenis titled Senapati and was an ally of the King of Magadh, Jarasandh. He was the first to be killed by Krishna who replaced him as the head of the republic. He killed next Shishupal, the king of a place called Chedi, now thought to be somewhere to be in the South of Magadh and an ally of the Magadh. Others to be killed or defeated included Narkāsur, Bān, Shālva, etc., all ruling in places in the periphery of Magadh. Ultimately he got the Magadh king himself killed by Bhim, the second Pandava brother, in a single combat. Thus we find that cult figure that he was, the cult developed due to the threat from the East.

The third story is the story of Arjun. Arjun of all the characters is truly an epic one comparable to Gilgamesh of the Gilgamesh epic of the Sumerians, Hercules of the Greeks and all other characters of similar epics. He is the incarnation of Nar, one among the saints Nar and Narayan, born to rid the world of evil. It is interesting to note that Nar actually means man. If we recall 'Purush' of that Sukta of the *Vedas* popularly known as the *Purush Sukta*'[1] who is the embodiment of the Creator, we will find that Purush also means man. Was the name Nar meant to identify him with the Purush of the *Vedas*? He was also the youngest son of Pandu, the king of Hastinapur. According to the story he is the third son among the five, the younger two being twins born to the second wife of Pandu. The author believes that he is actually the youngest, because the kingship remained among his children and not among the children of the eldest. If we look at the record of the kings of this line, kingship remained all along among the youngest of the sons. The progenitor of the race Puru was the youngest of the five sons of king Yayati, who in turn was a younger son. The great grandfather of Arjun, Shantanu was the younger son. His grandfather Vichitravirya was the youngest of the three brothers of whom Bhishma was the eldest and his father Pandu too was the younger of the two brothers and thus kingship was to pass on to his son, but as he was killed in battle it passed on to his grandson, Parikshit. In his childhood Arjun learnt archery and became the greatest archer in the world and even acknowledged to be his equal by his teacher Drona. In the contest for displaying the skill in archery for the hand of the most beautiful princess in India, held in Panchal kingdom, he easily succeeded where all others had failed and when the disappointed suitors combined to defeat him and wrest the princess he single-handed routed them all. However, all the five brothers married that princess. When they returned back their uncle instead of handing over the kingdom to them divided it and retaining the urban and better part gave them a forest as their portion of kingdom. Once when Arjun and Krishna were wandering on the banks of the Yamuna looking for a site for the kingdom, they were approached by Agni, the god of fire, seeking their help in burning a forest. On enquiry they were informed that he was prevented by Indra, the god of rain and the king of gods, and whenever he tried to burn the forest rain extinguished it. Arjun readily consented to the request of the god of fire, to help him in burning of forest. The god of fire gave Arjun a celestial bow, a quiver which would never empty, a celestial chariot which could not be destroyed and four horses who would never die and never tire. He stood on guard and allowed the forest to burn. As the fire started burning the forest the rain clouds gathered but were dispersed by Arjun with his celestial weapons. Enraged the God Indra engaged Arjun in battle, Krishna being his charioteer, but was repulsed and had to retreat. While the fire was consuming the forest a man trapped in it sought refuge and Arjun gave him place in his chariot. The man who was saved was a famous builder and in his gratitude built a beautiful capital where they established their kingdom. The defence of the poor fell to Arjun. As all the brothers had married a common princess a code of conduct was established between them and whoever broke it had to go into exile for twelve years. Arjun had to save a man from robbers and the code was broken. He left and wandered over whole of India. During his wanderings he married several princesses and the sons born to them became the kings and established a line of kings. He married the princess of Manipur and her son became king. He married the snake princess Ulopi and her son became king. Lastly he married the sister of Krishna and her son was to become king of their kingdom but as he was killed his grandson became king instead. As soon as he returned they decided to celebrate a sacrifice indicating sovereignty over the whole earth and Arjun went to the Western quarters to defeat the kingdoms in the West and to bring tribute. He defeated all the kings between the Yamuna and the Red Sea. After the sacrifice his brother lost everything in a gambling match to their cousins and became slave along with his brothers and wife and their wife was insulted and humiliated. However, their freedom was restored and they were asked to wander in the forest for twelve years and to spend one year in concealment with the clause that if they were discovered during the year of concealment they would have to wander again for twelve years. They went into the forest and enraged Arjun decided to placate Shiv, the god of Destruction among the Hindu trinity and get the ultimate weapon from him. He went to the mountains and engaged there in the worship of Shiv. Shiv in order to test him came before him in the form of a man from the Kirat tribe and engaged him in battle. He was pleased by the skill and prowess of Arjun and gave him his ultimate weapon. As Shiv disappeared the gods led by Indra appeared and took him to heaven. They too gave him their weapons. In heaven he defeated a group of demons who were troubling the gods and could not be destroyed by them. In heaven too he was given lessons in music and dances which made him a perfect musician and dancer. Gods also sent temptations to him in the shape of the most beautiful of the celestial nymphs, Urvashi, who expressed her love for him and desired him to marry her and stay in heaven. Remembering his purpose to eradicate evil he spurned her offer and returned back to earth and his brothers. The year to be spent in concealment was fast approaching and where the greater warrior who could be recognised anywhere was to remain hidden. He did what nobody could imagine. Dressed as an eunuch he hid in the women's apartments of king Virat of Matsya kingdom teaching his daughter music and dance. Nobody could suspect that in that eunuch was hidden the great warrior. We may remember that in the Greek epic poem, *Illiad,* the great warrior Achilles also tried to hide among the women in the women's apartments but was discovered by Ulysses. No such success came to Arjun's cousins and the year was spent in concealment. Towards the end of the period great events took place in Matsya. The king's commander-in-chief, a very powerful man in his audacity insulted their wife and tried to force her into his house. Enraged Bhim, the second brother killed him along with his brothers. Suspecting that that could only be done by Bhim, the Kauravas, the cousins of Pandavas attacked the Matsya kingdom. They devised a strategy of attacking with a weak force first and while the army might be engaged with that force they might capture the cows, of Matsya, the most famous in the country. When the weak force attacked, the army of Matsya along with the four Pandava brothers all in disguise went to battle leaving the defence of cows and the realm in the hands of the prince. Nobody thought of the eunuch teaching dance and music. Then the Kaurava army struck capturing all the cows. According to Kaurava's calculations there were a few days still remaining for the end of the year, but not so as per the calculations of Arjun. The Prince left to defend the kingdom was not even having a charioteer and boasted that if he might have a charioteer he would rescue the cows. Arjun offered to drive his chariot. What an odd couple they were, the prince, a mere stripling and the charioteer, an eunuch. On seeing the mighty Kaurava army with its world renowned warriors the prince lost heart and ran away. Arjun too jumping from the chariot, caught hold of him and tried to encourage him. Then he revealed his identity to him and persuaded him to become his charioteer. The chariot was driven to a hiding place where Arjun got his celestial weapons, his bow and quiver. When the Kaurava army saw them whom they thought ran away returning with the eunuch holding bow and arrow ready to fight and the prince driving the chariot, they simply laughed, and were much amused. Imagine their surprise which rapidly turned to consternation when they heard the dreaded sound of Arjun's bow and two sharp arrows were discharged, one of which fell at the feet of the teacher and other passed near his ear. The teacher explained that the one which fell at his feet meant that Arjun saluted him and the one which passed near his ear meant that he had enquired his welfare. Meanwhile Arjun persued the cows, killing the watchmen who were taking them and when he blew his conch the cows terrified ran back to the city. He then faced the Kaurava army and defeated them all. He returned back to the city taking with him their clothes leaving the most famous warriors naked on the field. This incident also reveals an interesting information regarding the existence of two calendars, the solar and the lunar. As per story while Arjun was rescuing the cows, the Kauravas felt jubilant that Arjun had revealed himself and as there were still a few days left, the Pandavas would have to go wandering for twelve more years. The matter was referred to Bhishma and he decreed that the lunar year had ended and not the solar year, but as they belonged to lunar race, they were in honour bound to accept the lunar year as final. This indicates that there were two calendar systems in vogue. Another interesting feature of the incident is the rescue of the cows. We may recall that the great achievements in the *Vedas* were invariably the rescue of the cows from imprisonment. Does it indicate that the people of the area who composed the great epic had not forgotten the *Vedas* and tried to carry forward its themes? Finally when the battle became inevitable and the armies arranged Arjun surveyed the scene and seeing all his relatives before him was filled with introspection and self-doubt regarding the killing of his elders and dear ones for the sake of a kingdom. His friend and charioteer Krishna gave a discourse explaining the religion and duty. His doubts dispelled, he fought furiously killing most of the enemies or else neutralising others who were destined to be killed by others. This is in short the story of Arjun.

Which was the story which formed the principal theme of the original *Mahābhārata* called originally *Jai Bhārat*? To find it we will have to look at the historical situation of the time. The principal threat to the region was from both the East and West, from the Magadh empire in the East and from the Iranian empire in the West. The threat from the East was dealt with in the story of Vāsudev Krishna who was made to destroy the Magadh empire in stories revolving round him. The threat from the West was to be seen and the only hero who could meet the threat and destroy the Kingdom in the West could alone be the hero of the epic. Neither Yudhister nor Vāsuḍev Krishna was shown as destroying the Kuru-Madra armies. It was Arjun alone who was shown as defeating the kings of the Western region when he marched to get tribute for the sacrifice of Yudhister and later destroying their armies in the field of Kurukshetra. The king of the Iranian empire Kurush (Cyrus) was said to have been killed on an attack on India and his army consisting among others his tribe and of Mada (Medes) was repulsed. That must have given rise to some euphoria and ballads must have been composed to sing of the victory and a personified hero was required who was created and made the subject of the epic. The ephithet 'Bhārat' was used in *Mahābhārata* only for Arjun. We find in the *Bhagwat Gita* which formed a part of the epic this epithet was used again and again for Arjun. Moreover Arjun had all the attributes of being an epic hero. He was born on this earth to destroy evil, he propitiated the supreme god of destruction Shiv and got his ultimate weapon, went to heaven to get more weapons, helped the gods in destroying their enemies, was tempted but spurned the temptation for his duty, was assailed by self-doubt and got it removed by a discourse by the Supreme God himself and almost single-handed destroyed the armies consisting of Kuru and Madra tribes. He had in effect removed the threat from the West. The main outline of the *Mahābhārata* might have been the same in *Jai Bhārat* but the principal story appears to be the story of Arjun. We may not forget here that Arjun was in that time as revealed in the Ashtadhyayi of Panini a cult figure and object of worship with a lot of his worshippers called Arjundevaks. The worshippers of Arjun in those times pointed out that he was regarded as a god and a fit person to be the hero of the epic. Later on lots of stories were added, existing ones enlarged, philosophical discourses added, polity and its principles embodied, ethics explained to make it a perfect epic, perhaps the longest of the epic in all languages of the world. We also find that the people had not forgotten the *Vedas* in composing that epic. The Purush of the *Vedas* was made into Nar of the *Mahābhārata* while the rescue of the cows was a theme recurring in both. The rescue of the cows is a recurring theme in the Vedas while it is one of the major events in the *Mahābhārata*. We thus find that it was inspired by real historical situation of the times and though it might have celebrated a real victory over Kurush (Cyrus) of the Achaemenid Empire it also reflected the emotional needs of the people to meet the threat of the empire by regarding resistance as their duty and religion. In conclusion we may note a coincidence in the epic. Arjun was addressed in addition to Bhārat as Pārtha. The other name of Kunti, the mother of Pandavas was Prītha and though the epithet could have been applied to all of them, yet it was applied to Arjun alone. However, we may note that a Parthian dynasty came to power in Iran in the 2nd century B.C., *i.e.*, 171 B.C. which ruled for about four hundred years and later known as the Pahlavi dynasty. Was there some connection between the two which the author and the people knew at that time but we do not know?

The question arises who composed *Jai Bhārat*? Was it Ved Vyas? We have no knowledge. Whether *Gita* was a part of *Jai Bhārat*? Again we are in the dark. But it appears that *Jai Bhārat* was a popular legend or a story and so were many others, among them the story of Bhim and Hidimbā, of the curse and ordeal of Yama who had to take birth as Yudhister, of Shāntanu and Devāpi, and similar others. Among these stories that of Shāntanu and Devāpi are found in the *Rigveda*.[2] A poet of genius appeared and he integrating all the stories formed them into the *Mahābhārata* which is in the present form. He had not only added all the stories and legends current in that time, *viz.*, story of Nala, of Rama *etc.* but added the philosophy of politics, of religion, of one's duty towards parents, towards wives, towards children, to society, etc. He has given the science of public administration and a whole Chapter is devoted to these. *Gita* might have been present in

Jai Bhārat in a nutshell but it is the present writer of *Mahābhārata* who gave it a larger form and its present shape. This poet of genius who did compose it was no other than Ved Vyas. Even the *Mahābhārata* mentions that Ved Vyas had composed the *Mahābhārata* in a Hundred Thousand couplets after a continuous effort lasting three years.[3] We find that all the stories in the literature of India since the earliest times are inevitably from the *Mahābhārata.* The stories of the dramas of Bhās known to be the earliest dramatist of India, many of the stories in the *Jātak* stories, other literature are from *Mahābhārata.* It must have preceded them by a few centuries at least.

Mahābhārata is described as a fifth *Veda.* It was truly the most powerful engine in the promotion of community feelings among the Indians of the time and afterwards. Looking to the list of kings who gathered in the field for the great battle we find that they range from Northern Himalayas to the South seas, from the modern Assam to Western Iran, the land of Madra tribes (now known as Medes). This must have bound them into a community conception. To a modern reader it may be a piece of literature but what it was to the people of those times is forcefully expressed by saying that it was the fifth *Veda.* The Ved Vyas was the educator of Indians and it can be said that a man can direct his whole life by what he learns from it and his religion from the preceptor and teachings specially in the *Gita.* This extravagant estimate of the greatness of *Mahābhārata* and of importance as it was not the estimate of a school or clique but a national estimate; and even those who might care little for this ethical aspect of the *Mahābhārata* attached a historical value to it and found in it a common ground. The importance of the poem is enhanced by the fact that the knowledge of it was disseminated among all classes by the professional reciters who wandered from city to city and recited at festivals. Furthermore *Mahābhārata* is in Sanskrit which was probably not a spoken dialect of that time and being a metrical language gave the impression of a poem of antiquity. Thus the very vehicle of the poem prevented it being anything less than a national possession though it is most clearly identified with the area around Delhi in Northern India. *Mahābhārata* was the embodiment of national Indian sentiments, of the consciousness of community, of race and culture. *Mahābhārata* also was in a sense the creator of Hindu religion inasmuch as the eternal type of divine characters which are the same for all Hindus were first clearly portrayed in it. The gods, Shiv, Vāsudev Krishna, Sun, Moon, Fire, Varun, Indra, and Wind etc were there portrayed with loving reality and sobriety and those were the gods who were common to all Hindus and worshipped everywhere although there were local differences in the attributes assigned to them. These distinctions, however, did not strike the Indians as we see from the fact that they could call by the same name their own deity which had a different name for them, *viz.*, the thousand names of Sun God, or of Shiv or of Vishnu. *Mahābhārata* embodied in noble and enduring forms the essential conceptions of nation respecting its divinities. This is the real meaning of the remark that it is the fifth *Veda* and that Ved Vyas gave the Hindus their religion by giving the gods their titles, prerogatives, and their personal and moral characteristics. The importance of *Mahābhārata* lies in the fact that of all the unifying influence at work upon the Hindus none was more powerful than that of religion, whether the older and more external state religion or the new form of the mysticism of the *Upnishads* and *Brahma Sutra*. The theology which is contained in *Mahābhārata,* specially the *Gitā* had the most profound influence on the Hindus upto the present time than all the *Upnishads,* other religious books, the theology of the Buddha religion or that of the Jains.

REFERENCES

1. *Rigveda* 10.90; *Atharvaveda* 19.6; *Yajurveda* 13.1; *Samveda* 4.10
2. *Rigveda* 10.98
3. *Mahābhārata,* Adiparva 62.52

THE AGE OF GITĀ

When was *Gitā* written or composed? This is a question which has agitated the scholars since *Gitā* became an important text of Hinduism. Various scholars had expressed their views to indicate the real period when *Gitā* was first composed and no two scholars agreed on it. However, they appear to agree that it must have been written somewhere between 5th century B.C. and 2nd century B.C. Those who advanced their views on the age of *Gitā* did so when the existence of Indus Valley Civilisation was not known and they knew nothing about the Indus script, *i.e.*, before 1931 A.D. After the details of Indus Valley Civilisation which flourished between 3000 B.C. and 1600 B.C. became known some of their arguments have lost force. They had somehow not taken care of some of historical facts in coming to their conclusions. We may, therefore, take into consideration the known facts based on archaeology, history, so far known texts and their interpretation and then begin our quest to establish the age of *Gitā*.

Archaeological Evidence

We know so far two inscriptions both belonging to 2nd century B.C. indicating the cult of Vāsudev Krishna as one of the dominant cults. The first inscription is at Ghosundi near Chittor which mentions the construction of a 'Pujā Shilpa-Prākar' in honour of Vāsudev and Sankarshan Balrām, the brother of Krishna. The other is the Garuda-stambha at Besnagar in Madhya Pradesh constructed and dedicated to Vāsudev, the 'God of Gods'. We have not got so far an earlier inscription about Vasudev but this indicates that his cult was widely prevalent in 2nd century B.C.

Historical Evidence

Among the historical evidence which may be of interest to us is the establishment of a dynasty of Pārth known as Pārthians in history in the neighbouring Iran, who ruled from 171 B.C. to 226 A.D.

Literary Evidence

Literary evidence is more ample. We may take the references to Krishna first into consideration which may indicate the prevalence of Krishna cult, Krishna story or an indication of knowledge of Krishna. We do not have, however, any reference to Krishna in the Vedas, *Brāhmanas, Āranyaks, Upnishads, Brahma Sutras* and other *Sutras* except a solitary reference. That indicated that the religious literature had not found it necessary to mention Krishna. The solitary reference is in *Chāndyogya-Upnishad* where it is mentioned that knowledge is also given to Krishna Devakiputra. However, there is reference to him in secular literature, *i.e.*, historical accounts, grammar and etymology.

The only historical account connected with our subject is that of Megasthenes who mentioned in his accounts, fragments of which are only available, that people in and around Mathurā held Herakles and Dionysus in special honour. He was wrong in interpretation for it must be Krishna and Sankarshan Balrām in place of Herakles and Dionysus. Megasthenes lived as Greek Ambassador to Mauryan Court from 305 B.C. to early 3rd century B.C. It indicates the prevalence of the cult of Krishna in his times.

Megasthenes (Frag. XLI) tells us: "Herakles was worshipped by the inhabitants of the plains, especially by the Sourseni, an Indian tribe possessed of two cities, Methora (Mathura) and Kleisobora (Krishnapura?) and who had a large navigable river, the Jobares (Jamuna) flowing through their territories." Curtius informs us that 'an image of Herakles was carried in front of the army of Porus as he advanced against Alexander."

We may now have a look at what the earliest known Etymologist Yāska had to say about the Krishna story. Yāska had not mentioned Krishna but in giving an example he says in his famous work *Nirukta* 'Akruro Dadāte Manim'; Akrura is adorning himself with Mani or Jewel. Akrura is associated with Krishna story and the famous incident of the 'Syamtak Mani' is an important event in the Krishna story in which Akrura took away the 'Syamtak Mani' leaving Krishna to shoulder the blame which led to many incidents with Krishna eventually fighting Jāmbavān, the bear king and marrying his daughter Jambawati and also Satyabhāmā. This mention of Akrura indicates that the Krishna story was widely known even though his cult was not prevalent. For otherwise Yāska would not have mentioned, of all people, Akrur. The question now is of the age of Yāska which as with other people, is obscure. However, Yāska is regarded as having lived in an earlier age than Pānini. Some people regard his age as 5th century B.C. while others take it to be 7th century B.C. and some even go as far as the 9th century B.C. However, none could give a cogent reason and their reasoning whatever it was, was arrived at before the discovery of Indus Valley Civilisation and the Indus script. The shades of the Indus script can be seen in the *Nirukta.* The Indus script, as we know, is a pictographic and ideographic script and for an etymologist the difference is seen in his interpretations. For one who bases his etymology on an alphabetical script he has to go to the basic meaning of the word or the root to explain the word or to suggest new word formation. For one who has before him the pictographic or ideographic script he goes to the picture or picture of the ideas or the base of the idea which gives rise to a particular word and its derivative for it must arise among the tribal society who first gave it the name. We find this in ample in Yāska. It is only Yāska who could have given the meaning of Vaishwānar[1] (fire) as 'Vishwānnarānnyati. Vishwa Énam Narā Nayantiti wā. Api wā Vishwānar Eva Syat', meaning thereby that it carries all people or people carry it or it is found in every thing. In early tribal societies the means of igniting a fire was only rubbing two dried sticks together till they became hot enough to give sparks and catch fire. They used that method only sparingly, used it only in ceremonial occasions and probably only once a year when there was a ritual of regeneration of fire on a single day. That day all the fire in every home was extinguished and the places used for keeping fire cleaned. Then the fire was generated and every hearth lighted their fires in their homes from that one. When the tribes moved from place to place the fire was taken along with them. This fire so taken was carried by the religious leaders or purohits in front of the group which moved. Therefore, the fire was called Agrani, one which was the first, carrying people to their destination, and it was carried by the people, and was found in every thing *i.e.,* even in dried sticks or even stones which might have also been used later to generate it. Yāska must have seen those ideographs in the Indus script for they were there and must have given the interpretations accordingly. Similarly was the word *Khal.*[2] The meaning of that word which Yāska had given was a battle and a store for grain. He had seen both in the script used for the two words occurring together and had derived the word *Skhal* meaning fall, for grain falls from the jar full of grain and a combatant falls in battle. It, therefore, appears that Yāska had written his work with Indus script before him. We know that the alphabetical Brahmi script was in vogue in the time of Ashoka, *i.e.,* in the 3rd century B.C. and the Sahgaurā plaque. The earliest known Brahmi script is conjectured to belong to the period of Chandragupta Maurya or slightly earlier, *i.e.,* 4th century B.C. To come so widely in vogue throughout the length and breadth of India must have taken a lot of time probably a few centuries. Therefore, Yāska must have lived few centuries prior to Mauryas and prior to Buddha. We should be inclined to take his period to nearer to 1000 B.C. rather than nearer to Pānini. If at that time the Krishna story was in vogue, then the cult of Krishna and the ideas associated with him which are the crux of *Gitā* must have arisen pretty earlier than we imagine.

We may now examine the reference to Arjun. We do not have any epigraphical reference of Arjun nor we find any mention in any historical account. The only reference we find is in Pānini as pointed out above where he is mentioned as a deity with a cult of his own. It may be pointed out that this coupling of his name with Vāsudev is very interesting. We do not have any other reference to Arjun in the religious works like the *Vedas, Brāhmans, Āranyaks, Upnishads* or *Sutras*. We are not considering *Purānās* because they are much later works. The only other interesting information is the presence of a tribe named *Arjunāyans* who lived in the Bharatpur-Alwar districts in North-East Rajasthan adjoining the Shaursenis of Mathura who had Krishna as their hero, or cult figure. The coins of *Arjunāyans* bear the legend 'Arjunāyanānām Jayah', victory of the Arjunāyanas. They were found in the early centuries of this era. Arjun ceased to be a cult figure sometimes after Pānini and if he was never a cult figure, then how he came to be mentioned by Pānini unless Pānini himself was an Arjunāyan. And if he is made the hero of *Mahābhārata*, then it must have been written or composed when he was a universal cult figure or if not then Ved Vyās, the author of *Mahābhārata*, must have been an Arjunāyan.

We may now examine the internal evidence in *Mahābhārata*. In the Ādi Parva it is mentioned that the number of couplets in *Mahābhārata* is twenty-four thousand[3] excluding the Upākhyāns, but the number in the *Mahābhārata* at present is approximately one lakh (a hundred thousand). That indicates that about seventy thousand couplets were later added during the course of centuries, and probably the whole plot of the original epic was thus so moulded that it changed the whole scenario and plot of the original epic. It is also mentioned that its original name was *Jai Bhārat*[4]. It, therefore, appears that originally there was a smaller epic *Jai Bhārat* which had only twenty-four thousand couplets and during the course of time other material was added and it assumed its present dimensions and as it became at least four times its original length it began to be called *Mahābhārat, i.e.*, greater Bhārat or a bigger book. We get confirmation of the existence of two different books in Rishi-tarpan section of Āshvalāyan Grihya Sutra: 'Samantu-Jaimini-Vaishampāyan-Pāil — Sutra-Bhāshya-*Bhārat-Mahābhārata Dharmāchārya'*.[5] Here two different books *Bhārat* and *Mahābhārata* are mentioned. Thus the smaller epic was enlarged and probably changed the whole drift of the story. It may be interesting to know the story and plot of the smaller epic but unfortunately no copy of the same or even an indication of its plot is available so far. We may, therefore, try to speculate on the contents of

that smaller one which may be a key to the period of the composition of the *Gitā*. *Jai Bhārat* being a smaller epic it must be having a single plot and a single story unlike the present one which is a tangle of a number of them and consisting mainly of the story of Yudhister as an incarnation of Yama, the story of Arjun, the story of Bhim and Hidimbā and the Krishna story. In the *Gitā* itself Arjun is addressed by Krishna variously as Parth, Bhārat, Kaunteya. We may note that Arjun alone in whole of extant *Mahābhārata* is variously described as Pārth or Bhārat. None others including
Yudhister, the eldest of them is so addressed though they all must have a similar title. Was Arjun alone a *Bhārat* and *Jai Bhārat* means the Victory of Arjun? Probably so. Arjun had all the attributes of an epic hero. He was a complete man for in addition to being a great warrior he was accomplished in arts like dance and music, conscious of his duty for which he had suffered a lot, highly religious to the extent that in quest of arms he even went to the heavens and was able to meet Shiv, one of the gods of Hindu Trinity and God of War. During his wanderings on earth his exploits were many. We may consider the main events of his life. As a student he was regarded as the finest archer in the world. On completion of his studies as price for teaching to be paid to his teacher he single-handedly captured his teacher's arch enemy, the King Drupad of Panchāl. For a contest in skill in archery for the hand of the daughter of king Drupad, Draupadi, he alone succeeded and won her hand though he had to share her with his other brothers. When his elder brother was given a forest to rule as his share of the kingdom, Arjun proceeded to organise it. Impressed by him as a warrior, 'Fire God' asked him to help him in consuming the forest given to his elder brother to rule. He readily agreed and promised to protect the 'Fire God' from Indra, the king of gods under whose protection the forest was. Fire God in gratitude gave him the divine bow 'Gāndiva' and his famous chariot. Arjun fought with Indra when he tried to prevent the 'Fire God' from burning the forest, and did not allow him to do so. Even though worsted the king of Gods was pleased. When the rule of his brother was established Arjun was given the charge of protecting the people. Once he was faced with a choice of

doing his duty and living in exile for twelve years or evading it and living in luxury. He chose duty and went in exile wandering all over the world for twelve years. During his wandering he protected peoples wherever he went and his exploits were many. During that period too he won the hands of three princesses, Subhadrā, the sister of Krishna, Chitrangdā, the princess of Manipur and Ulupi, the Nāg princess. When his brother lost his throne and everything in a game of dice and they had to wander in the forest for twelve years with one year in hiding, Arjun decided to go to heaven and to get all the divine weapons. He accordingly went to heaven and was tested in a combat by Shiv, the God of Destruction, himself. Pleased with his valour and determination he gave him his own favourite divine weapon. Other gods too gave their favourite weapons and polishing his lessons in dance and music by the divine teachers in heavens Arjun returned to earth. When twelve years passed and the time came for going into one year of hiding the problem arose of keeping Arjun himself hidden. Others could be hidden but not Arjun, the great warrior, who could not remain in concealment. Arjun himself solved this problem by wearing the garb of a woman teacher of dance and music. He lived for one year in the women's apartments of the royal palace of King Virāt. Who could have thought of searching for the great warrior among women? Those familiar with *Iliad* of Homer may recall that Ulysses sought out Achilles from among the women where he so chose to hide. Arjun was not detected. After the exile was over he single handedly defeated the Kaurava army when they rightly suspecting that the Pāndavās were hidden there attacked the kingdom of King Virāt. When the great *Mahābhārata* war ensued and the two armies stood face to face and like in a perfect epic Arjun was in a fix to fight or not to fight and the thought of killing his near and dear ones while doing his duty made him uneasy and filled his mind with self-doubt. He also felt a desire for renunciation. It was at such moments that a saint came and removed his doubts. But that time it was Krishna, the incarnation of Vishnu or the God other than Shiv among the Trinity who gave him the sermon and removed his doubts.

That sermon was the *Gitā.* We may see that of three gods of Trinity two helped him. The war was actually a war between Arjun on one side and Kaurava army on the other. He single-handedly destroyed the once mighty army and gave the kingdom to his brother to rule. But we may note that it was his progeny not that of his brother Yudhister who succeeded to the throne. He thus founded the dynasty. His going to heaven in search of something and other exploits on earth is found only in one other epic, *i.e.,* the epic of Gilgamesh, the Sumerian Epic attributed to a period between 2000 to 3000 B.C. and conceived in Sumer which was situated in Southern Iraq and was the earliest civilisation of the worlds. Looking to the epic dimensions of his personality and exploits it appears that Arjun was the hero of the earlier *Jai Bhārat* and *Gitā* was a part of it.

Before trying to determine the age when *Gitā* was written, we may have a look at *Rigveda* where though there was no reference to Krishna or Arjun, yet it mentions certain incidents which find reflection on *Mahābhārata.* Who can say if it had not a bearing on *Mahābhārata*? In the *Rigveda* are described two major battles, the battle at Hariyupiā and the one called 'Dāsrāj' battle. The battle at Hariyupiā was fought between Abhyāvarti, son of Chayaman and Vrichivān, the sons of Varshikh.[6] Abhyāvarti, son of Chāyamān is also described as a *Pārth:* Abhyāvarti, son of Chāyamān of Parth dynasty gave us alms and things. So Abhyāvarti was son of Chāyamān and a Pārth. The other battle, the *'Dasraj'* battle was fought between Sudās, son of Chāyamān, belonging to Bharat tribe and ten kings or heads of ten tribes.[7] So Sudās was a Bhārat and son of Chāyamān. His father is also called Pijvan. Were the two, Abhyāvarti and Sudās one and the same personage, the son of Chāyamān or were they different? We do not know for due to the obscurity of the *Vedas* we find it difficult to get at the real thing. People get different names in different context. But the fact is that one of the victorious kings is a Pārth and the other is a Bhārat. We may have a look at the tribes who opposed Sudās in the battle of ten kings, the 'Dasraj' battle. The whole of Sukta 18 of Mandal 7 of *Rigveda* is devoted to the description of this fight. The opposing tribes are Turvasu, Dhruhyu, Anu, Puru, Yakshu, Bhrigu, Pakhtha,

Bhalānsa, Bhananta, Alināsa, Vishānin, Shiv. The interesting thing to note is that five tribes Yadu, Turvasu, Druhyu, Anu and Puru are always mentioned together in *Rigveda* and are said to be living together and the *Purānās* also name them to be the children of Yayāti and thus brothers. In the above fight only four of them Turvasu, Druhyu, Anu and Puru fought Sudās. Of these Puru is the one who is said to be the progenitor of both Pāndavas and Kauravas. Why Yadus had not fought when they were living with other four tribes? Did they remain neutral? This is a solitary instance in *Vedas*. In the *Mahābhārata* war Krishna who was a descendant of Yadu too remained neutral just like his ancestor Yadu in the *Dāsrāj* war. Was it just a co- incidence? We may not forget that all the scholars and Rishis, especially Ved Vyas, the author of *Mahābhārata* were well versed in *Vedas* and might have remembered that Sudās was a Bhārat.

From the above facts known to us it can be said that by the time of Pānini, there was a cult of Arjun and of Vāsudev and that somehow the two cults came to be clubbed together. However, we do not find any evidence of the continuation of the cult of Arjun thereafter. It appears that as the cult of Vāsudev continued to grow, that of Arjun dwindled and came to be confined to the tribe named after him, *i.e.*, Arjunāyans. Hence, the *Jai Bhārat* and *Gitā* could only have been written when the cult of Arjun was in vogue. That was necessary for the epic to become popular. Thus it should be written in or about the time of Pānini as the later date and not afterwards. As the names of other important personages of *Mahābhārata*, Yudhister, Bhim etc., are already found in Pānini's works, *Jai Bharāt* or even the enlarged *Mahābhārata* must have been written prior to Pānini, *i.e.*, prior to 4th century B.C. We accordingly may discount it being written after the Pārth dynasty came to rule over neighbouring Iran in 171 B.C. to glorify them or to glorify the Arjunāyans for then it might have a limited audience and not the wide popularity it had.

If it was composed before Pānini, *i.e.*, 4th century B.C., then when its period can be fixed? If we believe that the echoes of the *Vedas* are there in the *Mahābhārata*, that probably it was composed keeping the two battles of the *Rigveda* combined together in view, if we take note of the interesting fact that both Yadu and his descendant Krishna remained neutral in the Dāsrāj battle and the *Mahābhārata* respectively and that it was not just a coincidence but was deliberately done, then the composition of the *Jai Bhārat* might have been made much nearer to the Vedic times, *i.e.*, the times of the Indus Valley Civilisation. The Indus Valley Civilisation, as we gather from the archaeological excavations, ceased to exist by 16th century B.C. probably due to the change in the course of the rivers, the Beās, the Ravi, the Satluj and the Yamunā and the disappearance of Saraswati which ruined the river based cities Harappa and Kalibangan and forced people to disperse. Similar thing happened with Indus and Mohenjodaro too which was made desolate. The people so dispersed moved to nearby areas. Their consolidation must have taken a few centuries. We may take this period to be at least 500 years. Thus by about 1000 B.C. people were settled, *Vedas* consolidated and studied and new literature of analysis, criticism, grammar and etymology began. It was sometimes about that period that Yāska must have written his *Nirukta* to analyse the word formation of the *Vedas* and *Brahmans*. It must also be that period when the Krishna story became popular that the epic *Jai Bhārat* must have been composed. With the growing story around Krishna and his mythology, the cult must have taken root and beliefs in his teachings must have taken shape which now form the basis of the *Gitā*. We may, therefore, take it that *Gitā* must have been composed much nearer to 1000 B.C. than to 400 B.C. when the cult of Arjun began to decline. The exact period is not possible to be determined due to the present state of our knowledge.

REFERENCES

1. *Nirukta* 7.6
2. *Nirukta* 3.2
3. *Mahābhārat*, Adiparva 1.10
4. *Ibid.*, Adiparva 62.20
5. *Ashvalayan Grihya Sutra* 3.4.4.
6. *Rigveda* 6.27.5
7. *Rigveda* 7.18. 6 to 9

LIKELY INFLUENCES OF HINDUISM AND OTHER RELIGIONS ON THE RELIGION OF THE JEWS

Was the Religion of the Jews entirely their own thinking? Did any other belief or religions have any perceptible or imperceptible influence on their religious beliefs? Did the Jews come into contact with other people, other religions, other civilisations during their wanderings prior to their final settlement in the land of Palestine, its expulsion from it and readmission into it? How far did it influence their religious beliefs and how far did these influences go towards making the beliefs of Christians as distinct from that of Jewish faith for Christians are Jewish in faith but are different from it?

These are the questions one has to encounter if one tries to understand the belief of the Jews that their religion is just created by God without any influence of other faiths or other religions. We may know that the Jews were constantly wandering from one land to another, from one civilisation to another, from one language area to another. It is inconceivable that they would not study the beliefs of other people and adopt some of them of their liking. They had matrimonial relations with people of other faiths and that too must have gone in making and enlarging their beliefs. Unfortunately, we do not have any old record about them and the latest or the earliest is the version of Ezra in about 450 B.C. who, it is said, had compiled the old texts; but those old texts themselves are not available. It is also said that the account upto the Exodus was written by Moses. We do not know if Moses was a real figure or a mythical one. There is no confirmation of their wanderings and coming into contact with other people except the version of the Bible. It may be a traditional account of them more in line with the *Purāṇās* of India. But taking their account, rejecting what may be improbable, modifying what may appear to be exaggeration we may proceed to examine the influences which they themselves admit they had absorbed during their wanderings.

Their history in brief is that they left Ur, an important city of Sumer in modern Iraq in its heyday and went towards the North and settled at Haran in modern Turkey. After living there for a generation they migrated South-West leaving a part of their people behind. They reached Palestine. They stayed there for two generations and left it for Egypt. They stayed there for a few centuries finally leaving it in 12th century B.C. and under the leadership of Moses came to Palestine. They settled in Palestine and remained there upto the 6th century B.C. when the Babylonians again took them captive and forced the whole population of Jews to move to Babylon. They remained there for a century when with the fall of Babylon kingdom and coming to power of Achaemenids they were allowed to go back to Palestine. In 70 A.D. they were again expelled and moved to different parts of the world and settled there but were always discriminated against. Or were they discriminating against other people? They moved from one place to another and from one country to another. We are mainly concerned with their movements upto 70 A.D. till such time their beliefs were crystallized and till about 6th century A.D. when the beliefs of Christians had also crystallised.

This in brief is their history. In their whole span of history they first met people of Haran, then of Cannan, Egypt, Palestine, Medes, Babylon and the various people who had to frequent those places during their period of sojourn. Who were those people at that particular time and what was their religious beliefs? It is rather difficult to say till we could establish the various periods and their probable dates when they lived at those places. Jews claim a great antiquity of their race and Christians to impress people about their faith too tend to support it but the modern historical and archaeological finds point to neither so great distant past nor so glorious one. We may take their dates and the probable ones to understand it. According to the Jews *Abraham* left Haran and went to Cannan in the year 2000 B.C. and he left Ur of the Chaldees along with his father a generation earlier. They settled in Cannan. Abraham got his son married to the grand daughter of his own brother, Nahor, who remained behind in Haran. This son Issac had a son, Jacob whom he sent to Haran again to seek a wife among the daughters of his wife's brother Laban. Jacob lived for 20 years in Haran and married Leah and Rachel, his cousins. He came back to Cannan. A son Joseph was born and it was this Joseph who was said to have been sold as a slave by his brothers out of jealousy and it was he who getting rich and powerful in Egypt invited his people to move to Egypt which they did. According to the Book of Genesis of the *Bible*, the age of Abraham was 175 years, of Issac was 180 years and of Jacob 147 years. The total period of the stay of those people, as calculated by adding to the period of each which he spent as head of the family, in Cannan comes to 210 years. They moved to Egypt in 1785 B.C. Joseph preceding them by about 10 years. If instead of such an exaggerated ages of the three generations but taking them to be normal Biblical span of three score and ten, then one finds that even according to the *Bible* they must have moved to Egypt in 18th century and in Haran at about a century earlier. We may now compare the historical dates, specially of those kings who were contemporary to Abraham and could be identified. This may be noted that in the earlier parts of the *Bible*, Book of Genesis attributed to Moses they were the only names which could be identified. Book of Genesis,[1] mentions four kings, Amraphel, king of Shinar; Arioch, King of Ellasar; Chedorlaomer, King of Elam; and Tidal, King of nations. Out of these only Amraphel king of Shinar which is Sumer in modern Iraq could be identified as Hammurabi, King of Babylon. We cannot say anything about others and Tidal king of nations might be a king of Hittites. Those were the contemporaries of Abraham but the dates of Hammurabi, King of Babylon who is known for his judicial codes are now regarded as 1728-1686 B.C. This implies that Abraham and his father must have been in Haran sometimes in about 1750 B.C. and that Jacob must have moved into Egypt towards the later half of 17th century B.C., *i.e.,* some where in 1630 B.C. taking 20 years for each generation. We may note that it is estimated that Hyksos (Egyptian-Hekachesut) moved into Egypt in about 1650 B.C. and ruled over it for about two centuries when they were overthrown by a local revolt which established an Egyptian dynasty and whose most famous king was Ramases II (1300-1234) and Merentah who succeeded him and was known for the Stele of Merentah of 1220 B.C. We thus find that the sojourn of the Jews in Egypt was contemporaneous with the rule of Hyksos. Actually, the Jews became important people serving the conquerors, manning their services and themselves waxed rich. We find from the Book of Genesis[2] that during a famine Joseph bought all the land of the people for supplying corn. People sold their land, their cattle, their horses etc. in distress. That land now possessed by Joseph in the name of Pharoah was rented out to the people again with the stipulation that a fifth of the produce would be given to the Pharoah.[3] It appears that Jews became instruments of the foreign powers and with their cleverness they could abet Hyksos kings to reduce the people of Egypt to penury and misery. But when the Hyksos regime was ousted from Egypt by a revolt of the people there was no future for the Jews in Egypt and they had to leave. We find from the Book of Exodus of the Bible that there was" a new king over Egypt who knew not Joseph".[4] The king was obviously a new one who had known Jews only as instruments of an odius and oppressive power. Therefore they had to leave. Whether they were expelled or left by themselves cannot be said with certainty. But they could not have remained in Egypt upto the 12th century B.C. or even the 13th as presumed. They must have left soon after the Hyksos, who left in about the middle of 15th century B.C., *i.e.,* about 1450 B.C. We find this in the archaeological finds of the letters of the Governor to the King of Egypt known as the Tell el Amarna documents found in the old palace at Tell el Amarna and dated between 1400 B.C. to 1365 B.C. In these letters the Governor of Palestine pleads to the Pharoah to send him some help and forces to counter the menace of a people who are entering Palestine in numbers and whom he is unable to resist. He names them as 'Habiru', who are nothing but the Hebrews. These letters confirm that the Jews left Egypt in the 14th century B.C. and came to Palestine. We thus find that in the earlier period they must have received influences of the culture and religious beliefs of Haran if they had any and later in Egypt they must have only come into contact with Hyksos and could not have established any rapport with the Egyptians whom they oppressed.

Influences on Jews in Haran and Egypt till they Came to Sinai

We may now see the cultural and religious atmosphere at Haran which could have gone to make up the religious beliefs of the Jews. We cannot know of their previous background at Ur for there was just a casual mention of Ur of the Chaldees in Genesis[5]. There was no more mention of Ur. There was no God-like the name Jahweh of the Jews among the gods worshipped in Ur or as a matter of fact in the whole of Sumerian or Babylonian Empire. This appears to be a myth or might be some small hamlet other than the Sumerian city of Ur. Had it been so, it would have been described as Ur in Shinar not the Ur of Chaldees. Moreover, it is only mentioned as their place of the nativity of Haran, the brother of Abraham.

Before proceeding further we may look at the important beliefs of the Jews upto the time they gathered at the foot of Mt. Sinai after their expulsion from Egypt. This can be only based on the Bible from the earlier parts attributed to Moses. The beliefs are just a few. According to the *Bible* it was God who created the world including Man in about six days, the name of the God is Yahweh, that he accepted more readily the sacrifice of animal than that of vegetable produce, that there was a deluge which destroyed every body who was wicked except a single family who escaped on instructions from God himself by seeking protection in a boat built for the purpose, that later mankind moving from the East reached the land called Shinar, that God had a covenant that he would protect man if he acted according to His command, that He had angels who worked for Him and sped to help a righteous man in trouble, and that the shape of God or Yahweh as seen and described by Moses was that of Fire. We may now see if these beliefs are originally their own or they could have borrowed from other people with whom they came into contact.

First we take up Haran. It is here that Jews are known to have first settled down. We will have to ignore Ur for had they been there for some generations or lived there in its hey day, they at least would have betrayed some knowledge of the gods and goddesses of Ur, its other beliefs and at least the name Yahweh would have been found among deities of Ur of Sumer which it is not there. Moreover they would have given the name Ur of Shinar and not Ur of Chaldees for the word Shinar recurs with some frequency in the Bible and in the chapter where Ur of the Chaldees is mentioned.[6] It is also said that first they came to Shinar from the East,[7] and that God dispersed them "abroad upon the face of all the earth"[8]. It is apparent that it is not the Ur of Shinar but some other Ur named after the great city and kingdom. Not knowing anything about the Ur of Chaldees let us see Haran and study the environment, both religious and culture, which Jews faced there and let us find out its impact on them.

Haran is situated in what is Turkey today at its border with Syria. It is situated in a mountainous country on the banks of a small mountain river which joins Euphrates a little upstream of the place where Khabur, another tributary of Euphrates, joins it. On the river Khabur was situated Wassuganni, the capital of the powerful Mitanni people. Haran was a part of the Mitanni kingdom and the people were Mitannians. We do not know whether the Jews were Mitannians themselves, but we note that of the children of Terah only Abraham moved out taking with him the son of his deceased brother also named Haran. The other brother Nahor and his descendants and probably other Jews continued to live in Haran and provided brides to the descendants of Abraham.

Who were Mitannians? What was their religion and what was their culture including their mythology if any? What might be their language? Nothing much is known of Mitannians. As a matter of fact their existence was even unknown just upto the last century. By sheer chance during excavations in central Turkey at Bogaz Que, a whole city, the ancient Hattusas, was unearthed. From the palace was also discovered a whole archive of ancient documents including treaties and diplomatic correspondence, between the Hittites whose capital was Hattusas and their enemies. From these archives were found a few documents throwing a light on the

Mitannians. There was a treaty between the Hittite King Suppiluliumas and the Mitanni King Wattiuza to whom the Hittite King, married his daughter after helping him to get his throne when his father died. The interesting thing to note are the names of gods who were cited as witnesses to the treaty by the Mitannians. The gods were Indra, Varuna, Mitra and Nāsatya. They were certainly Vedic gods. Some names of the Mitanni kings were Saushstar, Tushrat. A 'Horse Treatise' meant for training of horses, was also recovered. This 'Horse Treatise' written by Kikkuli had freely used Sanskrit terms for training of horses like ek vartan, dui vartan, tri vartan etc. The immediate neighbours of the Mitanni kingdom were the Assyrians with their capital at Assur. They were frequently at war. Earlier the Assyrians were under the Mitanni rulers. Saushsatar, the most important Mitanni king ruled over an area from Zagros mountains to the Mediterranean. King Tushtar defeated the Assur king and sent the holy statue of goddess Ishtar of Nineveh to the Egyptian Pharoah, as a mark of his respect. Later the Hittites and Assyrians jointly attacked the Mitanni kingdom and destroyed it. It was at about the time when the Mitannians were completely defeated sometimes between the 1300 B.C. and 1200 B.C. that we find the huge migrations into Greece and Western Turkey called the Aegean migration and the Dorian migration respectively. The migrants are said to be from European main land. Were some of them the refugees from Mitanni kingdom?

We thus find that the Mitannians were a people who believed in the Vedic Gods. The use of the Sanskrit words in the Horse treatise of Kikkuli makes it abundantly clear that their language was either Sanskrit or akin to Sanskrit and probably they believed in the mythology of the early Hindus. Can it be possible that they may not be aware of the *Vedas* while believing in the Hindu Vedic gods? It appears to be improbable that one may believe in gods but not the mythology and the hymns accompanying it originally. We may believe that they must have been aware of the *Vedas,* specially the *Rigveda* and the early *Brāhmana, i.e.,* the *Shatpath Brāhmana*. This should not be strange for we find that the area from Mitanni to India was occupied by a people believing in the Vedic gods Varuna as Ahur Mazda and Mitra with Avesta as their religious Book which is as old as the *Vedas* with some common hymns. The whole area believed in those gods though after some time Indra and Nāsatya were regarded by these people as evil beings. Can it be possible that when Moses in the eleventh chapter of the Genesis mentions that the people came to Shinar from the East, he might not be thinking of the people of Shinar, *i.e.*, Sumerians but of his own ancestors as coming from the East, *i.e.*, India or of the Mitannians coming from India?

We may now see how far the beliefs of the two, *i.e.*, Jews and the Mitannians or the Vedic Hindus are similar. The most remarkable similarity is the story of the Flood or Deluge. Unlike the Sumerian version both Jews and *Shatpath Brāhmana* believed that the Noah, for the Jews, and Manu, for the Hindus, built a boat directed by the God and forewarned of the flood by the God. They kept in the boat their immediate family, every kind of animal, every seed of a plant on the earth. Manu kept in addition the seven Rishis too. The flood was for seven days and after the floods the boat landed at a high peak. For the Hindus it was the Meru but for the Jews it was Mount Ararat which was the highest peak in the Mitanni territory. Mitannians probably believed themselves to be the chosen few of the God, something which the Jews believe even to this day. The second point of similarity may be the concept of the Creation. *Rigveda* describes the Creation in the Hymn known as the Nārāyaniya Hymn or the Hymn of creation which mentions that the God created the world out of Nothing.[9] This is what is described in the first chapter of Genesis. The similarity is striking. We know that Fire was worshipped both in India and in Iran in olden days, in the second Millennium B.C. Even in the third Millennium B.C. in India we find from the Indus Valley towns of Harappa, Mohenjodaro and Kalibangan fire-pits indicating the worship of Fire. Fire may not be the God, the creator, but it was the only forın of God known. Jews, we find that, when they gathered at the foot of Mt. Sinai after their expulsion from Egypt saw God only in the shape of Fire.[10] We know from a study of *Rigveda* the belief that nobody knows God and He may not be known even by the gods[11], that the various gods fulfil the work assigned to them and that the gods help man in time of trouble, specially one who cries to them in need and is righteous one. Most of the Hymns of *Rigveda* devoted to the Nāsatya twins mainly sing of their readiness to help men in trouble or need. We find the gods termed as Devtā or Deva in Sanskrit were transformed into angels, by the Jews, who did the work assigned to them and also helped righteous men in distress.

We may now examine the kind of thing offered to propitiate the God. In this the practice and theory both of ancient Hindus and Jews differ. *Bible* mentions that Abel and Cain, sons of Adam, brought their offerings to God, Cain, the first born, the produce of ground, while Abel the sheep or goat; God accepted the offerings of Abel and rejected that of Cain.[12] So God accepted the animal as sacrifice. This reminds us of the interesting controversy on the issue in India between learned men mentioned in the *Purānās* and *Mahābhārata.* It is said that scriptures said that *'aj'* is to be offered to god and that Nārad held that *'aj'* meant grains and some other among them Parwat held that it meant a goat. Finally it was decreed that it meant grains and that vegetable produce only is to be offered. This dissimilarity only indicated the debt which the Jews owe to Mitannians and hence to Vedic Hindus. Vedic Hindus accepted grains as offerings for the simple reason that India mainly produced vegetable food and the Jews accepted animal offering because they could easily offer an animal, goat or sheep, while grains or produce of earth was difficult to obtain. Or it might be a controversy in which those who sided the animal for sacrifice were able to influence the people of Mitanni simply due to the above reason. And through them the Jews also believed in the sacrifice of animal rather than grain.

How the Jews came to name their god as Yahweh? Is there such a god in either the Sumerian, Assyrian, Zoroastrian or the Mitannian civilisations? If we look at the known features of the Sumerians from where people feel that Jews actually came as mentioned in the *Bible* we do not find any such name as Yahweh or Jehova, as called later by the Jews, among those found in the records. Even in Ur we do not find any such name. Among the Assyrians too there is no mention of such a God named as Yahweh. Among the Zorastrians whose pantheon is much clearly known to us through the Zend Avesta we do not find such a name. Some scholars feel that probably it is a form of the name of Ahura, the God of the Zorastrians.[13] It was Bal Gangadhar Tilak who in his book *Orion* and in the Introduction to his *Gita Rahasya,*[14] dealing with *Gitā* and *Bible,* first pointed out that the Yahweh is the word taken from the *Vedas.* He had given this opinion when the existence of the Indus Valley Civilisation was not known nor that of the Mitannians speaking Sanskrit and having Vedic gods as their gods. According to him the word Yahweh is used in *Rigveda* for Soma[15], for Fire god[16], for Indra[17] and address to the Fire as Great[18]. Also he pointed out that the word is found in earliest book of Grammar and etymology *Nighantu* and *Nirukta* of Yāska. *Nighantu* is the book having a collection of words used in *Vedas* and *Nirukta* is the work which explains the etymology of those words. The *Nirukta* is said to be an earlier work than that of Panini and belongs probably to seventh century B.C. In *Nighantu* the word Yahaha is used in the sense of water[19], as power[20] and as somebody great[21]. He has explained the meaning of Yahweh as great in *Nirukta*[22]. Anybody having Indra, Varun, Mitra and Nāsatya and Vedic gods as their gods presupposes that they must be having the knowledge of *Vedas,* specially *Rigveda.* We cannot say that in those times there were communications between the two countries, Mitanni and India but the knowledge and religion must have reached there somehow. Whether or not Jews were a part of Mitanni people or living there in Haran surrounded by them they had learned enough and at least picked up a name used in *Rigveda* for different gods and this name Yahweh embodied in itself the attributes of all the gods mentioned in the *Rigveda* and later of the unnamed Creator itself.

Did the Jews reveal any other sign of borrowing from the *Vedas* or carrying the precepts of *Vedas*? In the *Bible* we do not find any indication of their religious beliefs till we come at the foot of Mt. Sinai where they gathered after they left Egypt pursued by Pharoah. Here too in the Book Exodus attributed to Moses, we find that in their camps were many images of gods other than Yahweh and that they still continued to make ones even there. Moses in their adversity taught them that they should strictly adhere to their ancient religion giving up whatever they learnt in Egypt. It is said that they still hankered after the Egyptian gods and goddesses. In probably a dispute as to whom they should worship they even made a statue of calf. Ultimately it was Moses who prevailed upon them to destroy all images and believe in the religion[23]. He told them that God had given him Ten Commandments which everyone had to follow. These Ten Commandments are the bedrock of the religion of Jews on which the rest of their religion and its rites are based[24]. Is there anything similar in the *Rigveda*? *Rigveda* mentions that learned men had established seven limits and anyone who crosses them is a sinner[25]. (Sapta Maryādāh kavayastatak shustāsāmekāmivbhyamhuro gāt)'.

Rigveda had not named these seven limits and assumed that men knew them and it might have been a convention observed by all. However, we find them named by Yāska in *Nirukta* while explaining the meaning of the word Anhur meaning sin[26]. Steyam talpārohanam brahmhatyān bhrunhatyān surāpānam dushkritsya karmanah punah punah sevām patkeanritodyamiti'. These seven limits are stealing, adultery, murder of learned men, killing of a child in the womb, drinking wine, doing evil deeds again and again and to tell a lie to hide his sin. In the Ten Commandments we have all of them except the drinking of wine. They prohibit stealing, adultery, widened the scope of murder by prohibiting any killing which includes that of learned men and a child in the womb, bearing false witness against neighbour and coveting the property of the neighbour which is covered under the limit of not doing a bad action, and not telling a lie of *Rigveda*. Stealing, murder adultery and speaking lie are things which are certainly common and the others are modified. The only additions are those relating to the regard that they should give to the God, not to make an image of God or of any living thing and not to believe in any other God. These were necessary for a people who were desolate and facing hard and uncertain times. They were added by Moses to prevent people from making images of calf or of Egyptian gods or to believe in other gods and thus create rift or schism in the people in distress when they could ill afford it.

Jews in Palestine

Alienated from the Egyptians during the Hyksos period and living in misery under the native Egyptian kings, the Jews by the middle of 14th century B.C. entered Palestine. They divided the various regions among tribes and settled in various parts of the land. By the time they settled down in the new land, the state of Mittani was destroyed by the Assyrians sometime in the middle of 13th century B.C. It may be interesting to note that it was at about this time, *i.e.*, 1250 B.C. that the presence of Etruscans was noticed in Italy and the Greek migration also called 'Dorian migration' began. Can it be linked to the destruction of Mitanni kingdom and the flight of its people who spoke a language akin to that of Greek, *i.e.*, Sanskrit and had similar Pantheon of gods having slightly different names? Dorians are said to have migrated from the North of Greece. Can they have among their midst the remnants of Mittanians? Running from the barbaric Assyrians and Hittites it is possible that some of them had managed to escape via the Black Sea and mingling with the local people the Dorians taught them the art of war and new speech and again tried to come near their home via Greece.

With the destruction of the state of Mittanni the Jews could not draw any further sustenance from their source of original inspiration. They were on their own in the land of Palestine which was their home for the next six to seven centuries. In Palestine they had not encountered a great religion backed by the might of a state power but the tribal religions of different people living among them, among them Philistines. These religions did not make much impact on the Jews and their beliefs. At the same time though the neighbouring great powers had an eye on Palestine for their territorial expansion, they had not bothered about the religious aspects of the territory. Thus it remained a battle ground between Egyptians, Hittites, Assyrians and Babylonians and some power or the other having some authority over at least parts of the land. Yet none appeared to have interfered in its religious affairs. Still we find the Jews from time to time worshipping images of gods of the other tribes. Old Testament of the *Bible* mentions these periods. We find in Judges[27] the Jews worshipping Baalim, and Baal-Berith became their god. It was just after the death of Gideon. Again in Judges[28] it is mentioned that the Jews began worshipping Baalim, Ashtaroth, gods of Zidon, of Moab, of Ammon and of Philistines. God became angry and made them subservient to Philistines. After great deal of suffering it appeared that the Jews were persuaded to destroy the images[29]. They became again independent. We again find that when Soloman became King of the Jews and inherited a stable kingdom he built temples for the deity of the Moab, Chemosh and to the deity of the Ammon, Molech, and also to the deities worshipped by his wives belonging to other religions.[30]

Were the Jews influenced by the neighbouring people of different races? Why did they worship images of different gods? Why they had a fascination for Baalim? We do not know why they worshipped images of different gods, specially that of Baalim, the calf. But it appeared that they were somehow worshipping the Calf or the Bull, Baal or Baalim. Egypt was a land where such gods with animal heads or forms were worshipped. Jews might have started worshipping them when they were in Egypt. We know that when after the Exodus they gathered at the foot of Mt. Sinai and Moses went up Mt. Sinai to commune with God, they took out the Calf and worshipped it. Later they were found to be worshipping it. We get references to their worshipping Baalim frequently. It appeared that they had always been worshipping Calf or Bull or Baalim since the very beginning of their identity and only the theology impressed upon them to worship a god who to them appeared to be imposing but dry. Whenever, the elders could impose their authority they suppressed the worship of Baalim but whenever their authority weakened the worship re-emerged. Or in other words when there was prosperity and relaxation of the authority of religious leaders there was the Baalim and whenever there was adversity the religious orthodoxy asserted itself. It also appears that the ceremonies of the worship of Baalim might have been a Saturnalia which the

Jews were reluctant to abandon. It was only when they received such a severe penalisation that the Jews utlimately gave up the worship of images. Jews' period of happiness and freedom came to an end swiftly in the 8th century B.C. and that too rather suddenly.

By the middle of 8th century Palestine was divided into two Jewish kingdoms, Israel with capital at Samaria and Judah with capital at Jerusalem. In 724 B.C. the Northern kingdom of Israel with Samaria as capital was attacked and after a siege lasting for three years it was captured. The attack took place when Shalmaneser V was king of Assyria. He was assassinated during the siege of Samaria and it was his son and successor Sargon during whose rule it fell. Probably Sargon II was not present when the city fell in 722 B.C. but the Jews were deported from Palestine. This was the first deportation they faced. In their place were also settled people of other races as deportees. They were from Babylon, Cuthah, Ava, Hamath and Sepharvaim as claimed by the *Bible*[31]. The troubles of Jews had not ended. In the 7th century B.C. the Southern kingdom of Judah was attacked by Nebuchadnezzar II of Babylon and in a siege lasting one and a half years Jerusalem fell in 687 B.C. when it was utterly destroyed. By 686 B.C. the Jews were deported to Babylon. Thus the later deported Jews came to Babylon while the earlier ones deported by Sargon II of Assyria in 722 B.C. were sent to the territory of the Mada (Medes) surprisingly in the neighbourhood of Haran from where they started earlier. They were according to *Bible* put in Halah and Habor by the river Gozan and in the cities of Medes.[32] Earlier it were the Mitannians and now it were the Medes. Probably the Mittannians were named as Medes and now the people of this same area are called Kurds. Are they the same people? Shifting of Jews to these area, *i.e.,* among Medes and Babylonians brought them into contact with major religions of the world. Formerly they saw the undeveloped religions of the various races in Palestine. Now they came into contact with Zoroastrianism, the dominant religion of the area professed by many races among them Medes and Persians. Medes and Persians not only professed this religion but with a true missionary zeal propagated it throughout the area and to everybody with whom they came into contact and Jews were no exception.

In 539 B.C. Cyrus captured Babylon and the Babylonian Empire came under the Achaemenid dynasty. Earlier the Medes had conquered the Assyrian Empire and destroyed all its cities, Ashur in 614 B.C., Nineveh 612 and Haran 608 B.C. These too formed a part of Achaemenian Empire under Cyrus. In 538 B.C. Cyrus by a decree freed the Jews and permitted them to return to their land and rebuild Jerusalem. The Jews returned back to Palestine under the leadership of Nehemiah and Ezra and began a religious revival. Was this a religious revival or was it a new religion?

Influence of Zoroastrianism on the Jews

What sort of influence the religion of Zoroaster had on the Jews? Did they include the principles of that religion in their own? What new features do we find in their religious theology and mythology after their return to Palestine from the captivity? Is there a significant difference or a cosmetic one? We may have to look into the scriptures, specially the chapters of the Old Testament from Chronicles which tell us the story of Jews after their return from captivity. In II Chronicles[33] we are told that Cyrus allowed them to return. In the Book of Esther we are informed that though the Jews were allowed to return, yet some remained in Babylon and entered the service of King Xerses I, Ahaseureus, of the Achaemenian dynasty and were appointed to important posts. They thus continued serving the Persian Empire which was the Empire professing Zoroastrianism. Thus that religion was no stranger to them.

In the Book of Job we encounter for the first time Satan. Was he not the same one who tempted Eve in the Garden of Eden and David? Actually it is not. The one who tempted Eve was just mentioned as serpent and was cursed to remain "a snake, and move about on his belly and eat dust".[34] He did not do further mischief. Nor do we find such a role later except in the case of David where Satan is just mentioned as suggesting to David to number his people which was not liked by God.[35] Upto now the Satan we find is an adversary of God. But in the Book of Job it is a new Satan. We find that the Sons of God assembled before God and Satan was among them.[36] God himself is said to have talked to him in a friendly way and to have challenged him to test Job.[37] We find Satan just a son of God, as is now a part of new mythology. He is no longer an evil adversary of God bent on destroying his creation but a son of God, created by Him, visiting Him when his sons assemble before Him and being challenged by God Himself testing and tempting people.

Again the Book of Job provides us a new view of God. Instead of a stern God, a flaming Fire, God appears before Job in a whirlwind and speaks reasonably and persuasively and explains his powers. He has not spoken like this even to Moses or David, his favourites. It is as if He is trying to justify his powers *vis-a-vis* Satan. Or is it like Ahur Mazda explaining to Zarthustra?

It was again in the Book of Ezekiel that we for the first time see God face to face. Earlier we had seen Him only in the shape of Fire when Moses and the people encounter Him at the foot of Mt. Sinai. Later it is His voice which is heard. But this time He is before Ezekiel in the shape of a human being sitting on a throne. We find that he has the shape of a human being, sitting on a throne made of sapphire and borne on their shoulders by four angels each having wings and having four heads each having that of a man, a lion, an ox and an eagle.[38] Is it not something like Ahur Mazda sitting on a throne talking to a Zarthustra?

Similarly, we find new concepts in the religion of the Jews. We find them to believe in angels created by God. We find them believing in the day of Last Judgement when the dead would arise and go before god to be judged for their actions in the world and to be assigned either heaven or hell according to their deeds to be judged on a balance. We thus find new concepts of heaven or hell.

In short we find new concepts in their religion, the concept of God as a King sitting on a throne, his having angels as attendants, the Satan as a creation of God who had gone against Him terrorising the people into cursing God and be alienated from Him, contest of God and Satan in the soul of man, the Day of Last Judgement, Heaven and Hell. From where the Jews borrowed these conceptions? There is no doubt that these concepts are found in the religion of the Zoroastrians. They have Ahur Mazda as the all powerful creator who rules the world. He had created the Angels and has also created the counterpart of Satan, Angre-Manyu. It is Angre-Manyu who through diseases torments the people. He also hurls calamities on the people. The contest between Ahur Mazda and Angre-Manyu is in the soul of Man. It is Ahur Mazda who explains to Zarthustra his powers, the creation of world, the Day of Last Judgement, the fate of man after death etc. and answers all and any questions asked by Zarthustra and satisfies him with a reasonable explanation. Again the concept of heaven and hell specially many heavens and many hells is found in only Zoroastrianism. The Talmud and Old Testament of the *Bible* now speak in this language. Gone was the stern voice of an invisible God and if visible only as fire and whirlwind. Gone are the harsh words and terse commands with which he had asked Abraham, Jacob, Moses, David etc. to hear what he says and to obey. Gone also was the time when anyone disobeying Him was punished; also if the nation as a whole disobeyed and deviated from the way laid down by Him, it was afflicted and even sent into captivity. After captivity it is a new Jewish religion and the ways of God had also changed. Man is to be punished only after the Day of the Last Judgement and that to be only after full balancing of his good and bad actions by angels. Now God does not punish him for deviation but Satan torments him to turn back on God. We thus find the Jews and their religion to have been materially influenced by the Zend Avesta of the Persians, the religion as taught by Zarthustra. Nehemiah and Ezra are said to have brought this religious revival by about 450 B.C. It is also said that Ezra found in the ruins of the old temple at Jerusalem, an old text of the first five Book of the Old Testaments now attributed to Moses. These are now the basic laws of the Jews modified as above by the Zoroastrianism. Did they have any other influence on their religious beliefs after that period?

Contact with Buddhism

Could Jews come into a close contact with Buddhism? In view of the fact that the evidence that Buddhist missionaries were active in that area makes it possible. What is the evidence? Are there any historical and archaeological records of their presence? In the Thirteenth Rock Edict Emperor Ashok claims that Buddhism had been established in various countries and he mentions "Yona king named Antiyoka and beyond this Antiyoka four kings named Turumaya, named Antikini, named Maka, named Alikasudara,". These are identified respectively with Antiochus II Theos of Syria, Ptolemy II Philadelphus of Egypt, Antigonus Gonatas of Macedon, Magas of Cyrene, and Alexander of Corinth. This Edict in view of the period of these kings must be somewhere near 250 B.C. This would also mean the presence of missionaries of Buddhism in Palestine. From Egypt some stones with Buddhist symbols of wheel and trident have been found but cannot be attributed to some particular date.[39] However, at Memphis in Egypt the discovery of some Indian figures made in mould about 200 B.C. points to these missions and an Indian colony there[40]. The above points out that the Buddhist missionaries did preach in Palestine. It remains to be seen if we find any evidence in the religion of the Jews of the precepts of the Buddha.

There are a few features which strike one immediately on looking at the Jews after 200 B.C. apart from the theology and mythology. First we notice the function of John, the Baptist. He had baptised some people among them Jesus Christ. We had not noticed before that period any baptism by the religious leaders of the Jews. Nor is it laid down in any law given to them. This baptism is something akin to initiation of Diksha typical of Buddhism or as a matter of fact is a typical Indian tradition. The second most obvious feature is the practice of ascetism. We find at this time a number of sects practising of ascetism by remaining away from habitations, living in a humble way, having the minimum possible needs and spending their time in meditation. They lead a celibate life never living among women. Such a sect known to us was the one known as the Essenes, in the times of Jesus and was mentioned by Pliny to have existed even a century prior to Christ.[41] It was deeply influenced by Buddhism and might have been a branch of Buddhism itself. Third feature is the practice of preachers and the teachers to move about from place to place preaching and never staying at a place for any length of time. These preachers too remained celibate and gave up all worldly goods depending for their feeding and lodging on the goodwill of people at large. We find as examples John, the Baptist, Jesus Christ and his disciples. This practice as we know was a practice adopted by the Buddha and his disciples and later became a part of the tenet of the Buddhist religious organisation known as Buddhist Mahasangh. When later Christian Church was organised, its organisation had a close resemblance to the organisational structure of the Buddhist Mahasangh with the Pope taking the place of the Mahasthavir, the chief of Buddhist Mahasangh, in the Christian Church organisation.

Among the beliefs we may have to again look at the transformation in the character of Satan. Satan is again changed out of recognition. He comes to Jesus and tempts him by offering him kingship over many lands only if he would worship him.[42] Satan as a tempter is a new feature in the religion of the Jews but certainly not among Indians or in the case of the Buddha. We know that when Buddha was meditating alone in the forest he was tempted by Mar or god Kamdev who is, according to Hindu beliefs, always sent by Indra to tempt any one practising meditation and likely to succeed in achieving God. This version of Mar tempting Buddha had gone and transformed Satan into a tempter but who does it with malice towards god. Transformation of Satan into a Hindu Mar is a sure evidence of the influence of Buddhism on the Jews of the time.

The full influence of Buddhism on the Jews can be seen in the career of Jesus and his twelve disciples and his teachings as recorded in the New Testament of the *Bible*. There is a close parallel with the life of the Buddha and his twelve disciples as well as in the teachings and theology. When Gautama, the Buddha was born, Asit, a revered ascetic came to his father and wanted to see him. When Jesus was born three Magi came there to see him. Both were born in the family of kings.

Both when meditating were tempted by Mar and Satan in the role now akin to Mar of Indian tradition. Both moved from place to place continuously never staying at one place for any length of time. Both were accompanied by twelve disciples. Was it a coincidence or did the writers of Jewish accounts borrow the stories about the life of Buddha to fit in with the life of Christ? The teachings of the Buddha are noteworthy for one aspect, *i.e.,* his compassion. He had a deep compassion for the poor, the downtrodden, the meek and even extended to animals. Anger, envy, jealousy etc., had no place in his view. We find the same compassion in Jesus Christ though it had not extended to prohibiting killing animals. He had the same compassion for all human beings and even was ready to forgive one who had committed crime due to ignorance, in a fit of anger or unintentionally. Both exhort people to have compassion on everybody even on enemies and to live a righteous life.

When people asked Buddha about the existence of God, he neither affirmed it nor denied it. He on the other hand exhorted the people not to think of such thing which do not concern them but to take to righteous conduct and compassion. If we look at the Gospels from the New Testament of the *Bible* we will find the same thing. Although the New Testament of the Bible which contains the preaching of Jesus Christ do not go to such an extent as to deny the existence of God for we hear quite often about the Kingdom of God, yet for all matters God has ceased to be an active force in the human affairs. Gone was the time when God would commune with Abraham, Noah, Moses, David, Job or even Ezekiel. Gone was the time when God would punish Jews for any transgression of his commands, or reward them for their steadfastness in obeying Him, rout his enemies and also give detailed instructions for any action to be taken by them even such mundane things like decorating or adorning His tabernacle. God is no longer taking any interest in human affairs. What we find that Man had to make or mar his destiny. He could do it only by righteous conduct, compassion, humility and serving the fellow beings in need which is like serving God. This is what Buddha preached. This was also a new religion not the old Judaic religion. The

Jews, specially the deeply religious ones steeped in old beliefs were fully justified in rising in revolt against that preacher of a new religion. Of course in what they were not justified was in getting him crucified through forcing a Roman Pilate.

If we analyse some of the sayings of Jesus Christ recorded in the Gospels we may find them as if lifted from Dhammapad. Some of them are as follows. "Woe unto you, scribes and Pharisees, hypocrites? For ye are like unto whited sepulchres, which indeed appear beautiful outward, but are within full of dead men's bones, and of all uncleanness"[43]. Also "And the Lord said unto him, Now do ye Pharisees make clean the outside of the cup and the platter; but your inward part is full of ravening and wickedness"[44]. Both these are echoes of Dhammapad 394. "But I say unto you, Love your enemies, bless them that curse you, do good to them that hate you, and pray for them which despitefully use you, and persecute you;"[45] This is similar to Dhammapad 5, 197 and 223. "For out of the heart proceed evil thoughts, murders, adulteries, fornications, thefts, false witness, blasphemies; These are the things which defile a man; but to eat with unwashen hands defileth not a man."[46] This has a very close similarity to Sutta Nipatta Anigandhsutta. "All therefore whatsoever they bid you observe, that observe and do; but do not ye after their works; for they say, and do not."[47] This may be compared to Dhammapad 51." And as ye would that men should do to you, so ye also to them likewise."[48] This may be seen in Dhammapad 130. "And why beholdest thou the mote that is in thy brother's eye, but considerest not the beam that is in thine own eyes"[49]. This had a close parallel with Dhammapad. We may see many more parallels both in sayings and in stories. What we may say in particular that the influence of coming into contact with Buddhism is seen in the new religion of the Jews which was preached by Jesus Christ and is now known as Christianity.

It was a long way from Haran but Jews during their wanderings had come into contact with every known religion of the then world. Jews were a restless people, who either voluntarily or forced, had constantly moved from country to country, more than any other people in the world. They came into contact with Vedic religion through the Mitannians, with the Zoroastrian religion through the Medes and Persians during their captivity in the land of Medes and with Buddhism in Palestine itself. They had absorbed something of each religion which could be traced. But they had also come into contact with numerous other religions like that of Egyptians, of Sumerians, Assyrians, and of Hittites which were in themselves great ones. In addition to these they had come into contact with a number of smaller ones, of the minor tribes living in their neighbourhood in Palestine. We do not know how much they had absorbed and how much rejected. But with the changes it became something unique which when blended with Buddhism into Christianity had so elevated the thoughts of man and his spirit that it swept off the whole of Europe and later the Americas. The scriptures of the Jews and those of the Christians were studied by Prophet Mohammad and some of the religious figures of both find a mention in the Holy *Kuran*.

REFERENCES

1. *Bible Genesis* 14.1.
2. *Bible*: chapter 47.20
3. *Bible, Gen.* 47.24-26
4. *Exodus* 1.8
5. *Bible Gen.* 11.28 and 31
6. *Bible Gen.* 11.28 and 31
7. *Bible Gen.* 11.2
8. *Bible Gen.* 11.9
9. *Rigveda.* 10.129
10. *Bible* Exodus 19.18
11. *Rigveda* 10.129
12. *Bible Gen.* 4.3-5
13. *Chips* Vol. I, p. 158 Dr. Speigel
14. In the Appendix to the Introduction Part 7.
15. *Rigveda* 9.75.1.
16. *Rigveda* 3.1.12.
17. *Rigveda* 8.13.20.
18. *Rigveda* 10.110.3.
19. *Nighantu* 1.12.
20. *Nighantu* 2.9.
21. *Nighantu* 3.3.
22. *Nirukta* 8.5.
23. *Bible* Exodus 32.
24. *Bible* Exodus 20.3-17
25. *Rigveda* 10.5.6
26. *Nirukta* 6.111
27. *Bible Judges* 8.33.
28. *Bible Judges* 10.6.
29. *Bible Judges* 10.16.
30. *Bible Kings* I, 11.7 and 8.
31. *Bible Kings* II 17.24
32. *Bible Kings* II 17.6.
33. *Bible,* Ch. 36.23.
34. *Bible Genesis* 3.14.
35. *I Chronicles* 21.1.
36. *Bible Job* 1.6.
37. *Bible Job* 1.8
38. *Bible Ezekiel* 1.10 & 26
39. *JRAS* 1898, p. 875.
40. *Petrie—Man* VIII (1908) No. 71.

41. *Historia Naturalis* Vol. V. 17.
42. *Bible,* St. Matthew 4.8 and 9; St. Mark 1.13; St. Luke 4. 4-8.
43. *Bible St. Matthew* 23.27
44. *Bible St. Luke* 11.39
45. *Bible St. Matthew* 5.44.
46. *Bible St. Matthew* 15. 19-20.
47. *Bible St. Mathew* 23.3
48. *Bible St. Luke* 6.31.
49. *Bible St. Mathew* 7.3.

Appendix-D

INDUS SCRIPT AND LANGUAGE : WAS THE LANGUAGE HINDI?

Script of Indus Valley Civilisation

What is the biggest unsolved mystery of the ancient world in the field of History? What do we miss in not solving it? One of the biggest unsolved mystery of the ancient world in the field of history is the mystery of the Indus Script. It remains undeciphered so far and because of it remaining undeciphered we do not know the language and what it contains and hence we do not know the history of Indus Valley Civilisation. Only if we know what it contains, in which language it is written, name of which god is written in it, if any, the name of any king if mentioned, then only can we be certain of the race, language and religion of the people who inhabited it and who developed it. Only then from the plethora of mythologies, history, religious beliefs available in India in the *Vedas, Brahmanas, Aranyaks,* and *Purānās* we may sift out those names and find and collect a proper history of the period. Only then we can be certain of their interaction with the neighbouring civilisation of Sumer and Akkad in Southern Iraq. We know much about Sumer and Akkad. Can we know enough even about Sumer if we do not know the result of interaction with the neighbouring civilisation of Indus Valley? Can we be certain that the word in use in Sumerian language is not a borrowed one from the Indus Valley? Can we be certain that the religion and culture of Sumer was not influenced by that of the Indus Valley due to interaction with its religion and beliefs? Probably not. The name of the mother goddess of Sumer was Ishtar and that of her son Tamuj, while the words Istri and Tanuj were used and are used as common names for woman and son in India. The name of the principal god of Sumer MARDUK is found in *Rigveda,*[1] as Mardeek and the name of Pishtin, the counterpart of Manu in their story of the

Flood is found as Pithinas again in *Rigveda*[2]. We again find common names parshu (axe), du (to go), Ishaku as Ishwaku (ruler) in both Sumerian and Sanskrit. Does it not show that there must be some interaction? Does it not indicate a relationship more intimate than imagined? It is obvious that without a knowledge of the history, language, religion and culture of Indus Valley we cannot fully understand the full history of Sumer, the formation of its language, religion and culture, and subsequently that of Akkad. How do we know anything about the Indus Valley Civilisation? Nothing can be known without knowing the Indus Script, the script of the Indus Valley Civilisation.

What is the Indus Script? Where is it found? Do we have enough material to try to understand it and decipher it? Indus Script consists of the symbols found on seals and other objects unearthed during excavations of the Indus Valley Civilisation. Indus Valley Civilisation was thus an old Civilisation like that of Sumer and Egypt which were once lost to history. However, like them when unearthed it is estimated that it flourished as a great cultural, religious and a homogeneous society prior to the 19th century B.C. It is presumed to have perished by 19th century B.C. because by then its great cities had ceased to exist and the other sites excavated so far also had ceased to exist probably earlier. What had happened to the people who inhabited it? We simply cannot say anything or even make a guess for we do not have enough material of the age or of the succeeding age to find a common ground. Do we have a historical record of the period either remembered in mythological accounts or described in any other context? India abounds in a plethora of mythological accounts and descriptions in its ancient texts but whether they pertain to Indus Valley period can only be said with certainty when the Indus Seals are deciphered and some of the names of gods or kings are also found on them. Of the Indus Valley civilisation so far about 800 sites were discovered. Of them about 530 were found on the banks of the river Saraswati, 200 in Kutch and Saurashtra, 70 late Indus in Uttar Pradesh and less than hundred in Indus Valley proper and Baluchistan. Bulk of the sites were found on the banks of the river Saraswati which is now extinct but which when flowing was a mighty river flowing from Himalayas through Punjab, parts of Rajasthan and lastly Sind where it was known as Mahamihran. It is possible that some of the sites which are now found on the banks of Indus might have been in those times actually on the banks of the river Saraswati which together with Indus changed courses frequently. Of the three major towns and smaller townships only Kalibangan was situated on the river Saraswati. The other major towns Mohenjodaro and Harappa were situated far away from the smaller sites on the river Saraswati. It is interesting to note that not a single site was situated anywhere near these towns. They were situated ensconced between rivers in safety from attackers from West and North respectively. Harappa was situated on the route from the North-West to the Saraswati while Mohenjodaro on the route from the West. It appears that their earlier establishment was to protect the population on the river Saraswati from wild tribes living beyond. Later they developed into Capital Cities. The other town Lothal is in Saurashtra peninsula interestingly enough bordering the mainland. The name Indus Valley Civilisation is a misnomer. Actually it should have been Saraswati Valley Civilisation. Now it is also known as Harappan Civilisation. Indus Script is found mainly on numerous seals unearthed during excavations in the Indus Valley Civilisation. It is also found etched on potsherds, bronze or copper implements, ivory pieces and such stray pieces. Few of the above are found in small villages sites. They are mostly found in big cities and smaller townships. The total number of objects having one or more symbols of Indus Script are 2906. However, there are 549 similar objects which either do not have any inscription on them or the symbols are missing, damaged or illegible. Of those, having the symbols, 1540 objects came from Mohenjodaro, 985 came from Harappa, 99 from Chanhudaro, 165 from Lothal, 99 from Kalibangan and 34 pieces from very small sites having a few each with Banawali having the maximum of 7. Interestingly we have 17 items from Western Asian towns of Djoka (Umma), Kish, Susa, Telloh, Ur and one from some unknown place in West Asia.

What are the Indus Valley seals? What do we have on them? How many symbols do we have on each seal? Seals are small square or rectangular pieces made of either baked earth or small stone pieces with length of sides ranging from .45″ to 2.65″. The smaller sealings have length from .35″ to .9″, width from .15″ to .3″ and thickness between .3″ to .05″. Some of the small sealings are also oval or round shaped. On the seals in the centre space is some picture and on the upper side are drawn the symbols either a single one, or in one line or two lines. These symbols are what is considered to be the Indus Script. However, there are a large number of these seals which do not have any picture at all but have instead these lines of symbols or Script. On the other hand there are seals which have only the pictures without any symbol. There are pictures and writing on both sides on some seals, interestingly both the pictures and writing on the two sides being different. Some seals have three sides with the scenes and writing different and if there is no scene but writing it also being different. What objects are shown in the seals? Usually there is shown an animal either a bull, a bull antelope, a tiger, an elephant, a goat, a buffalo or a rhinoceros. However, by far numerous in number is shown an animal which is like a bull but has only one horn in front, and named by archaeologists as unicorn. There are a few seals which have some scenes showing human beings along with animals busy in some ritual or activity or of animals alone shown in some unusual activity. The majority of the texts are in single lines only. The maximum number of lines is 7 in a text which does not have a picture in the middle. Again it is three on one side of the object which has a picture. The length of a line of text varies from 1 to 14 symbols. The maximum length of a text is 26 signs in three lines, one each on three different sides of a three faced seal but we do not know if the three lines are a text in continuity, or express the same meaning in different symbols or are even different. Most of the texts are, however, much shorter. The usual length of a text is 5 signs only.

On the seals which show some scenes of human activity or some ritual being performed or in other words show the incidents from the life of a deity surely we should find the incidents from the life and incidents connected with Shiv, whom the archaeologists and historians have identified as the deity of the Indus Valley Civilisation. Certainly not. We do not find any such incident connected with Him in the extant mythology of Shiv. The corpus of that mythology is enormous and is not likely to miss even incidents believed in those remote times. Do we find those incidents or scenes from the life of any other deity found in the Indian mythology? We do. In *Mahāpurān* which gives in detail the life of Rishabh, the Jain Tirthankar and also regarded by Hindus as an incarnation of Vishnu, various incidents of his life are mentioned in detail. A number of such incidents described in it are found depicted on the seals. Even the Seal No. 420 from Mohenjodaro, known as the Pashupatinath Seal on the basis of which scholars had identified him as Shiv, is actually described in *Mahāpurān*. Thus the deity of Indus Valley Civilisation is not Shiv but Rishabh. We do not know if he was known as Rishabh and a separate deity in Indus Valley or was identified with some other deity like Vishnu or Sun.

Script and Language

Do we know anything about the language and Script of the Indus Valley Civilisation? We unfortunately do not know anything about the language spoken and language written in the Indus Script and also which word is conveyed by each individual sign of the Script. Unlike other ancient languages of the world we do not have even a long text on which scholars may work. Can it be that the Script may not be a script and the signs may be just designs jumbled together on the seals? Does not the absence of long text just suggest that? Why long texts are not available? All the above can be possibilities and at the same time they may not be. The absence of long texts during excavations can be explained by the fact of the use of cotton cloth as a material for writing. It is found that clothes made of cotton were worn by the people. It is just possible that this cloth made of cotton was used and writings were made on cloth which perished. Also as referred to in ancient books the bark of silver birch and palm leaves were also used for writing purposes. All of which is lost due to the ravages of time. About use of inscriptions on stone slabs long in use in other civilisations of Egypt and Mesopotamia and also later from the age of Mauryas onwards, and their absence in Indus

Valley is surprising and cannot be explained. The only things discovered are seals made of baked clay or stone with the writings. To which use were the seals meant to be put? Were the seals used by the rulers to authenticate the materials to be exported and for similar purposes? We also cannot say. We cannot even say if the symbols on the seals were jumbled together and have no meaning. However, if we look at the seals there is a regular pattern in their setting of symbols and therefore these must be writings which conveyed definite message. They can be seals of rulers or of merchants but looking to the fact that some of them have religious scenes, showing some rituals being performed, some of them are certainly amulets to be carried on person or kept in the house for good luck. All this can be found only when we discover the language in which they were written and the message they convey. Hence, it is essential to study them and further to find out the language in which they were written and which words or word each symbol conveys.

What was the language spoken in the Indus Valley? Unfortunately the question of language is bogged down in controversy, and certainly round the personality and identity of the figure in Seal No. 420 from Mohenjodaro, known as Pashupatinath seal. In this seal is shown a nude man sitting on a stool with the headgear of the horns of bull, surrounded by four animals lion, elephant, rhinoceros and buffalo while under the stool again are sitting two goats. Marshall who wrote the first report on excavations jumped to the conclusion that as Shiv is the Lord of beasts, this deity must be Shiv. He also propounded the hypothesis that as Shiv is the god worshipped by Dravidians and specially Tamils the original inhabitants of Indus Valley must be Dravidians probably Tamils. He believed in this by the story in the *Bible* of Noah landing on Mt. Ararat and later his progeny so multiplying that they had to migrate to various lands giving rise to the belief that Aryans migrated to Indus Valley driving out the Tamils. All the presumptions of Marshall are as we know not correct. As seen earlier the deity on the Seal No. 420 of Mohenjodaro is not Shiv but Rishabh, who is now regarded by Hindus as the incarnation of Vishnu. We do not know if he was so regarded as an incarnation in Indus Valley times.

Moreover, Shiv is not exclusively a Dravidian deity. He is worshipped as extensively in North India. The first reference to Shiv is also in Sanskrit where Patanjali in the second century B.C. mentioned that the Maurya's sold the statues of Shiv for money.[3] This is the earliest reference unless we are prepared to believe that both *Ramāyān* and *Mahābhārat* which contained extensive references to Shiv were composed much earlier, before the 1st millennium B.C., which is more likely specially the first version of *Mahābhārat,* reference to which is made in later version of *Mahābhārat* itself. This is much before the Tamil references which were made only in the earlier centuries of the Christian Era. As far as *Biblic* Version of the Flood Story is concerned the reference to migration from Mt. Ararat and its implication to migration in India, is a wrong interpretation of the statement. The *Bible* clearly mentions that when the people overcrowded around Mt. Ararat they migrated but it never points out the exact location of the mountain. On the other hand it says that the people migrated into Mesopotamia, the ancient Sumer, from the east, "And it came to pass as they journeyed from the East, that they found a plain in the land of Shinar; and they dwelt there"[4]. Thus even if we believe in the story of the Bible, then according to it the people migrated into Sumer from India and Mt. Ararat may be a reference to some mountain in India. The arguments in favour of migration of Aryans into India are not convincing and therefore we may also consider the possibility of any of the language still spoken in Northern India as the possible language which took birth in Indus Valley.

What can be the language of the Indus Valley Civilisation if we consider it to be one of the languages still spoken in Northern India? Obviously it can be only Hindi and it is that dialect which is still spoken in the area where the Indus Civilisation once flourished. This area is the northern part of the present State of Rajasthan which is today mainly a desert. Is it not so that the language then spoken might have been considerably changed out of recognition during a period of 4000 years when a number of foreign people came into India? They must have brought their own languages which must have influenced that language. Moreover, a number of Empires flourished which imposed their own languages, Pali during the Mauryan times, Persian during the Muslim rule and lastly English. Can we say that the language must not have changed? Probably not. As a matter of fact the tract was an arid tract but for the river Saraswati and its tributaries notably the Dhrishdwati. But when the Saraswati dried up the area became a real desert and few people ventured into it. The people who inhabited it were left to fend for themselves in the widely scattered oases of the desert undisturbed by others including the empire builders. The language must have retained its pristine purity. How can it be said that the language was Hindi and not Sanskrit? Is it not said the original language was Sanskrit, specially Vedic Sanskrit and that all the later languages including Hindi were evolved from Sanskrit? If it is not Sanskrit then surely it may be the original Indo-European language which scholars after great effort established as the original language from which both Sanskrit and Greek took their classic form? Language when it evolves from the mutterings of the tribals in the long forgotten age has to be simple, monosyllabic one. Sanskrit is a language which is hardly monosyllabic and full of compound words. It is an artificial language which could hardly be a language of common conversation. Moreover, we have an indication that it had a parent in another language. Yaska in the *Nirukta* points out "Athapi bhashikebhya dhatubhyo naigmah krito bhashyante"[5], words of Vedic language were formed from the language spoken by people. He also points out that these Vedic words so formed were later used in the language spoken by the people too. Yaska was the earliest etymologist who commented on the evolution of the words of *Vedas*. Though the scholars regard his date to be only prior to that of Buddha, *i.e.*, in the 7th century B.C. yet it is possible that he might have lived much earlier. Surely if it is not Sanskrit then it must be Indo-European language from which both Sanskrit and Greek and Latin evolved. Again probably not. This so-called language was painstakingly constructed taking a mean word from similar words, *i.e.*, Sanskrit on the one hand and Greek and Latin on the other. It is nowhere found to be spoken. It is again an artificial language with a lot of compound words, which is not a natural growth or evolution. We must look for a simple monosyllabic language to be the original language not only in Indus Valley Civilisation but in Sumer and Egypt as well which were the other two most ancient Civilisations of the world.

What is the proof of Hindi being the language of Indus Valley Civilisation? Where can we find the proof? As to the place where such a proof can be found, every evidence however slender it may be points towards Sumer. Indeed Sumer is the ancient Civilisation which was the contemporary of Indus Civilisation and had some relationship with it. The only other Civilisation, Egyptian Civilisation though contemporary, was too remote to be likely of any help. The relations with Sumer were quite close though the modern scholars of Sumerian Civilisation discount any relationship with India depending only on Sumerian texts but failing to either refer to Indian sources or to remember that the then name of India is not known and that it might have been mentioned even in the Sumerian Texts. What are the proofs on which we can depend for basing our theory of Indus-Sumerian relations? One of the evidences is the mention of Sumerian gods and personages in the *Vedas*. The names which can be easily spotted are 'Mardeek'[6] and 'Pithinas'[7], one a god and the other too an important Sumerian personage in the folklore. There are extensive references to Sumer as the abode of gods in the *Purānās* and other religious scriptures and epics, where Sumer is described as a mountain, and the abode of gods. We have found a large number of seals of Indus Valley in various cities of Sumer some probably made in Sumer itself indicating the presence of Indus people there and the possibility of even Indus Colonies in various towns of Sumer. The scripts of both Indus Valley and ancient Sumer are very similar; the scripts, not the cuneiform, but the earlier ones, *i.e.*, one belonging to Uruk period, which has upright pictograms, those belonging to 3100 B.C. when the script was turned 90 degrees to the left and the script belonging to Jemedet Nasr period, 2800 B.C. Similarity, if script indicates that there are common symbols then the words indicated by that symbol might also be common. Finally there is the version in the *Bible* of people of Indus Valley settling in Sumer mentioned earlier. This part of the *Bible*, *i.e.*, the first four

Chapters which includes 'Genesis' where this statement appears is said to be written by Moses. He lived in the middle of the second millennium B.C., a period too close to the Sumerian Civilisation, which ended by 19th century but its remnants must have continued till very late and specially they may have retained the memory of earlier ages. If it was actually written by Moses then there should not be much doubt about its veracity. However, we may not entirely agree with Moses in deducing from the Biblic version of migration from East into Sumer that Sumerian was a form of the language of Indus Valley itself and that the culture of Indus Valley Civilisation dominated that of Sumer. Still there are possibilities of a large number of words being found in Sumerian language in addition to the grammatical forms.

But is it not a fact that Sumerian language—Indus Valley language connection had been very exhaustively studied and could not be proved? A large number of books on Sumerian-Indus Valley connection are in circulation. They have not been able to establish the connection. That is true. But surely we can look at it from a new angle. Moreover, we have not been able to find out the real Sumerian language as spoken or for that matter the spoken Akkadian, Hittite languages and similar languages of the Middle East found written in the Cuneiform script, but not spoken anywhere now. The languages spoken in the Middle East for more than two thousand six hundred years are mainly Arabic, Persian, Kurdish and Turkish. Although a large number of texts in Sumerian, Akkadian and Hittite were found but they were in Cuneiform script which could not be understood. It was only when Behistun inscription was found which had the same message written in two different scripts, Persian and Cuneiform and three different languages, Sumerian, Akkadian and Persian that they could be read and values assigned to various symbols in Cuneiform script. Meanings of the Sumerian and Akkadian words could also be ascertained. However, the pronunciation remained a distant dream. The words could be read but could not be properly pronounced simply because the pronunciation could not be grasped due to the deficiencies of the Persian script. What are the deficiencies of the Armaic script which evolved into the

Persian and Arabic scripts of later period, as compared to the Latin alphabet or Hindi alphabet? The Latin alphabet has twenty-one consonants and five vowels whereas the Armaic, Persian and Arabic scripts have much less consonants and even lesser vowels. For vowels they use diacritical marks. In Hindi script there are on the other hand forty consonants and twelve vowels, each having a separate sound. Moreover, by joining letters many more sounds could be represented in Hindi. Thus for every sound represented by a letter in Latin alphabet there are two or more different variation of that sound in Hindi alphabet. Similar is the case with vowels. There are twelve vowels which when joined to a consonant produce a much greater variety of sounds than is possible in Latin alphabets and much less in Armaic, Arabic or Persian scripts. As the Hindi script had almost double the number of consonants many of the sounds its letters represent are just missing in Latin and Persian scripts. In Persian script such sounds may not be expressed at all and those variations may actually be expressed by a single sound making it impossible to understand the pronunciation. This is noticed in the Sumerian language whose knowledge came down to us through the Persian script. Thus many different characters of Sumerian language are found to have the same sound and sometimes as many as 14 different characters are represented as having the same sound which is not possible and it is likely that they are variations of phonetic sounds which could not be identified. The problem is clearly defined in the *Encyclopedia of Language and Linguistics.*

> "In ideal circumstances the Sumerian writing system would have been reasonably simple and straightforward. But there were several factors which led to complications. Ideograms, for instance, often represented several related ideas, for example, Fig. 2(a) could be sun, or day, or bright; Fig. 3 could be interpreted as leg, or stand, or walk. Each variant meaning was of course expressed by a different word in spoken Sumerian, and so many written characters developed more than one phonetic value. Conversely the spoken language had large number of words which, as far as is known, were identical in sound—so many, in fact that it has been suggested that the language had phonetic tones which the writing system fails to

> differentiate. The result is that often a considerable number of different ideograms (sometimes upto 14) represent what appears to be identical phonetic values, and have to be distinguished by diacritical marks in modern transliteration (*e.g.*, ba, bá, bà, ba_4). These two principles of polyphony and homophony are basic features of Sumerian and all later Cuneiform writing..."[8]

Similarly in *Sumerian Dictionary* (Vol. A, Part I, p. 29, University of Pennsylvania) it is mentioned that in OB Nippur texts, the sign 'A' had five phonetic values and more are found in other texts. Can some concrete examples be given to illustrate the point? The example of two Sumerian words can be given. agi_6 uru_{16} is a Sumerian word meaning high tide[9]. Here 'a' stands for water and is probably not pronounced. But how 'giuru' meaning high tide is pronounced is not known. May be it can be 'jwār' meaning high tide in Hindi. Similarly 'a-gur-ra' means a vessel or pot.[10] But though there is sound 'r' in it the sounds 'gh' and 'rd' are not available in Sumerian script or for that matter in Latin or Persian scripts. The word may be 'ghadā' meaning a pot in Hindi. Persian script had been the tragedy of Sumerian language and it has reduced it to an unintelligible spoken language, a gibberish. Similar had been the fate of Elamite, Hittite, and Akkadian languages which had to be similarly expressed through Armaic script. They can be read but the pronunciation of words is not known. This Sumerian, an unintelligible gibberish, was made the base through which people tried to find similarity with either Tamil or Sanskrit or even the laboriously constructed Indo-European language. Thus making the Sumerian language, an unintelligibly spoken one the base for finding the roots of another highly artificial language, Sanskrit, was bound to have only one result—failure.

This earlier failure should not prevent us from making further attempts in probing Sumerian-Indus Valley connections. But this time our attempt should be in a reverse direction. We should not try to find out the Sumerian words in Indian languages supposed to be spoken in Indus Valley simply because the Sumerian words do not give us the correct pronunciation. We should on the other hand try to find out if the Sumerian language has words of Indian languages. This task has been made easy by the projected compilation and publication of *Sumerian Dictionary* (By University Museum, University of Pennsylvania) a few volumes of which have come out.

Has anyone attempted this approach? If so what are the results? Attempt was made by the author to find out such words in the Parts I and II of Volume A (five parts) of *Sumerian Dictionary*. The results are startling and interesting. In Part I 27 Hindi words are found while in Part II the number of such words is 40. The list of such words is appended. Are the words alike and their meaning the same too? Some of the words are exactly alike including their meaning, and thus the pronunciation of Sumerian words becomes clear. The Dictionary does not give the pronunciation because they do not know. Some words are slightly different in pronunciation but have the same meaning making it possible to conjecture that either the words in Hindi may be a correct spelling and a correct pronunciation in Sumerian or that the pronunciation and spelling had changed during migration from one country to another for such words are obviously borrowed by one language from another and this process might have been carried out on the parts of both. What are the other salient features of these common words in Hindi and Sumerian language?

(a) All these words are monosyllabic.

(b) These words in the attached list are also shown, written in Hindi script. It will be noticed that in some words the pronunciation of some sounds is such that it cannot be written either in Latin or Arabic, Persian or Armaic scripts. They can be written only in Hindi script which is a phonetic script.

(c) Some of these words belong to a dialect of Hindi still spoken in an area which was once the heartland of Indus Valley Civilisation but is now a desert. They were preserved in the widely scattered oases. The four words at serial Nos. 5, 8, 9, 27 in list of Part I are spoken exclusively in this area and might not be recognised in any other part of Hindi world as belonging to Hindi.

(d) The words which relate to water in Part I though begin

with 'a', are not found to be pronounced with 'a'. Probably 'a' is only a determinative. Similarly other words in Part II which also begin with word 'a' are also not found to be pronounced with 'a'. Here also 'a' is a determinative. But there is a difference between the two. The 'a' in Part I is shown as a simple 'a' while the 'a' in Part II is shown as 'a_2' which means that it is a different ideogram in Sumerian script and that there must be a different pronunciation and different meaning of the two.

(e) The words at serial No. 4 and 7 in list of Part I, are not spoken now but were found mentioned in the earliest collection of words of Vedic Age in India, *Nighantu.*

(f) The meaning of some words change during a long period of time and specially so when the period is 5000 years. It is interesting to note that such words in the Dictionary, which when found to be similar to Hindi words, have that meaning which they had in the earlier times. As an example the word 'Pirig' at serial No. 23 in the List for Part II, is Sumerian meaning lion. The counterpart in Hindi is 'mṛig'. We don't know if the difference in pronunciations is due to the migration of the word from one country to another or it is because of wrong reading of the Sumerian script. The meaning for 'mrig' is 'deer' in the present times but it was not always the same. In earlier classical times it was for animals in general. But still earlier it was meant exclusively for lion. In *Nirukta* the earliest collection of Vedic words, the meaning for 'mrig' is given as lion[11]. Thus the words in Sumerian has those meanings of Hindi words which were prevalent in those contemporary times.

Thus we find that there are a large number of common words in Sumerian and Hindi languages. As and when all the volumes of *Sumerian Dictionary* are published and the common words sorted out, we may not be surprised to find that the number of common words may be considerably more than 1000 words. We may not agree with the statement in the

Bible (Genesis) that it were the Indus people who colonised Sumer and thus the language of Sumer is either Hindi or one of its dialects, but the implication of far more closer contact and intimacy is indicated, to the extent of their enriching the two languages by loaning their words and also probably grammatical forms.

How this is going to help us in deciphering the Indus Script? Can it be possible that there may be common symbols for each word? If there are common symbols then as the Sumerian symbols are already identified, can we substitute them and find out the meaning of writings on the Indus Valley seals? The scripts of Sumer and Indus Valley Civilisation are apparently very similar. If the words of one language are borrowed by the other then it is very likely that the symbol denoting that word would also have been borrowed. If there is a difference it can be in adaptation of the symbol in accordance with the writing material and writing practices of the two scripts. Are not there a number of scripts of Sumerian language? To which script should we turn to find out the Indus script? Sumerian has four variations in its script. The last one known as the Cuneiform will not be of help simply because there is no parallel in the Indus Script. The earliest writing in Sumer consisted of pictures of animals, foodstuffs, textiles and other such commodities thus providing a simple method of recording number of animals and quantities of goods. The number and quantity was indicated by lines. We do not know in which language or languages the texts were written. But this pictographic system whatever the language became the basis of writing in Sumerian. The earliest texts came from the site of Uruk and are believed to be dated to 3300 B.C. At this stage many of the signs were still recognizable pictures; but the pictures were already to some extent stylised and simplified, and in some cases the presumed original pictographic forms are totally unrecognizable. By about 3100 B.C. the signs were for some reason as yet obscure were turned through ninety degrees to the left. In the Jemdet Nasr period, 2800 B.C. many of the lines in the old pictographs were given up making the writing simple but stylised so much so that some of the pictures could be barely recognized. In the classical Sumerian,

2400 B.C. the forms were further so simplified that the pictures could not be recognized. Do we have any similarity of Indus Valley script with that of any of the above three variations of Sumerian script? If so with which one? As a matter of fact we have elements of such similarity partly with all the three. Some of the characters are easily recognizable upright pictures of animals and birds, and trees, and other things of common use like utensils, drinking vessels etc. Some of them are turned ninety degrees to the right while some are turned ninety degrees to the left. In some the forms are so simplified and stylised that they could not be identified with any thing known. They could not be recognized, as depicting anything known.

Having known and found the symbols of Sumerian Script and Indus script and believing that the symbols might also represent the words in Indus script in case such a similar symbol is found in Indus Script as well, how that is going to help us in deciphering the Indus Script? The deciphering of the Script in that case will be easy. We have to substitute the word which is both Sumerian and Indus against the symbol. As the writings on the seals consist of usually three to five symbols the meaning may become clear. If it becomes clear then we may be sure that we have been successful in deciphering the script. Can we not do so immediately? We cannot do so immediately. The number of words so identified is still too small. We may wait till more words are identified and the symbols of Sumerian Script for them determined. Only then an attempt should be made to ascertain their meaning.

Should we adopt this process for other languages of the Middle East? We would not be able to do much with the script of these languages for they are all in the Cuneiform script. But it appears that the languages of the area as spoken earlier were related to Sumerian. Hence they must be having a large number of common words with Hindi. We should try to find out common words in Hindi and in those languages. It will help in getting at the correct pronunciation of these words and will enrich our study and may help us in understanding the origin of words. Thus knowing the correct pronunciation of a substantially large number of words will help in determining the pronunciation of a still large number of words in Sumerian and may help in making Sumerian instead of an unintelligible gibberish, a language intelligible, with body and soul of its own. So it may help other languages. We should not only try this method on other languages of the Middle East, Akkadian, Hittite, Elamite and Assyrian, but we should try to find out common words in Egyptian language as well. Will it not be farfetched to include Egyptian within our purview? It is just possible. We should not forget that along with the Sumer and Indus Valley, Egyptian was the only other Civilisation with a language and script. It must have had trade and other exchanges with at least Sumer if not with India as well. Some Egyptians hieroglyphs are similar to Sumerian and Indus symbols.

Thus having identified a pretty large number of common words in Sumerian language and Hindi, we have taken a step towards resolving the question of the identity of the language of the Indus Valley Civilisation. Hopefully scholars may now agree that it was a form of Hindi. The question of whether it was the gift of Sumer to Indus Valley Civilisation or *vice versa* can only be decided by scholars and may be after some clues are found. Hopefully it is a matter of time when the Script will be deciphered and we may be able to read the writings on the seals. This may give us some glimpses of the history of the Civilisation, the people who lived there, their lives and also their religious beliefs. We may get the names of certain chieftains and kings, which if found in the *Vedas*, Epics and the *Purānās* may help in establishing the historical goings-on in the Valley. Till then we have to wait.

REFERENCES

1. *Rig* 4.18.12.
2. *Rig* 6.26.6.
3. *Mahabhashya* 05.03.99.
4. *Genesis* 11.2—*Bible* (Authorised Version).
5. *Yaska-Nirukta* 2.1.2
6. *Rigveda*, 4.18.12.
7. *Rigveda*, 6.26.6.
8. *Encyclopaedia of Language and Linguistics*, Volume VIII, p. 4405
9. *Sumerian Dictionary* Vol. A, Part I, p. 87
10. *Ibid.*, p. 93
11. *Yaska-Nirukta* 1.6

SUMERIAN DICTIONARY

Volume A Part I

Common Words in Sumerian and Hindi / Sanskrit

S. No.	*Page No.*	*Sumerian Word*	*Meaning*	*Hindi/ Sanskrit word*	*Meaning*	*Written in Hindi*
1	3	a-du-ga	Sweet water	dudh	milk	दूध
2	3	a-kum	Hot water	garm	hot	गरम
3	5	a-tal	Broad water	tãl, tãlab	tank	ताल, तालाब
4	6	a-da-ri	lasting water	adri	rain cloud	अद्रि
5	6	a-he-gal-la	abundant water	hagla sagla sajal jalwã	all all with water well	हगला सगला सजल जलवा
6	12	a-dadag	clean water	tadãg	tank	तड़ाग
7	20	a-nam-ti-la	water of life	amrit	water of life	अमृत
8	50	a-bar-ra	adopted child	tãbar	child	टाबर
9	52	a-da-ab	a musical instrument	dhab	a musical instrument	ढब
10	68	a-gaigi	rear, back, backroom, front	ãg-e	front	आगे
11	70	a-ga-am	swamp, marsh, reed lagoon	*agam*	place where one cannot go	अगम
12	75	a-a-gu-la	great waters, flood, flooding	*kulyã*	river	कुल्या
13	78	a-gar-gar	dropping, dung (sheep, gazelle)	*gobar*	dung	गोबर
14	82	dug-a-gi-a dug-aga	a vessel	*dongã* *dongi*	vessel boat	डोंगा डोंगी
15	84	a-gi-a-um	a garment	*angiãn* *jãngiãn*	garment of upper body garment of lower body	अंगिया जांगिया
16	87	a-gi-uru	high tide	*jwãr*	high tide	ज्वार

S. No.	*Page No.*	*Sumerian Word*	*Meaning*	*Hindi/ Sanskrit word*	*Meaning*	*Written in Hindi*
17	93	a-gur-ra	vessel for pouring water	*gurhã*	pot for water	घड़ा
18	93	dug-a-gur -ra	vessel for pouring water	*dukdã*	vessel used in feasts	दुकड़ा
19	103	a-la a-a-la	a metal object, Part of metal object, a device for hoisting water	*ãlã*	instrument, tool	आला
20	114	a-mah	massive waters, flood	*meh* *maha*	rain cloud very big	मेंह
21	124	dug-a-nag dug-a-na-na	vessel for drinking water	*dongã*	vessel for keeping foodstuff	डोंगा
22	135	a-ra	a wooden object	*arã*	spokes of a wheel	अरा
23	140	a-ra-zu	pray, please, at your service (a term expressing obedience, submission) prayer (to god), supplication, intercession	*arch*	prayer	अर्च
24	153	a-ri	enemy	*ari*	enemy	अरि
25	32	a-a (Pro-nounced aia)	father	*ãrya*	respectful address	आर्य
26	33	ama	mother	*ammã*	mother	अम्मा
27	100	nagar	carpenter	*jangarh*	carpenter	जांगड़

SUMERIAN DICTIONARY

Volume A Part II

Common Words in Sumerian and Hindi/Sanskrit

S. No.	*Page No.*	*Sumerian Word*	*Meaning*	*Hindi/ Sanskrit Words*	*Meaning*	*Written in Hindi*
1	4	a-tu-lu (tu-ul)	to let one's arm be slack, to become inactive	Jhool thool	to hang, to become slack	झूल थूल
2.	10	a-bar	the outer side of wall	bãrh	boundary wall	बाड़
3.	10	a-mah	great power, huge strength	mahã	great, huge	महा
4.	12	a-le-um-ma	side board (a partof the plough)	hal lãngal	plough	हल लांगल
5.	29	a-u-zal-le-da	day-break	ūjãlã ushã	light dawn	उजाला उषा
6.	30	a-ag-ga	(issued) order, decree (given) instructions command	ãgyã	orders command decree	आज्ञा
7.	37	ki-a-ag-ga	place where orders/decrees are issued	ãgãr	hall	आगार
8.	46	a-bulug	hole, nook	bil	hole made by mouse	बिल
9.	41	a-an-kar	a weapon	ankush	a weapon also used in controling elephants	अकुंश
10.	45	a-bad	cover, protection shelter	bãrh	outer wall to protect cattle, boundary wall	बाड़

S. No.	*Page No.*	*Sumerian Word*	*Meaning*	*Hindi/ Sanskrit Words*	*Meaning*	*Written in Hindi*
11.	48	a-dam a-da-am a-dam	habitation settlement (and its inhabitants)	dhãm	habitations, settlements including inhabitants	धाम
12.	57	a-ma-al am-ma-al-la	mighty, able, capable	malla	mighty, powerful	मल्ल
13.	65	a-gid-da	spear	gadã	mace, club	गदा
14.	69	a-gu-sar-ra	path, road	sarhak	road	सड़क
15.	99	a-sikil	pure	shukla	pure, white	शुक्ल
16.	100	a-bi-se	now, this moment	abhee	now this moment	अभी
17.	102	a-sita	equipment, implement of agriculture	sitã	part of plough furrow	सीता
18.	110	a-tir	wings	teer	arrow	तीर
19.	120	a-zi-da a-si-da	right arm right side	sidhã	right side, right arm, right leg	सीधा
20.	129	a-ab-ba	father, old man, elder	abbã bããp bãpu	father, elder	अब्बा बाप बापू
21.	133	ab-ba	1. body of water sea, lake (in general) 2. sea (as a geographical term)	ããp ã ãb jal	water (Di-jal ã Tigris)	आप आब जल
22.	172	ab-subur	an animal, pig?	suvar	pig	सुअर
23.	12	pirig	lion	mrig	lion, (but now used for stag)	मृग
24.	21	bahar	potter	kumhãr	potter	कुम्हार
25.	2	dub-ba	basket	dubbã	basket, box	डिब्बा
26.	48	uru	city, town	pur	city, town	पुर
27.	49	u-dagal-la	sunlight	ujãlã	light	अजाला

S. No.	Page No.	Sumerian Word	Meaning	Hindi/ Sanskrit Words	Meaning	Written in Hindi
28.	56	a-gab-bu	left	khabba, khabbu	left, left handed	खब्बू
29.	56	igi	front	āge	front	आगे
30.	67	uz	goat	aja	goat	अज
31.	69	a-gu-zi-ga	early morning	ushā, ujālā	morning, light	उषा
32.	88	tir	tree	taru	tree	तरू
33.	109	tarah (dara)	ibex	dhor	domesticated animals	ढोर
34.	100	ma-gur	boat	magar	crocodile	मगर
35.	109	mas	goat	mesh	ram with broad tail	मेष
36.	122	Dur	male donkey	khar	male donkey	खर
				gardh-abh gadh-ha		गर्दभ गधा
37.	157	gun-a	multicoloured	gunā	multiply	गुणा
38.	164	si-ab si	cow horn horn	seeng	horn	सींग
39.	181	ku-ra-ka	netherworld	narak	hell	नरक
40.	159	Gu	ox	Gau (Ga-oo)	cow	गऊ

INDEX

Abdur Rahim Khānkhana, 320
Abhidhamma, 311
Abhijnam-Shākuntalam, 136, 145
Abhyāvarti, 54, 97
Abortion, 301
Achaemenids dynasty, 236, 237, 243, 244, 341, 368
Achaemenian, 212
Achaemenian Empire, 200
Acharya Jinsen, 122
Ādi Shankarāchārya, 284
Ādityas, 33, 39, 41, 56, 135, 317
Administration, 170, 173, 175, 182, 204, 230, 259, 285, 304
Aegean migration, 360
Afghanistan, 46, 48, 55, 148, 187, 190, 199, 204, 257
Age of Gita, 344-48
Age of reason, 204
Aggalassoi, 177, 178
Agni (fire), 42, 44, 56, 111, 205, 336
Agnimitra, 221, 322
Agnirdham, 124
Āgrā, 320
Agrani, 347
Agrasenis, 192, 253
Agriculture, 27, 57, 60, 75, 84, 85, 171, 198
  discovery, 78
  new techniques, 76
Ahur Mazda, 160, 369, 370
Aikshvakus, 186
Aj, 324
Ajanābh, 126
Ajātshatru, 27, 174, 184, 190, 230, 295, 298
Ajivakas, 215, 287
Ajmer, 72
Akrura, 346
Alexander, 23, 26, 176, 177, 178, 180, 186, 188, 189, 236, 239, 240, 244, 245, 250, 251, 252, 253, 296, 345, 371
Alikasudra, 371
Allah, 295
Allāhabād, 49
Allahabad-Kosam pillar, 282
Amarkosh, 225
Amir Khusro, 320
Āmrapāli, 183
Anabasis, 240
Anatolia, 139
Andhra Pradesh, 274
Anga, 169
Animals, 34, 73, 75, 216
  incarnations, 143
  seals, 86, 116, 117, 119-21, 128, 129, 380
Aniruddha, 144
Anjasi, 98
Anu tribe, 56
Aparājita, 214
Arab nations, 22
Arabic script, 388
Ārams, 303

Āranyaks, 141, 155, 206, 297, 322, 345
Aradha-Magadhi, 230
 dialect, 320
Ārjikia, 46
Arjun, 209, 213, 234, 292, 305, 332, 335, 336
Arjunāyans, 178, 180, 193, 210, 295, 348
Armaic script, 387
Arsian, 188, 189, 295
Artifacts, 82
Artisans, 172
Arya Samaj, 280
Aryans, 24, 142
 civilisation, 43, 66
 gods, 111
Ashoka (Emperor), 28, 115, 122, 141, 167, 237, 249, 260, 284, 285, 289, 291, 306, 307, 312, 314, 304
 administration, 267-68
 successors of, 286-88
Ashokan inscription, 256
 pillars, 248
Ashokavādan, 266
Ashrams, 303
Ashtadhyayi, 207
Ashtapād, 227
Ashwamedha, 94, 97
 yagna, 135
Ashwini Twins, 33, 59, 160, 161, 205, 221, 300
Assyrians, 187
Asurs, 93, 205, 207
Atharvaveda, 33, 34, 37, 38, 42, 59, 97, 119, 130, 159, 205, 228, 289
Atithigva, 54
Atri, 42
Aurangzeb, 320
Avestā, 158, 159, 162
Ayodhya, 47, 183
Aztees, 148

Babylonians, 355
Bactrians, 312
Bairāt, 248, 263, 277
 inscription, 275
Bairāt-Bhābhru, 292
 rock-edick, 241
Bākhtris, 285
Balram, 144, 292, 344
Baluchistan, 46, 76, 113, 151, 154, 170, 190, 273, 274, 378
Banjara, 83
Barābar Cave inscription, 263, 264, 275, 287
Beās river, 46, 52, 61, 90, 92, 134, 198, 304, 353
Behistun inscription, 189, 386
Besnagar, 210
Bhadrabāhu, 258
Bhagwat-Gita, 333, 340
Bhagwat Puran, 115, 135
Bharadwāja, 42, 232
Bharat tribe, 60
Bharatas, 96, 97
Bharatpur, 180
Bhāvya, 99
 rules, 54
Bhawani, 315
Bhim, 332, 341, 349
Bhimji-ki-Dungari, 248
Bhishma, 212, 331, 332, 339
Bhojpatra, 170, 290
Bible, 112, 354, 356, 358, 362, 366, 370, 372, 373, 382, 383, 385, 386, 391
Bijagarh inscription, 195, 200, 252
Bimbisār, 27, 183, 184, 196, 298, 300, 320
Bindusār, 256, 258, 259, 260, 267, 268, 269, 356, 358

Black magic, 85
Black sea, 164, 165, 365
Bodhisattva, 312, 313
Bogāz Que, 162, 221, 359
Brahmā, 161, 209, 211, 279
Brahmā Sūtra, 322, 345
Brāhmanas, 50, 55, 141, 155, 206, 297, 322
Brahmi script, 26, 147, 289, 321, 323, 347
Brāhat kathā, 225, 241
Brāhuis, 149
Buddha (Lord), 31, 49, 113, 119, 128, 144, 145, 169, 208, 214, 217, 218, 230, 249, 261, 267, 275, 281, 291, 294, 298, 300, 371, 373, 384
  teachings of, 24
Buddhism, 122, 213, 217-18, 285, 291, 298, 301, 309, 371, 373, 375
  adoption of, 308
Buddhist Council, 284
Buddhist Mahasangh, 372
  monastries, 305
Buddhis Sangh, 281, 282
Bureaucracy, 313, 319
Burha Pushkar Lake, 72, 83, 84

Caityas, 214
Calamities, 293, 370
Calcutta, 88
Calcutta-Bairat Edict, 264
Calcutta-Bhābhru Bairat Edict, 275, 276
Calcutta Museum, 241
Cambodia, 235
Cannan, 355, 356
Cape Comorin, 67
Caspian Sea, 164, 165
Caucasian Mountain, 66
Central Asia, 112
Ceylon Dipvansa, 261
Ceylonese Chronicals, 255, 265, 268, 272
Challenges, 21, 59, 60, 77, 223, 312, 313
Champā, 265
Chāṇakya, 185, 187, 231, 232, 233, 238, 242, 243, 250, 251, 255, 256, 290, 306
Chāndyogya-Upnishad, 345
Chandragiri, 246
Chandragupta Maurya, 23, 24, 26, 177, 186, 231, 232, 234, 237, 242, 246, 250, 252, 255, 259, 260, 268, 274, 286, 287, 289, 296, 306, 314
  administration, 290-95
  appellation of, 318
  problems of, 323-25
Charuvaki, 288
Chāymān, 97, 351
Chedi, 191, 335
Chenāb river, 195, 304
China, 226, 286, 298, 313
Chitrangdā, 350
Chittor, 178, 193, 315, 394
Chola, 274
Christians, 354
Christian Church Organisation, 372
Christian fundamentalism, 66
Christianity, 25, 148, 297, 309
Coins, 245, 306
Communications, 84, 320
Copper coins, 178
  implements, 82
Creator, 55, 63, 156, 301, 306
Criticism, 353
Crocodiles, 127, 133, 144
Crops, 58, 72, 73
Ctesias, 188

Cultural influences, 22
Cuneiform script, 386
Cyrus (Kurush), 190

Dadhrikā, 34, 37
Dandaka, 164
Dān-Stutis, 55, 62, 102
Dāshrāj, 93, 96, 352, 357
  battle, 102
Dashrath, 136, 163
Dasyus, 93
Dayaram Sahni, 248
Dāyarvush, 189
Deepvansh, 270, 282
Deities, 120
Delhi, 88
Delhi-Topra pillar, 279
Desiccation, 81, 114
  challenges of, 86, 154
Devalokas, 214
Devānam Priyadasi, 318
Dhamma, 275, 278, 279
Dhammapada, 374
Dharma, 217
Dharma Sūtras, 232
Dhauli, 263
Dhrishdhwati, 47, 98
Dhritrāshtra, 330
Dhruva, 97
Digambar Sect, 284
Disputes, 309, 310, 324, 325
Divodās, 36, 48, 49, 53, 60, 95
Divyāvadān, 265, 266, 276, 287
Diwali festival, 59, 80, 107, 108
Dorian migration, 360, 365
Dream of Merudevi, 215
Drahaya tribe, 56
Draupadi, 331, 349
Drupad, 333
Dravidians, 110, 111, 149
  languages, 114, 148
Drona, 332, 336
Drughan, 35
Durgā, 221, 222, 293, 294, 305, 315
Duryodhana, 245, 330, 331, 332
Dushyant, 96, 136
Dwārkā, 88, 100, 137, 153, 212

Education, 304, 305
Egyptian, 25
  civilisation, 295, 385
Ellasar, 356
Emergencies, 202
Employment, 181, 197
Excavations, 62, 82, 88, 103, 113, 192, 378, 379
Ezekiel, 373

Fateh Singh, 108, 111
Festivals, 44, 80, 107
Fire God, 37
Fire discovery, 78
Food problems, 76

Gāndhar, 169, 177, 181, 191, 331
Ganesh, 315
Ganeshwar hills, 82
Gangā, 47, 49, 68, 69, 95, 151, 152, 155, 192, 198, 383
Gapsāgar tank, 145
Garrisons, 92
Garuda-Stambha, 344
Genesis, 91-94
Ghosundi, 315, 344
  inscription, 210
Gilgamesh, 335, 351
Girnar, 263
  inscription, 256
Gita, 26, 213, 234, 341, 344, 349
  archaeological evidence, 344

composition of, 349
literary evidence, 345-46
Gita Rahasya, 363
Gods and Goddesses, 93, 105, 137, 155, 156, 212, 214, 248, 293, 297
Gold ornaments, 62
Gordon Childa, V., 74
Gospels, 374
Graha Sutra, 232, 322
Grains, 73
Greek version, 22, 23
Gṛtsamada, 42
Gujarat, 153
Gulf of Cutch, 68

Haran, 358
Harappa, 26, 27, 41, 43, 45, 47, 48, 52, 53, 66, 68, 88, 90, 93, 97, 99, 100, 103, 105, 130, 131, 138, 152, 160, 198, 302, 353, 361, 379
Harivansh Purān, 333
Hariyupiā, 54, 102
battle of, 154
Harsh, 259
Haryana, 152, 153, 192
Hastinapur, 153, 330, 355
Hidimba, 341, 349
Himachal Pradesh, 152
Hinyān, 261, 313
Hindu Mythology, 126
Hinduism, 122, 283, 291, 308, 310
Hindukush mountain, 27, 46, 52, 196, 204, 313
Hiranyagarbh Sukta, 63
Hiranyakashyap, 121
Hittites, 163, 359, 360, 375
Holi festival, 58, 80, 107, 108
Horse sacrifice, 54
Huen Tsang, 241, 248, 267
Hydrakes, 189
Hyksos, 356, 357, 365
Hymns, 33, 35, 37, 42, 48, 55, 59, 62, 80, 158, 205, 300, 301

Ikshwaku, 138, 186
dynasty, 125
Illiad, 350, 358
Indra, 37, 63, 211, 205, 341, 343, 361
Indonesia, 235
Indus Script, 110, 111, 347, 380
Indus Town Planning, 100
Indus-Sumer relationship, 136-38
Indus valley civilisation,
areas, 24, 67
deities, 108, 315, 380-81
discovery of, 346
estabilisation, 71
founding cities, 100-102
habitations of, 45
houses of, 77, 101
influences of, 302
inhabitants of, 142
language spoken, 109
major towns of, 26
mature phase of, 88-92
physical aspects, 32
political life, 210-12
presiding deities of, 133
problems of, 110-11
religion and culture, 378-80
script of, 377-80
seals of, 42, 86, 302, 379, 391
society, 32
stirring of, 27
symbols of, 143, 146
totem-turned-deity in, 42
Iran plateau, 157
Irāwati, 46
Islam, 148, 297

Ishāvasyo, 205

Jai Bharat, 329, 339, 340, 348-49
Jain Bhagawati Sutra, 169
Jain mythology, 24, 122, 125, 126, 144, 302
Jainism, 122, 213, 218, 291, 298, 301
Jaipur, 88
Jammu & Kashmir, 77
Jāmbavān, 346
Janpadas, 171, 174, 175, 200, 210
Janpada Kalyāni, 265, 266
Japan, 109
Jātaka Kathas, 283
Jātaka stories, 213, 218, 342
Jerusalem, 370
Jesus Christ, 371, 372, 373, 374
Jewellery, 88
Jews, 25, 273, 274
  influences of, 358-59
  religion of, 354-55
  worshipping, 366
Jews in Palestine, 365-66
Jhelum river, 23, 195, 304
Jiggurat, 105
Joseph, 357
Judaism, 25
Junagarh inscription, 194-95
Justin, 241-43
Jya, 61

Kalhan, 286
Kāli, 315
Kalibangan, 45, 48, 49, 52, 54, 85, 86, 90, 92, 98, 100, 103, 105, 138, 160, 302, 353, 361, 379
Kālidas, 136, 145, 195, 211, 221, 318, 322
Kalinga, 186, 263, 272, 314,
  war, 115, 264, 273, 274, 275, 276, 277, 286
Kambojas, 169, 181, 191, 191, 192, 285
Kamdev, 372
Kansa, 335
Kanva clan, 42
Kapilvastu, 303
Karna, 213
Kārtikeya, 163, 193, 194, 292, 294, 306
Kāshi, 164, 184
Kashmir, 286, 287
Kathāvatthu, 282, 311
Kātyāyan, 176, 208
Kauravas, 338, 339, 352
Kāutilya, 214, 232
Khal, 347
Khang, 223
Khari-Boli, 320
Khātusās, 162, 163
Kikkuli, 163, 360
King Bāli, 317
King Bharat, 133
King, Bhāvya, 50
King Chitra, 54
King Kanishka, 313
King Khārvel, 272, 314
King Lodi, 326
King Sranjaya, 102
King Kirat, 332, 350
King Yayati, 93
Kleitarchus, 240
Korān, 298
Koshāmbi Edict, 264, 282
Krishna, 143, 144, 213, 220, 234, 245, 292, 294, 305, 329, 333, 336, 340, 343, 344, 350
Kshetra, 139
Kshatriyas, 186, 247, 305

Kuber, 144
Kunal, 287
Kuntābh Suktas, 228, 229
Kunti, 341
Kurdistan, 114
Kurds, 367
Kuru, 139, 191, 212, 226
Kurukshetra, 153, 191, 335, 340
Kushan tribes, 114, 312, 313
Kutsa Angiras, 49, 98, 99
Kuyava, 49, 98

Lakshman, 234
Lakshmi, 80, 81, 145
Languages, 45, 108, 111, 112, 143, 204, 207, 222, 225, 226, 230, 295, 322, 381, 383
Linga, 105
Lingua-franca, 319
Lothal, 88, 92, 137
Lunar dynasty, 50, 51

Macedonia, 180
Madas, 187, 188
Mādhyamika, 178
Magadh, 23, 155, 169, 174, 270, 272, 303, 335
Mahābhārata, 25, 26, 55, 136, 153, 156, 176, 192, 194, 211, 213, 232, 233, 234, 241, 245, 265, 322, 329, 339, 340, 342, 343, 348, 350, 362, 383
  war, 332, 333
Mahābhāshya, 149, 220, 238
Mahadevan I, 108, 111
Mahapadmanand, 186
*Mahāparinibhan Sutt*a, 247
Mahāpuran, 122, 131, 135, 381
Māhavansh Tika, 239
Mahāvansa, 267, 276, 286, 311
Mahāvir (Lord), 122, 171, 208, 213, 217, 218, 230, 275, 292, 298, 299, 300
Mahāyān, 25, 201, 313
Mahisha, 123
Makhli Goshāl, 215
Makhaliputra Goshāl, 292, 298
Mālavas, 28, 170, 178, 180, 194, 199, 253, 287, 288, 291, 295
Mālva, 317, 318
Malaysia, 235, 313
Maldive Island, 202
Mandals, 33, 42, 63
Māndavya, 329
Manifestation, 294
Manu Smriti, 290
Marshall, 113, 121
Mātarishwā, 78
Mathurā, 193, 210, 220, 229, 292, 333, 345
Mātrabhumi, 226
Matsya kingdom, 338
Matubhumi, 139
Mauryan Age, 236
  language and literature, 319-25
  people and society, 289-95
Mauryan coins, 258-59
Mauryan dynastry, 286
Mauryas, 25, 26, 37, 51, 209
  religion, 291-93
Maxmulleur, 21
Mayurposhak, 246
Mecca, 314
Medina, 314
Mediterranean Basin, 74, 114
Megasthenes, 185, 188, 239, 259, 292, 345
Mesopatamia, 74, 383
Migration, 66, 112, 150, 152, 382, 383

Milind Panha, 238, 255
Minar Rock Edict, 271, 275
Mittanians, 162, 163, 164, 187, 359, 360, 361, 367
Mitra, 41, 160, 205
Modern Iraq, 22
Modern Satellite imagery, 66
Moggaliputta Tissa, 310
Mohanjodaro, 25, 27, 40, 43, 45, 47, 48, 52, 53, 54, 67, 85, 88, 90, 93, 97, 99, 100, 103, 105, 127, 128, 130, 138, 148, 151, 153, 160, 223, 302, 353, 361, 379
Monarchies, 167-69, 170, 174, 175, 182, 225
Monastries, 304, 305, 310, 312
Monks, 311
Moon, 343
Moriyas, 247
Mount Kailash, 126, 143, 221
Mt. Ararat, 382
Mt. Sinai, 361, 363, 369
Mudgal, 35, 36, 53, 96, 134
Mudrā Rākshas, 238, 242, 290
Muslim nations, 22
Myanmar (Burma), 313
Mystic religion, 316

Nadi-Stuti, 46, 70
Nagarjuni hills, 287
Nakul, 332
Nānāghat, 315
Nandas, 23, 28, 186, 231, 237, 285, 289, 295, 314
Narakas, 214
Narbada river, 152
Narkāsur, 152
Narsingh, 121, 145
Nāratya, 162, 360, 361, 362
Natural calamities, 150, 214
Neolithic Age, 67
Nepal, 337
New challenges, 57
New discoveries, 26
New Testament, 372, 373
New York, 88
Nighantu, 206, 207, 215, 222, 224, 363
Nile Valley, 74
Nirdhum Agni, 124
Nirukta, 181, 206, 207, 208, 222, 223, 225, 290, 323, 346, 384
Nirvān, 312, 313

Obligations, 296
Old Testament, 366, 368, 370
Oligarchies, 182, 265, 303
Orissa, 115
Orthodox church, 308
Oxydrakoi, 177

Pahlavi dynasty, 341
Painting, 204
Pakhtoon tribes, 55, 199
Pakistan, 53, 66, 68, 94, 153, 154, 181, 196, 199, 236
Palestine, 25, 161, 273, 354, 355, 365-67, 371, 375
Pali, 230, 231, 281
Pali chronicles, 261
Pali language, 320, 383
Panchalas, 186, 191, 212, 330, 331
Panchjanāha, 135
Pāndavas, 212, 335, 338, 339, 352, 341
dynastry, 183
Pāndu, 330
Pāṇini, 149, 176, 191, 207, 208, 212, 220, 225, 231, 232, 290, 292, 390, 347, 352

Parishishta Parvan, 246, 258
Pariyātra, 241, 248, 278
Pārvati, 221
Parthavas, 50, 54
Parsees, 107
Parpola, 111
Parshuram, 186
Pārshwanath (Jain Tirthankar), 261
Parikshit, 336
Pārthians, 345
Pashupatinath seal, 27, 40, 41, 103, 110, 115, 117, 120, 121, 123, 125, 133, 143, 149, 215, 216, 217, 381
Patanjali, 149, 176, 208, 209, 220, 225, 246, 254, 280, 290, 307, 322, 383
Pātliputra, 184, 185, 186, 239, 254, 271, 320
Peacock coins, 246
Persian script, 388
Pharoach, 357
Philippines, 313
Philosophical religion, 298-99
Pippalivan, 239, 249
Polyglottic words, 139
Porus, 23, 253
Post-Indus interregnum, 141-152
Pottery, 79, 101
Pradumn, 144
Prag-Jyotishpur, 212
Prahlad, 145
Prātisākhyas, 232
Prince Vijaya, 202
Pujā-Shilā-Prākār, 210
Pujā-Shilpakar, 344
Punjab 46, 68, 77, 91, 153, 178, 191, 379
Purānās, 23, 36, 49, 50, 51, 53, 93, 96, 122, 124, 141, 153, 156, 176, 182, 186, 192, 234, 241, 278, 292, 317, 322, 352, 354, 362, 377, 385
Puru, 150
  dynasty, 96
  tribe, 56
Purush Sukta, 119, 120, 130, 335
Pushan, 41
Pushyamitra, 28, 221, 287, 316

Quetta, 113, 149, 157
Queen Kaluvāki, 264

Rain God, 41
Rajanya Janpada, 191, 193
Rajasthan, 70, 72, 82, 170, 379
Rajgrih, 170
Rajgarh, 320
Rākshasas, 233
Rāmā, 220, 234
Rāmāyana, 55, 156, 176, 220, 232, 233, 234, 265, 322, 383
Rann of Cutch, 154
Rao, K.V.N., 108, 117
Rao, S.R., 111
Rāvi river, 47, 52, 68, 90, 92, 97, 134, 198, 304, 353
Recent discoveries, 178-79
Red Sea, 337
Religions, 205-10, 292-94
Religious faith, 105
Revealed religions, 298-99
Rigveda, 25, 33, 34, 35, 37, 42, 53, 62, 79, 94, 119, 152, 159, 205, 228, 310, 363, 377
Rishabh, 96, 122, 123, 126, 127, 130, 132, 143, 145, 161, 215, 216, 302, 381
  life of, 125-26
Rishis, 35, 54, 206, 361
Rock and Pillar inscriptions, 321-22

Rodhesia, 75
Rudra, 205
Rudradāman, 286

Schismatic monks, 311
Sahdev, 332
Sahgaurā, 167
  copper plate of, 141, 227
  plaque, 321, 322, 347
Salvation, 312
Samudragupta, 259
Sāmveda, 33, 42, 62, 119, 159, 205, 228
Samvashran, 126
Sānchi, 264
Sanghabheda, 311
Sanghamitra, 267
Sankarshan, 209, 210
Sanskrit literature, 231
Saraswati river, 27, 46, 49, 52, 55, 56, 68, 69, 84, 90, 92, 155, 156, 198, 378, 384
Sarma Paṇnat, 60
Sārnath, 216, 264
  Stupa, 246
Satan, 368, 369, 372
Satluj river, 47, 52, 67, 68, 69, 90, 150, 151, 198, 304, 353
Satyabhāma, 346
Satyavan, 333
Saurāshtra, 46, 160
Savitri, 353
Sawai Madhopur, 178
Seals, 39, 40, 44, 55, 56, 86, 101, 109, 110, 116, 117, 119, 130, 132, 378, 379, 380, 381, 382
Seleucas Nikator, 236, 257, 292, 296
Seven Pillar inscription, 264
Sexual intercourse, 301
Shābazgarhi, 264
Shaktāl, 241, 242
Shakuntalā, 96
Shākyas, 171, 217
Shalya, 332, 333
Shāntanu, 55, 336, 341
Shinar, 358, 359
Shishunag dynasty, 186, 236, 295, 298, 320
Shishupal, 375
Shitlā-Matā, 39
Shiva, 161, 221, 279, 294, 337, 343
Shankarāchārya, 281
Shramans, 304
Shunga dynasty, 209, 221, 322
Shursenis, 305, 333, 335
Sībis, 178, 180
Sind, 170
Sindhu, 199
Singhalis, 202
Singhasan Batisi, 318
Sir Mortimer Wheeler, 21
Skhal,, 347
Skanda, 210, 220
  cult, 315
Slave dynasty, 319
Smrities, 290
Snake princes, 126, 132, 145
Solasamahajanpada, 169
Sopura, 263
Sri Lanka, 165, 170, 218, 267, 270, 313
Stone age, 36
  implements, 83
Subhadrā, 350
Sudās, 48, 49, 53, 60, 135, 199
Suktas, 46, 64, 119
Sumerians, 25
Sumerian-Accadian languages, 140
Sumerian civilisation, 161, 385, 386

Sumerian Dictionary, 388-90
common words, 394-98
Sumerian languages, 377, 391-93
Sun god, 37, 41, 56, 205
temples, 145
Sungas dynasty, 316
Surya, 41
Śwetamber Sect. 284

Tāmbbarni, 285
Taranath, 286
Tārak, 211
Tārkshya, 34, 38
Tathāgat, 217
Taxilā, 177, 220, 230, 231, 263, 266, 268
Terracotta figures, 105
Thailand, 235, 313
Third Buddhist Council, 310, 311
Tibet, 286
Tirthankar, 96, 122, 123
Tissa Mogaliputra, 263, 276, 282
Tokyo, 88
Totems, 38, 41, 293, 307
Toynbe, Arnold, 74
Translation compounds, 225
Tribes, 50, 56, 61, 93, 94, 99, 333, 352
Trishadhasta, 70, 155
Tri-Vikrama, 314, 317
Turkey, 25, 355, 359
Turkish plateau, 163
Turkomania, 164

Udaipur, 72
Udvraj, 49, 53, 95, 97
Ujiayani, 266
Ujjain, 169, 180, 316
Ukraine region, 164
Ulopi, 335, 350
Ulysses, 338
Unicorn, 39, 105
Universal Teaches, 215, 216, 227
University of Pennsylvania, 389
Upnishads, 141, 155, 205, 208, 209, 232, 297, 300, 322, 345
Ur of Chaldees, 358
Ur of Shinar, 359
Uranjira, 46
Urvashi, 337
Uttar Pradesh, 170, 193, 305, 378

Vaikarna, 61
Vaishāli, 170, 174, 183, 194, 217, 230, 303
Vaishavānar, 44, 45
Vaishwānar, 56, 346
Vaishyas, 171
Vaital Pachisi, 318
Vājarsaneyi Prātisākhya, 232
Vajji, oligarchies of, 103
Vajjlies, 186
Vajrajangh, 144, 216
Vajrayan, 261
Vāmdeva, 42
Van-char, 83
Varruchikātyāyan, 225, 231
Varshikh, 97
Varuna, 144, 160, 205, 343
Vashist, 318
Vāsudeva, 209, 210, 213, 292
Vedas, 24, 26, 31, 32, 35, 42, 45, 48, 55, 59, 62, 78, 80, 92, 93, 98, 103, 107, 112, 119, 120, 123, 130, 134, 154, 157, 158, 198, 205, 210, 223, 225, 228, 297, 324, 345, 348, 360, 362, 384
Vedic Hindus, 362
Vedic Sanhitas, 33
Ved Vyas, 159, 234, 330, 352
Vichitravirya, 329

Videh, 155
Vidisha, 315
Vidur, 329
Vietnam, 313
Vihārs, 303
Vikramaditya, 316, 318
Vindhya mountains 296
Virāt, 241
Vishākha, 149, 209, 210, 220, 246, 280, 307
cult, 315
Vishākhdatt, 255
Vishālakshā, 232
Vishnu, 96, 121, 143, 145, 161, 205, 211, 218, 279, 294, 315, 317, 343, 350
incarnation of, 381
Vishwamitra, 33, 42, 48, 70
Vishwadevās, 56
Vitāshoka, 265
Vocabulary, 222, 223, 224
Vrichivants, 50
Vridhyāshva, 54
Vrita, 208, 209
Vrshasena, 287
Vrishnis, 153
Vyādi, 225

Washington, 319
Wind god, 38, 41, 213
Wooden club, 63

Xenophon, 188
Xerxes, 190, 368

Yadus, 56, 93, 150, 153, 199, 212, 220
Yagna, 79
Yahweh, 25, 258, 362
Yajurveda, 33, 42, 62, 119, 154, 205, 228
Yakshu, 199
Yama, 144, 213, 329, 350, 331, 333
Yamunā river, 47, 49, 68, 150, 155, 180, 192, 198, 295, 304, 352
Yāsks, 44, 46, 206, 207, 208, 221, 225, 225, 301, 323, 345, 347, 363
Yaudheyas, 23, 28, 170, 177, 180, 191, 193, 200, 210, 241, 246, 253, 266, 268-70, 281, 287, 291, 295
Yavans, 250
Yayati, 335, 352
Yazili-Kāyā, 163, 222
Yerragudi, 263
Yoga-Shatak, 322
Yogic posture, 121, 124
Yoginis, 293, 315
Yona King, 270
Yonas, 285
Yoni, 105
Yudhister, 329, 330, 340, 341, 349, 351

Zagros mountains, 360
Zambesi, 75
Zarthustra, 159
Zena Avesta, 370
Zoroastrain, 362, 363, 370, 375
Zoroastrainism, 300, 367
influence of, 368-70